THUNDER OVER NEW ENGLAND

Benjamin Bonnell The Loyalist

A Loyalist Story & Family Genealogy
Including Other Loyalist
Bunnell/Bonnell
Genealogies

Revised and Updated

By Paul J. Bunnell, FACG, UE

HERITAGE BOOKS
2009

HERITAGE BOOKS
AN IMPRINT OF HERITAGE BOOKS, INC.

Books, CDs, and more—Worldwide
For our listing of thousands of titles see our website at
www.HeritageBooks.com

Published 2009 by
HERITAGE BOOKS, INC.
Publishing Division
100 Railroad Ave. #104
Westminster, Maryland 21157

Copyright © 2003 Paul J. Bunnell, FACG, UE

Previously published by Paul J. Bunnell, FACG, UE
Copyright © 1988
Christopher Publishing House
Hanover, Massachusetts
All rights released back to the author
Library of Congress Catalog Card Number 86-71836
ISBN: 0-8158-436-9

All rights reserved. No part of this book may be reproduced or transmitted in any form or by any means, electronic or mechanical, including photocopying, recording or by any information storage and retrieval system without written permission from the author, except for the inclusion of brief quotations in a review.

International Standard Book Numbers
Paperbound: 978-1-58549-850-5
Clothbound: 978-0-7884-8072-0

Table of Contents

Table of Contents	i
A Special Dedication	ii
Foreword	iii
Preface	iv
Chapter 1 – 1840's	1
Chapter 2 – New Jersey 1744	3
Chapter 3 – Beginning of A Civil War 1775	9
Chapter 4 – Refugee's From New Jersey	19
Chapter 5 – New York City – Eye of The Storm	30
Chapter 6 – September 6, 1781 – The Massacre	39
Chapter 7 – Fleeing New York City	56
Chapter 8 – Settling The Wilderness	66
Chapter 9 – A Real Home	76
Chapter 10 – Death of A Loyalist	96
Chapter 11 – 1840's – The United States of America	106
Chapter 12 – Possible Parents of Benjamin Bonnell & A Future Monument	108
Chapter 13 – Curiosity Brought Him Back – You Decide – Is It Benjamin?	110
Chapter 14 – Recognition	118
Chapter 15 – Notable Family Members & Mariners & Ship Owners	121
Chapter 16 – Bunnell – Bonnell Loyalist Genealogies	128
Endnotes	285
Name Index	321
Other Publications by The Author	333
Author's Biography, Credits	Back Cover

A Special Dedication

To my Loving wife,
Leslie Diane (White) Bunnell

To my children,
Matthew Paul and Jeannine Marie Bunnell

To my Son and Daughter In-Laws
Eric Napoleon Smith and Taylor Morris (Soon Yung Choo)

To my Grandchildren,
Rebecca Marie, Amanda Marie, Hannah Marie Bunnell
Timothy Conn

In Loving Memory of my parents,
James Henry Sr. and Lorraine Muriel (Violette) Bunnell

To my brothers,
James Henry Jr. and Michael Norman Bunnell

To my sister-in-laws,
Janet and Lorraine

In Loving Memory of my mother-in-law,
Patricia Doreen (McCoy) White

In loving Memory of our Siamese cat who was named after Benjamin.
Ben Bunnell
Born 1 Sept.1979 Sandwich, Ma. Died 9 Nov. 2002 Amesbury, Ma.
(Who died at the completion of this revision) Age 23 Years, 2 Months.

And Not To Forget
My Special Relationship With
Corpl. Benjamin Bonnell Jr. & Sarah Jones, U.E.

FOREWORD

Thunder Over New England, Benjamin Bonnell, The Loyalist, can only be described as a struggle for individual rights, and survival during the American Revolution. Between 1770 and 1783 in the American Colonies, many people suffered during that struggle. There were losers and winners. Nearly all levels of the economic ladder had suffered. The common everyday farmer, the laborer and the small businessman were caught making the difficult choice of freedom, the rebel way, or keeping the course and serve their King and God. The latter choice created "The American Loyalist."

In the case of the American Loyalists, when the war was over, they were promised their rightful place in the new society. And this was even guaranteed by the rebels in the "Treaty of Paris," the document that was supposed to end all hostilities and bring everyone home. Even though the new Congress agreed to these principles, the states did not. The plan was a good one. One of forgiveness, and the guarantee to the right to continue on with their lives as they were before the war. But instead, each state ruled not to accept that part of the "Treaty" and ran all the Tories/Loyalists out of town and state and confiscated everything they owned. Many were neighbors and family members. Being loyal to King George III cost the Loyalists dearly. This rejection resulted in burning them out, tar and feathering, even execution by hanging and placing hateful anti-Loyalists signs on their bodies. The ones that got away, transformed into refugees and they headed for the British stronghold, New York City. There were between 30,000 to 40,000 Loyalist refugees living in or around that metropolis area. It was the one strategic place the British commanded throughout entire war.

The American Revolutionary War was not a popular uprising. One third of the population wanted to split from Britain, but one third did not, and the other third did not choose sides. One good example was the Quakers. Many did not like how Britain was treating the colonists, but their mostly non-violent way of life forbid revolting. This is how many became Loyalists. Choosing not to rebel made them automatic Loyalists. Nearly everyone was tired of the high taxes that supported European power struggles. The French and British were at odds several times in Canada, mostly in Acadie (Nova Scotia/New Brunswick) changing authority as each major battle ended. The final struggle left many of the Acadians without a home. The British shipped them out of Acadie to far away places, like New Orleans, France, the Carolinas, not to forget Boston, Philadelphia and other areas. Since 1755, the British had been achieving dominance all along the Eastern Atlantic shoreline.

One of the main personalities of the American war was Benedict Arnold. Fighting on both sides, he was considered one of the best generals of the American Revolutionary War. Even though Loyalist regiments were operational throughout the war, Benedict Arnold, after changing sides to the British cause, saw a great opportunity to recruit more American Loyalists. By this action he proved to the jealous British generals that the colonists were excellent soldiers. Later, after serving gallantly, the Loyalists were offered land grants in Nova Scotia (including New Brunswick), Quebec, Ontario, Prince Edward Island and the Bahamas, Bermuda and Sierra Leone.

Before and after the war three major groups of people were displaced; the French Acadians, the Loyalists, and let's not forget the oppression of the North American Natives. The Acadian and Quebec French peoples of Canada came to North America well before (1604) the Pilgrims landed at Plymouth, Massachusetts in 1620, but were persecuted and run off their land like the Indians.

They adapted well to the harsh climate in the north and became very successful farmers. The British tried everything to get rid of them, but failed. Even the great deportation of the mid-1700's later brought many back. The struggle for their own identity today is one of the biggest challenges facing Canada.

After the American revolt, Cape Breton, Upper and Lower Canada along with New Brunswick and Nova Scotia provinces quickly became the location for the Loyalists' resettlement. A new revolution nearly broke out in the streets of Saint John, New Brunswick and Shelburne, Nova Scotia from unfair land grants awarded to special interest groups. The United States thought this to be a great opportunity to invite New Brunswick to become the fourteenth state, but that offer failed. The War of 1812-1814 was another failed attempt to bring Canada into the United States, but by then both sides of the New Brunswick/Maine border was well populated by Loyalist and Acadian descendants and the desire for war was very minimal. One humorous incident stands out when Calais, Maine ran out of gun powder for their fourth of July celebration so they asked their good neighbors in St. Stephen's, New Brunswick for a loan from their powder house that was built for the War of 1812. Being good neighbors they accommodated with no reservations. I realize that this war was fierce in the Ontario and Great Lakes area and on the high seas, but many Canadians (mostly Maritimes) were not interested in another war sponsored by the British.

The Canadian Confederation was born in 1867 and relations between the United States and Canada are among the strongest in the world. Today, we are also the largest trading partners with the longest unfortified border anywhere (excepting after the September 11, 2001 terrorist action from foreigners). One thing that must remain between both people; the education and teaching of this period in history, of the cultures of the African, North American French Acadian, Quebec Francophone, the Loyalists (Black and White), and the Native American heritage. We have all heard of the Patriot cause, but the nearly 100,000 Loyalist refugees deserve a place in history along the side of these other groups. This book is designed to help you find and understand your Loyalist ancestor. The bloodlines of these very brave people run today in Great Britain, Australia, Sierra Leon, Bermuda, Bahamas Islands, Canada, and millions of people in the United States.

I congratulate the peoples of North America for creating the greatest melting pot in the history of the world. We must cherish our common relationships between Canada and the United States and know that there are tens of millions of us who carry this Loyalist heritage today.

Paul J. Bunnell, FACG, UE

PREFACE

I would like to thank all the people and institutions that made this book possible, especially Christopher Publishing House of Hanover, Massachusetts who gave me my first chance at this creation. And Heritage Books Inc. of Bowie, Maryland, who believed in my work and who later took on many future projects for me. And, Willow Bend Books of Westminster, Maryland who showed so much interest in the update and republication of this book.

During my travels throughout New England and Canada, I experienced a true interest by every person that I encountered regarding not just the establishment of my Loyalist lines and other family genealogy. But my main desire was to put the record straight concerning historic people like Benedict Arnold, and the true interpretation of why these Loyalists stood behind their King and fought for what they felt was right.

A special thank you to the people of New Brunswick where much of my lineage comes from on both sides of my family. They made my visits there comfortable and many went out of their way to help. I also met and helped bring together many family members who had their lines possibly hidden for over one hundred years or more. The families who had lived (or still do) on Benjamin's last property (Devil's Back, Greenwich Parish), like the Rathburns, Hewitts, and Delongs, were always so kind in helping me locate any landmarks and recalling old stories of the area. The fine employees of the New Brunswick Museum in Saint John and the Provincial Archives located on the beautiful campus of the University of New Brunswick went out of their way to assist me in finding Benjamin Bonnell and his family. The wonderful people of Saint John and Fredericton, New Brunswick who were all so kind during my visits. I want to congratulate all the people of New Brunswick for their New England and Maritime hospitality. I felt that I came home.

I do not wish to exclude all the wonderful and helpful people throughout the United States who gave their assistance to my research and who acted like true professional genealogists. I have never experienced so much interest in another's genealogical problems as they displayed. The long distance calls and the follow-up letters that came in regarding the establishment of Benjamin's record were overwhelming and heartwarming. Two men (William Austin and Claude Bunnell) and the members of the Bunnell/Bonnell Newsletter organization who have been extremely helpful in bringing Benjamin's line into the mainstream line of Bunnell/Bonnells. My sincere thanks to you all.

I feel that I made Benjamin the obsession of the entire North American continent and England. The employees at Augat Inc., Mashpee, Massachusetts always showed a sincere interest in my research on Benjamin that increased my drive for the truth. Like a family, they too were part of Benjamin's life. They had no choice. The plant of two hundred and sixty employees became victims of the downsizing era of 1995 and finally closed down in 1996. This family had died, but like Benjamin, the memory of them will always live on.

It was unbelievably shocking to have this same tragedy happen again in 2001 with my next employer, Arrow Electronics in North Reading, Massachusetts. Those people were equally brave and with great leadership we left our wonderful accomplishments in that business as our legacy. Big business has still got a lot to learn from its employees loyalty.

During those working years, much of my vacation time was spent on research. I appreciated the support from my wife and children while I crawled around on library floors looking for lost records. My education increased as I studied the American Loyalists, finding this part of history that was hardly ever taught in school. I began to understand both sides of the American struggle, and why many groups of colonists including the Quakers did what they had to do. I was a mediocre student attending Canoga Park High School in Canoga Park, California. I had no interests in history. But as this developed on my own, I learned to quickly appreciate history and genealogy together, especially when discovering the Nathaniel Bonnell House in Elizabeth, New Jersey (my direct ancestor) built around 1696. And walking onto the grounds of Fort Griswold in Groton, Connecticut knowing that Benjamin fought a terrible battle there under the leadership of Benedict Arnold sent chills through my body. They destroyed New London by fire and killed nearly all the Patriots at the fort. Long hours of prayer and thought went into that fort as I sat on the grassy knoll contemplating what had gone through Benjamin's mind at that time.

The thrill of finding the two hundred acres that King George III granted to Benjamin for his service in the American Legion and the Kings American Refugee Regiment during the American Revolution sent chills through my body. Located at the end of Long Reach (across from Westfield), Kings County, New Brunswick, I drove off the ferry that lands there today. And again, I was very moved. This was the place he settled, bringing his family to safety. The place he built (the Harding House which is part of Ben's house today). The land he farmed. All this was and still is a paradise overlooking the head of the Grand Bay on the Saint John River. The month was August and the year was 1986, exactly two hundred years almost to the day that Benjamin was granted this land (August 1786) that I set foot onto. I did not discover that similarity until later on in my research.

The following years carried me through his past in such a way that I felt he was with me. I talked about him and to him. I dreamt about him, and I drove my friends and family crazy over him. I felt Ben never wanted to see modern times or progress of the early eighteenth century. Because of increased settlement in the area and the birth of the river steam boats, Ben and his family made one last move: across the river just north of Westfield in the Parish of Greenwich Village just south of Brown's Flat. There around 1811 he sold Long Reach and bought 200 acres from John Crabb (also a Loyalist). The land was split. One hundred acres, lowland, the other hundred acres high up on "The Devil's Back" overlooking the Saint John River. This is where he died on 17 February 1828. The end of an era! The end of a great and average man!

My last thoughts and praise goes out to all the Bunnell/Bonnells. I wrote this book for you. Know your family history and you will know who you are.

Chapter 1

1840's

    Benjamin had felt strongly about this decision. For the past several years he saw that all the big opportunities were centered in Boston, Massachusetts. He didn't want to be a farmer like his father and grandfather before him. His misadventures in the shipping trade were not as successful as his brothers and other family members were. Knowing down deep that they would not agree with him right away, and even though his loyalist grandfather was already in spirit, he gave the thought of going to "The States" much time. First going into the lumber business, then shipping and now, of all things, going to "The States" as Canadian's called the United States of America. This would change his family forever.

    Ben's father had said; "If your grandfather were alive today, he would surely be lost for words to see his grandson going to the country that rejected him and his king during the American Revolution".

    On that big day, the fog was exceptionally thick in the Bay of Fundy. Benjamin wasn't the only young man leaving for Boston that day. Many others looked just like him; wearing old worn clothes, carrying a soiled suitcase, and traveling alone. This was a big step for him, as he had never left home before except to work the lumber mills or sailed a bit on the Saint John River.

    Ben knew it would be difficult in the States because the newspapers reported that the Irish were coming over to North America by the boatloads dropping them off on Partridge Island located just off the Saint John Harbor (an Emigrant processing point for Canada) and all point in the States. The potato harvest in Ireland had been a disaster for the past few years and many Irish families were starving. North America was the land of opportunity for many hard-pressed people of other countries. The Irish were going to Canada and the States. These events still did not stop Ben from taking his trip to Boston. He made his mind up and being young and adventurous, naturally presented the challenge before him. Right now, most of the jobs were in the States. That was all he could think of.

    Ben's mother and father were the descendants of American Loyalists, which didn't make his trip any more popular in the family. His mother, Sarah was the daughter of John Day, a staunch Loyalist from New Jersey and who had many landmarks named after him in New Brunswick, Canada. Ben's father was Benjamin Bonnell (3rd.), the same name running directly from the Loyalist Benjamin Bonnell (Jr.), of the American Legion, and from Morris County, New Jersey. He was a corporal who served under the great and honorable Brigadier General Benedict Arnold.

Ben (4th.) had heard the stories so many times before. He could recall nearly every word spoken from his grandfather's wrinkled lips. Grandpa would sit in his rocker on the back porch with all the children. Just beyond him was his blossoming apple orchard in back of his log cabin surrounded by a stone cellar that his sons help him build. Grandpa would prepare us all for his war stories of the great American Revolution, and stories of the tough years that followed in New Brunswick after the province was carved out of Nova Scotia for the Loyalists. The stories were always very interesting coming from a man who walked in those shoes trying to stay loyal to King George III in a country falling apart. During the mid-eighteen-twenties, Grandpa was now one of the very few loyalist left alive as many had already died off.

Grandpa Benjamin died in 1828, which gave Ben (4th.) a few years of his exciting stories because he was born in 1820. His father continued some of the stories, which kept grandpa's memory alive. Ben (3rd.) had a sister, Sarah, who was born in the States and even though she was under ten years old when they came to Canada, she remembered the hardship they all went through as refugees.

As Ben's (4th.) ship, The Gypsie left the Saint John harbor he looked up at his brother Simeon Bonnell commanding it out to the open sea. He marveled at how the town had grown from what his grandfather had described in his tales as a city of ten thousand tents. He felt a lump in his throat as the ship sailed off, leaving the early morning city lights fading into the thick fog. He quietly said goodbye to his homeland. Loneliness pitted his stomach and he wondered; was this what his grandfather felt when he left New York City in the Great Loyalist Exodus of 1783?

He squeezed himself into a corner of the ship and watched as the billowing sails above took him to a new and unknown future. His brother Simeon had his family back in New Brunswick and sailing was in his blood. He was happy with that kind of life just like thousands of other Canadian's in the Maritime's. The Bonnell's were adventurous and always stood up for what they believed in and never stepped aside because of adversity. If only all the stories of Ben's (4th.) grandfather were saved and passed down through each generation the family would know its past and find that their ancestors were very brave people.

Later on, Ben stood up and noticed that the fog had lifted. For the first time, he saw this land of his grandfathers; The United States coastline. So much like home, but so alive with the sounds of his grandfather's stories. Fantasy suddenly took over his mind. He slid back down again to cover himself from the cool and wet sea breeze. He closed his eyes as the ship sailed along the Maine coast. He started to recall his grandfather's stories. There, old Ben was sitting in his rocker cutting up a piece of dried wood, ready to tell his story from the beginning as each child listen as if in a trance.

Chapter 2

NEW JERSEY - 1744

He shot out of the clouds like a shooting star. The misty cool sea breeze was no obstacle for this brave creature trained so perfectly by nature. The near collision with the rolling waves heading ashore did not frighten him either. Just above the waterline he displayed more aerial skills. There! In front of him was the New Jersey beaches and coves. The Seagull headed inland. There was something taking him there. Something special.

The entire area of Essex and Morris County, New Jersey was covered with a thick layer of fog with heavy dew that crawled in from the ocean and Great Swamp Plain not too far away. Soon it would become another hot and humid summer day with one small change, the birth of Benjamin Bonnell, the son of Benjamin Senior, a farmer, frontiersman, Quaker and one of the settlers of Essex and Morris County. The doctor arrived to assist Eleanor the mother to be because it was not going to be an easy birth. Having trouble with the other children, they thought best to have him present. Just before the doctor arrived, he stopped by the Great Swamp to pick needed herbs and roots for possible treatment of Mrs. Bonnell. Many physicians spent many hours in the swamps searching for leaves, seeds, roots and bark for various ailment remedies for their patients. They advertised their expertise by going from town to town telling all of their most recent finds that would cure all kinds of sicknesses.

Many Quaker families were living in this area that the Dutch once owned. The Elizabeth Associates were one such lot of English colonists who was granted said lands in East New Jersey. Nathaniel Bonnell who was this family's ancestor was one of them. The witchcraft scares of the late sixteen hundreds were beginning to fade. Salem, Massachusetts's residences were still basking in their embarrassment from the witch trials and nearly every God-fearing colonist treated only their king second to him. The dark ages were slowly fading away with the church still firmly in control of many areas.

Benjamin was a small baby, which made the birth easy. The outcome was a happy one. Celebration was in order. His father was very proud to have another son. That meant prosperity to his family. Many boys meant more men to work the farm. Colonial life was very harsh with many dangers lurking around every corner, such as disease, Indians, many outbreaks of war between the European colonial powers who were constantly trying to dominate the American continent.

Jacob, Benjamin's older half brother, was so excited to have another brother. He stayed by the small crib for hours just watching the child inside. Later, he nearly killed Ben by trying to feed him some Indian cornbread. His mother explained the difficulty of a young child eating and the need to nurse without hard food in the beginning of life. This nourishment would continue for many months.

Time seemed to travel very fast that first year. By the next, young Benjamin was now walking and getting himself into trouble. His brothers, Jacob, David and Nathaniel were already out working their father's fields while their sisters took turns watching Ben as they did their own daily chores. One day Benjamin slipped outside without notice. The entire world suddenly opened up before him. Hugging the side of the cabin he walked around it holding one hand on the timber wall heading out back where he noticed a small trail of ants coming from the cabin going out into the woods. This first encounter of Mother Nature intrigued him. So off he went to find the destination of the hard working ants. The brush was very thick and his little feet were tired after a few steps of exploring. Then before his eyes was the ant hole. He squatted down to get a closer look into the small opening and watched the steady stream of insects traveling in and out. Then suddenly, a large dark shadow appeared overhead.

He turned around cautiously and found a giant black cow standing right in front of him. Frightened to death, he cried out. His father didn't own a cow so the beast was very strange to Ben. He ran back to the side of the cabin after a couple of tumbles. The feel of the wooden wall brought back his secure feeling. He hugged the side of his house until the others came running. Upon finding Ben, they discovered the cow that did not belong to them. Not many people owned cows, and by law Mr. Bonnell had to attempt to find the owner. He put the cow up in his barn and placed an ad in the New Jersey Gazette telling the readers that he had a lost cow. Several days later the rightful owner came by to collect it.

When Ben was six years old his father took him on a short trip from their Mendham farm to purchase whale oil for their lamps. Whaling was a very big industry for the colonies. Upon arriving at the processing plant, Ben discovered the large bones from the Whale lying about. Feeling a little sorry for the beast of the ocean he later learned that many parts of the Whale were used in everyday life, from the meat, ivory, bone, sperm and oils, etc.

The Woodbridge/Rahway Meeting House for Quaker worship was where Eleanor made sure her family went every Sunday for quiet prayer. It was hard on the small children like Ben because the service was always in silence, with just a scattered few words spoken. One Sunday Benjamin was very restless and his mother feared he would disrupt the service somehow. She lectured him all the way into the meetinghouse. One last assurance was to keep him seated at her side. The hall was so silent! The lack of sound was so torturous it drove Ben crazy. His mother knew this and she peered down at him with an evil eye. Benjamin Senior noticed the glares and anticipated an outburst from his little son who had Great Spirit. The child's eyes deepened with evil.

There was no stopping him now. His older siblings and a few parishioners who knew Ben waited for the disturbance to start. A devilish smile came over his face. He had his idea in mind. Now, to carry out his dirty deed. Before he could create his disturbance, a small church mouse ran right down the center of the gathering that faced each other. Shock and surprise painted across everyone's face. All they could do was watch the little creature run from one end of the meetinghouse to the other. No one could strike it down before it reached a small crack in the far wall. After the end of the incident, Ben ducked in fear of being blamed for the mouse. Instead, all the members laughed out in joyous unison. It was the only time he heard laughter in the meetinghouse. Every Sunday after, he watched out for that tiny mouse.

    The family had now added one more boy to the family. Aaron Bonnell was born 30 March 1749. Benjamin Senior was now the proud father of four boys. They lost a fifth boy, Simeon in earlier years but he had died shortly after birth.

    Young Benjamin wanted to learn to write and read books. But he knew time on the farm would not permit it. He felt very strongly about getting an education. His father knew how to read and write, and he wanted too. Opportunity would soon come his way. One day after his chores were done, he and a few other boys went over to a relative's, Nathaniel Bonnell's mill to play on the waterwheel and swim in the small pond. The outer rim of each wooden slat was slippery and slimy from the green moss growing there. This added to their fun as long as a long splinter in the wood did not get in the way. After getting run off it by old Nathaniel, they next went skinny-dipping in a pond nearby. Many of his young years were devoted to work and play.

    When Ben was ten years old he, like most boys that age, was full of hell. One day while his sisters were working in the herb garden in the back of the cabin, he chased a chicken right through it breaking several small stems of various herbs that the girls had so patiently planted. His father took him out back to the barn and beat him with a willow branch. This did not slow him down. The following day he crawled on his belly around to the back of the chicken coop and jumped out and scared one of his sisters half to death. She dropped all the eggs onto the ground, breaking six of them. She looked over at her playful brother and knew what was in store for him, but the two were very close, and she later told her mother that a snake crawled up behind her, scaring her into dropping the eggs. She ended up going to bed without dinner that night but she knew that was a lot better then seeing Ben beaten with that awful branch.

    One cool spring day in 1755, Benjamin, Jacob, Nathaniel, David and their father went to Morristown to trade their farm goods for supplies. Their now younger brother Aaron was left at home. While the two older boys went in with their father, Ben was ordered to stay behind and watch the wagon. It didn't take long for Mr. Bonnell to start haggling over prices of the goods he wanted. While Ben was petting the horses, suddenly coming down Main Street was a drummer, a bagpiper and an officer playing a marching tune. They were recruiters for the French and Indian Wars.

They walked right up to where Ben was standing and stopped. The young boy was mystified by the event. People gathered around to hear the soldier. The soldier sang out the words of Patriotism, and called out to serve the English king against the French tyrants. Ben was hypnotized by his spell. Then suddenly two boys not much older then Ben jumped up and said they would volunteer, shocking their family members standing next to them. The glory of battle for the king excited many young men.

Though the call was hypnotic, Ben and his family felt much differently about war. Maybe it was because his parents were farmers and Quakers? Eleanor, Ben's mother would never agree to see one of her boys run off to war. Her strong Quaker belief would never allow it. There was too much work to do around the farm then to run off and be shot at. He watched the Drummer, Bagpiper and Soldier march down the street with their new recruits. Their sounds faded as his family appeared out of the store baring smiles over the deal they just struck.

In 1757 news came about a very big battle up around Albany, New York. The French and Indians had killed many young recruits and Ben soon heard that two of his friends were among the dead. They were so young and it was such a terrible waste. That sad day he wanted to be alone. His father allowed him to do whatever he wanted to do.

Ben retreated to his favorite spot on a hill overlooking the Great Swamp. The view was breathtaking as he could see the ocean in the New York Bay in the far distance on a clear day. High winds raced through the lower valleys and across the Great Swamp ripping the leaves from their branches. Ben sat down under a white birch and rested the back of his head against its trunk. There, he closed his eyes and fell into a trance, listening to the wind race around him. He felt very comfortable, nearly to the point of falling asleep. A few minutes later, he did just that. The sun was going down when he woke. He felt a cold shiver run through his body. The breeze was cooler. After getting up he grabbed both shoulders, shaking from the chill, and ran home.

One day, other news spread about a Bonnell boy who was struck by lightening in the Great Swamp while he was playing on a large old tree. He was killed instantly and this added to many other superstitions about the swamp. Ben thought of his lost cousin and wondered if his spirit still haunted the area. Would he come across this lost soul during one of his silent moments there?

The colonies were heavily dependent on London for many of the special things in life like manufactured goods. Because of the great distance involved many new trades were being created setting into motion a more independent America. Taxes were always levied upon the colonies for various European operations. In 1764, the Sugar Act was enacted and this made many people angry. Soon smuggling became a way of life. Great Britain made this practice illegal and demanded stiff penalties to be applied. If any ship owner were caught smuggling sugar in from the West Indies, they would have their ship confiscated.

Several riots broke out over the Sugar Act and later the Stamp Act would nearly seal the fate of the American-English relationship. America did not want to finance wars all over the world for Great Britain. The idea of separation was still unthinkable because of the loyalty to God and King, but it wouldn't be long for that idea to turn to reality.

At twenty years old, the life around Ben appeared very exciting. Wars raged everywhere in the world and becoming a military man was a very promising career. He thought his duty was to be a farmer like his father and a good Quaker. Wanting to read and write was now a priority. He got his chance in 1760 when a young schoolteacher by the name of Dorothy Ellis took him aside. They met every chance they could after Ben's chores were done.

The education that would come to Benjamin was something he would never forget. They got permission from the Brotherton family to use their barn for Ben's classroom. One afternoon, while they both sat in the barn on a small bale of hay, Miss Ellis held a little gray chalkboard on her lap that she used to instruct her students. It suddenly fell onto the ground. Benjamin jumped down to retrieve it and as he did, he placed his hand on the lovely lady's thigh. He had never been with a woman before and when this happened, the blood rushed through his body like the rivers of spring bursting loose after winter. Their eyes met as Miss Ellis grabbed his hand and held it there. She knew that now she was going to be his teacher in the subject of lovemaking.

His eyes told her that he fancied her. That afternoon was especially quiet because everyone had gone to town except Mrs. Brotherton who was baking in the house. Without warning, Miss Ellis left Ben's side and went over and closed the barn door. And as she did, she untied a small ribbon from her hair letting her beautiful blond curls fall to her shoulders. That afternoon, Benjamin became a man.

It wasn't long before tensions in the Bonnell home increased. One very strong issue of difference was the increasing problem between England and the colonies. Ben's education gave him many opinions about politics, and his religion. His sisters never mentioned politics or any other subject that was considered a man's issue. They still had their points of view, but their father would never allow such views to be expressed in his house. Ben was often found at meetings in town concerning the high taxes the King was imposing on his colonial subjects. Many discussions ended in near violence in the streets with dedicated King's subjects, as Ben was. In general, the Quakers were against any violence and by nature stayed loyal to the Crown. Being a revolutionary was out of the question.

When Ben came home from such meetings, his father would forbid any political talk in his house. Everyone knew that he sided with both points of view, but being a simple farmer and Quaker, and having taken an oath to the King and God that he would never support any other country. This left him no choice but to stay out of the problems surrounding him, but also on the side of the British in his heart, but a Patriot in his community.

He felt like most others around him. One never went against God and King, lest he be struck down in his tracks by the almighty. Many times Ben had loud screaming matches with his father over the issues. His father was very sorry to see his son with an education because it brought on more grief. As time went on, making a living seemed to be a much bigger effort. The war debt of England was starting to take its toll. Everyone, rich or poor, was beginning to feel the pinch. Sometimes Benjamin's stances were now making sense, depending on ones point of view. His father saw that the need to take sides was at hand and a young overly opinionated man as Ben was, he could see that this son was not like his other boy's. He would have to find his place in life and take the consequences of his actions.

All four Bonnell men were very good looking. Many girls were there for the picking. The first to marry was Jacob. On 27 Nov. 1760, a large wedding was going on at Schooley Mountain. A simple Quaker ceremony was conducted at the Rahway/Plainfield Meetinghouse, New Jersey. And the bride was Mary Schooley. The second to marry was David to Mary Ann Master just around 1761. Nathaniel was still too young but would marry Elizabeth Likens lastly, who was from Virginia they say.

A Bonnell cousin that lived in Perth Amboy, New Jersey was very well known. As the sheriff of Perth Amboy, Isaac Bonnell was also involved with horse racing. On 7 April 1768, the Advertiser General and the New York Journal his add for a race to be held in May for any horse, mare or gelding, not more than half blood could run the two-mile heats. The winning purse would be fifty dollars. Richard Carnes Jr. and Isaac Bonnell would collect the three-dollar entrance fees. Little did Isaac know that his life would soon be changing[1]?

1770 was a bad year for farming. The weather was terrible and crop failure hit almost every farm. At times the Bonnell's thought of going to England, but they knew the colonists were not well treated there. They just had to make the best of the times and being such hard workers, they did manage to pull through the bad spells.

Benjamin was somewhat involved in the smuggling trade that was entering into some of the New Jersey ports at night. He managed to make a few connections with some highly placed men who had a great deal of goods coming in from many parts of the world. His father didn't like it, but sometimes they had no choice, because of the scarcity of many supplies. This was one area that would get Ben more involved with the Crown's future war effort.

By the time 1774 came around, the political issue concerning the colonies wanting more independence from England was at its height. News was coming in almost daily about riots or protests. The issue was one that caused families to split up. The backing of a complete separation from the mother country was not a popular one. When war did break out, one-third of the population was for the revolt, one-third against, and one-third didn't want to get involved.

---

[1] From A Glance Back in Time, by Richard B. Marrin, Pub. By Heritage Books Inc.

Chapter 3

BEGINNING OF A CIVIL WAR - 1775

News quickly spread from Boston. The first shot was fired. Officially, The American Revolution started at Lexington, Massachusetts. Soon, the entire thirteen colonies heard of the events seemingly overnight. Troops were being mustered openly where there were no British troops to stop them. Underground clusters of Patriot rebels were organizing quietly where the British were at their strongest. Vital and strategic information was being passed on quickly among the colonists, where the same took up to two weeks or more to reach England. This was a clear disadvantage to the British. Conditions were not the best for a war. Men needed special arrangements from Congress in order to sign up for short periods of duty so they could tend to their farms in-between the growing seasons. Congress also allowed substitutions of one man to use another so they could go home on leave to harvest the crops. The first military company in Morris County, New Jersey was formed near the township of Whippany in the fall of 1775, under the command of Captain Morris[2].

In New Jersey, Governor William Franklin, Benjamin Franklin's son was the last Tory governor to leave office. He was taken prisoner in 1776 and placed into custody at Perth Amboy, New Jersey and was later sent to a Connecticut prison. The news was devastating to his personal friend and cousin to Ben, The High Sheriff, Isaac Bonnell. He and his wife Grace Fox were very close to the family, not to mention faithful Loyalists. When their son was born, they made the ex-loyalist governor, godfather and also gave their son the same name, William Franklin Bonnell. Grace Fox died shortly after and disaster struck that Bonnell family. Isaac soon found his entire estate confiscated and sold off for being Loyalist. He was taken prisoner, but later released where he and the remaining members of his family fled to New York City, a stronghold for the British throughout the war, and the main haven for Loyalist refugees from all the colonies. Governor William Franklin was also released, stayed in New York for a time and then fled to England where he led a very unhappy life in the shadows of his popular father.

At Morristown, New Jersey, things were looking pretty bad for the Loyalists. In 1777, Washington took over the town for his headquarters, first at Arnold's Tavern. This was the turning point for Benjamin and his remaining life in New Jersey. The family kept a low profile and their lives were at stake now and his father was sure to feel the pain of a split family. Washington's Army was also encamped at Morristown during January 1777 after the battles of Trenton and Princeton. His mobile headquarters was moved to Freeman's Tavern and he worshipped at the Presbyterian Church there[3].

---

[2] From Historic Roadsides of Morris County, New Jersey, History of Whippany during the American Revolution.
[3] From Historic Roadsides of Morris County, New Jersey, History of Morristown during the American Revolution.

Ben felt surrounded. The Iron works at Hibernia and Mount Hope became a valuable asset to the Patriot Rebels for the production of cannon balls, grape shot and other iron ore items needed for war.

Conditions were getting worse. Benjamin heard that some of his friends were still smuggling for the British. They were being paid good hard cash for their efforts so Ben decided to look into the venture again. On May 8, 1777, Washington outlawed playing cards, dice and any other games that could take advantage of his troops. While waiting for battle, there was a lot of time on their hands. Many shrewd men were cheating these fellow Patriots out of what little they had. In Mendham, New Jersey, a little closer to home, Washington converted the Hill Top Church, located on Main Street to a military hospital during the winter of 1777[4]. One neutral spot for both sides during the war was the home of Lucas Von Beaverhoudt at Troy Hills. Here, British and American's sought out his hospitality and entertainment; A strange and real break from battle.

Benjamin decided to contact the group of smugglers and started to train. Philadelphia had just fallen to the Patriots and on June 25, 1778, Clinton of the British army decided not to go by sea with all those men, women and children who were now fleeing Loyalist refugees from that city. Clinton also felt that Patriot ships awaited him at the bay's entrance so he decided to quietly sneak 14,000 men and their families, and 1,500 wagons ninety miles across New Jersey to New York City safely behind British lines. This was a very bold move because Washington was located at Valley Forge just a few miles away from Clinton's column of refugees.

When the wagon train was finally on its way, it included herds of cattle, livestock, horses and any other means of transportation extending over twelve miles. The temperature was in the nineties and after being sighted by Washington troops, suddenly; the high temperature was not the main problem anymore. They all waited for an attack. The British troops stretched the entire column along the mountaintops watching for the Patriot rebels below. Attacks came from several angles and positions. Every rebel desired the capture of wagons and booty, but the column kept up their exodus towards New York. Gunfire and attacks were heard from miles away. With casualties on both sides, the British and Loyalists did make their final destination. This upset Washington dearly. His constant pain over the lose of New York City and area to the British was always a thorn in his side. Now, he lost a great opportunity to take a huge spoil from them. There were a lot of badly needed supplies in that historic twelve-mile column.

Washington's constant attempted attacks on New York left him in deep depression as each failure occurred. On one such occasion, he was beaten back to the New Jersey shore with his troops. Extremely depressed, he stepped out of his boat setting foot onto the beach and fell to his defeated knees and openly sobbed in front of all his men, a sight not seen from such a high official as he was.

---

[4] Also from Mendham History.

The chief and leader of the Revolutionary War were at his most vulnerable frame of mind. He took possession of a nearby farmhouse and stayed secluded there for days until he was rejuvenated again for battle.

The then Patriot rebel, Benedict Arnold was assigned to control Philadelphia after Clinton left there. Shortly after that, Arnold was at odds with Congress and other high officials while he governed that city. He was living like a king while many colonists were without food and proper clothing. By 1778, Major General Arnold had to appear for a trial at the Norris Tavern located at the corner of Water and Morris streets in Morristown, New Jersey. He was being charge with unmilitary like conduct in Philadelphia and Valley Forge that year. Little did Robert Norris know that his tavern would go down in history as a famous historical site? The trail was unsuccessful because they could not find enough evidence to convict the Major General, the same results in many other attempts to disgrace him. Arnold made many enemies, and several wanted him removed from his position. General Washington always came to Arnold's rescue, standing behind who he thought was the greatest general and military man he had. Still, many attempts to try him of treason continued.

The flood of goods and materials into New York City from the Patriot controlled areas of the colonies never let up. Badly needed cash and trade took priority with the farmers, especially in nearby New Jersey. Congress forbids any intercourse with the enemy without written approval. Wood was one commodity in high demand. The Raritan River area in New Jersey was heavily wooded and it was owned mostly by John Stevens, Esq. By March 4, 1779 he had developed a large business with the British selling his wood for their construction needs and fireplaces for heat.

During this same time, Benjamin met with the smugglers and made a deal to furnish them with information, and in addition agreed to help pass counterfeit money the British were manufacturing in high volumes. The economy of New Jersey was one of their main targets. Ben was able to make a great deal while working with the smugglers. His luck did not last long!

With thirty dollars in bad bills he bought some goods from Enos Jaquish. Poor Enos passed the phony bills on to a store clerk in town that identified them and summoned the sheriff. They quickly surrounded the Jaquish home and took Enos into custody. It didn't take long to track down the source of the money. Enos was let go and was taken off the hook. Now the attention was on Benjamin.

Original New Jersey Counterfeit $3 Bill

In that same month of March 1779, the rebel authorities had enough on Ben to request the Supreme Court in Succasunna, (Succasunny) (Roxbury Township) Morris County, New Jersey to place him under indictment for passing counterfeit currency.

March 1779, This State vs. Benjamin Bunnel junior of Succasunna (Succasunny) in Morris County places in the Supreme Court an indictment of Benjamin Bunnel for passing of counterfeit currency of true and lawful paper bills of credit, committed by the Honorable (not legible) of the United States of America, made current in this state, and each of the value of thirty dollars of lawful money of this state unlawfully, fraudulently, and deceitfully did utter, and pass to Enos Jaquish for and as true good, and lawful paper bills of credit so as to committed by the Congress of, and each of the value of thirty dollars lawful money of this state, he the said Benjamin Bunnel then and there will knowing this said paper bills to as of by him utter and paid to have been counterfeit, false and forged as aforesaid to the example of all others in the like case offending and against the peace of this state, the government, and dignity of the same.

Signed, William Paterson, Attorney General

William Paterson was a hard man to deal with. He wanted every loyalist eliminated. Born in 1745, County Antrim, Ireland, he came to the colonies at age two. His father was a tin ware salesman. They lived in New Castle, Delaware, then New London, Connecticut before settling in 1750 at Princeton, New Jersey where he began to manufacture tin goods. William attended college of New Jersey (Later Princeton) and took a B.A in 1763 and an M.A. three years later. He settled near New Brunswick at his Raritan estate in 1779 at the time of Benjamin's indictment. William Paterson served in the provincial congress (1775-76), then on the council of constitutional convention (1776), legislative council (1776-77), council of safety (1777) and was on the militia commission. From 1776 to 1783 he was attorney general of New Jersey. He married Cornelia Bell, and later to Euphemia White. They lived in New Brunswick City from 1783 to 1787. Was elected to the U.S. Senate (1789-90) and was governor of New Jersey from 1790-93). He also served as associate justice of the U.S. Supreme Court and died Sept. 1806. Paterson, New Jersey was named in his honor.

William Paterson

Benjamin's life in New Jersey was now over. He had to go underground, and do it quickly. Just thirty dollars changed his entire life. One morning as he was walking down a farm road towards Morristown to buy some goods he saw a small pose of rebels suddenly appeared. Muskets already drawn, he knew within seconds that his capture was at hand.

"Are you Benjamin Bonnell?" the Captain asked.
"Yes!" Ben replied sadly.
"You are under arrest," demanded the Captain.

Benjamin did not put up a fight. He handed over his musket and jumped up into their wagon as ordered. They had already captured two other men who were in the wagon. Everything was now in the open. His father would soon find out and the family would bare the pressures from other Rebel supporters. As the wagon sped off and the troops began their search for others, Ben thought he had to do something fast. He was sure to get the death sentence. The wagon and rebels approached a farm of another suspected Loyalist. Ben watched them confront the occupants of the farm. Like a wild animal, Ben followed every move they made. The captain walked up to the house and called out. The two horsemen who covered the rear of the wagon slowly moved to the front to help reinforce their captain.

This left the back of the wagon wide open. The other men knew what Ben was up to. He had to decide now. There was no waiting. He slowly slipped down off the wagon as the other two prisoners looked on. They were too frightened to follow Ben. He quickly slipped into some bushes on the side of the road and took off as fast as his legs could take him. There was a nearby cord field. That would surely hide him. He reached the middle and stepped up onto a small mound to take a peek at where his pursuers were. To his surprise, he noticed them all still talking with the farmer. They never notice his escape. Now, Morris County was no longer safe for him. He headed for Egg Harbor where many smuggling operations were going on. He could find shelter there. It wasn't long before he spotted a few familiar faces, some loyalist members of the Day, Steeves and Wright families. Out of breath, he sat back onto some new spring swamp-grass and told the others about his close call. They all listened closely to Ben's story because most had already been in his shoes and knew about all the fears he was expressing. This kind of treatment was not uncommon. In fact, the loyalists retaliated by targeting the faithful rebels of various communities to confuse the Patriot authorities. They recalled one special attack.

One early target was poor Joseph Curtis of Morristown who received a barrel of counterfeit bills on February 27, 1779 with a letter directing it all to him. This was obviously made to look like he ordered the phony bills. He was so outraged that he put an ad in the newspaper with a two hundred dollar reward for the person or persons who had committed this crime against his character. He had been jailed for that alleged crime and stayed very upset for some time after his release.

Benjamin managed to get back to the area where his family was and he was soon able to get some information on rebel troop movements to the British side. Washington's main artillery regiment was located at Succasunna, just above Morristown, his home.

On November 30, 1779, several residents of Morris County were apprehended and secured in jail for possession of counterfeit money, and for passing those bills of credit around the area. This scared Ben because he was part of this gang and he didn't want to get his family involved. The counterfeit money helped them all, but now it was his ruin.

Colonel Robinson and Chevalier Massillon took over the Drake House not more than one mile outside of Mendham during the winter of 1779-80. This location was their headquarters for a while[5]. The circle around Ben's home was closing in.

Somewhere along Ben's travels, he met Sarah (Sally) Jones who was from possibly Bergen County, New Jersey. He loved her very much and planned to take her for his wife. Their marriage and family began somewhere along the refugee trail, but a church record has yet to appear. His family kept a very low key and stayed out of rebel notice.

---

[5] Also from Mendham, NJ History during the American Revolution.

A meeting was held between a few smugglers who had just escaped the rebel authorities the night before. Ben attended that meeting and became very upset over the agenda. They felt they knew who the informants were and they plotted to have them killed. Just as the lynching crowd was leaving to find the informants, Ben jumped to his feet in protest. He pleaded for them to think it over. The would-be victims, John Ward and Nathaniel Camp of Newark had been their friends at one time. As a once peaceful Quaker, Ben begged them to not go out and kill these men who had families. After a half hour, Ben could see that he persuaded a few not to go out and murder these men. After more deliberations, they all decided to go out and deliver sentence for the crime they committed against them and their King. That night, they quietly went out and set fire to both men's barns without anyone seeing them or without any casualties.

On January 18, 1780, the next load of goods and counterfeit bills were about to arrive at the Sandy Hook lighthouse coming by ship through the ice-laden bay from New York. There were about ten men who were to meet there and carry off the booty. That night was very dark and freezing. Ben went with three others in a small rowboat. The icy ocean swells were high near the lighthouse. Other men were already on shore as Ben made his careful landing. Without a single word spoken, they all climbed up the small hill to a one-room cabin at the base of the light. The British had already made their drop and when the men entered the cabin their eyes beheld one of the biggest shipments yet. Over $45,000 in counterfeit bills and a large quantity in good hard currency. They had traded several large cases of dry goods that went to the British as part of the business transaction. The fruit of their hard labors were before them. The British got their goods, the smugglers their bogus money to use in the New Jersey monetary system, and income for their families.

Just as everyone was beginning to leave, a shout came from outside the cabin. It was not a friendly voice!

"This is Captain Rudolph of Major Lee's Rangers! I have a sergeant, a corporal and eight other men out here. You must surrender immediately or be shot!"

There was no time for thought or words. Shooting broke out as soon as Captain Rudolph ended his demand. Before the Patriot rebels could cover the back door, Ben and two others slipped away into the darkness.

Within minutes, Captain Rudolph and his party took the cabin and the Loyalists were taken prisoner. Ben and the other two men split up with Ben jumping into the frozen harbor and swimming across to safety. Exhausted and nearly dead from exposure, he laid on the beach for what seemed like half the night. He never swam so fast and couldn't feel a nerve in his ice-covered body for several hours. Later, he made his way back home.

The next day, he heard of another raid by the Patriot rebels. It was at Egg Harbor, a very popular drop off point for the British. This time there were deaths reported. Ben's good friend and captain of a fine schooner, Robert Campbell, of New York was killed along with several other Loyalists. Another large amount of counterfeit bills were seized.

During the winter of 1779-1780, the New York Bay froze to such an extent that the British Cavalry crossed it to invade New Jersey. Washington still had his headquarters in Morristown at the home of Colonel Jacob Ford, and his troops guarded the Chatham Bridge day and night fearing a sneak attack by the British. At times this location was also the spot for exchanging prisoners[6]. The Morristown area was becoming a very historic place. Not too long ago The Dickerson Tavern on Spring and Water Streets was the location of another attempted Court Martial of Benedict Arnold that Patriot General Robert Howe presided over. Later in 1780, the British nearly surprised Washington at Morristown, but by the time they reached Bottle Hill, the snow, rain and hail made the roads impassable and they all had to retreat[2].

The rebels were really putting on the pressure. Ben wasn't sure if one of the loyalist captives would reveal his location. Congress had passed a bill that now dealt with the counterfeiting problem; jail, trial and death! Not necessarily in that order. Ben feared his capture was at hand. He did not know whom to trust anymore. Later on during the war, a Bonnell relation who lived at the Chatham Bonnell homestead on Watchung Avenue baked bread all night for the traveling soldiers going to Yorktown, Virginia to battle[8]. Even a family member was capable of turning him in.

A meeting was planned with his family. He could no longer stay in New Jersey. Everything was at its lowest point, and with the times being as they were, a great fear was yet to come. On May 19, 1780, the bright mid-day sun turned into night. Times were pretty bad but no one thought the end of the world was a hand! Fear struck many as a dark cloud covered every bit of sky and sunlight. Only historical accounts would later shed light on the strange occurrence that terrified all of New England. A great number of forest fires raged throughout western New York and Pennsylvania, and without knowing the cause, the frightened population witnessed what they thought was a clear sign of the beginning of the end.

Benjamin was home with his wife during this trying moment. They sat in silent prayer and hoped that the end was not at hand. Soon, the clouds passed by and the smell of burning wood dissipated. Ben focused back into his immediate situation and sat Sarah down next to him looking her closely into those beautiful eyes.

---

[6] From Historic Roadsides of Morris County, New Jersey, History of Chatham during the American Revolution.
[7] From Historic Roadsides of Morris County, New Jersey, History of Morristown during the American Revolution.
[8] Also from the History of Chatham, NJ during the American Revolution.

"My dear! I must leave! This is no place for me here anymore. I'll go to New York City where it is safe. After the British take control of this uprising I can return. Right now I fear we are in danger with me hanging around this bailiwick."

Sarah started to cry. A child was on its way and difficult times lay ahead with Ben not at home to support them. The loyal family members would now take that burden. Ben explained that he would return to get her once he found a place. They embraced within a multitude of tears and then he left for his father's house to pass on the news.

The fire was high in the fireplace. Benjamin Senior and Eleanor were snuggled around it trying to keep the chill off their aging bodies. It was a hard days work and the warm fire felt good on the sore muscles. How familiar it was, as Ben looked through the front window. His parents had a sad and tiring look across their face. The thought of his leaving brought tears to his eyes once more. He loved his family very much, but now he needed to look to the future for his new family, Sarah and his future child. Without notice, he opened the front door sending a startle through them. Eyes were upon him at first in silence. Eleanor jumped up and embraced her son while his father walked over and carefully looked out the window just before closing the curtains.

"They are all out looking for you my son," his father said.

Ben told them all of his plans. He had to make New York his home for the safety of all. That statement caught his mother by surprise. He explained that he would send for Sarah and the baby later, once he secured a safe place. Eleanor was crying by the time Ben finished. They gave each other hugs and kisses as his father walked back to the fireplace. Ben looked over at him. He walked over and placed his hand on his shoulder from behind. He just kept staring into the fire. Silence took over the cabin as all eyes were on him. Then, Ben spoke!

"Father! I know I've placed you in some difficult spots during the past few years. I'm sorry for that. I had to do what I had to do. Our Quaker faith called for us to never revolt against our country. Now, I find that I still must fight. I'm sorry for that and I hope you understand."

Benjamin waited for his father's reply! The senior's eyes filled with tears while he still remained frozen gazing at the flames. The flicker danced all over the water that formed around his pupils.

Then suddenly, he turned around and looked closely at his Loyalist son, and said.

"I think my Quaker religion is still compassionate and I'll always love you my son. You do know the meetinghouse must disown you for taking part in this war?"

He took Ben into his arms and embraces him with his love and understanding.

Tears filled the room. His father sat back onto his chair filled with emotion and grief. His advanced years could not take the torment his family was going through. Everyone soon came together in one mass of family love. They had silent prayer together, until...

That precious moment was blown apart with the sound of several horses pulling up front of the cabin. A quick peek revealed rebel soldiers. Suddenly, they scrambled to get Ben out the back door before the soldiers made it back there. Ben's father opened the front door to greet the men. He noticed it was the same captain who was looking for Ben all along. Without mixing many words, the captain came right to the point.

"We know he is around here. Have you seen him?"

The captain motioned a horseman around back of the cabin. Without a second thought, Eleanor acted like she slipped off the front porch right into the path of the horseman, stopping him for just a few seconds longer from entering the back of the cabin. The rebel soldier jumped off his horse and assisted Eleanor off the muddy ground. She acted as if she sprained her ankle. After helping her to a bench on the porch he re-mounted his animal and continued around back. Ben was already long gone across the fields heading for Egg Harbor hoping to jump a Tory ship for New York.

Gov. William Franklin
Son of Benjamin Franklin & last Loyalist Governor of New Jersey

Chapter 4

REFUGEE'S FROM NEW JERSEY

When Benjamin arrived at the harbor, the night was a murky black one. The water was still with just a slight breeze brushing across it. It took just a few hours for a faint light to flicker over the bay telling him a ship was coming. He watched quietly as the familiar event started to unfold. As the ship slowly approached Ben noticed a candlelight coming from some bushes not far away from him. The night was still enough to hear a dory dropping into the distant waters. A few minutes later several men appear from the bushes heading for the beach as the dory came ashore. Ben recognized the people and found it safe enough to whistle a common secret signal they all had. Slightly startled, the men took notice and relax after seeing Ben. After the transactions were completed, the men slip back into the bushes and the dory now carrying Ben floated back into the darkness of the sea night.

By the time Ben arrived at the Wall Street dock in New York City the sun was beginning to rise. Just catching a little sleep, the bright sunrays blasted through his eyelids waking him facing the Queen Ann's British flag flying high atop the ships mast. Just then a passer-by sailor telling him they were entering the harbor kicked him. He jumped to his feet. There in front of him was the only major colonial city controlled by the British Empire in America.

Ben watched as the city came closer. He saw two ghostly ships anchored far offshore. They were serving as prison ships, housing captured rebels of the King. He read about the conditions on those ships and the low percentage of captors who were fortunate to leave them. Focus went back to the city in front of him. Looking at this city as a safe haven for the loyalists, little did he know it was only the beginning for millions of other types of refugees from around the world in the future to find refuge, seeking asylum at its gates. His thoughts now went to finding job and his home back in New Jersey. Disappointment controlled his mind. He felt lost. The dock area was crowded with wagons, horses and people traveling in every direction. Some ships were being unloaded while others were setting sail. Many privateers were delivering their spoils from raided coastline towns and ships of the open sea.

Shock and disillusionment set in as he saw people sleeping in the streets. Conditions were poor and overcrowded. It was much worst than what he heard. After the ship was secured at the dock, Ben disembarked and was greeted by a half dozen children begging for change. He didn't know how to accept this kind of poverty. It was sad. All he could do was brush the children aside and walk quickly away. After all! He was no better off then they were.

Benjamin knew of one location in town where he could make his start. He read about the Loyalist clubs in the city from the Royal Gazette newspaper printed by the notorious Loyalist editor, James Rivington. He read about the many loyalists from different areas of the colonies gathering in Pubs that represented their locales. The New Jersey one would be his target. It was still early in the day as the streets were bustled with activity. Troops were everywhere.

After a few questions, it wasn't long before Ben found Leonard's Tavern, a favorite meeting place for New Jersey men. The place was not open yet, so he went around back and found a comfortably place to bed down. He was exhausted.

It wasn't long before Benjamin was awakened by many loud voices coming from within the Tavern. He jumped to his feet and brushed off the dirt and dust. Spit in his hands and rubbed them over his hair giving the slight appearance that it was combed. He pulled open the heavy door and entered a smoke filled room. As he drifted through looking for a familiar face he heard stories jumping about, most quoted by Rivington's gazette.

"Did you know that Martha Washington left the General? She finally got smart!"

"George Washington and Benjamin Franklin were killed in an ambush!" stated another Loyalist.

The Royal Gazette started many rumors that gave the Loyalists badly needed moral until 1783 when it finally went out of business.

Benjamin finally spotted John and William Day and Titus Brown, three friends from Northern New Jersey. They were happy to see him too. After a short update of their lives and conditions, the subject changed over to the war. They heard some land would possibly be offered to loyal subjects after the hostilities. The American colonies were already expending westward and the British thought this area would be the loyalist prize for their service.

The visit to the Tavern paid off for Ben because one of his friends offered his floor to him to sleep on while he looked for a job. John Day worked at a warehouse as a hay loader and felt there could be a position there for Ben. Any job in New York at this time was paying very poorly. There were very little jobs and plenty of workers needing them. Many children were sent out into the streets to beg for what little they could get.

Ben sent off a letter to Sarah telling her of his safe passage and arrival. It was now September 1780 and in a few days, history would stand at a delicate balance. Just a short trip up the Hudson River events were unfolding. Benedict Arnold had just heard that John Anderson had been captured.

He sat down at the breakfast table with his aids but couldn't eat a thing. Anderson was his courier who carried a note, which contained all the plans of the surrender of West Point, a very strategic fort, and the capture of General George Washington when he arrived to meet Arnold there. Anderson was really Major John Andre of the British army. Arnold's plan had failed and soon he would be discovered. Arnold sat there wondering what to do next. He got up and went to his wife Peggy's room where he broke the news to her. She immediately became hysterical as he told her that he had to leave and would later send for her. Their plan was for her to deny the knowledge of the entire episode and break down into tears when she was told what Arnold had done. After a quick kiss, Arnold darted out of the room and into the countryside.

Andre's ship, the Vulture, was still anchored in the Hudson waiting for him to return. They had already suffered damage from a rebel gun and most men on board were getting anxious. Suddenly, they saw a small boat approaching bearing a flag of truce. To their surprise, it was Patriot, Benedict Arnold, not Andre. When Clinton heard the news, he abandoned the plans to attack West Point. They headed back to New York.

When General Washington arrived at West Point and heard the startling news, he and his men went to Peggy Arnold, who played her role so well that Washington later gave her safe passage to New York. On September 22, 1780 the American Revolution could have ended in favor of the British, if Arnold's plans had been successful.

On board the Vulture, Arnold asked to use the captain's cabin to write his desertion letter to Washington. The following is what he wrote:

"The heart which is conscious of its own rectitude, cannot attempt to palliate a step which the world may censure as wrong; I have ever acted from a principle of love to my country, since the commencement of the present unhappy contest between Great Britain and the Colonies. The same principle of love to my country actuates my present conduct, however, it may appear inconsistent to the world, who very seldom judge right of any man's actions."

When Arnold arrived at New York, the British kept their promise by giving him the position of Brigadier General and would soon raise a regiment for him consisting of American Loyalists. He was also given 6,315 pounds in cash for the loss of his property and a commission of 200 pounds a year, as well as a yearly stipend for his wife and children. This outraged many British citizens and high-ranking military men who were getting much less then he. He became a threat to them, because they all knew about his aggressive personality and his keen sense of military matters. He was labeled a traitor. Even by the British.

Washington was very upset over Arnold's actions. After he read his letter, he made one famous statement;

"And now whom can we trust."

Later, history would report that Benedict Arnold was the best battlefield general that served both armies of the American Revolution. Even when he lost some engagements, his blow to the enemy was lethal enough to cripple them for months. The battle against the British at Lake Champlain with the Green Mountain Men was one great example. And his march through Maine into Quebec was another great feat worth mentioning when he paid his men from his own pockets to keep their services after Congress refused to do so. His attacks against the Patriot rebels would soon prove to be just as devastating.

Now, the propaganda war was on the side of the British. Rebel conditions were poor, and after Arnold changed sides, many followed him. One very such mutiny occurred near Morristown when the Pennsylvania Regiment deserted and shot their Captain Adam Bettin on 1 January 1781 on Hollow Road[9]. This kind of desertion disturbed Washington the most. By January 3, 1781, bulletins were coming in stating the Patriot Rebel collapse was beginning. Washington's most outstanding outfit commanded by General Anthony Wayne, the Pennsylvania line of 2,500 men, became mutinous at Morristown, New Jersey. Their reasons were: lack of pay, no clothing or food, plus complaints about the terms of their duty. Many marched to Trenton, New Jersey to protest.

Hearing these developments disturbed Benjamin. He wondered what the conditions were like at home. So much history was unfolding around his family. He prayed they were safe. The suffering was high and many farmers were being robbed by troops from both sides. The rebels took goods in the name of Congress, and the British took in the name of the King. Was Sarah and the expected baby all right? Was the family farm still standing? Letters had not arrived in such a long time, he wondered!

Washington started to execute some of the mutineers to present an example to the rest of his troops that these actions would not be allowed anymore. Some flogging sentences were increased to five hundred lashes after Congress approved it. Many American rebels were nicknamed "bloody-backs." General Clinton enjoyed hearing that kind of bad news. He passed on every bit of those stories to his troops to keep their spirits high in the belief that the uprising would soon be over. But Washington still managed to hold on to many others.

---

[9] From Historic Roadsides of Morristown, New Jersey during the American Revolution.

Against his friends' advice, Benjamin decided to go back to Morris county to get his family out of there. He knew the trip would be very dangerous. On one cold winter's night, he managed to get a lift on a Privateer ship heading over to New Jersey to pick up more contraband. This time he slipped into the icy waters in the Perth Amboy harbor area at nine o'clock at night. The air was freezing cold. The wind off the ocean made it twice as cold as it really was. This return trip was just the beginning. There was over fifty miles to travel yet. Knowing he was an already wanted man, the thought of stealing a horse. It was not out of the question. When he got as far as Woodbridge, he did just that. Riding hard, the thought of hanging raced through his mind.

By the time he got to Rahway, three miles up the road, he caught a death of cold from his freezing body and wet clothes. He road three more miles where he finally collapsed into a ravine just outside of Westfield. The next morning he was awaken by the crow of a rooster. It was hard opening his eyes. Exhaustion and cold had taken its toll. Before him he saw two faded shadows. After a few attempts to focus his eyes, he discovered a couple in advanced years staring down at him. The old woman had some hot broth filled with several herbs in a pewter bowl. The old man came right to the point.

"Are you a Loyalist?"

Ben didn't know what to say at first, but the old lady added some security.

"Don't worry! We are not committed to either side. We are Quaker."

Before answering, Ben thought; "So was he, but somehow he got caught up into this war and now he had no way out."

"Yes! I am too!"

Ben sat up in bed and reached for the broth. The old couple was of the FitzRandolph family. Very well known in New Jersey, and one that was deeply split over the war. He recalled a Robert FitzRandolph who had already fled to New York as a Loyalist around the same time as Isaac Bonnell, the sheriff of Perth Amboy. This branch of the FitzRandolph's married into the Bonnell family. The thought made Ben feel safe. His recovery took two days and when visitors stopped by, he hid in the barn. He didn't' want to give them any trouble. When he left them they promised to pray for a peaceful journey for he and his family. Nighttime was much safer to travel.

Ben arrived near his family farm. It was close to sunrise. Along the way, he discovered much destruction. Many more farmhouses were burnt to the ground. He hoped to find his fathers place still standing. One high rolling hill was all that was left before he could see it. A heavy frost lay over the golden color grass. The damp chill shot right though his bones, but the rising sun was as bright as could be. When he reached the top, he had to cover his eyes from the blasting rays. In all its glory, there it was, still standing, everything! His father still managed to keep to the middle of the struggle without harming the family or farm.

It still was not safe to just ride down there, so he concealed himself next to some high bushes and watched the place for a while. After feeling pretty secure, he descended down the hill to the homestead. It looked so peaceful as a narrow stream of white smoke drifted into the crispy air from the chimney. Ben could smell something cooking. God was he hungry. A couple of scrawny chickens ran across the yard, being chased by his father's dog. He saw someone walking about inside the cabin as he dismounted his stolen horse.

Ben walked into the cabin as if he always did, startling everyone within. His father, and mother were getting ready to eat. Eleanor cried out and ran to her fugitive son. His father went to the windows and closed the curtains as he did in the past when Ben was on the run.

"We must get your horse out back before someone spots it," his father said and then followed his own command by going out to remove the horse himself.

"How are all the others?" Ben asked.

"They are fine, Eleanor answered.

His father came back into the cabin and walked over to his son giving him a big hug.

"I've missed you my boy."

It seemed like all reunions brought tears as everyone there started to feel the pain of separation. Senior Ben was getting old and with sons split in this war, it was starting to bring him down. Eleanor was sickly and hated to see her Quaker family fall to the side.
"But wait!" she thought. There was some good news.

"Ben! Sarah has had her baby. She named her Sarah." Eleanor smiled.

Ben got so excited that he picked his frail mother up and swung her around. He couldn't wait to get to his family. They all sat around the table and talked late into the night, filling Ben in on all that had happened while he was away. Many battles were fought around the area, and many friends and neighbors were killed. By the end of the evening, Ben announced that he had to take Sarah and the child back to New York City for their safety. He told them that they might never see each other again, unless the British won the war.

Brigadier General Benedict Arnold was forming a Loyalist refugee regiment after proving to General Clinton that the loyal colonists had potential military strength in the battlefield. Ben was planning to join. He really had no choice. He explained to his family that there was a plan in case the Patriots won. To relocate dedicated Loyalists and their families to Nova Scotia where plenty of land grants would be awarded for their service. Eleanor started to sob. She had never heard of Nova Scotia before and knew it must be far away. Ben explained that it was still in America, in a place called Canada located in the north.

The final good-byes were sadly expressed. Ben knew that hugging his mother and father this time would be the last. He mounted his horse and despondently rode off to meet up with his Sarah and children. As he road off, he wept as he heard he parents openly weeping back at the cabin.

Benjamin traveled in the waters edge of the Whippany River in order to hide his tracks. The area was crawling with Washington's troops. At one point, he was spotted. Knowing the territory, he outran them, but he knew they would now be on the watch for him. Sarah's family, like the Bonnell's was split over the revolution. Also being Quakers did not help their standing in that Meetinghouse in Bergen County. This area was not populated as much as his fathers place so it was much easier to hide someone. Soon he saw their small cabin nestled in a tiny ravine by the river. It was a very peaceful location, very much secluded. He hoped to have a place of his own just like that someday.

The opportunity was perfect. There was Sarah, outside fetching some water by the river, probably for their new baby. His insides were jumping with excitement. He wanted so much to just ride down that hill screaming out his love for her to the entire world, but he knew this could not be done. The entire area had to be checked out before he would quietly go down there. His approach was slow and calm. He got off his stolen horse and stepped down into a small brook that ran in back of the barn. There, he slowly crept around one corner and saw Sarah not more then ten feet away. Hardly containing himself, he managed to softly call out Sarah's name. When she turned around, her beauty was more as ever. At first her eyes looked sad, probably from the vacancy of her husband, but when their eyes met, she dropped the bucket of water and ran to his arms.

Their embrace seemed to last forever. All the agony and pain came to the surface as Sarah cried out. She had just lost her brother to this terrible war and thought she would never see her husband again. They cried together for nearly ten minutes before saying a word. Ben broke the bad news about them leaving New Jersey. There was no choice. Sarah started to cry again. She knew she had to go with her husband and never see her family again.

Suddenly, they heard several horses coming down the road. It was the militia looking for Ben. Sarah told him to hide in back of the barn in the abandoned underground root cellar that she and her brother use to play in when they were children. The door was covered with grass that had turned brown with the season. He jumped into the small opening and closed the lid as the horsemen rode up.

Sarah's father and mother came out to see what was happening. The troop consisted of some of their neighbors and friends that chose the rebel side. They also knew Ben, and figured he would show up someday to see his wife and children. One of the men was Sarah's close friend, James Day. He knew Ben also and was more understanding then the others.

"How have you been Sarah?" James asked.
"I'm gett'in by," Sarah replied coldly.

They asked to search the area because they got reports of someone looking like Ben was around. One man dismounted and followed Sarah's mother into the house while the others went through the outbuildings with her father. Sarah stood frozen while James Day and another man went around back looking through the brush. She decided to follow them seeing that they were the closest to her husbands hiding place.

Benjamin was at a real disadvantage, not able to see where they were and who they were. He just listened. Suddenly, James Day stepped on the wooden door covered with dirt and grass. Small amounts of dirt fell all over Ben's face and hair. Sarah was about to faint. The other man walked around to the front of the barn while James stood over the hiding place. Not moving, he just stood there.

"Sarah! Do you remember when we were kids and we played out back here?"

Sarah nearly wet her pants over his words. What should she do now? How should she answer that question? She wanted to lie down and just cry. James continued:

"It always amazed me how you got away and hid somewhere. How did you do that?"

Sarah stuttered a bit and tried to answer him, but he broke her thought by reaching down and quickly opening the door to the root cellar. Ben was startled, looking up at the rebel soldier. Sarah quietly cried out for mercy to her friend. Ben just sat there waiting for the order to get out. Everyone stood still looking at each other, except for Sarah who was still pleading. Unexpectedly, the commander yelled to James if he had found anything. James looked into Sarah's tearful eyes, and then down at Ben's pleading expression. His officer called out again!

Ben broke the silence by telling James that they were in the process of leaving the area for good. A few more seconds past until James broke the silence. With a swift kick of the door it slammed down onto Ben's face covering him with more dirt.

James yelled out:

"There is nothing back here sir. I'm on my way back."

Sarah reached out to her childhood friend and thanked him. He walked towards the front of the barn, but stopped one last time and turned to Sarah:

"Get him out of here quickly."

He joined the others as Sarah followed behind. James mounted his horse and they all rode back up the road.

Sarah turned and ran to the back of the barn leaving her parents wondering. They followed their daughter and discovered her in the arms of her husband. Ben explained that they had to leave immediately. He picked up his belonging and retrieved his horse from over the hill where it thankfully wandered too. They went into the cabin where Ben saw his child. The baby was beautiful. She was a true vision of Sarah. They then sat down and planned the trip to New York.

Sarah had saved several furnishings and belongings that she hoped someday would abound her own house. Her father gave them a wagon and Ben loaded it for the morning departure time. When the first signs of dawn came, Sarah lay there and watched Ben sleep. She listened outside to all the familiar sounds of her parent's farm. She would surely miss it very much. One part of her cried out with pain, the other was happy to have her husband back. She broke her trance and woke Ben up. They had to get going.

Breakfast was muted, even after silent prayer. Later, the farewell was just as quiet until the moment of departure. Sarah had the baby wrapped in a soft wool blanket to protect her from the cold and dust. Ben secured the back of the wagon and thanked Sarah's father for everything.

His stolen horse was now tied to the wagon. He jumped up onboard after saying goodbye. Sarah was resisting her departure with small delays, but finally hugged her parent's goodbye. Little did she realize that she would never see them again?

They had a long hard road to travel and Ben changed his clothing hoping that would alter his appearance. He took an old straw hat out of the barn to help. They had to travel north and then east across the Hudson River. Washington's troops were everywhere, but many didn't bother to stop traveling families unless they decided to rob them for supplies. The danger was all around them. Sarah's parents watched as their daughter rode off into eternity. As the day rolled on, they managed to ride right past many heavily armed rebels and their strongholds.

Their first night on the road was spent very close to the campfire. The icy cold stars danced around the sky making them both fall asleep early. They both held each other with the baby close to them. Like two scared children themselves, their dreams were filled with unsettling episodes of nightmares as to where they would end up. When morning broke, Sarah found Ben already loading the wagon. He had some food out and a hot brew of tea going in the fire. It wasn't long until they started their journey once more.

Ben kept to high ground when he could. This way he could see more and hopefully ward off any trouble before it started. It wasn't long until he spotted smoke right in the path of their travels to the Hudson. It was about five miles off. He decided to circle around a hilltop, keeping a distance, but able to see what was happening. After getting close enough, they saw a farmhouse and barn totally engulfed in flames. There were no troops or occupants around as far as Ben could determine. He decided to descend into the tiny valley to investigate. When he reached the bottom he instructed Sarah to stay behind while he checked out the area. He left them at a large clump of trees. The fire was decreasing in size as the buildings collapsed into charred ruins.

He walked over to where the house had been and discovered a murdered baby boy laying face down with a bullet hole through his head. In the charred doorway was a burnt body of what looked like a woman, probably the boy's mother. She was reaching out her arm to her dead son. Over near the collapsed barn, hanging from an old oak tree, was a man. Ben walked over to him and discovered a note pinned to his body.

It read:

"TORY - DIRTY TORY."

Ben cut the poor man down and dragged his stiff body over to lay with his wife and son.

He couldn't believe this was the work of rebel soldiers. He found it hard to think they would stoop so low as to kill woman and children. Now, he was concerned more about his family's safety. He made haste returning to Sarah and the baby, before she decided to investigate herself. He felt very weak and pale, so he took a few deep breaths and returned to the hidden wagon. He told Sarah about the man that was murdered, but he refused to tell her the rest of what he saw. They left that area as quickly as they could.

They finally saw their destination. Dobbs Ferry, New York. It was a long three days of journey only because they had to travel carefully. This was the crossover point to the British controlled area of New York and the gateway to New York City, Freedom! Opposing forces stood on each side of the Hudson River controlling entry and departure. Treatment was cruel and inhumane. Towns-people and children stood by threatening Loyalists of tar and feathering, stoning and calling out terrible names like traitor and disgusting obscenities. The rebel soldiers wanted the fleeing refugees to feel like dirt by degrading them all during their evacuation.

As they approached the ferry, Ben noticed the conditions of the soldiers. Many were dirty and poorly clothed. Conditions were bad. It was obvious that the war was taking its toll. Firewood was very scarce. This made Ben feel that the end of the war was very near. They couldn't hold out much longer, he thought. Morale was very low. Young boys looked tired and hungry and by their looks, recruiting age was getting younger by the day. They pulled their wagon over to designated spot and the clearance process would hopefully come by morning.

It was early the next morning when approval came. Excitement was high, but so was anxiety. The hecklers were all waiting for more Loyalists to cross. As they approached the ferry people started to gather and yell out curse after curse. Some spit on them and called them animals and traitors. Sarah couldn't take it any longer. She broke down and cried as they boarded the ferry. Her life was at its lowest level, she thought. It seemed like eternity, but the ferry finally left the rebel side and headed for the British side.

The Tory side of the Hudson River was less populated and very quiet as they landed. The small crowd just looked into the weary eyes of the new refugees, studying the emotional beating they just took. A file of wagons and horses with several people on foot silently departed the ferry in shame. The column just slowly headed in the direction of New York City, the capital of refuge and despair.

Chapter 5

NEW YORK CITY - EYE OF THE STORM

The trip back down the east side of the Hudson River was just as frightening. Every few miles they experienced Check Points. Everyone was stopped and searched by the British soldiers or other refugee loyalist Militiamen. Sarah couldn't stand then going through their personal effects. Her nerves were breaking apart. After a full day of travel, New York City appeared in all her glory. It was truly a welcome sight. Ben had to find his friend who offered them a place to stay. Hopefully, the invitation was still standing. He headed straight for Leonard's Tavern.

The establishment was packed with New Jersey Loyalists, as usual. Ben found his friend sitting at a table heavily covered with clouds of smoke as they all drank ale. The news was not good. His friend had given the room away to another Loyalist. He could only offer Ben and his family his old barn. They had no choice. They made all the arrangements and got directions. Ben took the bad news to Sarah who waited outside. With renewed strength, Sarah accepted the results and talked positive about it. This surprised Ben, but he did not question it. The barn was not far from the Wall Street dock area. The same place Ben had landed earlier and witnessed all the poverty and confusion. Now, they would be part of it.

To their amazement, the place was not bad. No sign of leaks, but it was damp and cold.

"A good fire will take care of that," Sarah said.

Ben pulled the wagon in and placed his horse in one stall. He pushed the wagon in another. A third stall would be their living quarters. Sarah started to clean and make the place into a home while Ben ran off to the tavern to learn more news.

He found the tavern still crowded and sat with William Wright and Joseph French. They were discussing events read in the Royal Gazette. Benedict Arnold had gone over General Sir Henry Clinton's head and wrote to London asking them for an independent Tory action under his leadership. This was his first step to get the American Loyalists into the conflict. He would need supplies and more men to end the war; the Loyalists were the answer. Most Loyalists were left out and wanted to help the cause so they could return home. The British from England in the colonies controlled the war and the loyal colonists did not like the way it was going.

Arnold was the best man to deal with Washington on the battlefield. Arnold's ambition ran high, even to the point of seeking and taking Clinton's command. Every military leader knew this, even Clinton himself. Benedict was already making many enemies on the British side. He had that talent to bring that out with everyone he dealt with. He had to take charge in such ruthless ways.

Never a politician, he entered partnerships with transport agents and leased eight vessels to the crown, securing for himself in just two months, six thousand pounds from an investment of only one thousand pounds. His actions were very questionable.

Arnold thought he got his first break with the death of General Phillips. This leadership past on to him, but it only lasted a few weeks before that battalion merged with Cornwallis. He was given the charge of fifteen hundred troops and sailed on transport vessels to the James River at Richmond, Virginia, and took that town without a rebel shot being fired. He burnt many public warehouse buildings and then returned to Portsmouth and was inactive until the spring. In October 1780, Sir Henry Clinton appointed Benedict Arnold Colonel of a regiment, and then raised his rank to Brigadier General.

While Ben was sharing his ale with William Wright and Joseph French, Wright recalled his plight in New Jersey. He had to sell his plantation in Chatham in July 1778. He became visibly upset as he described his eighty-one acres, fifty acres of which were excellent English meadow and produced upwards of fifty tons of timothy and blue grass in one season. The remaining was wooded and level with a nice house containing two fireplaces and a small bedroom. He said the water was the purest around Chatham and his orchard produced a bountiful crop every year. The place was fit for a gentleman, merchant or tradesman, and it was one of the best farms around[10]. Later, he purchased a small place in Woodbridge, New Jersey, thinking that he would be all right and go unnoticed. But on April 6, 1780, his house was seized and auctioned off along with that of Isaac Bonnell, sheriff of Perth Amboy for both being Loyalists.

Wright said that he and Isaac were good friends, and when Isaac's wife, Grace died he managed to sneak back to New Jersey to attend her funeral on Saturday, September 30, 1780, where at her graveside at the Trinity churchyard, he bid her farewell. The New York Gazette and Weekly Mercury ran her death notice on October 16, 1780. William Wright hung his head in sorrow after telling his emotional story. He just starred solemnly into his warm ale.

Self-confessions continued with Joseph French telling his story of woe, recalling his ordeal of despair. He placed his farm in the care of Lefever Legrange, thinking it would be safe in someone else's hands. It was a beautiful one hundred-seventy acre farm, located south of Fox Hill in the township of Mendham. Ben remembered how truly beautiful it was, agreeing with French as he spoke. It was one of the finest farms in the county. When the rebels found out that he joined the British army, Legrange's position was exposed and an inquisition was brought up against French on April 13, 1779 in Essex County. They sold his fine property. It all became final at ten o'clock on April 5, 1780 at an auction on the green at Morristown.

---

[10] Found in New Jersey Newspaper Extracts.

Silence hung over all three men. They did not hear even the roar of voices around them. Benjamin started his story of woe, and when he finished they all were depressed and weakened by the entire session. Suddenly, Joseph shot out of his chair and went over to the bar to get more ale. He did not want the others to see his tears in his eyes. Ben knew this and watched his friend wipe his eyes clear as he walked away.

The next few days Benjamin found himself wandering aimlessly through the streets looking for work. Most people felt pretty safe in New York. After all, the British army and navy had occupied the city since July 12, 1776, and by the end of that year controlled the entire lower Hudson area and managed to keep that control throughout the entire war. This drove Washington crazy. His attempts to take New York became an insane passion.

Ben hoped that he and his family would be able to go back home soon to be a simple farmer again. He heard that the British for their goods were now paying some farmers in gold. As he walked the city streets he stopped at the corner of Fair Street and Broadway and watched some refugee men present their certificates of loyalty to Captain Homfray before signing up under his command. Ben thought that he too might have to do the same thing to keep food on his family's table. When he arrived home that day, Sarah had some bean soup on the fire. Her father had given them a very large bag and it sure came in handy during the leaner periods. She knew how to prepare then several ways to make each meal different.

Ben noticed Sarah's face through the flickering of the fire. It had a special glow. It made her look heavenly. She had a glowing smile. Ben knew that something was up. He couldn't imagine what could make her appear so calm and content, and happy at such a low point in their lives. He whispered into her ear, asking her why she was so. She sat back from the fire watching the beans simmer, grabbed her knees up to her chest and just stared into the flames with her glowing smile.

"When are you going to tell me what you have on your mind," Ben finally pleaded.

"I am bearing another child," Sarah calmly replied.

Ben's face lit up like a lantern and he jumped over to her side and gave her the biggest kiss and hug. He hoped this one would be a son. Their night was full of love and compassion instead of loss and desperation.

The next day, he went to see another friend. John Day! Remembering that he once offered him a job in a warehouse where he worked. John was able to persuade the head master to hire Ben. It did not pay very much, but it was all there was. Life stabilized for a few months and Sarah was now very big with child.

Her appetite increased accordingly too. There wasn't much food, so Ben cut back his portion to supply the difference. One expense he had to continue and that was the money for the tavern visits. Any information about the war or news coming in from home was very important. He managed to spread his two allotted drinks throughout the evenings.

One afternoon, when Ben was minding a store on Wall Street for a friend, he noticed a New Jersey newspaper lying in the street. He had to read it. Then went out into the street and picked it up from the wet muddy gutter. He knew that it would be full of rebel propaganda, but it still had interests to him, especially if he read between the lines. Like a kid, he came running back into the store, sat behind the counter on a tall wooden stool and fumbled through each soggy torn page.

One article, written by a rebel, did catch his attention. It was an invented dialogue with Satan and Benedict Arnold. It quoted Satan speaking to Arnold:

"My worthy good fellow; I love you much better than I ever did;
You live like a prince;
But mind that you, do just what I bid."

Arnold's reply:

"My friend, do not doubt me; I will strictly adhere to all your great views;
To you, I'm devoted, with all things about me;
You'll permit me I hope, to die in my shoes."

At that moment, Ben got up and threw the newspaper across the store back into the street and walked about cursing Washington under his breath. Captain Thomas Ward put many ads in the New York papers, asking Loyalist refugee men to help him conduct raids into New Jersey. Ben remembered Ward contacting him on one occasion especially after a raid had failed, looking for more recruits. They had raided rebel farms in the Hackensack area not far from New York and carried their booty back to the British side. In December of 1780, the Bergen militia broke this ring by surprising them with fourteen men. They were thrown into the Morristown goal. Captain Ward wanted men like Ben, and after he asked for his services, Ben said that he would have to consider it awhile. He never got back to Ward because his own life turned into chaos.

That evening, he met up with his friends at the tavern. Titus Brown told Ben that he saw in a New Jersey newspaper an article mentioning the arrest of a Benjamin Bonnell of Captain Mead's Company. He, John Burnet, and John Yherts deserted on December 12, 1780. There was a three hundred dollar reward for his capture. Titus continued to explain that they were finally captured and thrown into the Newtown goal and secured there by James Morrow, town jailer, on January 7, 1781.

Titus asked Ben whom this Ben was, continuing with a joke about him serving both sides of the war. Ben said that he had a cousin who lived near Elizabethtown, New Jersey with the same name as he. They were a very active rebel family and thought that was probably him. The name Benjamin was very common in his family.

Joseph French told Ben that he had just heard that Patriot troops were keeping a close watch out for Benedict Arnold and that he was spotted with a number of British vessels from New York off the coast of New Haven, Connecticut. The report said that he had 4000 troops on board under his direction. Ben said, that he thought the British commanders wanted the rebels to watch out for Arnold. This would give them more time to plan the real theater of war. Arnold would not let them use him very much longer.

The main topic of discussion was the signing of the "Associated Loyalist Declaration" which was at the core of many Loyalist aggravations with their British rulers. They all felt that they were being used by London and that no one knew of their capabilities in this battle. The following is that declaration:

By the Honourable Board of Directors
Of Associated Loyalists,
A Declaration

From the commencement of the present unnatural rebellion, it has been often wished that some regular and efficient system was adopted, for employing the zeal of that Class of his Majesty's Loyal Subjects in North America, who from their peculiar circumstances, were unwilling to become Soldiers by profession, though ardently inclined to take up arms, and contribute their aid towards reducing the rebels. For want of such a system, the spontaneous exertions of the Colonial Loyalists have been confined within limits no ways proportioned to the extent of their inclinations. But, narrow as their shere of action has hitherto been, they found room to display such courage and abilities, as fully evinced the propriety and utility of giving further scope to that spirit of enterprise by which they were actuated.

His Majesty has therefore been induced to signify his royal pleasure, that a Board be established for embodying and employing such of his faithful Subjects in North American, as may be willing to associate under their direction, for the purpose "of arraying the sea coast of the revolted Provinces, and distressing their trade;" either in "co-operation with his Majesty's land and sea forces," or "by making diversions in their favour when they are carrying on operations in other parts."

In pursuance of his Majesty's gracious intentions, his Excellency Sir Henry Clinton, K.B. and commander in chief, has been pleased to issue a commission under his hand and seal, constituting William Franklin, Esquire, Governor of New Jersey, Josiah Martin, Esquire, Governor of North Carolina, Timothy Ruggles, Daniel Cox, George Duncan Ludlow, Edward Latwyche, George Rome, George Leonard, Anthony Stewart, and Robert Alexander, Esquire, a Board of Directors, for the conduct and management of this business.

That zeal which should animate every Loyal Subject of his Majesty, and that sympathetic regard which the Directors feel for their fellow sufferers amoung the Loyalists of America, have determined them to undertake the execution of the commission. In performing this duty to the best of Sovereigns, they are authorized to assure all those who may become Associators of the following benefits and rewards for their encouragement,
Viz.

1. That all persons willing and able to bear arms for the suppression of the present rebellion, and who engage to form under the direction of the Board, agreeable to this establishment, will be subject to the command of those officers who may be recommended by the Board, and commissioned by the Commander in Chief, during such term only as they may previously agree upon.

2. That the Associators are to be furnished with such ordnance and stores, small arms and ammunition, as may be judged proper for the service.

3. That they will be supplied with rations of provisions when they are going upon service, and during their continuance thereon.

4. That all captures made by the Associators (when not acting in conjunction with any of his Majesty's land and sea forces) will be their entire property, and distributed among them in such shares as shall be settled by the Board, and specified in the articles of Association.

5. That they are to be furnished by the Commander in Chief of his Majesty's ships on the North American station with such shipping, to be manned by themselves, as may be thought necessary for the service, from among the transports or other vessels in his Majesty's pay, and not commanded by the King's officers.

6. That their mariners will not be impressed into any other services during their continuance in the Director's employment.

7. That the prisoners they take will be exchanged only for such Associated Loyalist as the Board may name for that purpose.

8. *That the sick and wounded of the Loyalist so associated will have the help and benefit of the King's hospitals.*

9. *That such as may at any time be called to serve the royal army as Guides, will be allowed wages during their service.*

10. *That such Associators who shall continue to act under the Directors orders, during the rebellion, will receive a gratuitous grant of two hundred acres of land in North America.*

This declaration goes on to explain what they wanted everything restored as it was before the outbreak of hostilities.

Signed on behalf of the Board, William Franklin, President, New York, December 28, 1780.

This made every refugee feel like they were part of the struggle. After all, it was their homeland they were fighting for. They British could go home to England when all was done, but the Loyalists had to live with whatever the outcome would be. Ben felt like he was being sucked farther into this situation. He prayed it would be over soon, before he had to sign up to fight. Military service was now mandatory in New York City, and everyone between the ages of sixteen and sixty had to serve in some form or matter. There were over 30,000 Loyalists refugees now living in or around the city, a growing power not to ignore!

One day while Ben was sitting in the tavern waiting for his friends to show up a familiar face appeared at his table. Ben couldn't believe his eyes. It was one of his old smuggling friends. They were very action in the counterfeiting trade. He sat down and presented him with an offer that he couldn't refuse. The call finally came. It was from a much higher authority than his friend. They were recruiting men for the American Legion of Refugees created by Brigadier General Benedict Arnold. A position of Corporal awaited him. This was considered a very high honor because any soldiers around Arnold were considered his personal guard. Did Arnold know of Benjamin's reputation? There was a big campaign coming and they needed many soldiers. The answer naturally had to be yes!

Capt. Nathan Frinks of the American Legion Cavalry began to recruit loyalists at Bergen, New Jersey, New York and Westchester, New York[11].

---

[11] From National Archives of Canada Pay Lists C4219.

Now, Ben had to break the news to Sarah. She was very close to delivery and prayed he would be by her side at that moment. It would not be so; for Ben left for Ireland Heights just outside the city. Sarah went right into labor. She cried out for Ben as a mid-wife assisted her. It was a boy! And again, her husband was not there by her side.

She lay in a barn stall, with her newborn baby. Her husband was gone off to possibly never to return and her post-delivery depression added to the misery. The baby needed a name and for the second time she had to do the job. Samuel... After Ben's grandfather.

Brig. General Benedict Arnold
Patriot, Traitor and Loyalist

Courtesy of Benedict Arnold, The Prod Warrior, by Charles Sellers, 1930

Chapter 6

SEPTEMBER 6, 1781 - THE MASSACRE

Benjamin enlisted on August 6, 1781 and on August 28; he mustered under Captain James Wogan of the American Legion Refugees, which was formed by the newly appointed Brigadier General, Benedict Arnold. Ben's rank was Corporal and he wondered what his first assignment would be. With this great general at his lead, he was sure it was going to be very interesting. The Legion's uniforms were very smart; Red coat, white waistcoat, turnback and pants, blue collar and cuffs. They were encamped with the Queens Rangers at Ireland Heights located between Flushing and Jamaica on the ground lately occupied by the British Grenadiers. The following list of men is the muster roll of the American Legion under Arnold.

Muster Roll Call - 28 August 1781
American Legion - Brigadier General, Benedict Arnold

Rank	Name	Enlisted	Absent
Captain	Wogan, James	10 Dec. 1781 (Commission)	
Sergeant	Mopley, William	5 Jan. 1781	
Sergeant	Bysell, Daniel	15 Aug. 1781	
Sergeant	Nubell, Nathaniel	?	
Corporal	Woodhouse, Phillip	8 July 1781	
Corporal	Ackins, George	27 June 1781	Sick
Corporal	**Bonnell, Benjamin**	**6 Aug. 1781**	
Corporal	Cooke, Jabez	13 Aug. 1781	
Private	Woodhouse, John	6 July 1781	
Private	Cranbury, Thomas	6 July 1781	
Private	Bruce, Thomas	7 July 1781	
Private	Ward, Wiatt	6 July 1781	
Private	Lovett, William	24 July 1781	
Private	Halstead, John	24 July 1781	
Private	Hanse, Isaac	21 Nov. 1780	
Private	Bowe, Thomas	24 Jan. 1781	
Private	Butt, David	15 July 1781	
Private	Harvey, Alligood	11 July 1781	
Private	Anguish, John	15 June 1781	
Private	Neal, Michael	27 June 1781	
Private	Coleman, David	26 July 1781	
Private	Ogden, Noah	6 Aug. 1781	

Private	Varrep, Laurence	7 Aug. 1781	
Private	Brown, James	9 Aug. 1781	
Private	Townsend, Robert	9 Aug. 1781	
Private	Campbell, Michael	15 Aug. 1781	
Private	Cocket, William	16 Aug. 1781	
Private	Tarron, Peter	1 April 1781	
Private	Woodruff, Daniel	1 Jan. 1781	
Private	Henyen, Daniel	?	
Private	Van Otto, Peter	?	
Private	Fletcher, James	30 July 1781	
Private	Warren, John	30 July 1781	
Private	Munrow, Albert	27 July 1781	
Private	Miller, William	27 July 1781	
Private	Hill, Briney	16 July 1781	
Private	Beaty, Peter	15 Aug. 1781	
Private	Ferguson, John	15 Aug. 1781	
Private	Reed, William	17 Aug. 1781	
Private	Gardner, Thomas	17 Aug. 1781	
Private	Heppard, John	10 Aug. 1781	
Private	Murrey, John	19 Aug. 1781	
Private	Anderson, Mathew	15 Aug. 1781	Sick
Private	Ferguson, Robert	19 Aug. 1781	
Private	Murphy, Timothy	26 Aug. 1781	

Note: From the British Military and Naval Records (RG 8,I), Public Archives of Canada, Ottawa, Ontario.

One evening, Corporal Phillip Woodhouse and Ben were sitting by the fire when Woodhouse told him something he had overheard. Captain Wogan said they would soon be moving out to sea on a very big assignment. A large battle was not far off, Ben thought as he stared into the blazing flames. That night he slept restless as he dreamt of fierce hand-to-hand combat. Several times he woke up in a heavy sweat. The following few days were shear misery. Waiting for the news to pull out still had not arrived.

On September 4, 1781, word finally came. They would sail the following night at 7 P.M., the destination still unknown. There were many ships anchored in the New York harbor. Much more then realized. This was going to be a big combat mission, one with hundreds of troops consisting of several regiments. Rumors were flying everywhere. One was a surprise attack on New London, Connecticut along with its protecting fortifications. Arnold was from this area, and he knew it like the palm of his hand. Connecticut Privateers were making a ton of money looting British ships and the New London warehouses were packed full of these trophies of war including lots of gunpowder.

This kind of move was very bold on Arnold's part. He knew where to serve a heavy blow to get the biggest impact. George Washington would surely take notice. The war was not going very well for the British and a major win was needed. The word finally was verified at 1:30 P.M., September 5, 1781. New London was the target. The regiment departed for Long Island where the fleet would join them. When all other regiments gathered together, the force consisted of two divisions.

Arnold had just returned from a great campaign off the coast of Virginia. This new order to attack New London came quick because reports of large quantities of West India goods and European merchandise was just delivered by various privateers. Warehouses were brimming full of goods and the possible capture of the ship, "Hannah" and Capt. Watson would be a rich catch to bring back to New York City.

The attack plans for New London was carefully conceived at Sir Henry Clinton's British Headquarters in New York. Arnold would secretly enter the harbor at night and destroy shipping, public offices, stores, merchandise and all fortifications on both sides of the river Thames before any considerable collected force could be mustered. No one knew how brutal this attack was going to be.

2 P.M., September 5, 1781

All troops were mustered together and assigned to their ships. Along with the American Legion Refugees, there were sixty Yaggers, which were Hessian (German) infantrymen, a very rough mercenary combat regiment. They were dressed in dark green uniforms with bright red trimmings. A few others were the 38th. Regiment, dressed in red, faced with yellow, and the Loyal American Regiment. Other vessels had regiments from New Jersey, Pennsylvania and New York.

7 P.M. September 5, 1781

News came late to the town that a British fleet was lurking off the shores of Long Island, nearly opposite the mouth of the Thames River, the lifeline of New London. Many ignored the alarm because so many came before. No precautions were taken to avoid the surprise attack. Many turned in for the night. Each lit window was beginning to extinguish for the evening. The British watch in glee.

The anchor was weighed and orders given, as the fair wind took the fleet to the shores of New London and Fort Griswold. Each military target lay at opposite sides of the Thames River from each other. A few smaller forts or military placement as Fort Trumbull were placed between New London and the Long Island Sound. Each fort had to be overtaken before getting to the city.

1 A.M., September 6, 1781

The fleet arrived offshore from the river Thames. The wind had suddenly shifted to the north keeping the larger vessels from entering the river. It wasn't until 9 A.M. before they could head in. Anxiety ran high amongst the troops confined onboard. Death and injury was on everyone's mind. Ben thought of his farming days, when life was more simple and peaceful. The thought of losing a limb meant devastation and even starvation for his family. He knew no other life.

The fleet now stood at thirty-two vessels of all classes and the troops would land using twenty-four transports; eight hundred on the Fort Griswold side and nine hundred to one thousand on the New London side of the river.

10 A.M., September 6, 1781

All troops got the word and started to leave the ships for the invasion. Benjamin's division was ordered to land on the Fort Trumbull/New London side of the river and the other division on the side of Fort Griswold.

There was almost no resistance upon landing. Ben couldn't believe his eyes. The path was completely clear except for the distant horns and alarm bells going off. A few cannon fire rang out the invasion warning too from most of the fortifications. Their orders were not to go up the main road along the river, and to avoid any thickly settled areas. Instead they were to march up the inland road to Fort Polly, a very small fortification along a thick swamp. As they started up from the beach and got into formation Ben noticed the landing-taking place on the other side of the river. He could see the 40th. And 54th. Regiments along with the 3rd. Battalion of New Jersey Volunteers, with a detachment of Yaggers and a very large artillery company under the command of Lt. Colonel Eyre. He watched them all start up the hill heading for Fort Griswold. They looked like invading ants. Arnold's exact report of the landing was:

"At ten o'clock, the troops in two divisions and in four debarkations, were landed, one on each side the harbor, about three miles from New London; that on the Groton side consisting of the 40th and 54th regiments, and the third battalion of New Jersey volunteers, with a detachment of yagers and artillery, were under the command of Lieut. Col. Eyre. The division on the New London side consisted of the 38th. Regiment, the loyal Americans, the American Legion, refugees, and a detachment of sixty yagers, who were immediately on their landing, put in motion."

11 A. M., September 6, 1781

The troops on the New London side were within a half-mile of Fort Trumbull that was commanded by Capt. Adam Shapley including Fort Polly with twenty-three men. Both positions opened fire on them. The strategists had no idea that the firepower from this small fortification was so great. Everyone took cover. Arnold's military tactic was nothing like the British approach. He ordered his men to march, but also to take cover when danger strikes.

As Benedict Arnold sat on his horse on a nearby high hill, Ben could see messengers coming and going with new battlefield information. Arnold chose to be on the New London side of the campaign so he could witness the triumph takeover of the city. The command to charge the small fort was ordered and it was quickly overrun with Loyalists. They soon found out why their firepower was so great.

There were six cannons mounted, and two dismounted guns. They all became very concerned what lay ahead at Fort Trumbull. The artillery would surely be heavier the closer they got to the city? As the troops entered Fort Polly, Ben turned to discover his general was right behind him. He decided to take up his position with their advancement. They gathered up what gear they found and headed for the next fortification.

Within minutes, the gunfire from Fort Trumbull started to fall upon the advancing Loyalists. Comrades fell on each side of Ben. Then suddenly; he was hit in the head from a shot. He grabbed his right side of his temple and fell to the ground. This was it! Ben thought he was dying. Blood was everywhere. A clear picture of Sarah and his little girl and son ran about in his head. As his life was flashing about before him, he studied his wound and found it was only a flesh injury, but the bleeding would not stop. He needed something to stop it. The fort was not far off and he discovered a dead rebel lying on the side of the road. With one quick pause at the dead mans face, Ben quickly reached down and ripped part of his shirt from his limp body to make a bandage for his head.

Rebel Capt. Shapley commanded his men to retreat to the shoreline of the river and as ordered by Ledyard embarked his men in three boats across to reinforce Fort Griswold. The Loyalist fleet was not far off and one vessel shot their muskets overhead, wounding several rebels and capturing one boat.

After securing his wound, Ben stopped one more time to study the poor man. He was only a young boy! Pity and remorsefulness came over him. He wanted to turn and walk away from the hostilities and find another part of the world less troubled. All this death was for very little, he thought. Then, he suddenly replaced the picture of the dead mans face with one of his family, and that made Ben come back to reality. He must fight to save his family, and his King's empire!

He marched forward to engage the enemy. Alarm gunfire was coming from Fort Griswold consisting of two regular guns at fixed intervals. This signal of distress would hopefully bring Patriot assistance from the surrounding countryside. Arnold was much smarter than the rebels. He gave instructions to one of his ships that if signal fire came from the fort to add one cannon fire to their volley of help. This great retarded the arrival of any outside militia.

Within a few minutes Ben caught up with his company along with Captain Frink and Captain Millet, and four companies of the 38th. Regiment who were about to attack Fort Trumbull, with Benedict Arnold leading the way. The fire was heavy, but as soon as they reached the gates, all grapeshot stopped and a small amount of hand-to-hand combat erupted which soon ended the struggle. The second fort had fallen to the Loyalists. Killed and wounded amounted to four or five men. The resistance was not high. The following is the exact account from Arnold:

"I had the pleasure to see Capt. Millett march into Fort Trumbull, under a shower of grape-shot from a number of cannon which the enemy had turned upon him, and by the sudden attack and determined bravery of the troops, the fort was carried with only the loss of four or five men killed and wounded."

Captain Millet ordered one company to stay behind at Fort Trumbull as the rest of the forces proceeded on to New London. Families leaped from their beds and fled to the nearby woods, taking very little with them. Some lucky ones had time to take some bread from the table, and other filled pillowcases with items. Others took their milk cows for their infants. When the loyalists arrived through Brown's Gate at the base of Town Hill, they were suddenly fired upon by a fieldpiece which turned out to be a small six pounder used for firing salutes. They took cover and soon sighted the enemy's position on Manwaring's Hill. Three or four men had already deserted that post after seeing the large invasion force. They headed down Town Hill for New London. Many rebel soldiers could be seen trying to get across the river to Groton Heights and Fort Griswold. The wind was not in their favor at the mouth of the Norwich River and soon several had to abort their attempts to escape. Running boys had tied stockings flung over their shoulders containing family valuables, money and silver. Some fleeing Patriots had time to hastily fill wagons and carts with furniture, animals and other items they wanted. Panic was now in full swing of the city. Country farmhouses filled with refugees. One poor man was seen carrying a coffin containing his son who died the day before. Upon arriving at the burial ground, he deposited the box in the waiting dug hole, quickly covered some of it and ran off into the woods to safety.

Benedict Arnold did not feel comfortable with the operations at Fort Griswold. His informant, whom he called, "friends to the government," told him after landing, that Fort Griswold had only twenty or thirty men there. There were much more, so he needed to move quickly to stop more boats going to their aid from his side of the river. He needed the fall of Fort Griswold rapidly. He sent an officer to Lieutenant Colonel Eyre on that side of the river to update him on the new intelligence report. Arnold's orders were to attack the fort as quickly as possible to assure their defeat. On the other side, Col. Ledyard had issued several dispatches for help from Governor Trumbull who was at Lebanon. Just before securing himself in Fort Griswold for his final last stand, he was quoted as saying:

"If I must lose to-day, honor or life, you who know me, can tell which it will be."

As the advancement commenced on to New London, Arnold rode up on a high hill that overlooked the city, and Fort Griswold across the river. His concern was over there. He found the fortifications there a lot more formidable than first imagined. His informant was not too clear on this. (Some say that his informant was James Tilley who lived on Bank Street in New London, and others say it was H. Jeremiah Miller. Both had lost their homes to the fire).

The latest observation showed that there were men now getting across the river successfully and making their way up the hill to Fort Griswold. This would surely prolong the battle. A favorable wind suddenly came up for the escaping rebels and their ships. Because of this latest development, many of them made their way up-river to safety.

Meanwhile, on the New London side, Benjamin found a small stream off the road and decided to take a few minutes to clean his wound. After receiving permission, he jumped down the small embankment where the stream was located. There he found another world. The sound of the stream was so peaceful as he sat down on a rock near the edge. He startled a nearby frog into the stream as he reached down for water to clean his head wound. He sat there cleaning and listening to a robin sing, and he started thinking that death and destruction couldn't be so near this place, but the sudden pop of gun fire brought him back to reality. He finished wrapping his head with the cloth furnished by his unwilling host and darted back up the road. To his surprise he discovered his Captain Samuel (James?) Wogan lying on the side of the road with a head wound. Ben raced over to him and helped some others stop his bleeding. He would live to see another day, and as a good captain, ordered Ben to rejoin the advancing Loyalist regiments heading into New London led by Col. Beverly Robinson's Loyal Americans, the New Jersey loyalist commanded by Lieut. Col. Upham, and the sixty yagers (Hessian light infantry). Lieut. Col. Upham submitted one report as follows:

"We proceeded to the town of New London, constantly skirmishing with rebels, who fled from hill to hill, and stone-fences which intersected the country at small distances. Having reached the southerly part of the town, the general requested me to take possession of the hill north of the meetinghouse, where the rebels had collected, and which they seemed resolved to hold. We made a circle to the left, and soon gained the ground in contest. Here we had one man killed and one wounded. This height being the outpost was left to us and the yagers. Here we remained exposed to a constant fire from the rebels on the neighboring hills, and from the fort on the Groton side, until the last was carried by the British troops."

Benedict Arnold immediately dispatched a boat and an officer to Lieutenant Colonel Eyre, changing his first order to attack the Fort, holding back until the situation could be reassessed, but it was too late. He would not get there in time to stop the attack. Captain Beckwith was already demanding the surrender of the Fort and a short rude refusal came back from the rebel force from within the walls. The battle started immediately and lasted for nearly forty minutes. The bravery of the men inside was heroic as they stood their ground without giving one inch. Some of the Loyalist troops were making it over the walls but were quickly cut down. Major William Montgomery was killed by a giant Negro man named Jordan Freeman. Others killed were Captain George Craigie, Lieutenant H. William Smith and Ensign Thomas Hyde. Outrage was spreading amongst the British ranks. Then their leader, Lieutenant Colonel Eyre was wounded near the walls of the Fort, and the command immediately shifted to Major Stephen Bromfield.

Still attempting to climb the steep hill, Lieutenant Colonel Alexander Van Buskirk of the New Jersey volunteers and artillery companies felt that his arrival to the battle scene would be too late. The British needed this heavy firepower to bring the invasion to a speedy ending. In the harbor, ten or twelve rebel ships were burning. The entire area was beginning to look like a disaster. Families were running in every direction as the Loyalist troops went out of control burning the city (which some accounts say was an accident). Every house was being looted. Some British officers were seen charging homeowners not to burn their houses. Ten pounds was the fee charged by most.

Col. Upham's party defiled Cape Ann Street and Lewis Lane with flanking guards setting fire to the home of Pickett Latimer on the old Colchester road (Now Vauxhall Street). The house was hastily filled with goods for safekeeping, but was the first building consumed. The main body of troops came onto Vauxhall Street and met half-armed citizens that stood their ground at the old burial-ground.

After a few shots, they fled into the woods. By noon, Col. Upham, refugee loyalists and Hessians took possession of the hill and placed a field-piece there that they took from Fort Nonsense to direct fire against any shipping. Many rebel vessels had already escaped upriver due to a favorable wind. A cannon ball went through the front door of Capt. Robert Hallam's house on Norwich road.

Colonel William Ledyard commanded the Fort and was the military commander in charge of the entire district comprising of the two forts, harbor and the towns of New London and Groton. He was very proud of his men, for they fought very hard despite the odds. (Compared to modern historical facts, this incident is easily compared to the Alamo stand). At the beginning, he had only thirty-one men, which numbers soon swelled to one hundred forty-five.

It was a peaceful, quiet night until Sergeant Rufus Avery alerted Captain Latham of the approaching British fleet. After that the entire river area became alive with cannon fire, which was the warning signal for an oncoming attack. After all, this seaport was the home of many Privateers who were raiding British ships for a long time, making lots of money. Now, it was their day of judgment!

Colonel Ledyard immediately sent another messenger to the governor and any nearby commanders for help. Gunpowder was requested from New London for Fort Griswold, as their stores were plentiful (Some accounts say it was all the gunpowder stored in warehouses that caused the fires in New London).

The idea of creating skirmishes in the woods as the Loyalists landed was rejected. Colonel Ledyard could now see that the attack was coming to both sides of the Thames River. The British were splitting their forces. Ledyard ordered one gun be manned on the east wall of the Fort (This same site, years before, was the scene of an attack on a Pequot Indian village by white men who were demanding satisfaction for killing two traders).

Colonel Ledyard could see that his volunteers were just young boys; Daniel Williams only fifteen, Captain Simeon Allyn's nephews, Benadam and Belton were very young, too. Younger children followed their brothers to the Fort, playing games along the way. Now these young boys would grow up fast and possibly die in a very short time.

The Loyalists had three miles to travel before they would reach the Fort. Ledyard could see little puffs of smoke coming from New London forward defenses. Fort Nonsense on Town Hill soon fell into British hands. Arnold then perched himself upon the earthen mounds of that crudely built fortification.

Meanwhile, back at Fort Griswold, they could see two groups of Loyalist infantry approaching from two different points. Colonel Ledyard was told that the British artillery would not arrive in time to help their troops. They were having trouble coming up the hill through the thickets and briar.

The invading troops approached the Fort from the southwest and due to the steepness of the hill; the Fort guns could not strike them. The gates were ordered shut and Corporal Andrew Billings was the last man to enter. Elijah Bailey could not make it to the Fort in time before the gates closed, so he hid in a cornfield.

Suddenly, three men appeared carrying a flag of truce. Colonel Ledyard ordered a shot fired to stop them. He sent three of his captains to meet with them - Amos Stanton, Elijah Avery and John Williams. They returned with the British demand for the Patriot surrender that Colonel Ledyard quickly rejected.

New London started to burn. This would surely affect the morale of all the men at Fort Griswold. A second flag of truce appeared. This time the demands contained harsh terms. "Surrender, or if stormed, expect martial law." All would surely die now! Captain Shapley sent back another blunt refusal to Captain George Beckwith who instantly told the troops to attack.

Each British officer took the lead in front of his smartly dressed columns. They all moved out into the opening and proceeded with the advancement. Rebel Captain Elias Halsey took deadly aim and ordered open fire, mowing down twenty or so Loyalists from their ranks.

In the middle of the heavy fire, the leader of the British troops, Colonel Eyre, was mortally wounded. A lull suddenly came over the entire battlefield! Most Loyalists took cover behind rocks and bushes. Heavy fire commenced and cut down the rebel flag at the southwest section of the Fort. A cheer rose up from outside the Fort as every able-bodied Loyalist soldier came to life and began the attack anew from all positions. Many men fell in pools of blood without reaching the Fort walls, except for one man who was killed instantly at the gate.

Another was approached the walls with better success. Scaling ladders appeared all over the south side while British major, Montgomery threw his body into the open, leading his troops into the fort and taking out one gun. Before he died there, his last order was, "put every man to death." After that, rebel Captain, Shapley, and Jordan Freeman pushed back the intrusion to the outside wall area. British forces overtook the entire Fort. The Patriots were outnumbered.

At that point, Colonel Ledyard signaled his men to surrender. They all lined up at the gate and ordered it opened, letting in the victorious winners of the battle. Colonel Ledyard and Captain William Latham turned to the gate after viewing their men. As the gate opened, the victors threw their hats into the air in jubilation (Some accounts report that they shot some rebels at this time).

The British Major Bromfield marched through the north gate to greet his captors. As he entered, he ordered:

"Who commands this fort?"

"I did sir, but you do now", replied Ledyard.

When Colonel Ledyard presented his sword for surrender, to the horror of his troops, he was killed instantly by his own. (Some historians claim it was his own sword). The following is a true quote from Sergeant Avery to Governor Trumbull, which appears to support the theory of a stabbing by the British with a British weapon.

"I took particular notis when the enemy came over the paripit by the gates, first cleared the platforme then open'd the gates then the enemy rusht in...came...to one of our men he askt them for Quarters they dam'd him and put him to death, likewise Colonel Ledyard fair'd his fait in the same manner."

At the Fort, the British opened up with gunfire, spraying the entire grounds. Madness broke out all over as each Patriot soldier tried to take cover. After all shots were expelled, the King's soldiers ran about stabbing anyone who was still alive. The scene was sheer terror! No more could be said; it was a massacre! At the end, rebel Lieut. Richard Chapman and Capt. Shapley had also fallen. William Seymour of Hartford, a nephew of Col. Ledyard had received thirteen bayonet wounds. Lieut. Parke Avery after losing an eye, had his skull broken, and some of the brains hung out, was also bayoneted in the side. He was left bleeding and dying on the ground. What is very surprising, he recovered and lived forty years afterward. It took eleven months for Lieut. Stephen Hempstead to recover from his wounds. One loyalist was heard saying:

"Stop! Stop! In the name of heaven, I say, stop! My soul can't bear it."

After the fury passed, most Loyalist and British soldiers just walked away in shock and wonderment of what they did. The only thing that could be determined was that insanity broke out from the high casualty rate on the British side, and the refusal of the rebels to surrender up front of the engagement. The situation then turned totally uncontrollable. News spread fast across the river to New London. As the men, husbands and boys lay dying on one side of the Thames, their homes and shops were being plundered on the other side. In the middle, their ships burned on the water. Arnold states the following in his report:

"Here the coolness and bravery of the troops were very conspicuous, as the first who ascended the fraise were obliged to silence a nine-pounder which enfiladed the place on which they stood, until a sufficient body had collected to enter the works, which was done with fixed bayonets, through the embrasures, where they were opposed with great obstinacy by the garrison, with long spears. On this occasion I have to regret the loss of Major Montgomery, who was killed by a spear in entering the enemy's works; also of Ensign Whitlock, of the fortieth regiment, who was killed in the attack. Three other officers of the same regiment were wounded."

"After a most obstinate defense of nearly forty minutes the fort was carried by the superior bravery and perseverance of the assailants."

    As they all gazed over the devastation, the Loyalist, including Benjamin thought it was well deserved. After all, this community was making a living from the spoils they plundered from the war, and every Loyalist had lost their homes, families and way of making a living. The survivors here could go back and start over, but the Loyalists had nothing to go back too. Later, a feeling of guilt mixed in with the victory. They were still shocked over all the destruction they inflicted.

    Arnold accompanied Col. Upham's through Hempstead Street taking control of the north end of town. They stopped above the meetinghouse and Arnold took his small spyglass out to survey the area. Then they turned their horses down Richards Street with his troops. He then commanded with his extended sword:

"Soldiers! Do your duty."

    Soon the printing office and town mill was set ablaze, then the Plumb house on Winthrop's Neck and the entire point, destroying the battery, shipping, warehouses and anything else that could be set on fire. The Merrill house was spared. Bradley Street was nearly left unharmed with eight out of ten homes spared.

    One interesting account of the raid in New London was at the corner of Green Street where a well-known tavern stood. The landlady who's husband was a rebel sergeant in the militia fighting away from the home/tavern filled her tablecloth with all her goods except for a meal set for her brother who was a loyalist under Arnold's command invading the city.

The first thing the loyalist Captain did was to visit his sister's house with other Tory soldiers. He found her not, but refreshed himself with her offerings. After the close of the war, this captain refugee was in declining health obtained a leave to return home where he died in the same house.

Benedict Arnold found time to seek out an old friend in town on Bank Street. They sat at the table for refreshments until they had to rush out from the flames that destroyed that dwelling. Some of these double-sided loyal friends got compensation from both sides at the end of the war. A sort of double dipping in loyalty.

Some prisoners were taken as families and survivors of the dead slowly came out of hiding to collect their loved ones' bodies. Weeping was heard from all around. Some heavy smoke settled to the ground in the city giving it a ghostly appearance. There were one hundred forty-three buildings, including homes, thirty-seven stores, eighteen shops, twenty barns and several other structures destroyed by the fire, not to forget several warehouses containing the Privateers booty.

Colonel Ledyard's wife came back down the Thames River after being pulled from her bed, just after giving birth at the beginning of the attack. She found her house burned to the ground and her husband murdered. All that remained to her life was her baby and a key to her front door. The beaten townspeople watched the retreating army march off to the mouth of the river, board their boats for the fleet that took them out to sea.

One homeowner returned to extinguished a fire just in time and upon entering it found a dying Loyalist soldier in one of his beds. He was crying out for water. Some neighbors had found him bleeding to death on the side of the road. They carried him into the nearest house. He lived for several hours, but before he died he gave the rebels his name and asked to send a dispatch to New York so his parents might know of his death. He was only eighteen years old, a loyalist refugee and son of refugees who would soon settle in Nova Scotia. Two or three other loyalists were found and they were all buried on the side of Williams Street in New London.

Benjamin looked back at the harbor area covered in a thick, white blanket of smoke with several flaming embers still burning out of control. His hand reach up to his wound as the pain surfaced from the aftermath of the adrenaline rush. After assessing the troops on board ship, the officers found that hardly any Loyalists had stolen goods from the homes and shops in New London. A few eyewitnesses saw several town vagrants prowling through the streets in the wake of the invasion, taking what they pleased. It was so quiet on board ship because every man contemplated what he had done on shore. Ben's wound had stopped bleeding, and the cool sea breeze felt good blowing onto his face as he watched the New London shore sink into the blue waters of the Long Island Sound.[12]

---

[12] Many of the accounts of the battle of New London was taken from History of New London, Chapter XXXII, pages 545-572, by Frances Caulkins, Pub. 1860, 2nd. Edition.

There were differing opinions on the statistics of this battle, but history will finally settled on the following unless more details surface in the future:

American Forces
Engaged: 400
Killed: 85
Wounded: 60

Loyalist/British Forces
Engaged: 1700
Killed: 48
Wounded: 145

Many loyalists latter died before they returned to New York, and were buried in the sea, or on the shores of Plum and Gardiner's Island where the fleet anchored. Some say the number killed jumped to 220. The American Legion reported that 1 rank and file killed; 1 captain (Capt. Samuel (Should this be James?) Wogan) and 5 rank and file wounded; 2 rank and filed missing.[13]

Note: Although this story establishes Benjamin Bonnell on the New London side of the Thames River during the invasion and the historical records attest to that, there is still question of how Captain Samuel Wogan, Ben's officer (American Legion Refugees) received wounds at the battle Fort Griswold as found in Benedict Arnold's report (footnotes in the Battle of Groton Heights, by Charles Allyn, 1882). It could be possible that Ben and others served on both sides of the river because there are reported crossings.

Patriot Rebel Forces at Fort Griswold 6 September, 1781[14]

Killed	Escaped	Wounded & Paroled
Adams, Nathaniel	Bill, Benjamin	Avery, Amos
Allyn, Belton	Bill, Joshua	Avery, Capt. Ebenezer
Allyn, Benadam	Holdridge, Benajah	Avery, Lieut. Parke Jr.
Allyn, Capt. Samuel	Jaques, Samuel	Daboll, John Jr.
Allyn, Capt. Simeon	Latham, William Jr.	Edgecomb, Samuel Jr.
Avery, Capt. Elijah	Leeds, Cary	Eldridge, Christopher
Avery, Capt. Elisha	Lester, Amos	Eldridge, Daniel
Avery, Lieut. Ebenezer	Mallinson, Thomas	Eldridge, Ensign John
Avery, Ensign Daniel	Mason, Henry	Gallup, Andrew
Avery, Sergt. Cristopher	Mason, Japheth	Gallup, Robert

---

[13] Statistics and reports from Great Britain, Public Records Office, Colonial Office, Class 5, Vol. 103, page 311.
[14] From the Fort Griswold State Park records.

Avery, Sergt. Jasper
Avery, Sergt. Solomon
Avery, David
Avery, Thomas
Babcock, John P.
Bailey, Sergt. Ezekiel
Baker, Andrew
Billings, Corp. Andrew
Billings, John
Billings, Samuel
Bolton, William
Brown, John
Burrows, Capt. Hubbard
Butler, Jonathan
Chapman, Lieut. Richard
Chester, Daniel
Chester, Sergt. Eldredge
Chester, Frederic
Chester, Jedediah
Clark, John
Colt, Elias
Comstock, Lieut. James
Comstock, William
Covill, Philip
Davis, Daniel
Eldredge, Daniel
Freeman, Jordan (Colored)
Halsey, Capt. Elias Henry
Hill, Samuel
Holt, John Jr.
Hulburt, Sergt. Rufus
Jones, Eliday
Jones, Moses
Kenson, Benoni
Kinney, Barney
Lamb, Thomas
Latham, Lambo (Colored)
Ledyard, Lieut. Col. William (Commander)
Ledyard, Capt. Youngs
Leeds, Capt. Carey
Lester, Daniel D.

Morgan, Elisha
Morgan, James
Moxley, Joseph
Prentis, John

Taken Prisoner

Abraham, Samuel
Avery, Caleb
Avery, Sergt. Rufus
Baker, Joshua
Beaumont, Samuel
Buddington, Walter
Bushnell, Reuben
Chester, Charles
Darrow, Nathan
Dart, Elias
Dart, Levi
Edgecomb, Gilbert
Eldridge, Daniel
Fish, Ebenezer
Harding, Jeremiah
Kilburn -----
Latham, William
Ledyard, Ebenezer
Minor, Jonathan
Morgan, Isaac
Rowley, Isaac
Sanford, Holsey
Smith, Corp. Josiah
Stow, Lieut. Jabez
Tift, Solomon
Wales, Horatio
Welles, Thomas

Hempstead, Sergt. Stephen
Judd, Corp. Jehial
Latham, Christopher Jr.
Latham, Capt. Edward
Latham, Jonathan, Jr.
Latham, Capt. William
Moore, Frederick
Morgan, John
Pendleton, Joseph
Perkins, Ebenezer
Perkins, Lieut. Obadiah
Perkins, Capt. Solomon
Prior, Elisha
Seymour, William
Stanton, Daniel Jr.
Stanton, Edward
Starr, John
Starr, Lieut. William
Stillman, Samuel
Wansuc, Tom (Pequot Ind)
Wiilliams, Sanford
Woodworth, Asel
Woodworth, Thomas
Woodworth, Zibe

Cont. Killed

Lester, Ensign John
Lester, Jonas
Lester, Wait
Lewis, Lieut. Joseph
Mills, Corp. Edward
Miner, Thomas
Moore, Capt. Nathan
Morgan, Corp. Simeon
Moxley, Joseph
Palmer, David
Perkins, Asa
Perkins, Elisha
Perkins, Elnathan
Perkins, Luke
Perkins, Corp. Luke Jr.
Perkins, Simeon
Richards, Capt. Peter
Seabury, David
Shapley, Capt. Adam
Sholes, Corp. Nathan
Stanton, Capt. Amos
Stanton, Sergt. Daniel
Stanton, Lieut. Enos
Star, Sergt. Nicolas
Starr, Thomas Jr.
Stedman, Sergt. John K.
Walworth, Sylvester
Ward, Lieut. Patric
Wedger, Joseph
Whittlesey, John
Whittlesey, Stephen
Williams, Daniel
Williams, Lieut. Henry
Williams, Capt. John
Williams, Thomas
Woodbridge, Christopher
Woodbridge, Henry

A monument commemorating the falling British Major William Montgomery is located on the spot he was killed by Jordan Freeman, a Colored Patriot Rebel. It reads:

The Death of,
Major William Montgomery
While leading the British
Attack on the fort at
This point
Sept. 6th.
1781

Loyalist fleet lying off Thames River 6 Sept. 1781

Chapter 7

Fleeing New York City

A few days before the "Great Exodus," the city appeared gloomy. Defeat and uncertainty was on everyone's mind. It felt like the end of the world was at hand as in the days of the great clouds that rolled over New England a few years past. Evacuation plans were set after the signing of the Treaty of Paris. High-ranking officials were now mostly commoners until they could re-establish a new position in the next society. Each day brought on more depression and helplessness. Washington waited outside the boundaries like a wild Tiger ready to jump its prey. What else could possibly add to the insecurities?

One of those anxious moments came early in the morning as most of these events occur. Ben and Sarah were in a sleeping embrace when suddenly Ben was awakened by a deafening silence that came over the entire city. Only seconds had passed during his investigation. He first opened his eyes to the lack of sound; he lifted his head to peer out the window from the bed. Even the occasional dog bark was not present, or the crow of the morning cock. Something was very wrong! Sarah woke as she watched Ben rise up more! She noticed him looking for his musket!

Then suddenly, without any warning, the entire building shook off its foundation. Their children woke up screaming. Was Washington invading after the peace treaty was signed? Everything on the shelves flew into the air. Their bed rolled around the floor and they helplessly moved with it. The Bonnell's heard screaming coming from others outside. What was happening? Was it the end of the world?

As quick as the attack came, it disappeared. Ben finally was able to jump to his feet and observe the panic outside. People below were running out of the buildings and scrambling in every direction, not knowing really where to go for shelter. Several nearby buildings suffered damage, bricks lay in the streets. Sarah ran to Ben's side holding both children. Looking out the window, they heard others say there was no attack, no explosion! The great tremor came from below the earth!

People all over were screaming out that the end of the world was here! This caused great concern. **"Thunder Over New England"** had hit this area in the form of an "Earthquake!" Ben and his family knelt in silent prayer and pleaded for mercy.

Note: This event was recorded just west of New York City in 1783. It was felt from New Hampshire to Pennsylvania and had an intensity of 7, and magnitude was unknown, but probably around a 5.5 based on the intensity. From the United States Geological Survey records.

It took a few days to get over the panic of the earthquake. It seemed like the planning and pace of the evacuation picked up as people wanted to get out of the city. The July fleet to Canada was at hand and Ben and his family would be on it.

Despite the early morning hour, New York City was a beehive of activity. People were rushing in every direction, completing last minute chores. The next fleet was getting ready to leave for Nova Scotia. There were approximately eleven ships, and the "William" would be the one that would transport Benjamin and his family. Sarah was dressing the children as Ben was reviewing the situation on the streets below his window. They had managed to get a small room in the remaining days. Their daughter Sarah was still very sleepy, and as she rubbed the sleep from her eyes, her mother tied her dress shut. Packing was completed as Ben got very impatient, scolding Sarah for being so slow. He wanted to get down to the Wall Street dock at Crugers Wharf to meet with the other provincial refugees of the King's American Regiment, Unit 15, and his captain, William Wright Sr., his friend from Woodbridge, New Jersey. Each Loyalist and their families were assigned into refugee units to keep some form of military order in case a need came up.

The exodus would total over thirty thousand when all fleets completed their evacuation mission from New York. General Washington and his troops were eagerly awaiting their triumphant march into the city after the British exodus. The date was July 8, 1783 and the trip to Nova Scotia would take nearly a month. As the Bonnell's worked their way through the crowds, Sarah was still complaining to Ben about the sale of many furnishings they had owned in New Jersey. There was not enough room on board the ships, and the selling price was insulting. Many of the rich were trying to buy a better spot on board, plus get their furnishing stored below. This made it very unfair for the average Loyalist refugee.

4 August 1783

The following ad is from the New York Gazette and Weekly Mercury newspaper dated Monday, 4 August 1783.

> For Halifax
> The Brig.
> WILLIAM
>
> About 160 tons, well found
> With sail the 15th. Intend... has
> Good accommodations for passengers
> For freight or passage, apply to
> The matter on board at Crugers Wharf
> To Michael Price at No. 15 Wall Street.

This ad appeared many times in the newspaper. It was also found on other dates. It is believed that this ship made many trips to Canada.

8 July 1783 (Approx.)

The third major wave of refugees destined for the new Loyalist city of Saint John (Parrtown) at the mouth of the Saint John River took ship at the end of June, departing New York about 8 July 1783. Although the size of the July fleet was comparatively small it patterned the June exodus in that all the companies it embraced went to Saint John rather than Annapolis or Shelburne, Nova Scotia. The first to reach port, the Ann, arrived by 24 July and the others soon followed. Refugees, Provincials and others in the July fleet were on the following ships and militia companies.

Ship	Captain of Militia Unit	Refugee Unit
Elizabeth	Richard Hill	5
Commerce	Peter Huggeford	7
Montague	?	?
Grace	Thomas Welsh	11
Three Sisters	Thomas Huggeford	14
William	William Wright	15
Lord Townsend	John Mersereau	16
Joseph	Donald Drummond	17
Aurora	William Perrine	19
Commerce	Peter Berton	21
Elizabeth	Nathaniel Horton	22

Sovereign	John Menzies	24
Ann	Robert Chillas	28
Lord Townsend	Jacob Cook	?
Aurora	John Oblenis	31
Three Sisters	William Olive	32
Elizabeth	?	?
Grace	Richard Squires	34
Grace	Daniel Fowler	35
	King's American Regiment	
Commerce	1st. NJ Volunteers, Adjutant Generals	Department
Elizabeth	Lt. Colonel Thomas Rogers	
Aurora	?	?

Benjamin and family came on the ship "William." The King's American Regiment was also on the ship "William."

The following record was found in the evacuation records of New York.

Benjamin Bonnell, farmer, from New Jersey, assigned to refugee unit number 15, Captain William Wright on the ship, "William," with wife, and two children under ten years of age, dated July 1783.

A census taken the following year, May 1784, shows the family had all survived in Saint John, Nova Scotia (later New Brunswick).

The following is a list of persons that were recorded on the ship "William" with Benjamin and his family.

Name	Trade	From	Children	Spouse	Other
Bonnell, Benjamin	Farmer	N.J.	2	wife	
Barlow, Ezekiel	Blacksmith	Penn.	-	-	
Barlow, Joseph	Farmer	Penn.	2	wife	
Barlow, Thomas	Sawyer	Penn.	-	wife	
Branscomb, Arthur	-	-	3	wife	
Bridegmor, John Sr.	Farmer	N.J.	3	wife	
Bridegmor, (widow)	Widow	-	-	-	
Bridegmor, William	Farmer	N.J.	-	-	
Dickinson, Henry	-	-	-	-	2 servants
Dickinson, Isaac	-	-	-	-	1 servant
Dillon, William	-	-	-	-	
Flewelling, Abel	Carpenter	N.Y.	4	wife	2 servants

Name	Trade	From	Children	Spouse	Other
Flewelling, John	Cordwainer	N.Y.U.C.	7	wife	
Flewelling, Morris	Farmer	N.Y.	-	-	
Fowler, Oliver	-	-	-	-	
Fowler, Thomas (?)	-	-	3	wife	
Gard, William	Tailor	Penn.	-	-	
Gregory, Moses	Farmer	N.Y.	-	-	
Malone, Thomas	Farmer	Maryland	-	-	
Newman, Charles	-	-	-	-	
Ogden, Jehu	Cooper	N.J.	2	wife	
Pinkney, Charles	Farmer	N.Y.	-	-	
Pinkney, David	-	N.Y.?	-	-	
Pinkney, John	Farmer	N.Y.	-	-	
Pinkney, Oliver	-	N.Y.?	-	-	
Purdy, Daniel	Farmer	N.Y.	-	-	
Sproul, James	Farmer	N.J.	-	-	1 servant
Sproul, James Jr.	Farmer	N.J.	-	-	1 servant
Stebbens, Cornelius	Saddler	N.J.	1	wife	
Supplee, Enoch	Schoolmaster	Penn.	-	-	
Thorpe, John	Farmer	Penn.	1	wife	
Tomlinson, John	Tailor	-	-	wife	
Tully, John	Farmer	N.Y.	-	wife	
Wright, William Sr.	Farmer	N.J.	3	wife	3 servants
Wright, William Jr.	Farmer	N.J.	-	-	1 servant

Men listed under refugee unit 15, but regiment and ship not mentioned, but possibly could be on the "William."

Name	Trade	From	Children	Spouse	Other
Alston, David	-	N.J.?	-	-	
Alston, Joseph	Printer	N.J.	-	-	
Clawson, William	Farmer	N.J.	1	-	
Clawson, John	Farmer	N.J.	-	-	1 servant
Glannon, Edward	-	-	3	wife	2 servants
Harris, William	Farmer	Penn.	1	wife	
Major, Edward	-	-	5	wife	2 servants
Ogden, Jacob	-	-	2	wife	
Welsh, Morris	Farmer	N.Y.	4	wife	
Wiggins, John	Farmer	N.Y.	1	wife	1 servant

Ref: Early Loyalist of Saint John, by D.G. Bell, published by New Ireland Press, 1983

The children did not fully understand why their home was being changed, but they did pick up the emotional atmosphere around them, parents included as they wondered what lay ahead of them. They finally made their way to the docks and there they were, the "Elizabeth," "Commerce," "Montague," "Three Sisters," the "Grace," "Lord Townsend," the "Joseph," "Sovereign," " Aurora," the "Ann" and of course, the "William." The fleet awaited their passengers to board. Ben checked in with his captain and met his good friend, Titus Brown. It took nearly all day to load the passengers and cargo. When the sails finally opened, the sight was beautiful. The harbor area filled with canvas and each ship marched out into the Long Island Sound.

With all the vessels stretching across the horizon, it gave one a feeling of power, even at the moment of defeat. Benjamin and Sarah managed to work their way to the back of the ship to watch their homeland slip into history, like most other families on board. The day was now at its end and the small New York City skyline sank into the amber sunset. The majestic sight from the air made this fleet look so grand in the deep golden colors of summer while the silvery shine of the ocean made it sparkle into the days end.

Ben and Sarah held each other as the children already settled down on the deck floor playing a game. Awe, the innocence of youth. It was so hard to imagine, in just a few years time, they had been displaced from two homes, wanted by the authorities, joined the ranks with Benedict Arnold, destroyed and fort and city, and now heading for a wilderness unknown.

Some of the passengers started to disperse in tears after the now small city lights disappeared, but Ben and Sarah stood there taking in every last minute of that ending sight, as the "William" and the other ships sailed along the side of Long Island heading east for Connecticut, Rhode Island and Massachusetts.

The next day aboard ship most people were sitting around talking about what their new life was going to be like. Those families talking were from well-educated and wealthy backgrounds. Ben and Sarah listened to them talking about the new plantations and estates they would soon own again in Nova Scotia. The King was surely going to take good care of them, one said. Even the farmers and soldiers, like the Bonnell's were going to be rightfully compensated for their loyalty and service.

That night, Ben took a few minutes and left his family below deck and went up top to look over a very familiar sight that was coming up. He thought he would never see that sight again. The evening was fairly still with a slight cool breeze blowing easterly. Ben walked nervously to one side of the ship, facing north. He rested his arms on top the sides and there before his eyes he spotted his uneasy desire.

There it was, all lit up like nothing had ever happened there. New London, Connecticut - a memory that he would never forget. Instantly, September 6, 1781 flashed into his troubled mind. What an awful day that was! Great emotions started to build up including revenge, sadness, victory, loss, hatred and terrible destruction. They raced around his head trying to escape, but they would be trapped there for the rest of his life. Peace now prevailed over this land and Ben, who was once a victor on that day, was now the loser. All that he could do was to stare into the flickering lights of New London until they faded away. He prayed that the memory would fade with it.

For the next few days, most passengers found something to do, but the following days after, they became restless and board. It seemed to take forever to get around Shoals Hope (Cape Cod). The arm of Massachusetts was so long, it jetted out nearly one hundred miles. When they reached the tip, concern grew throughout the ship. The captain announced that the current going around the Cape was treacherous.

Many ships lost the fight to shifting sandbars and rough seas. It was a tense few hours, but the entire fleet made it around with no problems. Martha's Vineyard and Nantucket Sound was also very good to them. Once the fear of nature was out of the way, the captain announced another great fear, the greatest of all! There was a rough and tough fighting rebel band of Privateers lurking the waters out of Cape Cod Bay. A small village of Barnstable was their host port, but scattered ships shot out of smaller harbors along the Cape looking for a chance to pick off a stray vessel from the fleet. The alert was from Barnstable to Salisbury and parts of southern Maine, another one hundred miles.

Whaling was the main industry in these waters and that made excellent seamen. The entire fleet was order to close ranks and stick together. It wasn't long until several Privateers were sighted. They followed a great distance, but were quick enough to change speed to overtake a stray vessel. Nearly everyone was on board to watch the threat in the distance. One vessel, possibly the "Elizabeth" fired a warning shot at one of them. The Cape Privateers faded off as the fleet approached offshore of Boston that evening. Most passengers were amazed at the size of the city. The lights stretched across what seemed like miles of coastline. Lantern lights were spotted from many ships windows. The harbor was huge.

The people of Boston left the fleet alone as they past. They knew of the retreating British heading north and at this night chose to let them be. The most annoying thing about the trip was the lack of docking privileges. Everywhere was enemy territory. This new nation was so large that it couldn't help but be a world power someday. After all, they just beat the greatest nation on earth!

As the fleet edged its way north along the Maine coast, Ben thought again about his loses the past few years. He had been displaced and replaced, and now he read that much of the lands going to the Loyalists were lands once belonging to the Acadian farmers. The battles were not always fought between the colonies; the British and French were fighting over North America for nearly two hundred years. The last victory was in 1755 when the French finally turned over the Canadian territories to England. Many of these poor Acadian souls were exiled in the greatest dispersion in history at that time. Splitting families up by forcing them farther north to Quebec where other French subjects lived or shipping them off to Boston, Virginia, the Carolina's, Florida and New Orleans (who became the Cajuns), and even sent them back to France. It took years for some families to reunite. Some never did. The British reasoning was that these people were too prosperous in Acadie (Nova Scotia) and were multiplying at a rapid rate, soon to give France a great economic power in that region.

On July 24, 1783, the ship "Ann" was the first of the July fleet to arrive at the busy harbor of Parr Town (now Saint John). Soon after, many other sails appeared on the horizon revealing the entire fleet. There was much activity on board ship. Families were organizing all their belongings beforehand so that they could view the shoreline of their new home. Like most families, Benjamin and Sarah were very anxious about the long awaited arrival. There were many pillars of smoke coming from the heavily settled area where the ships were heading. Sarah studied her two children very closely as the ship approached the harbor, wondering what the future held for them.

She looked up and saw the most frightening sight. There in front of her, and all the weary passengers, was a city of thousands of tents and lean-to houses which made up approximately ninety percent of the entire city of Parr Town. Panic struck most women and bewilderment covered every man's face. The region was still very primitive and hostile, and more fleets were to follow throughout the year. Where was the food going to come from to feed all these people? Every tree in the immediate area had already been cut down. Scarcity was seen very easily from the ship.

Before landing, most Loyalists already called this new promise land, Nova Scarcity. Sarah suddenly couldn't contain herself any longer. She followed most of the other women by openly sobbing. There was nothing Ben could do to get her through the panic and depressed feeling.

How could it possibly get any worse? Where were they going to live? How were they going to eat? Many people were going to die that first winter. One man cried out,

"Our King sent us all up here to die."

Some wanted to go farther up the Saint John River, but stories of ships braking up on the rocks with no survivors spread fast, squelching that idea. This added more fear to the destitute, homeless Loyalists, including the thought of wild Indians ripping them apart in the deep woods. Everyone quickly agreed the tent city was the best place to land.

Many curious people were waiting at the docks to greet each ship unloading more weary passengers. The Bonnell's disembarked into the thick blanket of spectators. They saw confusion in every direction they looked. Sarah held onto the children as Benjamin held onto their few possessions. The passengers were then instructed to stand by for directions on where to go for supplies and living arrangements. Town criers were at every corner announcing city affairs and world events.

The hasty directions were given and the Bonnell's walked down a muddy street to several covered wagons where they received a large canvas sheet to use as a tent and living quarters. Included were some pegs, a couple sakes of grains and foods, and rope. In shock, they were escorted to a small plot of land to set up their tent. The children were given some blankets to carry along with the old ones they brought with them. After completing their camp, Benjamin set out to find anything he could about the promise land grants the King was offering all Loyalists. There were many different meeting spots throughout the tent city. Benjamin tried most of them only to find that they all had the same answer - no land available until the property could be properly surveyed.

This brought out violent outcries from every direction of the refugee community. While Benjamin fought his way back up the muddy streets to his tent, he noticed many sick and hungry people. Several odd services were being offered to raise a British cent piece. The children had settled in and were playing in one area of the tent when Ben arrived. Sarah had already feared the dangers outside when he told them what he saw. She prepared their bedding as their first day ended in the new land. Like a blanket, tucking them in, the thick Bay of Fundy fog rolled into the region as it does most nights. The night was very wet and damp, very common for this area. As the Bonnell's laid under the covers, they heard coughing and moans coming from outside. The population of Parr Town was now at 10,000, most living in tents.

The next morning was very chilly and wet, however, new information came in regarding the food and supplies situation. Ben was already down at the waterfront picking up any news. Each family would receive five hundred feet of lumber with bricks and some shingles to construct their dwellings. The fleet of ships that brought Benjamin and his family was now departing the harbor for the return trip to New York City. Each sail was set and a quiet somber mood soon fell over the dock area. The loud noise and heavy activity had passed away with their departure. A feeling of loneliness returned to this outpost in the north. During one meeting Ben heard stories of families being robbed by New England Privateers along the coast. They rowed ashore and held them up like bandits.

Most Loyalists wanted immediate action and demanded protection from the regular British army while they tried to establish their new lives. After all, the King promised this! There were many outspoken Loyalists who were very familiar with the present situation and who were getting upset over the inaction on surveying the region in a quick fashion so the new settlers could get their promised land grants.

The following few months brought on food riots and fights over supplies. Many children were stealing for their families or for themselves, and corruption was spreading everywhere. Many Loyalists were thinking of returning to the States to face whatever action or treatment by the rebels, just to get food and housing for their families. Many did just that, but hundreds never went back to their birthplace. Instead, settled in northern states like Vermont, New Hampshire, Maine and New York starting a new live in the new nation.

September and October were the coldest months on record according to some of the old French residents and Indians. There were many cases of pneumonia and tuberculosis throughout the population. Blankets soaked up the night moisture chilling the already cold temperature bringing on all types of ailments; many cases being fatal. The wind and fog off the bay was especially harsh. Some of the upper class Loyalists were beginning to lose their well-educated manner and dignity and the regard for other people and took up rude talk and theft. They thought that they would never feel the hardships as the common Loyalists.

The land grant issue was a very touchy one. There were many crooked deals going on in order to catch the choicest properties. This was an area where upper class did score. They were the decision-makers when it came to land grants. This made many of the common Loyalist refugees rise up in anger and demand their rights. For a short period of time, the newfound society appeared to be crumbling.

When winter arrived, the supply lines dwindled to a crawl. It was very hard to store food in the tents, so the few wooden buildings available were used for storing all the perishable supplies. Most Loyalists could not have imagined the winters in Nova Scotia. With exception of the people from northern New York, one could never believe that snow could get so deep, or such a large river as the Saint John could freeze over. Ten-foot snowdrifts were very common and many people froze to death from exposure.

Chapter 8

Settling the Wilderness

The Loyalists thought the spring would never come to this frozen land of Canada, but one day it did manage to appear with some startling effects. That particular morning was very quiet and peaceful. Everyone was doing his or her chores as usual when suddenly the cracking of gunfire was heard up the Saint John River valley. All the women and children took cover, as every man that could be mustered ran for his musket. They never thought that the Americans could manage an attack from the north. Everyone headed for high ground overlooking the reversing falls and waited quietly for the first signs of the attackers riding down the frozen Saint John River. Suddenly, there it was again, not far off this time. The echo reached them much faster this time.

Benjamin lay on his belly holding his musket. He looked at all those frightened faces and thought his and their life would never be peaceful again. He was now concerned about the safety of his new homeland. There it was again - this time many cracklings and, therefore, it was decided to send a scout up the river to a higher point to see what was taking the advancing army so long to attack the line of defense at the Falls. The scout rode up the river along an Indian trail and stopped at the bend where the Loyalists could clearly see him. There it was again! Everyone figured that the Americans were taking shots at the scout. Judging by the echoes, the enemy had to be face to face with the scout, but he remained in the open still sitting on his horse, clearly in the open. After a few more shots were fired, the scout turned around to his Loyalist comrades and waved like he was on a picnic, then returned to them. They waited in anticipation for his insane assessment.

Puzzled, they watched him ride up with a wide grin across his face. By the time he reached his captain, he was in total laughter, like a young child. He dismounted in hysteria as he studied all the concerned faces. The captain stepped forward with great seriousness and demanded the refugee to stand. Still laughing, he pointed back up the river and said:

"Our enemy is the melting Saint John River!"

The coming spring and Mother Nature had fooled the Loyalists and the good news made them all break down into laughter along with their scout. The women and children surfaced to find their irresponsible husbands acting like children. Once they too found out the news, all in joy and singing out greeted the relief. They all needed that moment very much.

The following months were much colder than their homes in the States. The planted season was retarded, making it much shorter. They had to learn to adjust. The census of 1784 showed that they survived. Many small gardens started to sprout up all over the city, some large lots and others, small and hugging the tents they lived in. It wasn't long until most poor Loyalist had to guard their gardens. The non-farmers, and the lazy rich refugees who did not want to grow their own food stole from the meager gardens. Beggars and thieves were on the increase.

The big break came in August 1784 when Ben quickly linked himself with a band of Loyalists who appeared to be getting closer to securing a land grant. He ended up being correct and on August 11, 1784, Benjamin was included in a one thousand, one hundred and twenty acre land grant in the county of Sunbury, partly within the township of Fonuray and partly within the unappropriated land of Carleton in the Province of Nova Scotia (later to be New Brunswick). This large grant started at the beginning of the Lower Falls of the Saint John River reaching all the way to the ocean. Ben was listed with Matthew Hains and one hundred eleven others, each to have ten acres of land.

He ran back to his tent to announce the good news to his family. The long hard struggle for land had finally paid off. They would make the trip the following day to get his ten acres stack assigned. A plan for their home started immediately with the allotted wood and supplies to be the starting materials. That night, they celebrated by purchasing a small amount of rum and ale, and some molasses sweets for the children.

The following day was disappointing to them all. When they arrived at the grant, they found it rocky and mostly unfit for planting. Sarah quickly gathered her thoughts and feelings and turned the rude surprise to a positive one. She scooped up a handful of soil and said:

"At least we can say this is our home, and we will work this rocky ground until we have enough to get a larger farm."

With that said, she reached for her children and placed her arms around her husband and after they hugged, she demanded they pace off the property asking Ben where he wanted their home to sit. All the while, Ben was staring out at the ocean. He came back to reality and helped to reinforce Sarah's shacking strength.

Later, all the documents were signed with John Parr, Esquire, Captain General Governor and Commander in Chief, approving the agreement and allocation on August 13, 1784. It was registered and signed by A. Gold and Ira Stupton and the final recording was performed on January 6, 1785 in the newly formed province of New Brunswick.

Note: Today (2002), this grant has a residential tract and railroad line on it.

Benjamin's lists of other grantees and document appears as following:

> Land Granted 11 August 1784, Ten Acre Lots Near Carleton, Nova Scotia

Matthew Hains and 111 others.

George the Third by the grace of God of Great Britain, France and Ireland, King defender of the faith and so forth. To all to whom these presents shall come greeting. Know ye that we of our special grace, certain knowledge and mere motion, have given and granted and by these presents for us our heirs and successors, do give and grant unto Matthew Hains, John Holland, Tomithy Witmore, William Tully, Samuel Clayton, William Young, Albert Ogden, Abraham Hesfand, Andrew Glover, Joseph Lingley, Samuel Welch, Daniel Ogden, Edward Duffill, John Witmore, William Willing, Nathaniel Osborn, Gideon Corey, Thomas Humbold, Freeman Smith, Abner Hampton, James Place, Justus Siely, William Witmore, Thomas Witmore, Stephen Hoyl, John Sefs, Walter Campbell, Michael Ambroise, George Hammilton, Nathaniel Dickenson, Jasper Ruggles, Adine Paddock, Thomas Yeareley, John Brundige, William Buckley, William Rodin, Jesse Lamereux, Barsers Davis, Lawrence Dawling, Luther Cutter, Lott Hrange, John Inis, Catherience McNeal, James Adams, Andrew Bowman, Mich'l Laffan, Richard Holland, Thomas Heston, Joseph Cronwell, John Hutchinson, David Blair, John Cock Simion, Timothy F. Witmore, Moses Knapp, William Clark, Anew Shaw, Acteon Jeffery, William Lucey, Theuben Myers, John Nicholas Blame, James Cram, Joseph Cooper, BENJAMIN BONNELL, William Cox, James Munger, Rober Herrett, William Harris, William Crofering, Frederick Maybec, John Taylor, Godfrey Kilbenbock, Jonathan Parker, Robert Peel, John Tool, Thomas Handford, David Cram, Anthony Recce, Daniel Lamoreux, Robert Gibbs, James Thanks, James Witmore, Humphrey Peel, Meranden Drummond, Calib Austin, Collin Campbell, Henry Redding, Philip Kustis, Joseph

Stackhouse; Jeremiah Brundige, Louis Beatis Lent, Andrew Sherwood, Thomas Green, John Dunham, Robert Stackhouse, William Olive, Reuben Judd, John Warde, Nathen Frink, Joseph Shotwell, Archibald McNeal, Widow Anne Boyer, David B. Witmore, Margaret Hearns, Donald McDonald, Josepg Burrell, John Challones, Peter Willing, Anthony Egbert, Adam McColgan, George Lane, John Crofts and Edward Taylor, their heirs and assigns, X a tract of land containing one thousand one hundred and twenty acres in the County of Sunbury partly within the township of Fonuray and partly within the unappropriated land of Carleton in our Province of Nova Scotia, bounded and abutted, situated laying and being as follows. Beginning at the lower falls of the river St. Johns on the western side to thence to run south fifty-one degrees west to the road thence running the several corners of the said road westward one hundred and twenty-three chains of four rods each thence to run South twenty-five degrees east until it comes to the sea shore thence running the several courses of the sea shore towards the mouth of Saint John River aforesaid until it comes to the back line of Carleton Town plott on until a line produced foeth forty-three degrees west comes to the said line and thence to run and continue that course until it comes to the river St. Johns thence to run up the course of the river to the bounds at the falls first mentioned contacting one thousand one hundred and twenty acres more or less, allowance being made for all such roads as may hereafter be deemed necessary to...this the...and hath such shape form and marks, as appears...plat thereof hereinto annexed together with all underwoods, timber and timber trees, lakes, ponds, fishings, waters, water courses, profits, commodities, appurtenances and hereditaments whatsoever there belongings or in any wise appertaining together also the privilege of hunting, hawking and fowling in and upon the same and mines and minerals, saving and reserving...to us, our heirs and successors, all white pine it any shall be found growing thereon, and also saving or reserving to us our heirs and successors all mines of gold, silver, copper, lead and coals, to have and to hold the said parcel or tract of one thousand one hundred and twenty acres of land and all and...other then promises hereby granted unto the said several and respective granters in severalty in the lots, shares and proportions as following to wit unto the said Matthew Haines (all the above names mentioned again) and each and everyone of them respectively ten acres apiece and in severalty unto their and every of their several respective heirs and assigns forever in free and common socage. The said several and respective grantees and their several and respective heirs or assigns yielding and paying therefore unto us our heirs and successors unto our Receiver General for the time being onto his deputy or deputies for the time being yearly, that is to say at the feast of St. Michael in every year at the rate of two shillings for every hundred acres, and so in proportion according to the quantities of acres hereby granted, the same to commence and be payable from the said feast of Saint Michael which shall first happen after the expiration of ten years from the date hereof provided always and this present grant is upon condition that the said several and respective grantees and their respective heirs or assigns shall and do within three years after the date hereof for every fifty acres of plantable land hereby granted clear and work three acres at least in that part thereof as respectively he, she or they shall judge most convenient and advantageous, or else to clear and drain three acres of swampy or sunken ground or drain three acres of marsh, if any such contained therein and shall and do within the time aforesaid...and keep upon every fifty acres thereof accounted barren...and continue the same thereon until three acres for every fifty acres be fully cleared and improved, and if there shall be no part of the said tract fit for present cultivation without manuring and improving the same respectively, he, she or they within the time aforesaid shall be obliged to erect on some part of his, her or their respective land one good dwelling house to be at least twenty feet in length and sixteen feet in breadth, and to put on his, her or their said respective land the like number of three neat cattle for every fifty acres or otherwise if any part of the said tract shall be stony or rocky ground and not fit for planting or pasture, shall and do within three years as aforesaid, begin to employ thereon and continue to work for three years then rest ensuing in digging any stone quarry or mine, one good and able hand for every fifty acres, it shall be accounted a sufficient seating, cultivation and improvements to save forever from forfeiture fifty acres of land in any part of the tract hereby granted and the said respective several grantees and their respective heirs and assigns be at liberty to withdraw his, her or their stock, or forbear working in any quarry or mine in proportion to such cultivation and improvements, as shall be made upon the plantable lands, swamps, sunken grounds or marsh herein contained, and of the said rent hereby reserved shall happen to be in arrear or unpaid for the space of one year from the time it shall become due, and no distress can be found on the said land, tenements and hereditaments hereby granted or if this grant shall not be duly registered in the registers office of our said province within six months from the date hereof, and a docket also entered in the auditors office of the same then grant be void, and the said lands, tenements and hereditaments hereby granted, and every part and parcel thereof shall revert to us, our heirs and successors, and provided also and upon this further condition that if the land hereby given and granted to the said several and respective grantees, and his, her or their respective heirs as aforesaid shall at any time or times hereafter come unto the possession and tenure of any person or persons whatever inhabitants of our said province of Nova Scotia, either by virtue of any deed of sale, conveyance,...or exchange or by gift, inheritance or descent devise or marriage, such person or person being inhabitants as aforesaid shall within twelve months after his, her or their entry and possession of the same take the oaths prescribed by law, and make and subscribe the following declaration, that is to say I, _____, do promise and declare, that I will maintain and defend to the utmost of my power the authority of the King in his Parliament as the supreme Legislature of the province, before some one of the Magistrates of the said province, and such declaration and certificate of the Magistrate that such oaths have been taken, being recorded in the Secretary's office of the said province, there person or persons so taking the oaths aforesaid, and making and subscribing the said declaration, shall be deemed the lawful possession or possessions of the lands hereby granted; and in case of default on the part of such person or persons in taking the oaths, and making and subscribing the declaration within twelve months as aforesaid, this present grant and every part thereof shall and we do hereby declare the same to be null and void to all intents and purposes, and the lands hereby granted and every part and parcel thereof shall in like manner revert to and became vested to us, our heirs and successors, anything herein contained to the contrary notwithstanding.

  Given under the great seal of our Province of Nova Scotia, Witness our trusty and well beloved John Parr Esquire Captain General Governor and Commander in Chief in and over our said Province this eleventh day of August in the year of our Lord one thousand seven hundred and eighty-four, and in the twenty-fourth year of our Reign.

By his Excellency's command   J. Parr
  Rich Bulkeley

Signed in Council
Rich Bulkeley

      Nova Scotia, Halifax,
      14 August 1784
      Entered at the Auditor's
       Office
      Frank Shipton

Nova Scotia, Halifax
Registered 13 August 1784
An Goold Reg.

New Brunswick
Registered 6th. January 1785

Note: Copied from the original.

New Brunswick was carved out of the Province of Nova Scotia in the later half of 1784, because of the unhappiness of the Loyalists regarding the management of the new territory. They wanted more recognition in government matters because their needs were not being met in Halifax. The land grants and Loyalist representation were the main issues.

Benjamin and Sarah were very concerned about their safety since moving to their new home. The ocean frontage posed a threat from Privateers who traveled up and down the coast searching for easy booty from the vulnerable settlers. Arms were always kept close by.

The lumber that was issued was not the best grade, but it was good enough to build a small, one room cabin to protect them from the harsh elements in the north. The upcoming winter would put them to the test. At least they wouldn't have to spend another winter in a tent. Being so close to the water meant seeing and meeting many different people who traveled the waterway for a living.

One morning as the fog covered their little cabin, tiny Sarah heard the crowing of Joseph Lingley's rooster next door. He just bought him the day before in Parrtown hoping to breed his hens. The new, early morning sound surely awoke many other folks. Sarah, still in her nightgown, and rubbing the sleep from her tired eyes, went to fetch the water bucket to fill it outdoors at a newly dug community well. Her mouth was very dry, due to the bronchial and sinus conditions she inherited from her family.

Everyone was still in bed, but she could hear her father stirring on his corded bed and mattress he made several days earlier. He soon was rising to the new day. She walked over to the door and unlatched its heavy leather noose that was tied to the wall and door. When she opened the door, she was expecting to catch a glimpse of the sun fighting its way through the fog as it does many mornings. With her bucket in one hand and a good strong pull on the door with the other hand, she managed to swing the door wide open.

Suddenly, to her surprise and horror, she found a giant man standing there. He filled the entire doorway. She looked up at him and saw that he was covered with furs from many different animals. His full beard hid his face except for his deep dark, piercing eyes, which were staring right through Sarah. He must have been over six feet tall.

With a terrifying scream, Sarah threw the bucket to the dirt floor and ran hysterically to her father's bedside. Ben leaped to his feet and started for his musket when the stranger said:

"Bonjour, I am very sorry for disturbing you and your family at this early hour of the day, but you see, my boat was damaged by some rocks at the entrance of the harbour."

Still very cautious, Benjamin retreated from his rifle and grabbed his trousers instead. He wife, Sarah was hiding under the covers, peeking out through a small moth hole.

The large man stepped back from the door showing Ben that he had no hostel intentions. He proved to be a very polite and gracious man.

"Just one moment," Ben replied as he finished buttoning his shirt. Sarah relaxed a bit but still remained under the covers, now with little Sarah who was still shaking. Ben then asked Sarah to not be frightened and to start a fire and put a pot of tea on.

The visitor was a Frenchman who lived up the Saint John River at the old French Village about fifteen miles away. His name was Oliver Thibadeau, and coming up from behind him was another Frenchman who introduced himself as Francois Violet. Francois had just finished dragging their small boat ashore. Ben started to feel a little more comfortable with the two men and invited them into the cabin for some tea. They told him their boat needed repairs. Their English was surprisingly clear, asking Ben permission to leave it there as they went to town for the materials to restore it. Ben had no problem with their request. After talking with them, he found that they were fur trapping to find extra cash. They were farmers, but needed more ways to support their large Acadian families.

Francois Violet was on his third marriage, as he had outlived two of his wives. All three relationships ended up with twenty-five children. Some of those children had already made Olivier and Francois in-laws. They new soon they would have to migrate north where other French Canadian's settled. The Loyalists were taking all the lands in the south of New Brunswick forcing the Acadian's to sell out or leave. This new territory to the north was called Madawaska. Olivier Thibodeau had just completed the sale of his land to Philip Weade, who later found that his small log cabin was haunted, and there were well-known stories about it all over the county.

Two bodies had been found murdered for no apparent reason on the dusty, dirt floor and Olivier would not go any farther than that in his story. Many Loyalist children in that area had already labeled the place "haunted" and many came from far off to frighten themselves from its reputation. An old lady named Mary Fisher was to blame for spreading the stories to the Loyalist families. The stories caused the price of the cabin to be reduced which sold separately to Mr. Ackerman and Mr. Vanderbeck.

The French Village was just sixty miles south from St. Ann's (now Fredericton). Olivier and Francois told Ben of the beautiful river valley and realizing they were all farmers, told him of the good fertile farmland along its banks. Hunting also was very good. Beaver, deer, and fish were there for the taking, even in the dead of winter.

Benjamin told them how unhappy the Loyalists were concerning the land grant issue. He expressed his sympathy about the way the French were being pressured off their lands and out of the area. The age-old British/French struggle for control over this territory left many homeless, especially back in 1755 when the British forcibly broke up Acadian families and shipped them to far away places like Boston, North and South Carolina, France, New Orleans, Virginia, Pennsylvania, etc. They did their damnedest to break up the successes of the Acadian's. The visit was an interesting one and the two Acadian's soon left for Parrtown to get supplies to fix their craft. The following day, their boat was repaired and they left, never again to cross paths until Benjamin's third great-grandchild married into their families bringing together the Loyalist lines with the Acadian and Quebec lines of the Violette, Thibodeau, Cyr, Hebert, Pelletier, Belanger, Gagne, Gagnon, Dumont, Michaud, Nadeau, Ouellette, Martin, Langlois, Beaupre, Leclerc, Dionne, Vaillancourt, Cote, Parent, Morin, Bernier, Talbot, Melanson, LeBlanc, Cornier, Roy, Boucher, Levasseur, Levesque, Tardif, Doucet, Marchant, Picard, LaTour, and hundreds of others, forever securing the Acadian genetic lines the English tried so hard to snuff out.

The following months were fairly good. Shelter was better and supplies were more plentiful, but many Loyalists did return to the States and endured whatever treatment came their way. By 1785, the time was right for Ben and Sarah to start thinking of continuing their family. The need for a better land grant was a top priority so he kept an eye out on daily developments. The lot they had did save their lives but was terrible for any length of time. He knew he had the right to two hundred acres and thanks to the information that Olivier and Francois gave him, he waited for something up into the Saint John River Valley. On 18 May 1785, the City of Saint John was created under the royal charter. Colonel Gabriel Ludlow of Queens County would become its first mayor and hold that office until 1795.

Chapter 9

A Real Home

In the spring of 1785, life was still a struggle, but compared to the previous two years, it was pure honey and molasses. Ben was working sixteen hours a day, but those hours were spent working on his own property. The land was really not fit for farming, but he tried his best to get the most out of it. He still managed to find time in the day to go to town to follow the land grant hearings.

One day, he and a few of his comrades from the refugee regiment went into town to keep themselves represented. The coffeehouse was a little more crowded than usual. Accompanying Benjamin were his Captain, William Wright Sr., and his son William, and Daniel Fowler, George Harding and his good friend, Titus Brown. A few others turned up later and by now Ben knew the game well enough, that he immediately grouped his companions together and told them to stay close by as the lobbying started.

One group had just been awarded a grant that they won the month before. The location was St. Ann's. Ben remembered that name from his French friends. The next grant was issued at the northern part of the Long Reach around a Connecticut Loyalist settlement called Kingston. He remembered this area to from the Acadian's. This was the area that had good soil, at least better than where he was now. Ben positioned himself closer to the platform where the chairman was conducting the session. Suddenly, the shouting started again, and this time Ben was right there.

This was his big chance for some choice property. His previous rank of corporal would entitle him to two hundred acres. King George owed him this and when the grant went to another group, he nearly cried out. Two representatives from that group stepped forward to collect the prize. It was Isaac Bunnell of Redding, Connecticut who served in the Prince of Wales Regiment, and Benjamin Keirstead, his friend and future in-law. They walked away in glee.

The last land grant issue of the day came up for grabs. It was the southwestern part of the Long Reach, which was surrounded by water on three sides. It lay across from the Loyalist parish of Westfield. The location would assure a cool cross breeze during the summer months. The shouting suddenly began. The fight was fierce but in the end Ben walked away with the grant in his hand, and as the chairman. His companions cheered in jubilation.

The record shows that Benjamin and sixty other Loyalists were granted the Long Reach property, which consisted of one thousand, two hundred and eighty acres, to be divided according to the rank of each soldier. The contract would be finalized much later, on January 24, 1786, but settlement could commence within several days.
Those loyalists were:

"Benjamin Bunnell, Enos Supple, Samuel Parmale, Moses Gregory, John Lee, Abel Haulling, John Smith, George Harding, Sarah Lester, Joseph Alston, James Lavison, David Cram, James Cam, Isaac Dickenson, Henry Dickenson, Robert Conrad, William Harris, Joseph Barlow, John Flewelling Jr., Amos Arnold, Titus Brown, Daniel Fowler, George McCall, John Bridgman, Morris Flewelling, John Johnston, Charles Looseley, John James Clemett, Henry Devober, Elizabeth Bridgman, John Flewelling, Samuel Austin, James Ham, Robert and Caleb Merrit, Elizabeth Vail, James Cram, Thomas Elms, Thomas Beam, Thomas Miles, Thomas Burtleys, Aaron Kingsland, William Wright Jr., Joseph Brothers, William Vermulle, Jonathan Burnham, Nathaniel Horton, James Lisk, Joseph Bidder, William Perry, Abraham Frost, Joseph Cooper, John James Clemett, Thomas Yearly, Mordecai Lesier, Jacob Holden, Jonathan Parker, Catherine Kautzman, Edward Sutton, Simion Mallary, Ensign Samuel Stricht." (Note: Spelling may not be exact due to clarity of the document so look for various versions).

It was a happy night at the Bonnell's cabin. Sarah next year would not repeat the planting in the small rocky ten-acre field. Plans for the new farm had to begin right away. The government-issued canvas would come into use once more as a temporary shelter, until the new home was constructed. Preparations to move up-river started too. Sarah had just finished making rag dolls for the children, and Ben traded Captain Wright Sr. some vegetables for a small amount of rum to help celebrate. In two days they would hire a boatman to go up and pace out their new property.

One quarter page photo of Land Grant from King George III to Benjamin and 60 Others.

Upper half of one-quarter page of land grant for Long Reach. First name listed is Benjamin.

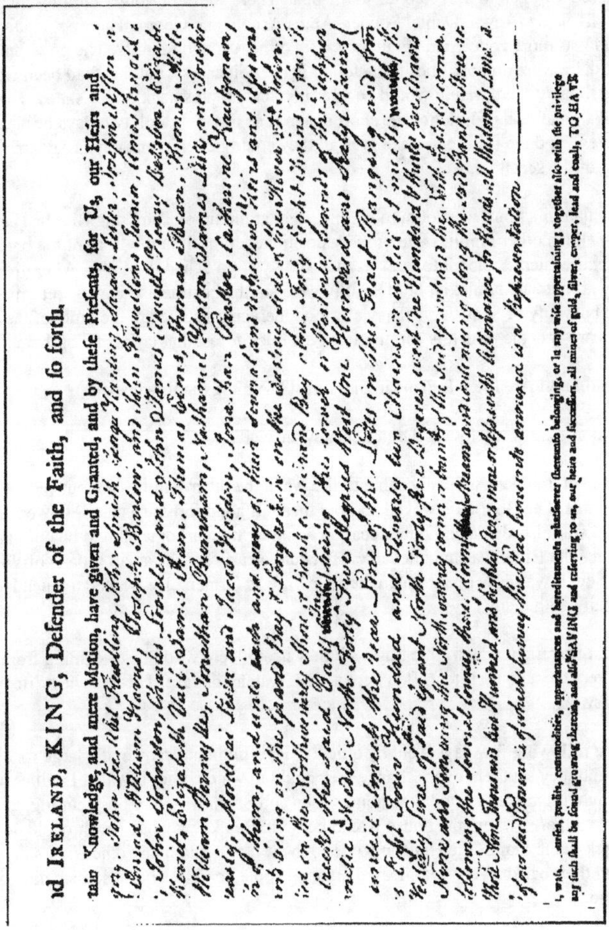
...nd IRELAND, KING, Defender of the Faith, and so forth.

...tain Knowledge, and mere Motion, have given and Granted, and by these Presents, for Us, our Heirs and
...gery, John Lee, Abel Fowlling, John Smith, George Harding, Sarah Lester, Joseph Alston a...
...Conrad, William Harris, Joseph Barlow, and John Travellens Junior, Amos Arnold a...
..., John Johnston, Charles Froseley, and John James Crowell, Henry Bettsher, Elizabe...
...Kenet, Elizabeth Vail, James Fram, Thomas Lens, Thomas Bean, Thomas Mile...
William Vermylle, Jonathan Burnham, Nathaniel Horton, James Lilk and Joseph...
...easly, Mordecai Lester and Jacob Holden, Jonathan Parker, Catherine Kautzman,
...n of them, and unto each and every of their several and respective Heirs and Assigns
...and being on the Grand Bay & Long reach on the easterly Side of the River St. John...
...ed on the Northwesterly Shore or Bank of the Grand Bay about Forty Eight Chains of the...
Creek, the said Creek being the lower or Westerly bounds of the upper
...ence North Forty Five Degrees West One Hundred and Sixty Chains
...untill it meets the rear Line of the Lotts in that Tract Ranging and from
...s East Four Hundred and Twenty two Chains or untill it meets [illegible] the
Westerly Line of said Grant North Forty five Degrees, west One Hundred & thirty five Chains...
Nine and Ten being the Northwesterly corner or bounds of the said Grant and the North easterly corner...
following the several Courses thereof down the Stream and continuing along the said Bank or Shore...
whole Nine Thousand two Hundred and Eighty Acres more or less with allowance for Roads and Wilderness Line...
...of our said Province of which Survey the Plat hereunto annexed is a Representation

..., wate[illegible]courses, profits, commodities, appurtenances and hereditaments whatsoever thereunto belonging, or in any wise appertaining; together also with the privilege
...any such shall be found growing thereon, and also SAVING and reserving to us, our heirs and successors, all mines of gold, silver, copper, lead and coals, TO HAVE

It was a beautiful flowering month in May of 1785. Maybe it was because everything was going so smoothly; life seemed to regain some order. Through George Harding's connections, they acquired a wagon to move goods to the boat. There were four other families on board with the Bunnell - Titus Brown, Daniel Fowler, Amos Arnold and George Harding. Upon leaving the city, Sarah was more concerned about the safety of her growing family. The government assured them that there were no hostilities to be found in the wilderness, but they had been wrong before - they had thought the uprising would be over in a few months back in the States. The trip consumed a great deal of time for the short distance of travel. It took two days because of the rivers current, and ten to fifteen miles was all they could travel in one day. They arrived at the beginning of the second day.

Benjamin's grant was lot number one, right at the tip of The Long Reach. They landed there with all the other families. He proudly positioned himself at the front of the boat to watch his two hundred acres come into view as they slowly approached the shore. After grounding the craft, they all unloaded quickly, but fearfully watched the boatman sail away, returning to the noisy and busy city of Saint John. They all stood there and listened to the quiet of their new land. All they heard was the birdcalls coming from the thick forest that lay ahead of them.

"Mommy! Are there Indians in that forest?" Young Sarah whispered.

"I don't know my love," Sarah honestly answered.

The still moment suddenly came to life when the other families announced their leaving for their grants. The Bonnell's waved and bid them all good fortune as the followed an old trail inland. Ben was already pacing out a location he thought their home should be built at. The view of the Saint John River was unbelievable. He could clearly see the small village of Westfield on the other side. It was now time to plan their new life as farmers. He wanted a much larger family, and hopefully with many boys.

That first night was frightening. All they heard were wild noises coming from the forest some got very close to their tent. Ben kept a close watch all night. This was how life would be in New Brunswick.

The following few days went by quickly. The children discovered a large rock partially in the water and they sat there every chance they could to watch other Loyalist families traveling up the river to their land grants and new homes. Ben and Sarah was very busy cutting down trees on the high ground area where the house would be built. Ben knew what a river could do in the spring. Back in the States, the Hudson River, in New York, and many other rivers in New Jersey overflowed their banks every year, leaving many people homeless because they did not built on high ground.

One day, Titus Brown showed up in a very unpleasant mood. He had discovered that most of his land was unsuitable for farming. He had no idea what to do and all he could think of was to seek out Benjamin for help. His guess was correct for Ben knew of another case during his long days waiting for a land grant. He instructed Titus to petition the registry for a new grant, calling his unfit for farming. Ben agreed to be his witness along with their Captain, William Wright Sr. Here is what that document said:

19 May 1785

To his Excellency and the honourable council. I, Titus Brown, having made application for a lot number nine on the east side of the Long Reach, on the river Saint John in William Holland" survey of the Hastings grant, do find an opposition made against me by Captain William Wright on behalf of Joseph and James Davison.

I would beg his Excellency's pleasure with your honourable consideration in the matter as the underwritten certificate doth mention.

I, Benjamin Bunnel, being present when the aforementioned land was issued do certify that the said lot number nine as likewise, number eight was condemned and thrown out as not fit for cultivation in the opinion of Captain William Wright, and some of the company likewise do certify that these two lots, that Captain Wright did at the same time draw number twenty-six in the same draft. His Excellency's pleasure would be thankfully preferred by your very humble servant Titus Brown and Benjamin Bunnel.

Finally, with all the paperwork and character references in order, Titus was awarded another land grant a little further up river and Benjamin went back to building his home and farm. His property would one day be called Harding's Point which would be named after his comrade and friend, George Harding, who would later purchase it from Ben and expand the home into a grand looking traveling Inn. At the far end of this property it would later be called Sand Point because of its beautiful sandy beach.

It was mandatory that most land grants given to the Loyalists are laid out in a defensive manner with quick access to river or ocean outlets in case of any future attacks from the United States, and the feeling of all was that it was inevitable. Benjamin wanted nothing further to do with the military involvement or future engagements. He suffered enough and the memory of new London and Fort Griswold came to mind frequently.

The Loyalist land grants and new Province meant a lot to the settlers and even though Benjamin could never bring himself to fight again, he did stand firm in his deeply rooted Quaker beliefs and the rights to his property with privacy. This new time in his life was hard and most everyone around him was poor, like him.

Early in the morning of July 23, 1785, as the fog was lying heavy over the river and nearby the shore, Benjamin was awakened by some movement in the brush not far from his cabin. He went for his musket, as Sarah quietly checked the children while they slept. Ben cautiously opened the door to his cabin and looked out to see who was on his property. There in front of him was George Duncan on the river in his boat fishing for an early morning catch. He surely was not the noise coming from the bushes. Ben finished securing his buttons on his trousers and pulled his straps over both shoulders and proceeded out the door. He crept around back fighting off four or five hungry chickens that thought it was feeding time. Their unexpected attack started his heart pounding elevating the suspense. He slowly advanced to the heavily wooded area just in back of the cabin where the noise was coming from.

George Duncan's attention was now drawn to the tense scene. He couldn't see whom Ben was checking on, but rowing his boat closer would keep him involved in the developing situation. He saw Ben point his musket into the air, and the loud musket shot rang out and awakened everything within hearing. The crackle from Ben's old musket sent several blackbirds and seagulls into flight. The blackberry bushes directly in front of him shook violently as the intruder jumped to his feet holding a large pale full of the fruit. Ben jumped back in shock as the frightened criminal revealed himself to Ben, and George Duncan who was now not more then one hundred yards away from the two men face to face.

This guy was familiar to both men. Everyone in the area was too poor to ignore suck a crime and here Ben's own neighbor, William Perry was the thief. Food and wood was a very vital part of survival in the beginning years of the settlements and taking resources off other Loyalists property was a major crime. At first Ben had no idea what to do or say to his neighbor who had one hundred-thirty acres down by Sand Point. They did not get along very well, and Ben could not bring himself to subdue him as William Perry suddenly took off like a rabbit heading back to his property. Ben looked over his right should to see that his witness was still taking in all that had happened; enough to press charges later with the proper authorities.

In August of 1785, a suit for trespassing was filed at Mr. Campbell's office against William Perry. The case would be heard by the Supreme Court. On July 23, 1785, Mr. Campbell requested the sheriff of Kings County to arrest William Perry and to hold him there until the first Tuesday of October when the hearing would be held in Saint John. Ward Chipman signed the documents on August 9, 1785 and George Duncan was Ben's witness. On the twentieth day of August, William Perry was arrested and held for the upcoming trial. Mr. Perry was delivered to Saint John for the hearing by Richard and John Roe (Doe) on October 21, 1785. There was no further documentation of this trial or the outcome, but it is certain that Mr. William Perry had to repay Benjamin for his crime.

The battle between William Perry and Benjamin Bunnel would not stop there. Perry was granted lot number fifteen which was included in the grants with Ben and 60 others on Long Reach. Though they all got access to those grants in 1785, it was finally registered on 1 Feb. 1786. Ben headed most functions because he was probably the only one that could read so much grant business got him involved. The next encounter between the two men was on 15 Sept. 1785 when William Perry petitioned for land. The record reads:

"William Perry states that Benjamin Bunnel refuses to pay him for his improvements. In Council 20th. Sept. 1785, B. Bunnel to show cause why he does not comply with the injunction to make compensation to Perry."

One assumption was that William Perry must have cleared land and for some reason was not paid his compensation (Land or money?) and filed the petition. He did receive his land grant in January 1786.

All of this activity in October put Ben behind in his farm work. One day as he was sowing winter wheat, he received word that his close friend, Colonel Henry Nase would soon be sailing for Poughkeepsie, New York on personal business. There were a lot of Loyalists who started to travel back and forth to the States regarding family matters, but the Colonel's reason was slightly different. When he hurriedly left New York he hid $1000 in a teapot and buried it under a large oak tree near his house there. He worried that his money would be found on him while crossing enemy lines during war. Times in Nova Scotia and New Brunswick were very hard and he needed the hidden treasure he left behind in New York.

On the first of November 1785, he left his manner, but did not sail until the eleventh. The trip took twelve days, and his desire was to pick up his money and return immediately before any of his old neighbors or enemies recognized him. When he arrived, he noticed that in the few passing years had drastically changed the appearance of the area. After digging around seven or eight large oak trees he broke down over his obvious new loss. The money was gone, or had he forgotten which tree had his treasure. His search ended coming to the conclusion that someone had found his fortune making it theirs.

By now, he was attracting attention from some nearby farms. On December second, he departed Poughkeepsie for the posts of New York City, and sailed home a broken man. The return trip took fourteen days, and upon arriving at Saint John he saw why that port city was the third largest shipbuilding seaport in the world at that time. He saw ship mast in various building stages dotting the coastline around the city. Some very large ships were nearly complete. The sight was beautiful. This infant city was growing to the largest seaport on the east coast except for Boston. This once commanding Loyalist stood proud looking at all His Majesty's ships that carried the tall mast from the Loyalist land grants.

From 1783 to 1816, many of the great pines located on Loyalist land grants were marked with a "Broad Arrow," making them the property of the British Royal Navy for use as mast on most of their ships. This was known as the "Broad Arrow Policy." On Benjamin's strategically located land at the end of the Long Reach played a large roll in transporting these mast to Saint John. The ten-mile peninsula jetted out into the Grand Bay heading to the city. Ben did not care for the invasion of his now private life, but it was his contribution to the Crown as long as he did not get involved in military matters as he was in the past.

When Colonel Henry Nase returned to Westfield, everyone wanted to know what life was like back in the States, how was his trip and treatment. They soon learned that he would not utter a word about his experience there. They knew not to question each other when returning from the lower x-colonies. Loyalists endured lots of renewed pain and bad treatment over their past involvements Only Henry's diary would tell what really happened during his haunting trip to New York.

At the end of 1785, life was centered on the farm and survival for family. In April of 1786, Benjamin started plowing his fields again, sowing his cabbage. He began to see first signs of vessels traveling up the river after the thaw. The ice had cleared enough for water traffic to flow. The month of May brought on the planting of potatoes, sowing of peas and planting more cabbage. In the summer of 1786, Benjamin and Sarah's parents pleaded to the Rahway/Woodbridge Meeting House back in New Jersey for relief help for their Quaker families who were suffering in Canada. Joseph Moore and William Wilson were assigned to execute the project that was later named the "Sufferings in March 1787." The actual visit is said to have occurred in the summer of 1786 and Ben and Sarah received a visit from some of these concerned Friends (Quakers) from Rahway/Woodbridge area in New Jersey.

There were many destitute families in New Brunswick and Nova Scotia that couldn't make a go of it and some of that bad news made it back home to the States. Concerned families established relief efforts and channeled their efforts and supplies through religious societies, mostly the Quakers. It is not known if Benjamin's family was really in need of help, but the Quakers did come to see them. Even though a few years they had disowned earlier Benjamin and his family because of the involvement in the war, they still found enough compassion to record Ben and his family as recipients for help. Joseph Moore of New Jersey who was one of the visiting Friends recorded this. The Philadelphia Yearly Meeting backed the entire operation. Robert FitRandolph was another who received aid and who was from Woodbridge, New Jersey[15]. The following are those Quakers visited:

---

[15] Records filed at vault of Philadelphia Yearly Meeting, for Sufferings, Miscellaneous Papers, box 19 at (Arch Street), # 302, Philadelphia, Pa.

List One
1. John Horner, farmer, Lydia his wife and four children, none of these were members.
2. John Strickland, Shoemaker, from Middletown, Bucks County, Pennsylvania.
3. John Dennis, Carpenter and boat builder, son of Henry Dennis formally of Philadelphia, and who is dead. Wife Martha and four children were from Bucks County, Pennsylvania. They married contrary to our discipline.
4. John Langhborough, Blacksmith, his wife Margaret is a member from Aldngan (?).
5. Samuel Fairbanks, Surveyor, his wife Hannah a member of Chester of Philadelphia and daughter of Francis Richardson dead. They have three children. Samuel has been concerned in war.
6. Amos Strickland, Farmer from Bucks County, Pennsylvania. Ma...? Out of our way.
7. Samuel Stillwell (Stithwell) innkeeper and carpenter. Wife and one child...? Of them members.
8. Jesse Woodward and wife. He was disowned. His wife a member from about C...wicks, New Jersey. He was a farmer.
9. Isaac Woodward
10. Jesse Woodward, son of Jesse Woodward disowned.
11. Anthony Woodward, Farmer, wife Kesiah from New Jersey. He was disowned. They have one child.
12. Joseph Th...?, a Mason. He wife Abigail and two daughters, Hester and Martha married and none of them are members.

List Two - River St. John
1. Caleb Powell, Farmer and his wife at Gagetown, New Brunswick. From Westbury, Long Island. He was disowned.
2. Marm.nike Hutchinson, Farmer at Maugerville, New Brunswick. From Crosswick, New Jersey.
3. James Powell, son of Caleb, Farmer.

4. Abner Hampton, disowned by Rahway Monthly Meeting (Rahway, New Jersey) for some inconsistent conduct in the war.
5. Andrew Hampton, supposed a member.
6. Benjamin Bunnell, wife and children from Rahway Monthly Meeting (Rahway, New Jersey). He was disowned for some conduct of a warlike nature.
7. John Lee, wife and children. Professors with friends from Rahway, New Jersey.
8. William Underhill on Spoon Island from New York Government.
9. Robert Comely from Horsham went out from Friends in the time of the late war.
10. (?) Cousins and son at St. John from Gloucester, New Jersey.
11. Hugh Cowperthwaite, Farmer. His wife Sarah and about 10 children from Salem, New Jersey, now at Sheffield, New Brunswick.
12. Joel Daniel, Carpenter, late of Alloways Creek, now of Maugerville, New Brunswick. His wife's former name was Clarissa Winn, late of Staten Island. He has never been treated with for going out in marriage.
13. Joseph Canby, wife and children from Bucks County, Pennsylvania now at Indian House Village. Thomas Canby, Blacksmith. Both were disowned for some inconsistent conduct in the late war. (Below at St. Marys Bay).
14. Anthony Hollingshead, Farmer and children from near Mooretown. His wife Elizabeth and three sons. He was disowned.
15. Lucy Smith, wife of Joseph Smith and their son from Squan, New Jersey. People of sober character.
16. Priscilla Harrison, wife of Christopher Harrison from Burlington with four children. Not members. She the daughter of Joseph Peddle.

That August they experienced a small frost and by the end of the month it had killed Ben's vines. The first snow arrived on the fifth of November 1786; more on the sixth and on the fifteenth a heavy snowstorm hit the area and froze most of the creeks. Six inches more fell on the eighteenth, which assured everyone that skate travel was now safe across the rivers.

The year ended quietly in good spirits. Christmas day was warm for that time of year, and looking outside the Bonnell's cabin window, one could see the river open to some travel after a thaw. It was a beautiful Christmas because on the twenty-first they had six inches of snow. Sarah placed a fine looking pheasant on the table, one that Ben shot the day before. They all sat down and prayed for a prosperous new year.

The winter of 1786 was oddly pleasant in New Brunswick. January, always a mild month, brought on an extended temporary thaw. When spring arrived in 1787, the crops were productive for the Bonnell's. It was a little safer knowing that many of the bears moved father north. The small cabin was finally completed and the fields were fully planted. Lumber was in high demand and each Loyalist cut a limited number to sell, but others unfortunate enough stole others good fortune. Many Loyalists put ads in the Saint John Gazette Newspaper warning thieves that their lives would be in dangers if trespassing on their property. There were many timber thieves in or around the Westfield area.

One unusually warm day in 1788, Benjamin was preparing his field for a potato planting when Sarah came to see him. She scared off three seagulls, which were watching Ben's every move, hoping to catch any interesting discarded materials of interest. As Ben looked up to see his faithful wife, he noticed the frightened gulls fly overhead. He stood up to embrace her and spotted a very familiar glow in her face. The glow that told him he would be a father again. He waited for her to confirm his thoughts, which she did. After a sweet embrace, he decided to call it a day to celebrate. More good news came on March thirteenth that year with the announcement of the marriage of Henry Nase to Jane Quinton. May 1788, brought on the usual planting of summer turnips and sowing of summer wheat and peas. Corn would complete May's planting. The year's end was quiet and quickly passed by.

1789 was another pleasant year. Sarah gave birth to a son, to whom they named Benjamin (3rd.). Ben always wanted a son named after him and his father. It was a name passed on in his family for many years, generation after generation. By the time that May came around Ben had planted corn, yellow beans, pumpkins and a small orchard of apples. October completed the potato harvest that was always a big project.

In 1790, the Bonnell's had another son whom they named Joseph, another old family name. Now Benjamin had two Canadian-born children and as the family increased in size, so did the fears of possibly losing one of them to the Saint John River. Many people, mostly children and old folks were drowning at an alarming rate. During the winter months, the frozen rivers became an easy travel route and playground. It was especially handy for the people living on the Long Reach wanting to go to Westfield across the river.

Traffic was heavy and movement was right by Ben's cabin, something he did not like very much. He enjoyed his privacy and his number one lot on Long Reach was one of exposure, and opportunity. Ben did not seek the opportunities though. When spring arrived, most accidents occurred then because the ice became thin and was very unpredictable. Tragedy struck nearly every family each year. After a slow warn start that year, winter hit hard in February. By the first of March 1790, the snow was very deep and the weather became very harsh, but by April second, the thaw began and on the third it started to rain.

Ben hoped for another good year as he began planting again in May. Corn, peas and beans were put into the ground first. Buckwheat and oats came next in June, and July saw green peas and turnips. The Indians didn't bother Ben and his family very much, but there were many terrible stories told around the fireplace at night by the neighbors.

As the year rolled by, Benjamin didn't pay much attention to world events, but close-by there were many changes, and some he did get involved in. Another child was born in 1797. This time a daughter named Eleanor Ann. It was time to add-on to the small cabin. The family was quickly outgrowing it and Ben with the help of his elder son Samuel started the construction. A few months passed and their cabin took on the appearance of a nice colonial home. They even added some boards to the once open-beam walls. This left Sarah furious one day as she searched all over for the child's blue loyalists jacket she had Samuel pass down to young Benjamin 3rd. He could not find it or his fishing pole his father made for him. Sarah kept insisting it was sealed up in one of the walls because little Ben always hung it on nails that protruded from the beams. Its fine brass buttons, and patched elbows would never be seen again in their lifetime. This was an expensive item to lose back in those days of scarcity. Little Ben surely got a whipping for his recklessness.

Many outsider people were in the area and some of the original settlers wanted to be left alone to live out their quiet, but narrow lives. The previous year (1796) Benjamin's friend, Colonel Henry Nase, had been insulted and abused and he was to take legal action to settle the problem. That same year, on April second, General Coffin gave land to the parish for the Church of England chapel. Abel Flewelling and Elias Scovil were witnesses to the signing of the deed, and later the Parishioners requested the election of Elias Scovil as pastor because of all the hard work and teaching he had done for the community. In 1798, Greenwich and Westfield each had their own church. And Ben and Sarah gave birth to another child. Ben gave this boy a very special name. His younger brother, Simeon had died young and what a nice way to honor him.

One clear and bright May afternoon in 1798, Benjamin was working his blue potato crop when his friend, Colonel Henry Nase, came by with some startling news about Jonathan Sherwood, the son of their friend, Andrew Sherwood of Hempstead, Long Island, New York. It took Benjamin several minutes to calm Henry. He kept mumbling and cursing Jonathan Sherwood. Without a warning, Henry scooped Ben up onto his feet and dragged him to his small boat and rowed off.

They arrived at a heavily overgrown beach, which hid their boat and them from what Henry wanted to show Ben. There, right in front of their eyes, was a sight that Ben thought he would never see near his home. Henry had to stop Benjamin from jumping out of the boat. He now wanted to kill Jonathan Sherwood.

There in front of them was a family of black people and Jonathan Sherwood who was inviting them into his house, an unheard of thing to do in those days. The entire town of Westfield would surely mark Sherwood. The black family appeared very poor and hungry. The children had no shoes and their clothing was tattered.

Henry and Benjamin left that scene for John Coffin's home to place a protest and complaint against Jonathan Sherwood for bringing such a family into the community. They did not want Westfield to support this family, let alone have them live nearby. They demanded that John Coffin take written action against Sherwood. Coffin had no choice but to write up a complaint to Abel Flewelling to take action against Sherwood. The following is what the complaint said:

Mr. Abel Flewelling, Sir,
Where as Henry Nase and Benjamin Bunnel has said complaint against Jonathan Sherwood for introducing a black pauper and family into the Parish.
You are hereby instructed to call on the said Sherwood to require of him security that the said Pauper does not become a Parish charge - Should he refuse you will promise to give legal warning to this Pauper that he may not gain a settlement.
Signed, John Coffin, Justice of the Peace.
June 1, 1798
A. Flewelling.[16]

This infuriated Sherwood to the point that during the following years, a feud broke out between him and Henry and Ben. Later, Jonathan's daughter, Jerusha married Isaac Bunnell, a Loyalist from Redding, Connecticut (unproven relation to Ben and Isaac Bunnell, b. 1745). The Sherwood's lived six miles north of St. George in Charlotte County, New Brunswick.

On May 11, 1805, Jonathan Sherwood got his revenge on Benjamin by filing a suit at the Supreme Court, an unknown complaint. Although there is no documentation available, it certainly had to do with the feud from the black family complaint. The court document that did survive reads as follows:

---

[16] Kings County New Brunswick Court records for under Bunnel vs. Pauper at Fredericton NB Archives.

Sherwood vs. Bunnell - For Capture, filed 12 July 1805 Kings Js. - Capture.... for Jonathan Sherwood against Benjamin Bunnell..... the Saturday next after the first Tuesday in July next. Signed, Ward Chipman 11 May 1805.

The traffic at the end of Long Reach, going across to Westfield was getting too much for Benjamin. He and Sarah wanted so much to live out their lives in semi-seclusion, away from the rest of the world. The family was the only thing that mattered. They now had eight children; Sarah, Samuel, Aphia, Benjamin (3rd.), Joseph, Eleanor Ann, Simeon and Isaac.

Benjamin's health was on the decline due to arthritic conditions attacking his entire body. Some of his old war wounds gave him much trouble, and he had congestive lungs. He never did join the New Brunswick Militia or any of their exercises, even when tensions were building again between the United States and England. The raid on New London and Fort Griswold, Connecticut in 1781 had left plenty of scars, enough to fill his heart with sadness for the rest of his life. It appeared that some of this anti-military involvement did rub off onto his children because there is no record of the serving in the military, defensive or offensively.

Ben and Sarah had their eyes on a parcel of land across the river on Greenwich Hill (Devil's Back), in Greenwich Parish, near Brown's Flat. It was an old Loyalist land grant given to John and Elizabeth Crab and John Crab Junior. Half of the 200 acres lay on top a plateau. It was like being far away from everything; natural springs bubbling from the ground; tall pine and birch and wild berries growing everywhere. Below the plateau was a pond with easements for the neighbors to use, the only allowed invasion from outsiders. On top the Devil's Back, just about 200 yards facing east from the Bonnell's future homestead was a 300 foot drop to the River Saint John, and the greatest breathtaking view one could possibly have of the Saint John River Valley and Long Reach located across its waters. This was truly heaven, and it didn't take long for Ben and Sarah to decide on relocation in the final stages of their lives.

Benjamin placed an ad for the Long Reach property as follows:

"Bonnel" of Westfield has property near the Coffin Manor for sale.[17]*"*

On May 25, 1809, and after living peacefully as a farmer for twenty-three years on the King's land grant, Benjamin and Sarah sold the Long Reach property to Tertullus Theal of Saint John for one hundred and twenty-one pounds, lawful money of the Province of New Brunswick. Ben, knowing how to write, signed his name and aided his wife with her mark.

---

[17] From People, Places, Things in New Brunswick, Vol. 1784-1809, by B.J. Grant 1990

This was done in the presence of John Coffin, judge of the court of common pleas. It was received on June 6, 1809 and registered on June 7, 1809 by Daniel Muheau. Enos Supple and Sam Parmale, who received lot number two on the Long Reach Grants, saw their old neighbors and friends off to their new home. They did not realize that in the near future, the land would change hands again to the Harding's, a well-known loyalist family. They would build Ben's property into a beehive of activity for travelers and riverboats. The simple Bonnell home would be transformed into a very large Inn overlooking the River Saint John. After many years as the successful Harding home, this spot served the Westfield Ferry that traveled back and forth between that town and Long Reach. Today, the Harding/Bonnell house still stands to remind us all of the Loyalist era in New Brunswick.

Benjamin knew that he had a large task in front of him; clearing the land for growing fields, raising a small two story cabin, and planting a new apple orchard. His boys were all able-bodied men that would be his main resource to complete the job. On January 11, 1810, Benjamin and Sarah completed the purchase of the two hundred acres of land from John and Elizabeth Crab for the sum of twenty pounds; A fantastic buy, giving them a one hundred pound profit from both transactions. They did not realize that in twenty-four years, Simeon, their son would marry Prudence Crab, John and Elizabeth Crab's daughter. The Devil's Back property would remain in the family for over seventy-five years later.

The bill of sale was drawn up as follows:

"The said Benjamin Bunnel, his heirs and assigns, all that parcel or track of land, lying and being in the Parish of Greenwich and Province of New Brunswick, bounded and described as follows, lying on the northwest side of the Long Reach in the aforesaid Parish of Greenwich, near the Devil's Back, so called, bounded on the northwest side of the river St. John, upon the southwest side adjoining upon Morris Kimble's land, upon the northeast side adjoining upon Jacob Bulyea's land and to run back from the said river until it makes two hundred acres which would be surveyed by Daniel Micheau, Engineer."

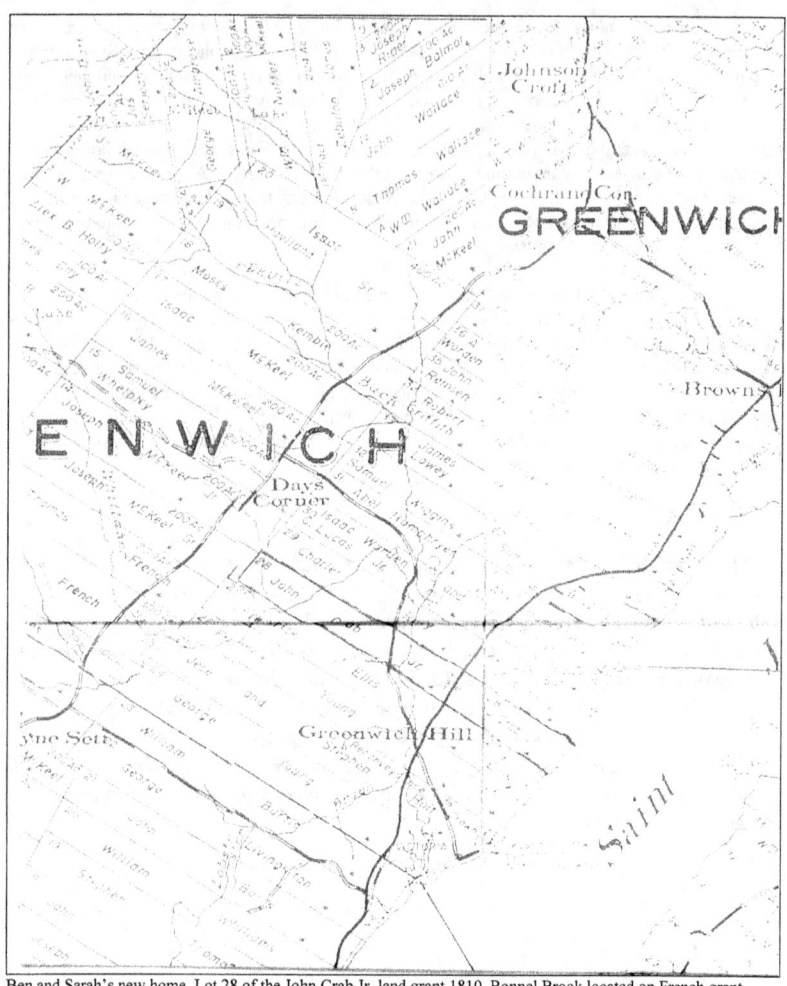

Ben and Sarah's new home. Lot 28 of the John Crab Jr. land grant 1810. Bonnel Brook located on French grant.

There was a lot of work lying ahead. Ben broke out the old canvas that was furnished by the King that he used twice before for their temporary shelter while they constructed a home. Sarah patched the few holes it had and they once again moved in under its protection. John Crab gave Ben a few good ideas about where to look for the best water source on the property. He also showed him where the abundance of wild berries grew, and where the best soil was for planting. Both families became very close. The Crab's lived in Kingston on another land grant John managed to get. They visited often while Prudence and Simeon courted. All the Bonnell boys were much taller then their father. Ben was short compared to them. The boys added to the future rumor that all New Brunswick men looked like "Lumber Jacks." It wasn't long after that Ben's son Isaac took a fancy to Lavina Kimble, their neighbors Moris Kimble's daughter.

By December 1810, the cabin was completed and the fields were cut out of the thick woods. Ben wasn't as able to complete it without his sons. The women completed the inside of the cabin, plus made chicken coops and prepared for the upcoming winter. Now it was time to sit back and rest through the winter, living off some of the Long Reach profit. Samuel Wiggins (Wogan), Captain of the American Legion lived just four lots up (Lot 32) from Ben (Lot 28).

When spring came, apple trees were planted and the fields were cultivated for planting. Life was much better up on the hill. The views of the Saint John River were breathtaking. Ben closed himself off from the outside world again, but the news of crowing hostilities between the States and England sent concern to all. There was not much concern over an attack by the former colonies in Ben's case because they would have to scale three hundred feet just to see him. They all knew that Canada would be dragged into a war again if England engaged one with the States.

The relationship status between New Brunswick and its neighboring States had changed drastically in the few short years after the Revolution. Families traveled back and forth over the borders. Trade with Boston was getting bigger, then with London. Loyalist and French families were related to each other. There were no borders to them. All of the New England States were in a very deep relationship with the Maritime Provinces. On one wanted to sacrifice the supply line, even while tensions grew between Washington and London.

It wasn't long until the British government ordered the construction of a few blockhouses along the border with the US. Hostilities soon broke out, but the majority of the people living in the north did not recognize it. Trade and commerce went on, even after an order went out to stop it. Most did not want to fight. A few outbreaks did occur in the northeast, but much of the battle of 1812 was fought around the Great Lakes and on the seas. One great example of the friendly relationship between New Brunswick and Maine/Massachusetts was when Calais, Maine ran out of gunpowder to celebrate their Forth of July festivities. They looked across the boarder to St. Stephen's, New Brunswick for help. The fine people of St. Stephen's quickly responded by breaking into the blockhouse and took out their gunpowder and loaned it to their neighbor across the border.

On a sad day, 21 Sept. 1816, Sarah awaked Ben while he was sneaking an early afternoon nap in his rocker on the back porch.

"Dear! Wake up dear! I have some sad news from the Peninsula (Kingston, Long Reach). Your old friend Titus Brown has past away."

"My God woman!" Ben cried out. He was only 60 years!

"The service will be tomorrow, 22 Sept. at the Anglican Trinity Church in Kingston," Sarah said.

"I must try to attend," Ben said sadly as he gazed down at the ground[18].

After the war, times got tough for the people of New Brunswick. The only strong sector of their economy was shipbuilding and other related trades from that industry. The United States finally felt that it gained its independence from England and continued to expand west to the Pacific Ocean and beyond. Money was tight in the Maritimes and Ben's son; Benjamin Junior wanted to invest into the shipping business. In 1818 while in Fredericton, New Brunswick, he borrowed ten pounds and promised to pay back ten pounds, fourteen shillings and five pence half for the loan. A contract was drawn up between himself and John Bentley. Ben went back to Bentley for another loan of Fifty pounds and when they came due, Benjamin Junior could not pay it. He avoided John Bentley until he had no choice but to call for his arrest.

John Bentley hired Charles J. Peters as his attorney, and he filed a complaint with the Supreme Court for action in June 1818. Mr. Odell issued a warrant out for Benjamin Junior's arrest. Chief Justice, Jonathan Bliss, Esq. signed the decree. The charges were for nonpayment of a note and trespass. After many attempts, the final warrant read:

"We command you as before, we have commanded you, that you take Benjamin Bonnell Jr. if he shall be found in your bailiwick and keep him safely until trial."

Finally, they caught up with Ben Junior and he repaid eighteen pounds, six shillings and three pence sometime during the summer. With the court's help, it appears that John Bentley finally received his money.

---

[18] New Brunswick, Generations, Fall 2001 edition by Gerald Bell, page 52.

Then, again in March of 1819, Moses Brundage hired the same Charles Peters, attorney at law, to prosecute Benjamin Junior along with Jonathan Purdy for not holding to a note they made with Moses Brundage in 1818. There were actually two notes, one for ten pounds and another for forty pounds. They too avoided Brundage until he had no choice but to take the matter to court. The court naturally ruled in Brundage's favor and demanded both men to pay up the fifty pounds due.

Moses Brundage was born in 1780 and along with his father, John and family, came to Saint John in 1783 as Loyalist Refugee's from Yonkers, New York, near the Hudson River area. Moses was the oldest child and he later settled in Greenwich, Kings County, New Brunswick, not far from the Bonnell's. In 1834 Moses bought the old Colonel James Brittain estate of two hundred acres.

Benjamin Senior and his daughter Sarah Purdy were outraged over the actions of Ben Junior and her brother-in-law Jonathan Purdy. They took a chance in the shipping business and lost. Ben Senior was furious with his namesake-son.

Benjamin Senior and Sarah now had two married children. Their daughter, Sarah had first married Joseph Purdy and some records show her marrying her brother-in-law Jonathan Purdy. Daughter, Eleanor Ann was next to marry, and on 20 August 1816 she became Joseph Fanjoy's wife. Both were from loyalist families that made Ben very happy.

The entire river area was growing at a rapid rate and there was talk going around about steam-powered boats running up and down the waterway. Many of the old loyalists were passing on. Each time Ben read an obituary in the Saint John Newspapers he reflected upon himself and his age. Many names listed were familiar to him. That made him even the more, take notice of his advancing years.

Ft. Griswold Monument, Groton, Connecticut
By Jacob Muller

Chapter 10

Death of A Loyalist

The year was 1821 and life was still peaceful and quiet for Sarah and Ben. The farm was maturing along and they both loved their mountaintop retreat. News and current events traveled slowly, sometimes a week later. The newspaper was the only link they had unless someone had returned from the city. The apple orchard was now producing fine fruit. Sarah had a beautiful flower garden on the sunny side of their cabin.

Many afternoons were spent just sitting on the back porch that their son Isaac help build. Ben's breathing problems gave him much discomfort and often became labored where his farm chores suffered. He was getting older and he knew that his days of work were limited. Sometimes the pain of his arthritis was too much to handle. He became aggravated and mean. Everyone around him knew his condition and just seemed to put up with his complaints.

News came one day about erecting a memorial for the dead at Fort Griswold in Connecticut. This disturbed Ben a great deal. He had pushed the memory of that terrible day deep into his depths of his mind. Now there was this talk of immortalizing this tragic event. The following two years left poor Ben reliving that battle. He even told his grandchildren of those days of glory and misery.

Many days passed with Ben whittling on a scrap of wood. The porch was his favorite spot and a tall pile of shaving covered the floor. Sarah was a very patient woman, but in times like this, she contacted her trusty son Isaac to do some of the chores that needed attending. Ben's age was now in the advance seventies. He also spent much of his time with the grandchildren, and a few others from the village. Several walked up the hill to Devil's Back and seek him out wanting to hear his stories of colonial America, the times of struggle, and the true loyalty to his King.

Benjamin did manage to come out of his self-imposed hiding on 31 May 1823. He attended his son Joseph's wedding. The marriage was a true loyalist one. Her name was Sophia E. Ward, a good woman. So far, all his children married other loyalists. That made him very happy. His other son, Benjamin Junior married Sarah Day, daughter of loyalist, John Day who was from New Jersey and served there and other areas during the war. And of course his daughter Sarah married into the Purdy family who came from Westchester, New York. And let us not forget his son Simeon married the daughter of John Crabb. His other son Isaac would soon follow suit as he was courting his future wife, Lavina Kimbell, another loyalist family. The wedding was simple and many faces were strange to Ben.

Benjamin couldn't believe how successful the Harding family had been with his old land grant on Long Reach. It was still a fine stop-off for travelers and the location of the home had a magnificent view of the Saint John River and Westfield on the other side. On a clear day, Ben could see his old place from on top the Devil's Back cliff overlooking the entire river basin below.

On November 13, 1824, Benjamin decided to sell one hundred acres of his property to his son, Isaac. He had a special place in his heart for Isaac because he felt that he would probably be the only son who would stay and work the farm. The other boys were very restless and carefree. Simeon wanted the other one hundred acres but had to wait till Ben and Sarah passed on. Benjamin Junior, in many ways, was very much like his father. He couldn't hold onto money very well and had a restless adventure about himself. And little Benjamin the third, showed even more adventurism running through his veins.

Benjamin the third, spent many hours listening to his grandfathers stories asking many questions about the world outside of New Brunswick. He always tried to imagine what was around every corner. He was a child that was never happy with what he had. He was always restless and looking towards tomorrow. The United States was always a subject he brought up, wanted to know what it looked like.

On 6 September 1825, the people of Groton, Connecticut gave a large and spontaneous celebration of the anniversary of the battle of New London and Fort Griswold. They expressed the need to erect a monument to the memory of the slain there. The state legislature granted a lottery to raise funds and by 6 Sept. 1826, the first corner stone was laid. It would take until 1830 for the completion of the native rock built monument that measured twenty-six feet square at the base, twelve at the top and 127 feet in height. The interior had 168 steps leading to the platform. This was truly a grand monument in the same image as the Washington Monument in Washington DC. To this day, the reenactment and observance still occurs every 6 September. Surely, Ben read about the proposed funding.

The following years were bad ones for Benjamin. His pain was much worse and his breathing labored. The fields were left for Isaac to work. The poor old man had to let go of being a farmer. He knew he was dying. Now eighty-two years old, he was outliving most of his loyalist friends. He watched the young child and wished he had that kind of energy. He glory days were coming to an end and one day in 1827, he sat down and wrote his last will and testament.

On 28 June 1827, the day was very bright and sunny. Benjamin sat out back on his porch at a small table. With pen and paper in hand, not knowing how to start his will, he hesitated many times before getting the rhythm of his words. He felt very fortunate to be able to write because like his wife, Sarah, and most other people did not have the education. For them, oral communication was their only means. The only traces they left behind were a lonely X on various documents.

Benjamin friend, Henry Nase, was still around and was still the probate judge for the area. Ben got the process of will writing from him, and with that, he was able to carry on with completing his will. Several times, he paused and looked out over his small apple orchard and fields, reflecting back over his lifetime and wondered about all the unjust things he had done. The war was the biggest disruption in his life, he thought.

Suddenly, he was brought out of his thoughts by a nearby sea gull squealing overhead. Back to reality, his pen pushed forward with those words all too familiar; "I Benjamin Bunnell (Notice the change in spelling), Senior, of Long Reach, Parish of Westfield and the county of Kings, Yeoman, being of sound mind and memory, although weak and infirm of body...." The old Loyalist completed his last words on paper and managed to live into the next year.

28 June 1827

Listed here is Benjamin's last will and testament.

In the name of God, Amen.
I, Benjamin Bunnell, of Long Reach, Parish of Westfield and County of Kings, Yeoman, being of sound mind and memory although weak and infirm of body, But knowing that it is appointed once for all to die - I do make and ordain my last will and testament in manner and form as follows - viz. principally and above all I give and recommend my soul unto the hands of the Allmighty God that gave it, and my body I recommend to the earth - to be buried in a Christian-like manner. Nothing doubting but at the general resurrection I shall receive the same again - THROUGH the mighty power of GOD. And as touching such wordly... as it hath pleased God to bless me in. I leave and bequeath it in manner and form as follows

FIRST
I allow all my just debts to be paid.

Secondly
I leave and bequeath unto my beloved wife Sarah - all the profits arising from the farm at the Devil's Back known by lot no. twenty-nine, it being the South half of the same containing one hundred acres more or less together with the use of two milk cows and six sheep - with all the moveables and household furniture therein during her natural period of life or while she lives -

Thirdly
I leave and bequeath to my son Benjamin twenty-five pounds currency. To my son Simeon fifty pounds current money. And to three of my daughters Sarah, Aphia and Eleanor, I bequeath ten pounds currency apiece or to each if it remains to be had after. The others get their shares - or otherwise whatever remains after my sons shares or what is mentioned is to be divided between the three Daughters mentioned. Each share and share alike. All these shares mentioned to be raised or got from the sale or profit of what I leave in my beloved wife's hands at her decease.

Lastly
I do make constitute and ordain
Thomas Fowler and Isaac Cawson both of the Long Reach and County of Kings to be my executors of this my last will and testament. Dated this 28th. Day of June in the year of our Lord One Thousand Eight Hundred and Twenty-Seven
Sealed and Delivered in presence of;

Signed sealed and delivered
In the presence of us
Joseph Purdy
Sarah Purdy   Benjamin Bunnell

The Seagull

As the winter sun came up over the Bay of Fundy on the morning of 17 February 1828, a lone sea gull left a cluster of rock formations in the bay and headed north of Saint John City, going up river just entering the mouth of the grand bay. The gull circled overhead without a sound, as the small city of Saint John still slumbered in the early morning fog. Each chimney-top emitted a stream of warm white smoke into the new chilly day. He left the city for better prospects of breakfast upstream. This graceful sea gull of the ocean headed for the Reversing Falls just outside the city hoping to capture a salmon tumbling from the falls. Many other sea gulls had the same idea. With no success, he slowly drifted farther upriver. Hunting up there always had less competition.

Patches of snow dotted the hillside as fishermen began to drag their boats into the yet unfrozen river hoping to make an early morning catch. He noticed other farmers moving about their grants as the landscaped barren land lay waiting for the first signs of spring, still two months away.

Upon arriving at the Grand Bay, there was move activity below. He heard the noisy farm chores awake the livestock into their new daytime schedule. Now this gull could find a good meal. His competitors were not far off, so he kept one eye on them as he descended. His touchdown was successful; a few egg shells, scraps of bread and chicken bones thrown out from the farmer's previous evening meal.

Now morning was in full operation. Wagons and animals noises were filling the air. The day was becoming clear, but cold. The sea gull was now full, but like most birds of prey, not yet satisfied. With a flutter of his three-foot wings, he started farther up the river in search of whatever suited his fancy.

After a few miles of gliding flight, he sighted a fisherman mooring his boat at the end of Long Reach. He was holding a large catch of fish. The gull's descent to the Harding House rooftop was quick. It was a grand place to view the entire Westfield and river area. The gull extended his neck and bellowed out a loud screech begging the fisherman for just one of his catch. He knew he would have to move fast to steal a sample. What seemed like a second, the gull attacked and scooped up a far size fish and raced across the river to Westfield.

He landed on a still quiet cabin and gulped down his latest meal. The entire village of Westfield was still as he looked around for other interesting targets. There wasn't much to offer him so his big and beautiful gray and white wings carried him up into the brisk sky. Slowly, he circled Woodman's Point where a marsh offered some possibilities. Now quite full, he spent very little effort in looking there. Maybe one and three-quarter circles and then drifted farther upstream to the Devil's Back Mountain.

The gull glided around a small two level log cabin in the village of Greenwich on Devil's Back. Curiosity caused him to land on that roof. A noise from within made his head tilt to one side as if he was trying to listen. It was sobbing coming from within. The man inside had died; Benjamin Bunnell had died. Sarah cried at her latest loss, her biggest loss. Another loyalist soldier was dead. History was slowly turning another page. The American Revolution was fading into the past.

The gull was intrigued and hung around the cabin for a couple days. Many people started to visit, bring food and creating much scrap that he ate when discarded. All the visitors cried and sobbed. Candles lit inside and outside the cabin at night. The gull rested next to the warm chimney and waited the next day for opportunities.

On 19 February 1828, dressed in black, elderly Sarah Bunnell, Benjamin's widow was being escorted from her house to a nearby wagon to her daughter, Sarah, and her husband Joseph Purdy. Many of the other children were there as they mounted their horses and wagons preparing for the short journey to the Westfield/Greenwich Saint James Anglican Church for the final service for Benjamin.

As the procession headed up the narrow dirt highway to the small chapel, one could see many loyalist families outside their homes visibly in grief. They were all too familiar; The families of Charles Reily, Isaac Warden, C. Lucas Jr., Abel Humphreys, Samuel Wiggins, James Lowey, Robert Griffith, John Remsen, A. Worden, Ebenezer Rider and James Suter.

The service was small, with just the family and a few friends attending. Sarah's health was too delicate to withstand a large gathering. The past two days and the trip to the church took much from her frail body. Their sons, Simeon and Benjamin each gave a short eulogy commemorating their father's deeds and historic life. "Loyal to his King to the end," one had said. They described events in Ben's life and the congregation couldn't help but feel proud of this man. One could almost feel the sorrow and loss when his sons retold the events in New Jersey and the happy life he and Sarah had there. They all knew the stories too well.

As the events were being recalled, the picture was very clear to everyone. Enduring the humiliating exodus from their property; the struggle as refugees in New York City; and the battles fought and lost with the final approach to a hostile land in New Brunswick. Sarah recalled them as if they happened yesterday. The sweet smell of the New Jersey meadows was a memory nearly fifty years old, but as clear as she was just there. The glory of the British fleet leaving New York harbor for a crushing battle at New London and Fort Griswold, Connecticut. Sarah and the others all remembered the tears that swelled in Ben's eyes as he told that story. He would never take up arms again to fight.

Benjamin Juniors wife, Sarah (Day) cried out as she knew very well what he went through from her father's own experience. John Day engaged in many battles too. Ben Junior would prove that this great mans name would be carried down through each generation in remembrance of him. Little Benjamin the third was just beginning to understand the importance of his family history. The son's final story of their father was when they arrived in Canada on the ship William with all the other ships in that July 1783 fleet. Leaving their homeland for a new one, and finding Parr Town (Saint John) very hostile to accept with wild Indians and unhappy Frenchmen.

After the sermon, the family members slowly left the chapel. Wife Sarah, sat atop the wagon and the neighbors watched the sadden column of people leave – the Purdy's, Steeves/Stevens, Crabb's, Day's, Ward's, Fanjoy's and the Kimbell's pass by them. Benjamin was always proud of his new family, with the entire above-mentioned loyalist's.

A few clouds started to form overhead, followed by a bitter-cold wind from the river. That time of day always brought the Saint John River breeze onto shore. The wagons and horsemen slowly started back up the Devil's Back to where the Bonnell's cabin was. Benjamin's body rested there in waiting on their cloth-covered table for his grief-stricken family returning from his own service.

A few other friends and relatives of the family waited outside the cabin as they approached – The French, McClean, Delong, Brundage and Perry's. They were all very close and a few were to marry into Ben's family in the near future. All, from true loyalist lines.

On the porch was Benjamin's carved wooden marker all ready waiting for his burial. Stone markers were very scarce in New Brunswick because the granite came from quarries in the States. No true loyalist would allow a headstone placed on their grave from somewhere in the States, like New Hampshire which had plenty of granite.

The era of the Loyalist in New Brunswick was coming to an end. From 1800 to 1835 most of all the Loyalists passed on from this earth. Canada, as we know it, would soon be created into an independent nation, and a new relationship would blossom into one of the closest partnerships in trade and customs the world had ever known. Any future hostilities are hard to imagine. Old memories do crop up once in a while but time inter-relationships has healed most of all that.

Benjamin was lying on the table that was placed in a small back room. He was surrounded by a glowing arrangement of candles that Sarah, herself, so painfully placed.

He looked so peaceful lying there in his Provincial uniform. Small grandson, Benjamin was outside frightening off a large sea gull that had been hanging around for the past two days.

Henry Nase registered Benjamin's will on 28 March 1828.

By his Excellency M. G..... Howard Douglas Baronet... and Commander in chief of the Province of New Brunswick... G Y do allow whom there... come or may.

An inventory was taken of all the goods and chattels of the late Benjamin Bunnell deceased in the Parish of Greenwich

April the 15 1828

	Pounds
One hundred acres of land	100.000.0
Three cows	12.000.0
Seven sheep	3.001.0
One bag	1.000.0
One bed and bedding	3.000.0
One wheel	5.0
One pot	2.0
One table	1.3
One half dozen chairs	012.0
One pale	1.3
One pare of andirons	5.0
Total	120.106.6

The inventory was taken by:
Anderson Warden
George Edward Neal

In later years (1906) the following search was taken.
Probate Court Kings County
Received from A.W. Baird Esq. the sum of 20cts in probate stamps for one search in Estate of Benjamin Bunnell 26 Nov. A.D. 1906

The announcement of Ben's death was in the New Brunswick Courier and City Gazette newspapers dated 5 April 1828. All it said was:

"Died, Long Reach, 17th. Feb., age 84, Benjamin Bunnell."[18]

The following poem was written as lyrics to a song, it is believed, titled *Old Song for Loyalist Day - The Sons of Eighty-Three*. It appeared in a Saint John, New Brunswick newspaper dated 1897. It was possibly written for music composed by S.K. Foster, Esq. in September 1848. Steven K. Foster was a leader in music around that city. In the article the newspaper made the following statement: "The song was found among some old books formerly in the possession of the Tisdale family. The writer is unknown."

*This is my own - My native land
The home where I was born, And near the spot where now we stand, I spent life's early morn;
Here oft in childhood's happy days - Beneath some aged tree- I've sat and listened to the ways which told of
"Eighty-three."
I sing not now of war and strife, Of battle and defeat,
Of pillaged homes and loss of life, Of rally or retreat;
For long, sweet peace hath spread her wings on this my native land,
And each revolving year still brings new blessings from her hand.
Through richer lands - in other climes - My feet have chanced to roam;
But midst their beauties there were times I fondly thought of home.
Of mountains wide and boundless woods, where sleep the inland sea,
Of silence in her solitudes, which all have charms for me.
Where're we stray, on life's wide track, What're our fortunes be,*

---

[18] New Brunswick Vital Statistics From Newspapers 1824-1828 by Daniel F. Johnson, 1983.

Fond memory still can bring us back the honoured and the free-
The loyal band that sternly strove rebellion's tide to stem,
And close in danger's path to prove their honor's stainless name.
Our fathers fondly prayed that we - Whom they so oft had blest-
Might guard their flag when they should be laid by that flag in rest;
Their dearest wish we cherish still- that meteor banner yet.
Floats proudly from you frowning hill, where by our sires 'twas set.
And we, their sons, beneath its shade, shall sing the songs of yore,
And tell our sons of those who led their grandires to this shore;
And with a parent's earnest love our latest breath shall pray,
That they, like us, may faithfully prove, and guard that flag for aye.

A quiet and peaceful road on Ben's Long Reach property

Chapter 11

1840s – United States of America

Benjamin 4th. was awakened suddenly by the loud banging of the ship's bell. When he opened his eyes, all that could be seen were legs running in every direction on board – all running to one side of the ship, crashing into its side rail. He lifted his stiff body up and walked over to where the excitement was centered, rubbing his eyes clear of the sleep. When he saw the sight too, he dropped his suitcase and forced his way to the rail to get a better look. He had slept through the entire trip, because before his weary eyes was the gigantic city of Boston.

It was morning and the harbor was a sight to be seen. Large sailing vessels were everywhere breaking their sails open to the wind, and the dock area was full of horse-driven carts and people going in every direction. He thought that this city's population must be as large as all of New Brunswick. Never had he thought this city would be so big.

Most people on board came to their senses and started to scurry around, organizing their belongings so they could quickly disembark and explore this new world. Benjamin's bag was trampled during the rush and he had to pick clothing that flew from it. After gathering all his things he pushed his way back to the ships side. Excitement was in the air. The passengers were talking and elated that the trip had no problems.

All along the coastline, one could see ships of all sizes filling every cove or harbor. Everyone in the States must own a ship, Ben thought. The docking took place at Charlestown. The area was bustling with people. Many shops and places of business lined the docks. Feeling a little afraid, Ben was amazed at the site. Boston had many riches and the signs of prosperity was everywhere. The plank was soon lowered and he disembarked the ship, and taking the first step onto his grandfather's homeland soil sent chills through all his bones. Was the old loyalist with him?

The first priority was to finding a place to eat and bed-down. Benjamin found a men's boarding house. Many there were Irish descent, and several wayward seamen. At the break of day he would be off to find a job. In many ways, the mix of people was the same as Saint John. All except the snobby rich Bostonians who made it very clear what you status was in town.

It didn't take Ben long to land a job. An apprentice brass finisher opened up his opportunities in this new land. What little free time he had, he managed to meet Mary Cottle, daughter of a ship's carpenter, Woodbury Cottle and his wife Sarah who were from Kittery, Maine. This was his love, and the soon married on 11 April 1847 at the High Street Baptist Church in Charlestown. They had thirteen children.

In 1859, news came from home that Ben's father (Benjamin Jr.) was ill. So the family moved up to New Brunswick, just before the second American Revolution started. Just after 1871, they all returned to Boston, the final trip. There, Benjamin the loyalist seed was planted back in the United States.

To Peace

    Imagine, if all the world could think as one
    At the time, a war had just begun.
    And all the parents' sons, to sons,
    Would stand up and say, "Put down your guns."
    We're no different, you and I.
    We all look up at the same colored sky.
    The Loyalists fought for what was right.
    They made their oath to God and King,
    To fight.
    The Patriots did the same,
    Except to tell, the Kings' insane.
    Now here I stand, a Loyalist son,
    Loving America, this grand union.
    I also love the land up north,
    The violet color, like woven cloth.
    New Brunswick, Canada, my land of past,
    I love you too, this land so vast.
    We now stand friends so close and far,
    All together, to follow one star.
    Someday the maple leaf, someday the stripes,
    Will come together, and form what's right,
    A North American union so strong and bold,
    Of all the greatest people in the entire world.

Chapter 12

Possible Parents of Benjamin Bonnell

Like many of us, our research for more records never ends. There is always something missing, something overlooked. Unfortunately for me, what is missing is 100% absolute proof of the parents of Benjamin and Sarah (Jones). Sarah's line may possibly be from the Jones family of Bergen County, New Jersey, but there is no proof of that yet.

Benjamin, like many loyalists, they traveled around, as settlers, soldiers, fugitives and refugees. To date, I have found him in Morris County, New Jersey, New York City, New London and Fort Griswold, Connecticut, and of course New Brunswick, Canada. Many New Jersey records did not survive the war, and this makes our search more complex. Ben's record is obscure in many areas. There are three Bunnell/Bonnell lines that look like good candidates for possible parents of our loyalist ancestor. Most recent developments and proof point to the last listed; Benjamin Bonnell.

Thomas Bonnel: Born approx. 1700-10. He was considered one of the first settlers of Morris County, New Jersey. He died c. 1790 at Hanover, New Jersey. Being a Quaker and having a few similar names matched up between both families, this looked like a best candidate but findings by William Austin on the below mentioned Benjamin line has changed that view.

Gershom Bunnell: Born 1 May 1707 Elizabethtown, New Jersey (East Jersey). He died 8 July 1758 at Danbury, Connecticut. Several of his children were loyalist, one settling in New Brunswick, Canada not more then 10 miles from Ben. There is no proof of any connection here even though in the very early stages and days of my research, it all pointed to this family.

Benjamin Bonnell: Born after 1700, possibly at Mendham/Dover, Morris County, New Jersey. He was the son of Samuel Bonnell and Abigail .....? It is this line that has the greatest possibility of being our Benjamin's parents (98% chance). William R. Austin of the Bunnell/Bonnell Newsletter has spent many hours breaking down the probable proof of this claim. Besides the similarities of family names in both lines (Simeon, Eleanor, Samuel and Benjamin) and a strong point is that Benjamin the loyalist and his wife Sarah were Quaker's who were from the Rahway/Mendham, New Jersey Meetinghouse of Friends (Quakers). The family of Thomas Bonnel/Bonnell was Presbyterian and I find no evidence of Gershom Bunnell being a Quaker.

Also the will and indictment documents of the loyalist Benjamin has recently revealed that he was listed as "Junior." His mother, Eleanor is not a very familiar name in the Bunnell family and Ben uses Eleanor as one of his daughter's name. Also the link and visit (1786 to New Brunswick) by Joseph Moore and other Quakers from Rahway/Woodbridge, New Jersey to see Benjamin and family ties another knot into this line. And the 1855 Henry Brotherton letter telling of the connections found by William Austin. So, it is the Benjamin Bonnell line that I will enter here.

A Monument In Honor

Several years ago I purchased twenty acres of Benjamin and Sarah's Devil's Back property. After keeping it into the family again for a few years, I sold it off but retained a one acre right of way on the main road (Rt. 102) to someday construct a loyalist monument in honor of our family who settled there. Sometime in the future I hope to afford to place a large stone with a plaque to help continue educate future generations on who the loyalists were and what they stood for including all the contributions they made to the history and future of New Brunswick.

Chapter 13

CURIOSITY BROUGHT HIM BACK
You Decide: Is It Benjamin?

The Case of the Haunting Ancestor of Benjamin Bonnell, U.E.

We all have had strange and funny feelings at times while researching our ancestors. An impulse to pull into a cemetery and finding a relative, the strong desire to open a certain book and discovering a record or history of on them, a compelling urge to look up a certain census suddenly finding your family you didn't know lived there. Or what about discovering a place you felt you have already visited? Better yet; how about being followed by your ancestor!

Most genealogists cannot deny not having at least one of these feelings. I want to share my very special and shocking experience, which opened my eyes to the unknown and unexpected.

Benjamin Bonnell, my seventh generation grandparent was possibly born in Morris County, New Jersey around 1744. After many years of intense research at the Trenton, New Jersey Archives, New York libraries, Connecticut historical sites, and the New Brunswick Archives at Fredericton, the Saint John Public Library, New Brunswick Museum and historical and genealogical societies throughout the Saint John area, I put together a fairly good picture of Ben's life. I found myself very attached to him, compared to other ancestors. This special bond grew with every bit of information gathered. Ben and I were buddies.

The record picks up with he and his family being disowned by the Quakers in Morris County, New Jersey for having been involved with the Revolutionary War. I found that he was an American Loyalist. Losing everything in New Jersey, he fled to New York City as a refugee with his two children and wife, Sarah (Jones). He signed up with Brig. General, Benedict Arnold in the American Legion in August 1781.

Took part in a terrible battle on 9 Sept. 1781 at New London and Fort Griswold, Connecticut. This I feel haunted him for the rest of his life.

Ben and his family left New York City in the Great Exodus of 1783 when the British lost America. Between 30,000 to 100,000 Loyalists had to evacuate to many areas of the globe, mostly to Canada. In the July fleet of that same year, Ben and family landed at Saint John with very little. Living in tents for several months he and his small family were granted 10 acres of land on the West Side of Saint John in 1784. Conditions were horrible. By August 1786, Ben was finally granted 200 acres, a real place to settle, lot number one at the very end of Long Reach in Westfield, Kings County, New Brunswick.

He built a modest home overlooking the Saint John River, carved out a beautiful farm and finally faded away from the Revolutionary War and all its terrible memories. They lived there from 1786 to 1811.

John Crabb, another loyalist, had a place for sale across the river slightly north of Westfield in Greenwich Village on Devils Back Mountain just south of Brown's Flat. After selling his Long Reach property, Ben purchased the 200 acres at Devils Back. High up on the plateau, Ben and his family commanded a million dollar view of the Saint John River Valley in that area. His final retreat from society lasted from 1811 to 17 Feb. 1828, the day he died.

Present Day

Giving you a general description of his life brings you right up to the time I went to his last resting-place on top the Devils Back Mountain in the village of Greenwich on Tuesday, 27 August 1985 between three and four o'clock in the afternoon. Present day Route 102 cuts right through the 200 acres, but a good 100 acres lay straight up the mountain to the area where Ben and Sarah lived and where Ben supposedly died. Butterflies fluttered throughout my stomach as I started to climb the steep hill. The Delong family was kind enough to give me permission to enter the past of my ancestor on top Devils Back. I was hoping to get pictures of a possible cellar foundation to his old cabin and an old overgrown apple orchard near it.

The feeling of awe ran through my entire body as I walked a narrow path by old farm fields overgrown, the apple orchard grown wild. I took my camera a snapped all around as I felt the history and life of my family tingling through my nervous system. In my mind I saw Ben's sons working the field, Sarah picking apples off the trees and Ben sitting on a porch whittling away on a piece of wood, rocking in his chair. What a beautiful life, I thought.

The day was perfect. The sky was crystal clear with very few clouds. There was no trace of fog from the river three hundred feet below. I wandered to the edge of Devils Back and found a view of the Saint John River that was breathtaking. What a paradise, I thought. Suddenly I got the sensation to turn around and take a picture of the small path I just came down. It had no meaning or reason to me, but I did. There was a funky old chair just outside the door of a run-down shack that the Delong family probably built around the 1920's. I did feel like a presence was around me but shrugged it off as my overall feelings of just being there.

A few minutes later, I found myself drifting slowly back down the path and taking one last look as I turned around viewing the overgrown farm of my family. Wild berries were growing everywhere and the water table was so high the small springs were sprouting up out of the wild grass everywhere. There still was some big trees, pine and birch that survived the cutters ax. I pictured family members sitting under their shady limbs, maybe beautiful Sarah Day getting her proposal for marriage from son Benjamin. I couldn't locate the house foundation so I just took more shots of the landscape around me. My body shook with excitement just knowing and feeling the family all around me.

My twelve-hour drive back home to Cape Cod, Massachusetts seemed to take one hour. I was in a daze the entire time thinking of the calm feeling I had while up on Devils Back. The following day I asked my wife to have my photos developed right away because I couldn't wait to share my experience, one quite similar to my visit to Fort Griswold, Connecticut where a terrible battle and slaughter took place in 1781 with Ben and Benedict Arnold and army burning New London to the ground and wiping out Patriot troops who were unarmed at Fort Griswold. So moved by that visit, I took a small brick fragment that I found from the center of the fort for a keepsake.

My wife, Leslie brought my pictures to my office and I gazed with pleasure as I showed her what moved me so much. She brought to my attention a few photos with spots on them (3), but one was very special because it stood out the most. I looked down at it in surprise. It was the one I turn and took the photo of the path and bushes for no reason, but a strong desire. The spot was bright blue and was drifting in the air in front of the bushes on the path. The strange spot was in the photo, not on the paper. I checked the negative and found the spot to be in with the grass and bushes, clearly not a developing problem. I looked up at Leslie and wondered; could it be?

The following few days took my wife to several photographers to examine the photo. All judged it to be genuine and in the photo on the negative and not a case of sun glares, flashes, smoke or haze. Our excitement grew and the following week we discovered a psychic fair was in town. We had nothing to lose so we took the photos and a grabbed my brick fragment to add to our upcoming reading.

Donna Miller was our choice of psychic, not ever meeting her before she had recently moved to Cape Cod from Florida. I felt that our $12, fifteen-minute meeting shot me like a bullet, a bullet to the heart. I first handed Donna the photos never saying a word about where, what or who they were. Without hesitation she looks up at us and says that this is my ancestor and he is following me around, wondering why I was looking for him and researching him for so long. He also wanted to know why I was up on his mountain.

Ghost photo 1985. Ben is blue cloud in background.

I nearly lost ten years of my life... How did this young girl know all this? I was shocked and surprise but not enough to hand her my little stone. This time she took a little time and held the stone in both hands closing her eyes. She suddenly became very upset and handed it back to me telling me she did not want to read into it any longer. Puzzled, I asked her what she saw or felt. She said; this stone is a very negative stone and I feel a lot of sadness with it. I see a lot of flames and fire with many bodies lying around a field.

My genealogical foundations were now shaken loose. I couldn't believe what this girl was telling me. She saw everything. I quickly invited her to our home for a private meeting because I had ten thousand questions and documents I wanted her to find for me. Those few days wait drove me crazy. I checked over all kinds of problems I was having in my research. I didn't know what to throw at her. Then I decided to stay on the same subject and the same man.... Benjamin.

I needed more information and proof of his birthplace and who his parents were. This would be the area I would concentrate on. Not telling Donna any new information or what I had on Ben in the colonies, I asked her to try to find any documents that could lead me to his home or just give me more information on him. This time she took a pencil and paper and closed her eyes and began drawing a map and to my surprise it was one of the New York/New Jersey coastline. Then she took her pencil inland from New Jersey and drew the near perfect shape of Morris County, New Jersey. She blew me away. She then made a dot in the middle of that county and tried to spell out a town. This ended up being Succasunna. She told me his records were burned in a public building of some kind, like a courthouse or schoolhouse. I could possibly find these records elsewhere regarding Ben at this location. She also told me that he moved around a lot and that Ben was now at peace. She felt the town of Dover would play a part into his mystery. That night we both felt his presence with us. Donna said there was a special connection between Ben and I. She said his parents were possibly Benjamin and Abagail.

The following day I put Donna's tale to the test. I wrote to the Trenton, New Jersey Archives and asked then to check their records on Succasunna for Ben. It didn't take long when I received a large envelope from the archives giving me the indictment papers for the arrest of Benjamin Bonnell in 1779 for carrying counterfeit money for the British. This document was from the New Jersey Supreme Court and recorded in the town of Succasunna, Morris County, New Jersey.

This story doesn't end here. I wrote a book on Benjamin's life and upon near completion I wanted the cover picture to really mean something to this project. One early morning at 3 AM in 1986 I was awaken by a dream like vision. I saw three figures; a young boy with a jacket on holding a fishing poles, a Farmer pushing a plow shear, and a revolutionary soldier.

What a perfect cover I thought. This vision presented the three phases in Benjamin's life. The next morning at work I asked another employee who was a very good artist if he would draw out this image I had. I showed him a picture soldier, a boy and a Farmer. He took them and returned in a few days with an oval drawing of all three together. It was exactly what I wanted. I rushed it to my publisher and they bought the entire and started the process in making my first book, "Thunder Over New England, Benjamin Bonnell, The Loyalist" which would be printed in 1988.

In Mid August 1986, I traveled to Westfield (Long Reach), New Brunswick, Canada to explore Ben's land grant that King George III gave him for serving in the American Revolution. We found a Ferry at Westfield that would take us across the wide Saint John River to the shores of the Long Reach.

As we approached the landing I noticed an old colonial building not far from the water's edge. In back was a large campground and the old house served as a store in the bottom section. A large historical sign said "The Harding House built c. 1790". I thought that this could not be true because I knew Ben was granted this 200 tract in 1786, and that the Harding family did not move into the house until into the 1800's. I suddenly realized especially after talking to the owners, Howard and Diane Heans that the backside of this house was built by Benjamin. When Howard took me for a tour, I felt as if I was walking through a great religious experience. I was truly moved by it all.

I did not realized until about a year later that I set foot on Ben's land exactly 200 years later in August 1986, the same time as he did.

The following year or two I kept in contact with the Heans family because Howard was restoring the home and was always finding artifacts. When my book was released in 1988, I traveled to New Brunswick for promotion and TV appearances. I made a point to stop by and visit the home. When Howard saw me he became very excited and led me into that old house to show me something.

He said that the past May, during the loyalist celebration of their landing back in 1783 his workmen found something in the back part of the house. The section believed to be built by Ben. His excitement drove me wild. He grabbed a large box and first told me the story about their find.

His workmen took down some old plaster exposing the opened beam wall to the original part of the house. And the found hanging on an old square nail the following items:

A young boys loyalist jacket
And a four-foot high twig fishing pole with the string still attached.

He said the find brought the TV news out and the New Brunswick Museum wanted desperately to get possession of it because they did not have many civilian clothes from the loyalist period. They dated the jacket to be at least early 1780's.

    I sat back against a table in pure shock. My god, this is my ancestor's clothing, and then I turned pale. Howard asked me if I was OK, but instead I grabbed him by the shoulder and instructed him to get a copy of my book I sent him a few months earlier. I stood there and stared at the jacket and pole until he returned. After he handed it to me, I pointed to the boy in my cover design, which became my logo, and then I pointed to the jacket and the pole that was uncovered from the wall. Howard stood back and now both our faces looked the same, My dream of two years earlier was before my very eyes.

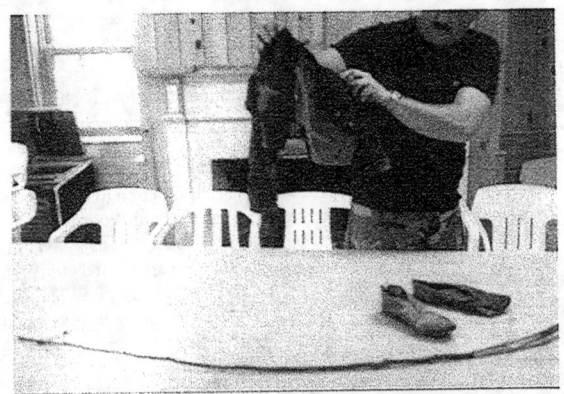

1780's Loyalist Child Jacket, shoes and Fishing pole with string found 1988 in Ben's wall.

Ft. Griswold stone read by psychic

My logo dreamt up in 1986. Notice loyalist child.

Nowadays, I look for anything leading me to my ancestor's records.... Believe me, I am now open to any method.

Update: 2 May 2002.

    Research conducted by William Austin regarding the identification of Benjamin's parents brought to light one more key area that Donna Miller had noted during her readings. She said the town of Dover would play a part in solving the mystery of Ben's source. In Mr. Austin's excellent find of Ben's parents, the major reference of proof comes from a letter dated 28 Nov. 1855 from Richard Brotherton to Charles Bonnell of Waterloo, New York telling him the parentage of Ben. Richard Brotherton was writing from his home in DOVER, New Jersey! This letter was miraculously saved throughout the years to finally help solve this case. Going back to Benjamin's indictment, I know find that after his name is a small entry that now clearly says, "Junior." This is more proof that his father was Benjamin. The name Abigail turns out to be his grandmothers name.

Strange Message? October 2002

    My daughter and husband found a mouse in Haverhill, Massachusetts lying on a schoolyard parking lot. He was maybe one day old. Nearly an inch long and still very pink and blind they brought it to me hoping that I could save it. The poor creature was lost, hungry and I suppose very frightened. I covered him in a small cloth and sent my daughter to the drugstore for an eyedropper, and some canned milk. My infant instincts took over. For the next few days I fed him every two hours and held him close, as a mother would do to comfort her child. At night he was placed under a lamp for heat and I got up every two hours for feedings.

I became very attached to the little fellow, and he to me. I spent hours just staring at him take the food, holding the eyedropper and try to walk on my chest. He soon developed a little squeak and I could tell when he was hungry or mad.

The outlook was not good after I checked out a care site on the Internet and found that the survival rate was only about 1%. That made me care for him even more. The poor little guy was so dependent on me for everything. I padded his small head and just kept him warm. I cleaned him as a mother would, but with a cloth to assure his toilet needs were met. But, on the fourth day I discovered my small friend had passed away sometime between 5:30 AM to 7 AM. I never thought such a short relationship could be so hard in accepting its loss. Living in an apartment gave me no choices for burial and the bathroom facilities in this case was not an option. So I chose a very special place in my town. The Amesbury Quaker Meeting House-ground. That was the spot I placed his very tiny body, wrapped in a sandwich zip-lock bag marked "Poor Little Mr. Haverhill Mouse."

When I sadly drove away after a brief service, I had suddenly thought what had just happened over the past four days. I had befriended a mouse that I buried at a Quaker Meeting House! If you recall at the beginning of this book, the fictional story I included about when Ben and his family were in the Rahway Meeting House for service and the little "Quaker Mouse" came running down the center of the room? This story was added in June 2002, five months before my encounter with a real "Quaker Mouse."

Section today believed to be Ben's outer building that is now in back of Harding House, Long Reach.

Chapter 14

Recognition

My Thanks to the Following Sources

1. Those Damned Rebels, by Michael Pearson, published by G.P. Putnam's Son.
2. New Brunswick Genealogical Society, Saint John and Fredericton, New Brunswick, Canada.
3. Early Loyalist, Saint John, by D.G. Bell, published by New Ireland Press.
4. September 6, 1781, North Groton's Story, by C. Smith & H. Vergasson, published by A. Printing Co., New London, Connecticut.
5. The Loyal Americans, by The Canadian War Museum, published by Alger Press.
6. Illustrated History of the American Revolution, published by American History Illustrated.
7. The Traitor and the Spy, by James Flexner, published by Harcourt, Brace and Co.
8. Mrs. Donna Miller, Psychic Research, Camp Edwards, Bourne, Massachusetts.
9. Documents relating to the revolutionary history of the State of New Jersey (5 volumes), newspaper extracts, published by State Gazette Publishing Co., 1917.
10. United Empire Loyalists Association of Canada, Toronto, Ontario, Canada.
11. New England Historical Genealogical Society, Boston, Massachusetts.
12. New Brunswick Historical Society, The Loyalist House, Saint John, New Brunswick, Canada
13. Kings County Historical & Archival Society (W. Harry Dalling), Hampton, New Brunswick, Canada.
14. Huguenot Society of America, New York, New York.
15. The Church of Jesus Christ of Latter-Day-Saints (Mormon), Salt Lake City, Utah.
16. Boston Public Library, Special Collections, Boston, Massachusetts.
17. Cleadie B. Barnett (Researcher), Oromocto, New Brunswick, Canada.
18. The New Brunswick Museum (all employee - many thanks), Saint John, New Brunswick, Canada.
19. New Brunswick Provincial Archives, (all employee's) Fredericton, New Brunswick, Canada.
20. Westfield Village Clerk's Office, Westfield, Kings County, New Brunswick, Canada.
21. Miss Vivian Wright, Rothesay, New Brunswick, Canada.
22. Elizabeth Sewell, Fredericton, New Brunswick, Canada.
23. Commonwealth of Massachusetts, Department of Public Health, Boston, Massachusetts.
24. Falmouth Public Library, Falmouth, (Cape Cod) Massachusetts.
25. City of Boston, Department of Birth, Marriage & Death Records, Boston, Massachusetts.

26. National Archives, General Service Administration, Washington, D.C.
27. Colonel Henry Nase diaries, (found at the New Brunswick Museum) Saint John, New Brunswick, Canada.
28. Duane Crabtree (Crabb genealogy), Massachusetts.
29. Department of Transportation, Fredericton, New Brunswick, Canada.
30. Department of Civil Engineering, Fredericton, New Brunswick, Canada.
31. The George Harding diaries, by George F. Harding (found at the New Brunswick Museum) Saint John, New Brunswick, Canada.
32. New Brunswick Courier, Saint John, New Brunswick, Canada.
33. The Battle of Groton Heights, by Charles Allyn, 1882, New London, Connecticut.
34. The Sons of the American Revolution (Located in the Nathaniel Bonnell House, built c. 1696)(Mr. Howard Wiseman), Elizabeth, New Jersey.
35. The Public Archives of Canada (now The National Archives), Ottawa, Ontario, Canada.
36. New York Gazette and Weekly Mercury. (Colonial newspaper of that time).
37. Fran Russell, Psychic Research, Cape Cod, Massachusetts.
38. The Genealogical Helper, Everton Publishers Inc., Logan, Utah.
39. The Sturgis Library, Rt. 6A, Barnstable (Cape Cod), Massachusetts.
40. Mr. Roy Delong, (Part owner of Benjamin's Devil Back property), Greenwich Hill, New Brunswick, Canada.
41. Mr. John Bonnell (A direct descendant to Ben), Saint John, New Brunswick, Canada.
42. Mrs. Ruth Duncan (Author of William Bunnell and his Descendants), West Simsbury, Connecticut.
43. Linda Gordon (Direct ancestor of Isaac Bunnell, also a loyalist), Saint John, New Brunswick, Canada.
44. Mr. Claude Bunnell, Haddonfield, New Jersey (now possibly lives in Florida).
45. Mrs. Paula Bonnell Sacco, Pittsburgh, Pennsylvania.
46. Mr. Charles F. Putnam, W. Acton, Massachusetts.
47. New Jersey State Archives, Trenton, New Jersey.
48. Mrs. Betty Grant, The Ocean County Historical Society, New Jersey.
49. James Rathburn, Westfield, New Brunswick, Canada.
50. Thomas B. Wilson, Lambertville, New Jersey.
51. Rutgers University, New Brunswick, New Jersey.
52. The Falmouth Genealogical Society, Falmouth Library, Falmouth, Massachusetts.
53. William Austin, past Editor of The Bunnell/Bonnell Newsletter, Laceyville, Pennsylvania.
54. Terry D. Porter, AGAPE, WGA/E Agent, Flatrock, Indiana.
55. Geneva M. Bodenmiller (Descends from Affie Bonnell and proved Sarah Jones last name in bible), Northville, Michigan.
56. Paul Bonnell (Direct descendant to Ben), St. Lambert, Quebec, Canada.

57. All the employee's who worked at Augat Inc, Rt. 28, Mashpee, Massachusetts (1979 to 1996).
58. Christopher Publishing House Inc., Hanover, Massachusetts (For giving me my first chance).
59. Howard & Diane Heans, Harding Campground, Long Reach, (Westfield), New Brunswick, Canada (owners of Ben's land and home).
60. Kings Landing, The Emporium, Fredericton, New Brunswick, Canada (A living history of the Loyalists).
61. Doug & Margaret Machado, Scappoose, Oregon (For starting me out in genealogy).
62. Bill & Rhonda Fitzgerald, Marstons Mills (Cape Cod), Massachusetts.
63. Thomas & Colleen Higham, Sandwich (Cape Cod), Massachusetts.
64. His Royal Highness, The Prince Philip, Buckingham Palace, England (Graciously accepting "Thunder Over New England" in 1989 after meeting with him at Lennoxville, Quebec, Canada.
65. The Bunnell/Bonnell Family In America, Vol. I, by William R. Austin, Pub. By Heritage Books Inc., Bowie, Md. 1999.
66. William Austin who has done much work on the entire Bunnell/Bonnell genealogy and many hours into research of who the parents were of Benjamin. I appreciate the help.
67. Mr. And Mrs. Thomas Lynch, Pocasset, (Cape Cod), Massachusetts. (For giving me the foundations of my computer knowledge).

If there are some I forgot to mention, my humble apology to you all. My final recognition goes out to Benjamin Bonnell and Sarah Jones, his wife, Loyalists, Greenwich Village, Kings County, New Brunswick, Canada.

Note: Some detail in this book has factual fiction added to bring real life to the characters. All research and documentation are authentic. This record will always need more research and documentation, as all genealogy requires. The seagull in this story is another thing.

1934 Canadian stamp in honor of UE Loyalists

Chapter 15

Notable Family Members

OUR NEW BRUNSWICK FAMILY WHO WERE MARINERS AND SHIP OWNERS

Simeon Bonnell, son of Ben & Sarah,
1825 Ship **Honesty**, owner #2 with 32 shares. Constructed 1822, 2 masted schooner 57 ft. long, 17 wide, 5 ft deep, 67 tons. Retired 1839.
1840 Ship **Primrose**, 32 shares, 2nd. Owner, built 1837, 2 masted 61 ft. long, 17 wide, 5 ft. deep, 45 tons. Retired 1847.
1847 Ship **Highway Mary**, owner #1, 64 shares built 1831, 2 masted, schooner, 62 ft. long, 17 ft. wide, 5 ft. deep, 51 tons, retired 1851.
1851 Ship **Roxana**, owner #2, 32 shares, built 1847, 2 masted schooner, 65 ft. long, 17 ft. wide, 5 ft. deep, 49 tons, retired 1851.
1851 ship **Linnet** Mariner owner #1 with 32 shares, owner with brothers Isaac & Benjamin, built 1848, 2 masted schooner, 68 ft. long, 19 ft. wide, 6 ft. deep, 56 tons, retired 1853.
1853 ship **Hyena**, owner #1 with 64 shares, built 1848, 2 masted schooner, 66 ft. long, 19 ft. wide, 6 ft. deep, 55 tons, sunk 1872 on Saint John River.
1840, ship Gypsie. He was the captain on voyage to Boston from Saint John, New Brunswick that brought his brother Benjamin to the States. Simeon could have also been a part owner.

Benjamin, son of Ben & Sarah,
1829 ship **Triumph** #2 owner with 32 shares built 1829, 2 masted, 60 ft. long, 19 ft. wide, 6 ft. deep, 83 tons, retired 1836.
1833 ship **Caledonia**, #1 owner with 64 shares, built 1833, 1 deck, 2 masted schooner, 69 ft. long, 20 ft. wide, 6 ft. deep, 115 tons, retired 1839.
1851 ship **Linnet** #1 owner with 32 shares, built 1848, 2 masted, schooner, 68 ft. long, 19 ft. wide, 6 ft. deep, 56 tons, Sunk at Mount Desert Island (Maine) 1866.

Simon Bonnell, son of Sarah Day and Ben Jr.
was #1 owner 1881 in ship **EM Bonnell** with 24 shares, built 1881, 2 masted schooner, 100 ft. long, 27 ft. wide, 10 ft. deep, 198 tons, sunk off Caicos Island, Bahamas 1882.

Samuel Bonnell, son of Ben & Sarah Day
1847 ship **British Queen**, #2 owner partnership with Brother Abraham, 32 shares, built 1835 2 masted schooner 63 ft. long, 20 wide, 5 deep, 98 tons, retired 1851.
1851, ship **Argyle** #1 owner with 64 shares, built 1837, 2 masted schooner, 67 ft. long, 19 ft. wide, 6 ft. deep, 52 tons, retired 1853.
1864 ship **Hall and Fairweather** #1 owner with 64 shares, built 1864, 2 masted schooner, 72 ft. long, 24 ft. wide, 6 ft. deep, 66 tons, retired at Long Reach 1888.
1867 ship **Bessie B (Bonnell?)**, owner #1 with 32 shares, built at Boston, 1 deck, steamer, 56 ft. long, 14 ft. wide, 6 ft. deep, 30 tons, 30 horse power, retired at Musquash (NB?) 1874.

Abraham Bonnell, son of Ben and Sarah Day,
1842 ship **Dolphin** #1 owner, 32 shares, built 1842, 1 deck, 2 masted schooner, 66 ft. long, 17 ft. wide, 6 ft. deep, 55 tons, retired 1845.
1846 ship **British Queen**, #1 owner with 64 shares, built 1846, 2 masted, schooner, 63 ft. long, 20 ft. wide, 5 ft deep, 98 tons, retired 1847.
1847 ship **Prince Albert** owner #1 with brother Graves, with 64 shares, built 1840, with 1 deck,. 2 masted, schooner, 66 ft. long, 19 ft. wide, 6 ft. deep, 53 tons, retired 1853.
1848 ship **Hazard**, was owner & builder with 64 shares, 1842, 1 deck, schooner 60 ft. long, 16 ft. wide, 5 ft. deep, 44 tons, retired 1852.
1852 ship **Collingwood**, was owner & builder with 64 shares, built at Long Reach NB 1849, 1 deck, 2 masted, schooner, 68 ft. long, 19 ft. wide, 6 ft. deep, retired 1853.

James Bonnell, son of Ben & Sarah Day
1835 ship **Dove**, #1 owner with 64 shares, built at Greenwich NB 1832, 2 masted schooner 58 ft. long, 17 ft. wide, 5 ft. deep, 70 tons, retired 1838.

Frederick Simeon Bonnell, son of Simeon Married Martha Richie, owned ships,
1881, **E. M. Bonnell** #2 owner with 16 shares, built 1881 2 masted schooner, 100 ft. long, 27 ft. wide, 10 ft deep, 198 tons, sunk off Caicos Island, Bahamas 1882.
1885 ship **Clifton** built 1885, 2 masted schooner, #1 owner with 12 shares, 100 ft. long, 28 ft. wide., 11 ft. deep, 223 tons, sunk off Santa Domingo Coast 1894.
1886 ship **C.E. White**, #1 owner with 18 shares, built 1886, 3 masted schooner 111 ft. long, 28 ft. wide, 11 ft. deep, 244 tons, sunk off Bay of Fundy 1889.
1888, ship **H.B. Homan** owner #14 with 2 shares, built 1888, 3 masted schooner, 132 ft. long, 31 ft. wide, 11 ft. deep, 319 tons, sunk in Saint John River 1905.
1889 ship **Martha L. Bonnell**, #1 owner with 14 shares, built at Saint John 1889, 3 masted schooner, 127 ft. long, 31 ft. wide, 11 ft. deep, 308 tons, sunk off Long Island Sound New York 1897 by fire. (Named after his wife. Paul has painting of).
1890 ship **Aldmyth** #1 owner with 64 shares, built at PEI 1884, 2 masted Brigantine, 106 ft. long, 25 ft. wide, 11 ft. deep, 230 tons, lost off Nassau Bahamas 1893.

ADVENTUROUS BUNNELL/BONNELL's ON THE CUTTING EDGE

1. **Abigail Bonnell**, (daughter of **Benjamin Bonnell** b. 1723 and **Rachel Van Winkle**). She and her husband **Jonathan Johnson** were one of the first pioneer families to settle Ohio in 1804.
2. **Abraham Bonnell (Bonnay, Bonneuil, and Bunnell)** was born c. 1290 in France. He left France and settled in Holland.
3. **Abraham Bonnell**, b. 1858 Prince Edward Island, Canada. He was the supervisor of Falconwood Hospital for 56 years.
4. **Alvah Alonzo Bunnell**, b. 22 August 1855 (son of **Eli**, and **M.A. Caulder**, b. 1819. After 1885, he became partner in the Cypress Shingle Mill in Flager County, Florida. In order to supply wood to the area for this business, a train stop was required which created the need to name this station. They named it "Bunnell" as it is named today. Somewhere around 1900 **Alvah** moves on, and his daughter did live in the West Palm Beach, Florida area at one time.
5. **Benjamin Bunnell**, b. 1600's. He was one of the early settlers of Wallingford, Connecticut and became a "Freeman" in 1670.
6. **Benjamin Bonnell**, b. c. 1744, (possibly) Morris County, New Jersey (American Loyalist). He was accused of carrying 35 dollars counterfeit money, which was made by the British in New York City 1779. He escaped to that place as a Refugee with his wife and two children under age ten. In August 1781 he signed up in the American Legion, serving under Brig. General **Benedict Arnold**. On 6 Sept. 1781 they invaded New London and Fort Griswold, Connecticut, burning the city down and killing many at the fort. In July 1783, all loyalists left New York City for Nova Scotia (over 30,000). Ben went back to farming there.
7. **Benjamin Bonnell Jr.**, b. 1751/6 (son of **Benjamin** (b. 1723) and **Rachel Van Winkle**). He enlisted in 1777 and served at the battles of Brandywine, Six Nations, Connecticut Farms and Yorktown as a Patriot. He also served in General **George Washington's** Body Guard Regiment as a Private.
8. **Benjamin Bunnell**, b.c. 1570 (son of **Thomas**, b.c. 1540 and **Jacque Bygote**). After his father left France as a persecuted Protestant the family settled in Norwich, England, later Ben moved to London where he joined the Dutch Church.
9. **Benjamin Bunnell/Bonnell**, b. 1742 (son of **Solomon**, b. 1705 and **Mary Holdren**), New Jersey. He served in Captain **Timothy Jayne's** and **Henry Shoemaker**'s companies during the American Revolution as a Patriot. He was one of the early settlers of Wyoming County, Pennsylvania.
10. **Benjamin Bonnell Sr.**, Esquire, b. 23 November 1723 (son of **Nathaniel Bonnell** and **Joanna Miller**). He was Justice of the Peace in New Jersey and active in the Presbyterian Church there. He died in a ferryboat accident in New York Bay. All aboard the ferry were lost.

11. **Charles E. Bunnell**, b.c. 1832 New York. Served in Civil War as Private in E Company of the New York infantry. He was promoted to corporal then reduced in rank. Service was from 5 September 1861 to 9 September 1864. He was wounded 2 July 1863 at Gettysburg, Pennsylvania.
12. **David H. Bunnell**, owner of P.C. Computer company in San Francisco, California. Was also published in Newsweek magazine.
13. **Etienne de Bonneuil**, b.c. 1200's, France. He was famous for making the plans for the Upsal Cathedral in Sweden. He was from the **Abraham Bonney/Bonnell** line, which settled Holland. He was an architect.
14. **Isaac Bonnell** Esquire, b. 1738, New Jersey (American Loyalist). He was High Sheriff of Middlesex County, New Jersey at the outbreak of war. Was taken prisoner by American rebels. He owned land around Perth Amboy, New Jersey and was close friend to the last British governor of New Jersey, **William Franklin** (son of **Benjamin Franklin**). Everything he owned was confiscated and later he fled to Nova Scotia, Canada (c. 1783). He named his son (**William Franklin Bonnell**) after his friend and made him his godfather. Isaac became Judge and Magistrate of Digby, Nova Scotia and was well respected there.
15. **Israel Bunnell**, b. 17 March 1746 (son of **Ebenezer**, b. 1713 and **Lydia Clark**). He was born in Connecticut and was a deacon and held many public offices.
16. **James Bonnell**, b. 1754, Elizabeth, New Jersey (son of **Thomas**, b.c. 1700). He was a Patriot Captain in the Revolutionary War and his activities are well documented. As of this date he and his father could be this **Benjamin Bonnell's** family, but it has not be proven.
17. **James Moody** (called Bonnell), b.c. 1740's. He was an American Loyalist who conducted many raids throughout New Jersey during the American Revolution. He fled to England and wrote many pamphlets about his exploits in Sussex County, New Jersey. There are no other records stating why he was called Bonnell.
18. **James Bonnell**, b. 14 November 1603, Geneva, Switzerland. He was also referred to as **Thomas Bonnell**. **Louis XIV** of France called him **Thomas**. He settled in Norwich, England and possibly became mayor there.
19. **John Sutherland Bonnell**, b. 10 January 1893, Prince Edward Island, Canada (son of **Abraham and Catherine**). In 1922 he was ordained a Presbyterian minister and went to the United States to become pastor of the Fifth Avenue Presbyterian Church in New York City, holding that position until 1962.
20. **Marie Catherine Bonneel**, b.c. 1650, Ypres, West Flanders, France (now Belgium) (daughter of **Jean Bonneel**, b.c. 1630 and **Jeanne Misseroen**). She married **Jean Leuridan** (son of **Feu Phillippe**) on 24 September 1672 in Comines, France. He was possibly from royal blood according to collection of Merghelinck of Noble Families, #33, Vol. 11, page 162.
21. **Matthew Bonnell**, b. 7 August 1785, near Elizabeth, New Jersey (son of **Daniel Bonnell**, b. 1749 and **Martha Hughes**). In 1828 his family moved to Clinton County, Indiana. They were one of five families first to settle that area.

22. **George Woodbury Bunnell III**, b. 9 June 1949, Lawrence, Essex County, Massachusetts (son of **George Woodbury Bunnell Jr.**, b. 1924 and **Nellie Giarrusso**). He is a member of the popular rock and roll group, The Strawberry Alarmclock during the late 1960's and early 1970's. The group received a gold record (Incense and Peppermints) for selling over one million copies. Presently, the group performs at oldies functions and also performs country and western music.
23. **Joseph Bonnell**, b. 1684, Elizabeth, New Jersey (son of **Nathaniel Bonnell**, b. 1644 and **Susanna Whitehead**). He was Supreme Court judge in New Jersey and was very active in government.
24. **Nathaniel Bonnell**, b. 1644, New Haven, Connecticut (son of **William Bunnell**, b. 1606 and **Ann Wilmot**). He was one of the original British associates (settlers) of Elizabethtown, New Jersey after the Dutch lost control of that area. He or his son **Nathaniel** built a home in Elizabeth which still stands today as the New Jersey Headquarters of the Sons of the American Revolution. He owned hundreds of acres of land and kept the old spelling of his surname "Bonnell".
25. **Peter Bunnell**, b.c. 1600, England. According to History of Wallingford, Connecticut, he came to Plymouth, Massachusetts on the Mayflower in 1620. There is no other written proof that he was listed elsewhere. Today's passengers list does not have him listed.
26. **Rachel Bonnell**, b. 29 May 1794, possibly New Jersey (daughter of **Paul**, b. 1762 and **Mary Parsons**). She and husband, **Aaron Jernell** were early pioneers to Indiana in 1837/8.
27. **Rhoda Bonnell**, b. 1763, Elizabeth, New Jersey (daughter of **Benjamin**, b. 1723 and **Rachel Van Winkle**). She and husband, **Calvin Morrell** were early pioneers of Clearmont County, Ohio in 1804.
28. **Richard Bunnell**, b.c. 1600, England. He came to Watertown, Massachusetts in 1630. His name may have been **William**, or he was possibly **William**'s brother. He disappears after ten years.
29. **Samuel Bonnell**, b.c. 1500's, England (son of **Daniel**). He became Accountant General for Ireland and was succeeded by his son, who later in life wrote about Archeacon Hamilton of Armagh.
30. **Solomon Bunnell**, b.c. 1750's at possibly Lanesborough, Massachusetts. He was an American Loyalist who during the battle of Bennington, Vermont shot two of his neighbors in the back. The record is draped in black in the town records. He fled to Digby, Nova Scotia in 1783 and who carried a curse with him (see #31).
31. **Solomon Bunnell Jr.**, b.c. 1780's, son of the above Loyalist, **Solomon Bunnell**. On 15 March 1794, he shot **Jane Fitz Randolph** of Weymouth, Nova Scotia. He foolishly pointed the gun at her and it went off accidentally. He left Nova Scotia and was never heard from again. **Jane's** father was **David Fitz Randolph**, a loyalist who came from New Jersey. They came to Nova Scotia in 1784. (From The Blazing Star newspaper, New Jersey).

32. **Spencer R. Bonnell**. He was a Worcester, Massachusetts graduate of Amherst in 1872 and was ordained and installed Pastor of the South Deerfield Congregational Church on 4 July 1878.
33. **Stephen Bunnell**, b. 1731, Scotch Plains, New Jersey. He was an early pioneer of Warren County, Kentucky, and later moved to Ohio in 1806.
34. **Thomas Bunnell/Bonnell**, b.c. 1540 possibly Ypres, West Flanders, France (now Belguim). He left France as a persecuted Protestant c. 1577/79. Lived in St. John parish in Wymer Ward, England and possibly became Mayor of Norwich.
35. **Thomas Bonnel**, b.c. 1700 (possibly England or New Jersey). He was one of the early pioneers and settlers of Morris County, New Jersey. He was referred to as **Bonhill** on one occasion. He could possibly be the father of **Benjamin**, which this book was written for, but their needs to be more proof of their relationship.
36. **Thomas Bunnell**, Captain of the sloop Elizabeth, which was captured by British troops during the American Revolutionary War in 1770-80's. It was turned over to a neutral ship, possibly Spanish and sent to New York. He was part owner along with **William Peatt**.
37. **William Bunnell/Bonnell**, b.c. 1606/17, Cheshire, England (son of **Benjamin**, b.c. 1570 and **Rebecca Brooks**). He was an early pioneer to Watertown, Massachusetts in 1630. Later he moved to Connecticut, but deserted his family many times to travel (possibly for business). His wife, **Ann Wilmot's** father, **Benjamin Wilmot** supported the family for many years as **William** went back and forth to England. It is said that during a return trip to Connecticut in 1654 he died in Barbados (1 Aug. 1678). He is considered the founding father of most **Bunnell/Bonnell's** in the United States today.
38. **William Franklin Bonnell**, b. 1778/80, New Jersey (son of **Isaac**, b. 1738 and **Grace Fox**). He was the godson to the last British governor of New Jersey, **William Franklin**, **Benjamin Franklin's** son. **William** later became the first postmaster of Gagetown, New Brunswick, Canada. Their family was highly respected and there is no proof yet as to the possible relationship to **Benjamin** of this book.
39. **William La Bunnell**, b.c. 1040, France. It is said that he was a Norman knight who came to England with **William the Conqueror** in 1066.
40. **Lafayette Houghton Bunnell**, b. 1824, New York. He was a doctor in a search party in that mid-1800's looking for Indians in central California. They were the first white men to enter the Yosemite Valley. He is responsible for naming the valley after the Indians. He was the author of The Discovery of the Yosemite Indians, 1880 and Winona (We-no-nah) and its Evirons on the Mississippi, 1897. He settled in Waynona, Minnesota and his house still stands today (open to the public).

41. **Benjamin Franklin Bunnell** (the author's godfather), b. 6 June 1929, Amesbury, Essex County, Massachusetts. Son of **George Woodbury Bunnell Sr.** and **Mary Bertogli**. He married **Madeleine M. Guilmette** of Amesbury, Massachusetts. He died 19 May 1967 working on the construction site of Route 495 at the intersection and off ramp of Route 95 in Amesbury, Massachusetts, crushed by a Backhoe/tractor.
42. **Benjamin Bunnell**, b. 1985/6 (son of **Albert Bunnell**). As of the earlier writing of this book, he was the last named **Benjamin**, but now there is a son **Benjamin** of **Paul** (son of above #41) and **Marcia Bunnell**.
43. **Matthew Paul Bunnell**, b. 11 Jan. 1973, Encino, California, son of the author became a Professional Wrestler out of Nashua, New Hampshire.

Listed on Page 122, The Martha L. Bonnell
Built 1889

The Price of Wales Elm

This Dutch Elm tree use to stand at Harding's Point just near where the Westfield Ferry lands to the far left of Benjamin Bunnell's loyalist land grant #1. On 4 August 1860, the Prince of Wales, future King Edward VII sailed by this tree on the steamboat Forest Queen going to Fredericton. It reminded him of the three feathers in his heraldic coat of arms so much that he ordered that ships captain to steer close to shore for a better view. This author was able to see and visit it before it was fallen by Dutch Elms disease. This mighty and popular royal tree must have been a young elm in 1786 when Ben was granted this land by King George III.[1] After the royal visit, the tree was known as the Prince of Wales Elm or the Prince's Feathers. It stood over 50 feet tall in 1986 just before it died.

Chapter 16

Bunnell-Bonnell Loyalist Genealogy

Loyalist
Benjamin & Sarah (Jones) Bonnell/Bunnell Genealogy

I. Benjamin^1 BUNNELL (Bonnell) Corporal, U.E was Farmer. He was born circa 1744-5 at possibly Essex County, New Jersey, English Colony.^{0} He was Quaker. He settled young circa 1745 at Mendham/Dover, Morris, New Jersey, British Colony with his family. Some of this information is from William Austin 26 March 2002 research letter based on the Quaker material in 1786. The Mendham meetinghouse was incorporated into the Rahway meetinghouse records. (Society of Friends).

---

[1] One report says it was on William Perry's land grant but Perry's grant #0 was at the opposite end of Ben's grant located near Sand Point. Controversy still goes on between William Perry and Benjamin Bunnell! From Kings County Memories newsletter October 2002, Vol. 42, #6.

He married Sarah (Sally) JONES after 1770 at New Jersey/New York, USA.[1] Ben was listed Supreme Court indictment (#34062) for passing counterfeit $30 to Enos Jaquish. Document signed by William Paterson, Attorney General who later becomes governor of NJ and has Patterson, NJ named after him. Enos was listed in tax ratable of Woodbridge, Middlesex Co., NJ. Woodbridge was one of the routes taken by the counterfeiting gangs. Location was in the Mendham/Dover area in Mar 1779 at Roxbury Township/Mendham/Dover area, Succasunna/Succasunny, Morris, New Jersey, British Colony. He immigrated after Mar 1779 to Refugee, New York City, New York, USA.[2] MILITARY: Enlisted in American Legion, Capt. James Wogan's Company serving under Brigadier General Benedict Arnold (New London raid records he was Capt. Samuel Wogan?). Ben's rank was Corporal. Muster in my file on 6 Aug 1781 at The Heights of Ireland (Near Jamaica/Flatbush), New York, British Colony.[3] They went on to destroyed by fire and plundered New London and Fort Griswold, Ct. 6 Sept.1781and attacking its defending forts, Fort Trumbull and Fort Nonsense on west side of the Thames River and New London. On the other side was Groton and Fort Griswold, Connecticut. Ben was deported on a fleet of 11 ships. He was on the "William" listed as a farmer from New Jersey assigned to Refugee Unit #15, Kings American Regiment of Refugees. Captain was William Wright. Ben left with wife and two children under 10 on 8 Jul 1783 at Wall Street, New York City, New York. When they arrived from NY on ship William, this new port was called Parrtown and the province was Nova Scotia at that time circa 28 Jul 1783. (Later to be Saint John, Saint John, County, New Brunswick, Canada.) He was given land/grant entered at Halifax, NS Auditor's office, signed 6 Jan. 1785, to Matthew Hains & 111 others listing Ben, asking for lands starting at Conway going south to Carleton Line then to the sea, with all rights of mines, minerals, timber, trees, underbrush, lakes, ponds, fishing, water and water courses, profits, common, hunting, fouling, hawking; all white pine. (Each lot was approx. 10 acres and was carved out of 120 acres. This was his first grant. This land was proved unfit for farming so they began to look elsewhere. Copy in my file. Ref. Ward Chipman papers (MG23 D1) listed as Benjamin Bennell, 1784 land grant, St. John Co. Series 1, Vol. 24, page 313 Microfilm #C-9818 on 11 Aug 1784 at Carleton/Conway Township, Sunbury, New Brunswick, Canada.[4] Ben was listed on land petition of William Perry, found at Fredericton NB Archives by Carole Bonnell of Bunnell newsletter on film #F1028 of RS108 index 1783-1918) in 1785 at Westfield? Kings County, New Brunswick, Canada.[5] He was again listed on land petition grant of Titus Brown as confirming his land was not good and wanted it escheated. Copy in my file and also found by Carole Bonnell of Bunnell newsletter on file # F1024 of RS108 land petition index 1783-1918 at the Fredericton Archives, NB. This was dated in 1785 at Long Reach, Westfield, Kings, New Brunswick, Canada.[6] Ben and family lived in 1785 at Long Reach, Westfield, Kings, New Brunswick, Canada.[7]

He later became an Anglican. He lived on 2 Jan 1786 at Lot # 1, Grant 15, 185 acres, Long Reach River, Kings, New Brunswick, Canada.[8,9] He was Quaker when Joseph Moore of Philadelphia and other Quakers came from the Rahway, New Jersey area to New Brunswick to help Loyalist Quakers in need. Ben and family were listed. Joseph was close to the Brotherton family who Ben's brother Aaron married Ann Brotherton. So this may have been some family relief from home in NJ.[10] Ben was listed on land petition of Joseph French, found at Fredericton NB Archives by Carole Bonnell of Bunnell newsletter on film #F1043 of RS108 index 1783-1918) in 1804 at Westfield?, Kings, New Brunswick, Canada.[11] After 23 years on this property, Ben sold it to Tertullus Theal of Saint John for 121 pounds on 25 May 1809 at Long Reach, Westfield, Kings, New Brunswick, Canada. Ben bought 200 acres from Loyalist, John & Elizabeth Crab/Crabb for 20 pounds located just across the river from his old land grant on 11 Jan 1810 at Devil's Back, Greenwich Parish, Kings, New Brunswick, Canada. He was a signer on land grant regarding Gilbert Cladian and Joseph Purdy. It mentioned granted to Ben & others in Jan. 1786. From Cleadie Barnett research & records on 22 Sep 1821 at New Brunswick, Canada. Ben sold off 100 acres of his property to his son, Isaac on 13 Nov 1824 at Devil's Back, Greenwich Parish, Kings, New Brunswick, Canada. He left a will on 28 Jun 1827 at Long Reach, Westfield Parish, Kings, New Brunswick, Canada.[12] HEALTH: He died of a painful ailment that he had for sometime. Source was obituary in Saint John, NB newspaper on 17 Feb 1828 at Devil's Back, Greenwich Village, Kings, New Brunswick, Canada. He died on 17 Feb 1828 at Home?, Greenwich, Kings, New Brunswick, Canada.[13] He was buried on 19 Feb 1828 at Westfield?, Kings, New Brunswick, Canada.[14] His estate was probated on 17 Mar 1828 at Greenwich/Westfield, Kings, New Brunswick, Canada.[15,16] Inventory taken of goods and chattles of late Benjamin Bunnell deceased, in the parish of Greenwich; by Anderson Worden & George E. Neil.

100 acres of land	100.0.0
3 cows	12.0.0
7 sheep	3.10.0
1 hog	1.0.0
1 bed & bedding	3.0.0
1 wheel	0.5.0
1 pot	0.2.0
1 table	0.1.3
1/2 dozen chairs	0.12.0
1 pale	0.1.0
1 pare of handirons	0.5.0
Total	120.1.6.6

on 15 Apr 1828 at Long Reach, Westfield Parish, Kings, New Brunswick, Canada. A Picture of his spirit was taken showing bright blue spot on photo. Experts claimed nothing was wrong with film, psychic said it was Ben following me around on his property. Also, that we had close bonds in Aug 1985 at Devil's Back, Greenwich Village, Kings, New Brunswick, Canada. First publication was Thunder Over New England, Benjamin Bonnell, The Loyalist (the book) in 1988. Proof of parents in Richard Brotherton letter date 28 Nov. 1855 to his cousin Charles Bonnel in Waterloo, New York, and the work that William Austin has done to prove this line in May 2002.

A. Sarah Elizabeth[2] BUNNELL (Bonnell)[17] She was a housewife. She was Quaker and later changed to Anglican in Canada. She was born circa 1779 at New York or New Jersey, USA. MILITARY: Child of UE Loyalist. (1779-1783) at New Jersey, British Colony. She immigrated in Jul 1783 to Wall Street Dock, New York, New York, USA.[18] She married Jonathan or Joseph Purdy, son of Gilbert Purdy I and Elizabeth Ogden, in 1816 at Westfield, Kings, New Brunswick, Canada.[19,20] at the Gagetown Anglican Church Records of Marriages (Record found in Generations (NB) Fall 1997 issues p.25 lists a Sarah Purdy marrying David Easty Brooks in Sept. 1814 in Hampstead, Kings Co., New Brunswick, Canada, possibly married by Rev. Estabrooks. (Is it this Sarah?) circa 1827 at Gagetown Anglican Church, Gagetown, York?, New Brunswick, Canada). She was mentioned in fathers will getting 10 pounds. Her and Joseph Purdy listed as witnesses on 28 Jun 1827 at Will of Father, Westfield/Greenwich Parish, Kings, New Brunswick, Canada. She appeared on the census of 1851 at Kings, New Brunswick, Canada.[21] She was age 72 in 1851 Kings Co.,New Brunswick Census in 1851 at Census, Westfield area, Kings, New Brunswick, Canada. She died after 1851 at Kingston Parish area, Kings, New Brunswick, Canada.

1. Emily Jane[3] Purdy married Arch McLean at New Brunswick, Canada. She was born after 1817 at Kings?, New Brunswick, Canada.[22] She appeared on the census of 1851 at Kingston Parish, Kings, New Brunswick, Canada.[23] She died in 1888 at New Brunswick? Canada? (Record from R. Lloyd Wood, 14 McLeod Cres., London, Ontario, Canada N5X 1S8 on Purdy family in Mar 1993).

2. Jesse Graves[3] Purdy was born after 1817 at Westfield?, Kings, New Brunswick, Canada. (Record from Linking The Past With The Present, Westfield newspaper article 26 June 1930 on the Purdy family). Question as to who is his mother; Mary #12423 or Sarah #169? on 26 Jun 1930.

3. Mary^3 Purdy married David Oram at New Brunswick, Canada. She was born after 1817 at New Brunswick, Canada. (Record from R. Lloyd Wood, 14 McLeod Cres., London, Ontario, Canada N5X 1S8 on Purdy family in Mar 1993).

    a) Sarah^4 Oram was born at New Brunswick, Canada. (Record from R. Lloyd Wood, 14 McLeod Cres., London, Ontario, Canada N5X 1S8 on Purdy family in Mar 1993).

4. Elmina^3 Purdy married Abram Holder at New Brunswick?, Canada. She was born after 1817 at New Brunswick, Canada. (Record from R. Lloyd Wood, 14 McLeod Cres., London, Ontario, Canada N5X 1S8 on Purdy family in Mar 1993).

5. Jesse H.^{3} Purdy married Joanna Wolsey Fowler at New Brunswick?, Canada. He was born in 1822 at New Brunswick, Canada. He died in 1905 at New Brunswick?, Canada? He was buried in 1905 at New Brunswick?, Canada? (Record from R. Lloyd Wood, 14 McLeod Cres., London, Ontario, Canada N5X 1S8 on Purdy family in Mar 1993).

    a) Fanny^4 Purdy. Her married name was Elkin. She married Robert C. (Rob) Elkin at New Brunswick?, Canada? She was born at New Brunswick, Canada. (Record from R. Lloyd Wood, London, Ontario, Canada N5X 1S8 on Purdy family in Mar 1993).

        (1) Frederick (Fred)^5 Elkin was born at New Brunswick?, Canada? (Record from R. Lloyd Wood, London, Ontario, Canada N5X 1S8 on Purdy family in Mar 1993).

        (2) Frank^5 Elkin was born at New Brunswick?, Canada. (Record from R. Lloyd Wood, London, Ontario, Canada N5X 1S8 on Purdy family in Mar 1993).

        (3) Florence^5 Elkin was born at New Brunswick?, Canada. (Record from R. Lloyd Wood, London, Ontario, Canada N5X 1S8 on Purdy family in Mar 1993).

        (4) Mable^5 Elkin was born at New Brunswick?, Canada. (Record from R. Lloyd Wood, London, Ontario, Canada N5X 1S8 on Purdy family in Mar 1993).

(5) Minnie G.^{5} Elkin. Her (1st.) married name was Chalmers. Her (2nd.) married name was Stockwell. She was born at New Brunswick?, Canada. She married A. L. Stockwell at Canada? She married ? Chalmers at Canada? (Record from R. Lloyd Wood, London, Ontario, Canada N5X 1S8 on Purdy family in Mar 1993).

b) Jesse^4 Purdy was born at New Brunswick?, Canada. He married A. J. (Allie) Machum at Canada? (Record from R. Lloyd Wood, London, Ontario, Canada N5X 1S8 on Purdy family in Mar 1993).

c) Anna T. (Annie)^4 Purdy was born in 1857 at New Brunswick, Canada. She died in 1921 at New Brunswick?, Canada. She was buried in 1921 at New Brunswick?, Canada. (Record from R. Lloyd Wood, London, Ontario, Canada N5X 1S8 on Purdy family in Mar 1993).

6. William (Will)^3 Purdy (Record from Linking The Past With The Present, Westfield newspaper article 26 June 1930 on the Purdy family). Question as to who is his mother, Mary #12423 or Sarah #169? He was born circa 1823 at Westfield?, Kings, New Brunswick, Canada. He appeared on the census of 1851 at Kingston Parish, Kings, New Brunswick, Canada.^{24}

7. Amanda Malvina (Mellie)^3 Purdy. Her married name was Wood. She was housewife. (Record from Barbara M. Love, 84 Clearwater Rd., Newton, Ma. 02162-1106 in Sept. 1997). She was born on 19 Jan 1827 at New Brunswick, Canada. She married James Robert Wood, son of Robert Wood Jr. and Elizabeth Hay, on 22 Sep 1847 at Indiantown, New Brunswick, Canada. She died on 16 Aug 1904 at New Brunswick, Canada, at age 77.

a) Thomas Frederick (Fred)^4 Wood was a farmer. He was born on 17 Jun 1859 at Kings ?, New Brunswick, Canada. He married Lettie Marcia Wetmore, daughter of Edwin Marshall Wetmore and Ruth Letitia Ann (Lettie) Flewelling, on 30 Oct 1888 at Clifton, Kings, New Brunswick, Canada. He died on 17 Jan 1953 at New Brunswick?, Canada?, at age 93. Record from R. Lloyd Wood, London, Ontario, Canada N5X 1S8 on his grandfather & Purdy line in Jan 1993.

(1) Frank Leslie (Les)^5 Wood was New Brunswick, Canada Dept. of Agriculture. He was born on 12 Feb 1894 at New Brunswick, Canada. He married Inez Evans Johnston, daughter of John Vicars Johnston, on 23 Aug 1922 at Nashwaaksis, New Brunswick, Canada. He died on 21 Mar 1974 at New Brunswick?, Canada, at age 80. record from R. Lloyd Wood, London, Ontario, Canada N5X 1S8 on his father & Purdy line in Jan 1993.

(a) Frederick Robert Lloyd^6 Wood was a Professor of Engineering. He was born on 22 Nov 1927 at Canada. He married Rosemarie Mueller on 21 May 1955 at Hamilton, Ontario, Canada. Record from himself living at London, Ontario, Canada N5X 1S8 sent Purdy line to me in Jan 1993.

8. Austin^3 Purdy was born circa 1829 at Kings?, New Brunswick, Canada. He appeared on the census of 1851 at Kingston Parish, Kings, New Brunswick, Canada.[25]

9. Albinia^3 Purdy was born circa 1834 at Kings?, New Brunswick, Canada. She appeared on the census of 1851 at Kingston Parish, Kings, New Brunswick, Canada.[26]

B. Samuel^2 Bunnell (Bonnel) was born after 1779 at (possibly) Westfield, Kings, New Brunswick, Canada.[27] He married Anne (Annie) P. Craig circa Mar 1850 at Saint John, New Brunswick, Canada.[28] He appeared on the census of 1871 at Canadian Census, Queens Ward, Saint John, New Brunswick, Canada.[29]

1. Mary E.^{3} Bunnell (Bonnel) was born circa 1851 at Saint John, New Brunswick, Canada. She appeared on the census of 1871 at Canadian Census, Queens Ward, Saint John, New Brunswick, Canada.[30]

2. Fannie (Fanny) Wood^3 BUNNELL (Bonnell) Record from RS141 A2/1 county vitals (1801-99),SJ,1-1,p.49,#49,F14037 (birth of Clarence). More records from "   "   " SJ,1-2,p.39,#401,F14954 (birth for Robert). Record from RS141 A2/1 co.vitals (1801-99),SJ,1-1,p.121,#46,F14037 (sons birth). She was born before 1871 at Saint John, New Brunswick, Canada. She appeared on the census of 1871 at Canadian Census, Queens Ward, Saint John, New Brunswick, Canada.[31] She married Thomas Clarence WALLACE before 1889 at New Brunswick, Canada.

a) Clarence Gardiner[4] WALLACE, Record from RS141 A2/1 county vitals (1801-99),SJ,1-1,p.49,#480,F14037. He was born on 11 Oct 1889 at Saint John, Saint John Co., New Brunswick, Canada.

b) Todd[4] WALLACE, Record from RS141 A2/1 county vitals (1801-99),SJ,1-1,p.121,#46,F14037. He was born on 3 Jan 1892 at Saint John, Saint John Co., New Brunswick, Canada.

c) Robert Samuel[4] WALLACE, Record from RS141 A2/1 county vitals (1801-99),SJ,1-2,p.39,#401.F14954. He was born on 10 Jun 1894 at Saint John, Saint John Co., New Brunswick, Canada.

3. Robert[3] Bunnell (Bonnel) was born before 1871 at Saint John, New Brunswick, Canada. He appeared on the census of 1871 at Canadian Census, Queens Ward, Saint John, New Brunswick, Canada.[32]

4. Bessie[3] Bunnell (Bonnel) was born before 1871 at Saint John, New Brunswick, Canada. She appeared on the census of 1871 at Canadian Census, Queens Ward, Saint John, New Brunswick, Canada.[33]

5. Alicia[3] Bunnell (Bonnel) was born before 1871 at Saint John, New Brunswick, Canada. She appeared on the census of 1871 at Canadian Census, Queens Ward, Saint John, New Brunswick, Canada.[34]

C. Benjamin[2] Bunnell (Bonnell) was Anglican or Baptist. He was a farmer. He was born circa 1789 at Long Reach, Westfield Parish, Kings, New Brunswick, Canada. He married to Sarah DAY (Dey), daughter of John DAY U.E. (Loyalist) and Tina (--?--), circa 1809 at Westfield, Kings, New Brunswick, Canada. He had a Judgment against him by John Bentley for Trespass and non-payment of loan. Record from Kings Co., NB court records, Fredericton Archives, NB. dated between May-July 1818 in May 1818 at Westfield?, Kings, New Brunswick, USA. He was baptized on 28 Apr 1827 at Greenwich/Westfield Anglican Church, Westfield, Kings, New Brunswick, Canada.[35] He was mentioned in fathers will getting 25 pounds on 28 Jun 1827 at Will of Father, Westfield/Greenwich Parish, Kings, New Brunswick, Canada. He was listed in shipping, Ben of Westfield, Farmer/Planter was #2 owner with 32 shares, Previously registered at Saint John 1829, constructed at Kingston 1829, 2 masted schooner, length 60 ft., width 19 ft, depth 6 ft, gross tons 83, year registered 1833, official year closure 1836, reason closure #4, place Saint John 1836 in 1829 at Ship

"Triumph", Kingston, Kings, New Brunswick, Canada.36 Again listed in shipping Ben of Westfield, Mariner, owner #1 with 64 shares, previously registered at Saint John 1833, built at Waterborough 1833, 1 deck, 2 masted schooner, length 69 ft, width 20 ft, depth 6 ft, tons 115, year registered 1839, official closure year 1839, reason closure #4 at Saint John, 1839 in 1833 at Ship "Caledonia", Waterborough, New Brunswick?, Canada.37 Again listed as Farmer/Planter and part owner in shipping with 32 shares Ref: AutoInc 33388 Reg. #J833075 from Ships & Seafarer's of Atlantic Canada CD, Newfoundland in 1833 at Westfield, Kings, New Brunswick, Canada. He was Mariner and part owner of a ship with 64 shares from AutoInc #34566 Reg.#J839018 found in Ships & Seafarer's of Atlantic Canada CD, Newfoundland in 1839 at Westfield, Kings, New Brunswick, Canada. Again listed in shipping Ben of Saint John, Mariner, owner #1 with 32 shares, previously registered at Saint John 1851, built at Grand Lake 1848, 2 masted schooner, length 68 ft, width 19 ft, depth 6 ft, gross tons 56, year registered 1853, official year closure 1867, reason closer #12 at Mount Desert Island 1866 in 1851 at Ship "Linnet", Grand Lake, Kings, New Brunswick, Canada.38 He appeared on the census of 1851 at Canadian Census, Westfield Parish, Kings, New Brunswick, Canada.39 And again listed as a Mariner with 32 shares in a ship ownership. From AutoInc #37818 Reg.#J853034 found on Ships & Seafarer's of Atlantic Canada CD, Newfoundland in 1853 at Saint John, Saint John, New Brunswick, Canada. He married again Henrietta (Heddy/Hatty) Day on 14 Dec 1859 at Saint John, New Brunswick, Canada. He left a will on 2 Aug 1866 at Westfield, Kings, New Brunswick, USA.40,41 He died on 10 Aug 1866 at Westfield, Kings Co., New Brunswick, Canada.42,43 His death rec.17 Aug.1866 Morning News on 17 Aug 1866 at Morning News, New Brunswick, Canada. His estate was probated on 4 Sep 1866 at Westfield, Kings, New Brunswick, USA.44,45

1. Polly (Mary Jane)3 BUNNELL (Bonnell) was Anglican. She was born in 1810 at Westfield/Greenwich, Kings, New Brunswick, Canada.46,47 She married Robert FRENCH on 23 Jul 1831 at Westfield Anglican Church, Westfield or Hampton, Kings, New Brunswick, Canada.48,49 Husband was from Kingston, New Brunswick on 24 Jul 1831. Her estate was probated on 2 Aug 1866 at Westfield, Kings, New Brunswick, Canada.50,51

2. James3 BUNNELL (Bonnell) was Anglican. He was born in 1815 at Westfield/Greenwich, Kings Co., New Brunswick, Canada.52 He was a Mariner and owner of 64 shares in shipping. From AutoInc #33789, Reg.#J835119 found in Ships & Seafarer's of Atlantic Canada CD, Newfoundland in 1835 at Westfield, Kings, New Brunswick, Canada. Listed again in shipping James of Westfield, Mariner, owner #1, 64 shares, previously registered at Saint John 1833, built at

Greenwich 1832, 2 masted schooner, length 58 ft, width 17 ft, depth 5 ft, gross tons 70, year registered 1835, year officially closure 1838, reason #4 at Saint John 1838 in 1835 at Ship "Dove", Greenwich, Kings, New Brunswick, Canada.[53] He married Mary Lingley in Feb 1837 at Westfield, Kings, New Brunswick, Canada.[54,55] His estate was probated on 2 Aug 1866 at Westfield, Kings, New Brunswick, Canada.[56,57] His is listed on 23 Aug 1877 at Daily Examiner Newspaper, Saint John, Saint John, New Brunswick, Canada. He died on 23 Aug 1877 at Saint John, Saint John Co., New Brunswick, Canada.[58] HEALTH: Possible bad liver on 23 Aug 1877. He was buried circa 25 Aug 1877 at Saint John?, New Brunswick, Canada.

3. Simeon[3] BUNNELL (Bonnell) Capt. Ref: Charlotte's at Adelaide Rd. Portland, Saint John, NB address. He was Anglican. He was born in 1817 at Westfield, Kings Co., New Brunswick, Canada? He married Prudence CRABB (Crab), daughter of John CRABB (Crab) U.E. and Elizabeth Bassett, on 6 Apr 1834 at Westfield/Greenwich Anglican Church, Westfield/Greenwich Parish, Kings, New Brunswick, Canada.[59] He was baptized on 2 Feb 1836 at Westfield/Greenwich Anglican Church, Westfield/Greenwich Parish, Kings, New Brunswick, Canada.[60] He was a Farmer/mariner, and Captain of ship Gypsie c.1840 taking his brother Benjamin to Boston to live. They landed at Chelsea, Mass circa 1840. He was into shipping listed as Simeon of Westfield, Mariner, #2 owner with 32 shares, previously registered at Saint John 1837, built at Kingston 1837, 2 masted schooner, length 61 ft, width 17 ft, depth 5 ft, gross ton 45, registered 1840, officially year closure 1847, reason #4 at Saint John 1847 in 1840 at Ship "Primrose", Kingston, Kings, New Brunswick, Canada.[61] Listed again as Mariner with 32 shares in shipping. From AutoInc 334940, Reg.#J840058, Saint John, found in Ships & Seafarer's of Atlantic Canada CD, Newfoundland in 1840 at Westfield, Kings, New Brunswick, Canada. He married Mary Jane Stevens (Steeves), daughter of Stephen Stevens U.E. and Eleanor (Hannah) Lingley, on 3 Nov 1841 at Westfield Anglican Ch, Westfield, New Brunswick, Canada.[62] He married ? ? (Bunnell)(Bonnell) circa Jan 1843 at New Brunswick, Canada. He married Elizabeth Sophia Stevens on 27 Apr 1846 at Westfield, Kings, New Brunswick, Canada.[63] Listed again as Mariner and owner of 64 shares in shipping. From AutoInc #36464, Reg.#J847040, Saint John, found in Ships & Seafarer's of Atlantic Canada CD, Newfoundland in 1847 at Saint John, Saint John, New Brunswick, Canada. And again as Simeon of Saint John, Mariner, owner #1 with 64 shares, previously registered at Saint John 1846, built at Kingston 1831, 2 masted schooner, length 62 ft, width 17 ft, depth 5 ft, gross tons 51, year registered 1847, official year of closure 1851, reason #4 at Saint John

1851 in 1847 at Ship "Highway Mary", Kingston, Kings, New Brunswick, Canada.[64] Listed again as Mariner and owner of 32 shares in shipping. From AutoInc #37525, Reg.#J851128, Saint John found in Ships & Seafarer's of Atlantic Canada CD, Newfoundland in 1851 at Portland, Saint John, New Brunswick, Canada. He was listed again in shipping as Simeon of Portland (NB), Mariner owner #1 with 32 shares (owner with brothers, Isaac & Ben), previously registered at Saint John 1850, built at Grand Lake 1848, 2 masted schooner, length 68 ft, width 19 ft, depth 6 ft, gross tons 56, registered 1851, official closure 1853, reason #4 at Saint John 1853 in 1851 at Ship "Linnet", Grand Lake, Kings, New Brunswick, Canada.[65] Listed again in shipping as Simeon of Saint John, Mariner, owner #2, 32 shares, previously registered at Saint John 1847, built at Kennebacasis 1847, 2 masted schooner, length 65 ft, width 17 ft, depth 5 ft, gross tons 49, registered 1851, official closure 1851, reason #4 at Saint John 1851 in 1851 at Ship "Roxana", Kennebacasis, Kings, New Brunswick, Canada.[66] And again as Mariner and owner of 32 shares in shipping. From AutoInc #37342, Reg.#J851013, Saint John, found in Ships & Seafarer's of Atlantic Canada CD, Newfound in 1851 at Saint John, Saint John, New Brunswick, Canada. Listed again as Mariner and owner of 64 shares in shipping. From AutoInc #37922, Reg.#J853093, Saint John found in Ships & Seafarer's of Atlantic Canada Cd, Newfoundland in 1853 at Saint John, Saint John, New Brunswick, Canada. Listed again in shipping as Simeon of Saint John, Mariner, owner #1 with 64 shares, previously registered at Saint John 1848, built at Grand Lake 1848, 2 masted schooner, length 66 ft, width 19 ft, depth 6 ft, gross tons 55, registered 1853, official closure 1882, reason #9 at Saint John River 1872 in 1853 at Ship "Hyena", Grand Lake, Kings, New Brunswick, Canada.[67] Listed again in shipping of Westfield, a Mariner and owner #1 with 24 shares, constructed at Saint John 1881, 2 masted schooner, length 100 ft, width 27 ft, depth 10 ft, gross tons 198, net tons 170, registered tons 198, year registered 1881, official year of closure 1882, reason #9 at Caicos Island, Bahamas 1882 in 1881 at Ship "E. M. Bonnell", Westfield, Kings, New Brunswick, Canada.[68] He died on 1 Feb 1882 at Westfield, Kings, New Brunswick, Canada.[69] He was buried circa 3 Feb 1882 at Stevens (Stephen)/Ingleside Cemetery (Brandy Point), Westfield, Kings, New Brunswick, Canada.[70]

a) Elizabeth[4] BUNNELL (Bonnell) immigrated.[71] She Not sure if mother is Prudence?(need birth). She was born circa 1838 at Westfield, Kings, New Brunswick, Canada. She appeared on the census of 1851 at Canadian Census, Sussex Parish, Kings, New Brunswick, Canada.[72] Record from Paul Bonnell, St. Lambert, Quebec, Canada 1989 in 1989.

b) Charlotte M.[4] BUNNELL (Bonnell) She was youngest daughter to Simeon & Prudence. She was born in 1856 at New Brunswick, Canada. She married Alfred L. COWAN on 24 May 1876 at Adelaide Rd., Portland, Saint John, New Brunswick, Canada. Marriage record from Daily Telegraph 26 May 1876,by Rev. D. McClellan (at her parents house) on 26 May 1876. She died in 1937 at New Brunswick?, Canada? Record from Paul Bonnell, Lambert, Quebec, Canada in 1989.

c) Jane (Janie)[4] Bunnell (Bonnell) Kings Co. Ceme.rec.2 of 6 says that she was the daughter to S. Bonnell (could it be Sineon?). She was born circa 1843 at Westfield, Kings Co., New Brunswick, Canada? She married ? McCordock circa 1863 at New Brunswick, Canada. She died on 2 Jan 1883 at Westfield, Kings Co., New Brunswick, Canada.[73] She was buried circa 3 Jan 1883 at Stevens Cemetery, Westfield, Kings, New Brunswick, Canada.

d) John M.[4] BUNNELL (Stone)(Bonnell) (adopted line) was also known as John Bunnell. He lived at New Brunswick, Canada. He was born circa 1844 at Westfield Parish, Kings, New Brunswick, Canada. He was born in 1843 at Lands End, Kings Co., New Brunswick, Canada. He appeared on the census of 1851 at Canadian Census, Westfield Parish, Kings, New Brunswick, Canada.[74] He married an unknown person before 1874. Record from Troy Stone 1991, Florenceville, New Brunswick, ancestor of above John in 1991.

(1) Louis[5] BUNNELL (Stone)(Bonnell) (adopted line) lived at New Brunswick, Canada. Record from Troy Stone of Florenceville, NB 1993. He was born in 1874 at New Brunswick, Canada.

(a) Ernest[6] BUNNELL (Stone)(Bonnell) (adopted line) Record from Troy Stone 1991. He was born on 2 Sep 1912 at New Brunswick, Canada.

i) Lewis[7] BUNNELL (Stone)(Bonnell) (adopted line) Record from Troy Stone 1991. He was born after 1930 at New Brunswick, Canada.

(a) Troy F. J.[8] BUNNELL (Stone)(Bonnell) (adopted line) died Living 1991 at Box 10 Si. Record from Troy Stone 1991. He was born on 29 Dec 1965 at New Brunswick, Canada.

i) Christopher[9] BUNNELL (Stone)(Bonnell) (adopted line) was born on 25 Sep 1990 at New Brunswick, Canada.

e) Mary Jane[4] BUNNELL (Bonnell) was Anglican. She was born on 2 Jan 1843 at Westfield, Kings Co., New Brunswick, Canada. She was baptized on 6 Jan 1843 at Westfield Anglican Church, Westfield, Kings, New Brunswick, Canada. She married David MCCORDOCK on 31 Jan 1873 at Adelaide Rd. Portland, St. John, NB(parents home). She was Married by Rev. W. B. Boggs on 31 Jan 1873. Marriage record from 4 Feb.1873 Visitor (private Somerville collection) newspaper on 4 Feb 1873. She died on 2 Jan 1883 at Westfield, New Brunswick, Canada, at age 40. She was buried circa 4 Jan 1883 at Stevens Cemetery, Westfield, Kings, New Brunswick, Canada.

f) Carl E.[4] Bunnell (Bonnell) Something is wrong with this record. Both parents died before his birth??? in 1889. He was born in 1889 at Westfield?, Kings, New Brunswick, Canada.[75] He was buried in 1927 at Stephen/Ingleside Cemetery (Brandy Point), Westfield, Kings, New Brunswick, Canada.[76] He died in 1927 at Westfield, Kings, New Brunswick, Canada.[77]

g) Melissa[4] BUNNELL (Bonnell) Not sure if Simeon's 3rd.wife is mother or even if parents are right, just buried w/them? She was born in 1846 at New Brunswick, Canada. She was buried in 1929 at Stephens Cemetery (Brandy Point), Westfield, Kings, New Brunswick, Canada.[78] She died in 1929 at New Brunswick, Canada?

h) Alfred Ludlow[4] BUNNELL (Bonnell) Not sure of mother?(need birth date). He was Baptist (John Stevens records show religion as Methodist?). He was born circa 1848 at Westfield, Kings Co., New Brunswick, Canada. He married Mabel DALTON after 1880 at New Brunswick, Canada?[79] Occupation was Sea fishery in 1881 at Fairview, New Brunswick, Canada. He appeared on the census of 1881 at Federal Census, Fairview, New Brunswick, Canada.[80] He was listed as a seaman in 1885 at Fairview Directory, South Bay, New Brunswick, Canada. He was Mariner and part ship owner. See above 1881 History in 1886 at Portland, Saint John, New Brunswick, Canada. He was Merchant. See above 1881 History for details in 1889 at Saint John, Saint John, New Brunswick, Canada. He lived in 1889 at North Section,

Fairview, New Brunswick, Canada.[81] He appeared on the census of 1891 at Federal Census - Portland Ward 1, Portland (Saint John), Saint John, New Brunswick, Canada.[82] He died on 22 Jun 1894 at age 46, Westfield, Kings Co., New Brunswick, Canada.[83] He was buried circa 24 Jun 1894 at Stevens Cemetery, Westfield, Kings, New Brunswick, Canada.[84] Record from Paul Bonnell, St. Lambert, Quebec, Canada 1989.

(1) Walter B.[5] BUNNELL (Bonnell).[85] He was buried.[86] Record from Paul Bonnell, St. Lambert, Quebec, Canada. He Not sure if Prudence is mother?(need birth). He was born in 1882 at New Brunswick, Canada. He married Lillie TUFTS before 1892 at New Brunswick, Canada? He died in 1906 at New Brunswick, Canada?

(a) Percival Lincoln[6] BUNNELL (Bonnell) record from RS141 A2/1 county vitals 1801-99,SJ,1-1,p.153,#1245,F14037 birth. He was born on 27 Oct 1892 at Lepreau, Saint John Co., New Brunswick, Canada.

(b) (male)[6] BUNNELL (Bonnell record from RS141,A2/1 county vitals 1801-99,SJ,1-2,p.173,#443. He was born on 24 May 1898 at Saint John, Saint John Co., New Brunswick, Canada.

(2) (--?--)[5] BUNNELL (Bonnell) Record from RS141 A2/1 county vitals 1801-99,SJ,1-1,p.20,#25. He was born on 11 Jan 1889 at Grand Bay, Saint John Co., New Brunswick, Canada.

(3) William R.[5] BUNNELL was born before 1890 at Fairview?, New Brunswick, Canada.[87]

(a) Willard[6] BUNNELL was born circa 1910 at New Brunswick?, Canada?[88]

(4) Allison Henry[5] BUNNELL (Bonnell) Record from RS141,A2/1,county vitals 1801-99,SJ,1-1,p.193 birth. He was born on 2 May 1894 at Sutton, Saint John Co., New Brunswick, Canada.

i) Freddie[4] Bunnell (Bonnell) It appears mother is Simeon's 3rd.wife? He was born circa Nov 1850 at Westfield, Kings, New Brunswick, Canada. He died on 17 May 1852 at Westfield, Kings, New Brunswick, Canada.[89] He was buried circa 19 May 1852 at Stephens/Ingleside Cemetery (Brandy Point), Westfield, Kings, New Brunswick, Canada.[90] Record from Paul Bonnell, St. Lambert, Quebec, Canada 1989.

j) Frederick Simeon[4] BUNNELL (Bonnell) It appears that Simeon's 3rd.wife is his mother? He was born after 1853? at New Brunswick, Canada. He married Martha L. RICHIE, daughter of Francis RITCHIE, circa 1877 at New Brunswick, Canada ? He was into shipping and from Portland (Saint John) owner #2, with 16 shares, constructed at Saint John 1881, 2 masted schooner, length 100 ft, width 27 ft, depth 10 ft, gross tons 198, net tons 170, registered tons 198, year registered 1881, official year of closure 1882, reason #9 at Caicos Island, Bahamas 1882 in 1881 at Ship "E. M. Bonnell", Saint John, Saint John, New Brunswick, Canada.[91] He was Ship owner in 1881. He was Part owner in shipping (16 shares), from AutoInc #44561, Reg. #J881001 found in Ships & Seafarer's of Atlantic Canada CD, Newfoundland in 1881 at Portland, Saint John, New Brunswick, Canada. Again listed as Merchant and part owner (12 shares) in shipping. From AutoInc #45591, Reg.#J885011 found in Ships & Seafarer's of Atlantic Canada CD, Newfoundland in 1885 at Portland, Saint John, New Brunswick, Canada. And again in shipping as Frederick from Portland (Saint John), Merchant,, built in 1885, 2 masted schooner, owner #1 with 12 shares, length 100 ft, width 28 ft, depth 11 ft, gross tons 223, net tons 184, registered tons 219, year registered 1885, official year of closure 1894, reason 15 at Santa Domingo Coast 1894 in 1885 at Ship "Clifton", Moss Glen, New Brunswick, Canada.[92] Listed again in shipping as Frederick S. from Saint John, Merchant, owner #1 with 18 shares, constructed at Saint John 1886, 3 masted schooner, length 111 ft, width 28 ft, depth 11 ft, gross tonnage 244, net tons 206, registered tons 228, year registered 1886, official year of closure 1889, reason 22 at Bay of Fundy 1889 in 1886 at Ship "C.E. White", Saint John, Saint John, New Brunswick, Canada.[93] Again listed as Merchant and part owner (18 shares) in shipping. From AutoInc #45772, Reg.#J886027. Found in Ships & Seafarer's of Atlantic Canada CD, Newfoundland in 1886 at Saint John, Saint John, New Brunswick, Canada. And again in shipping as Frederick S. Bonnell of Saint John, Merchant, owner #14 with 2 shares, constructed at Portland (Saint John) 1888, 3 masted schooner, length 132 ft, width 31 ft, depth 11 ft, gross tons 319, net tons 269, registered tons 299, year registered 1888, official year of closuer 1905, reason 9 at Saint John River 1905 in 1888 at Ship "H.B. Homan", Portland (Saint

John), Saint John, New Brunswick, Canada.[94] Listed again as Merchant and part owner (2 shares) in shipping. From AutoInc #45919, Reg.#J888025 found in Ships & Seafarer's of Atlantic Canada Cd, Newfoundland in 1888 at Saint John, Saint John, New Brunswick, Canada. And again as Merchant and part owner (14 shares) in shipping. From AutoInc #46088, Reg.#J889025 found in Ships & Seafarer's of Atlantic Canada Cd, Newfoundland in 1889 at Saint John, Saint John, New Brunswick, Canada. Again in shipping as Frederick S. Bonnell of Saint John, Merchant, owner #1 with 14 shares, constructed at Saint John 1889, 3 masted schooner, length 127 ft, width 31 ft, depth 11 ft, gross tons 308, net tons 254, registered tons 297, year registered 1889, official year closure 1897, reason #10 at Long Island Sound 1897 in 1889 at Ship "M.L. Bonnell", Saint John, Saint John, New Brunswick, Canada.[95] He immigrated in 1889.[96] He was Merchant and part owner (64 shares) in shipping. From Ships & Seafarer's of Atlantic Canada CD, Newfoundland AutoInc #46316, Reg.#J890021 in 1890 at Saint John, Saint John, New Brunswick, Canada. He was in shipping again as Frederick S. Bonnell of Saint John, Merchant, owner #1 with 64 shares, constructed at Prince Edward Island 1884, 2 masted Brigantine, length 106 ft, width 25 ft, depth 11 ft, gross tons 230, net tons 175, registered tons 218, year registered 1890, official year of closure 1893, reason #7 at Nassau 1893 in 1890 at Ship "Aldmyth", Prince Edward Island, Canada.[97] He died in 1917 at New Brunswick, Canada ? He was buried in 1917.[98] Some record from Paul Bonnell, St. Lambert, Quebec, Canada in 1979.

(1) Edwin[5] BUNNELL (Bonnell) was born in 1878 at New Brunswick, Canada. He died in 1927 at New Brunswick, Canada ?

(2) Francis (Frank) Simeon[5] BUNNELL (Bonnell) was born in 1879 at New Brunswick, Canada. He died in 1954 at New Brunswick, Canada ?

(a) Jean[6] BUNNELL (Bonnell) married E. J. R. WRIGHT. She was born circa 1899.

(3) Ralph[5] BUNNELL (Bonnell) was born in 1881 at New Brunswick, Canada. He died in 1948 at New Brunswick, Canada ?

(4) Fenwick[5] BUNNELL (Bonnell) was born in 1884 at New Brunswick, Canada. He died in 1949 at New Brunswick, Canada ?

(5) Kenneth Frederick[5] BUNNELL (Bonnell) was born in 1886 at New Brunswick, Canada. He married Helen Louisa JOHNSTON before 1916. He died in 1973 at New Brunswick, Canada ?

(a) John Wran[6] BUNNELL (Bonnell) was born in 1916 at New Brunswick, Canada. He married Ruth THURSTON circa 1936. He lived in 1990 at Pickering, Ontario, Canada.[99]

i) Brian Peter[7] BUNNELL (Bonnell) was born after 1936 at New Brunswick, Canada. He lived in 1990 at Pickering, Ontario, Canada.[100]

ii) Robert Kenneth[7] BUNNELL (Bonnell) was born after 1936 at New Brunswick, Canada. He lived in 1990 at Pickering, Ontario, Canada.[101]

(b) Paul Ritchie[6] BUNNELL (Bonnell) U.E was born in 1927 at New Brunswick, Canada. He married Ruby L. ALLEN in 1950? at Canada ? He was Retired Salesman. (surname spelled Bonnell) before 1989. He lived in 2002 at 216 Regent St., Saint Lambert, Quebec, Canada.

i) Susan E.[7] BUNNELL (Bonnell) was born in 1951 at New Brunswick, Canada.

ii) Peter R.[7] BUNNELL (Bonnell) was born in 1954 at New Brunswick, Canada.

(a) Eric[8] BUNNELL (Bonnell) was born at Canada. He immigrated.[102]

k) Harry E. or F.[4] BUNNELL (Bonnell) Mother not known because Crab d.1841,Mary J.d.1843?Possibly Simeon's 3rd.wife? He was born in 1858 at New Brunswick, Canada. Lost at sea.[103] He died on 21 Feb 1883 Lost at sea.[104] He was buried at Sea.[105] Record from Paul Bonnell, St. Lambert, Quebec, Canada in 1989. He is possibly related if not son of Simeon Bonnell #130 in 2000.

l) Walter B.[4] Bunnell (Bonnell) was born in 1882 at Westfield, Kings, New Brunswick, Canada. He died in 1906 at Westfield?, Kings, New Brunswick, Canada. He was buried in 1906 at Stephen Cemetery (Brandy Point), Westfield, Kings, New Brunswick, Canada.[106]

4. Benjamin[3] BUNNELL (Bonnell) 3rd was born circa 1820 at Saint John/Westfield, Saint John/Kings, New Brunswick, Canada.[107,108] He was Baptist. He was Laborer circa 1840 at Ships Passenger list, on ship, Gypsie from NB to Boston, Boston, Suffolk, Massachusetts, USA. He immigrated in 1840.[109] He married Dora DAY (?) (Daye) before 1847 at St John, St John County, New Brunswick, Canada?[110] He married (2nd.) Mary Sohpia COTTLE, daughter of Woodbury L. COTTLE and Hannah (Margaret) D. SKINNER (Skimmer), on 11 Apr 1847 at High Street Baptist Church, Charlestown, Suffolk, Massachusetts, USA.[111,112] He appeared on the census of 1850 at Census, Boston, Massachusetts, USA.[113] He appeared on the census of 10 Dec 1851 at Canada Census, Westfield, Kings, New Brunswick, Canada.[114,115] His estate was probated on 2 Aug 1866 at Westfield, Kings, New Brunswick, Canada.[116,117] He appeared on the census of 1871 at Canadian Census, Fredericton, York, New Brunswick, Canada.[118] He was Free Christian Baptist. He died on 3 Jul 1891 at 73 Lenox St., Boston, Suffolk, Massachusetts, USA. He was buried on 5 Jul 1891 at lot 146 Field of Heth Forest Hills Cemetery, Dorchester (Boston), Suffolk, Massachusetts, USA.[119] Donna Doscher has 25X30 painting of yarn of St John c.1848-58 by Charles, Ben's brother after he broke his leg Anne #106 had it until her death circa 1995.

a) Sarah Elizabeth[4] BUNNELL (Bonnell) Record from RS141 A2/1 county vitals 1801-99,Yo,10-3,p.13,#2496,F14025 birth of George. She was born on 30 Dec 1848 at Chelsea, Suffolk, Massachusetts, USA.[120] She appeared on the census of 1850 at US Census, Charlestown, Suffolk, Massachusetts, USA.[121] She married Robert Bruce Segee (Leger), son of John Peters SEGEE and Mary Ann BLACKBURN, on 29 Jan 1870 at Fredericton, York, New Brunswick, Canada.[122,123] She immigrated in 1871.[124] She was Free Christian Baptist. She appeared on the census of 1871 at Canadian Census, Fredericton, York, New Brunswick, Canada.[125] She died after 1872 at Massachusetts? or Canada? She Richard Segee July 1997 in Jul 1997.

(1) Bessie^5 SEGEE. Her married name was Butler. She married Frank BUTLER circa 1870 at Boston, Massachusetts? She was born after 1871 at Boston, Massachusetts? Record from Richard Segee of Ontario, July 1997 in Jul 1997.

    (a) Willard^6 BUTLER was born at Boston, Massachusetts? Record from Richard Segee July 1997.

    (b) Norma^6 BUTLER was born at Boston, Massachusetts? Record from Richard Segee of Ontario, July 1997.

    (c) Audrey^6 BUTLER was born at Boston, Massachusetts? Record from Richard Segee of Ontario, July 1997.

(2) George Woodburry^5 Segee (Leger) Miss.Annie Mae/James Bonnell of Boston, listed as kin. Birth record says Segee last name. After Loyalist Building was built was Janitor til death. Record from RS141 A2/1 county vitals 1801-99,Yo,10-3,p.13,#2496,F14025 birth circa 1801. He was Free Christian Baptist. He appeared on the census of 1871 at Canadian Census, Fredericton, York, New Brunswick, Canada.[126] He was born on 4 Feb 1871 at Fredericton, York New Brunswick, Canada. He married Margaret Maud MCKENZIE, daughter of Thomas MCKENZIE Capt. and Hannah WILSON, on 8 Jun 1909 at New Brunswick Canada. MILITARY: Sadler in WWI circa 1917. He immigrated in 1917.[127] Service at 2 PM by Rev. JW Bartlett in Nov 1936 at McAdam's Funeral Home, 651 King St., Fredericton, York, New Brunswick, Canada. He was buried in Nov 1936 at Rural Cemetery, Fredericton, York, New Brunswick, Canada.[128] HEALTH: Stroke,Paralysis,died in Nov 1936 at Fredericton, York, New Brunswick, Canada. He died on 7 Nov 1936 at (In AM), Victoria Pub Hosp, Fredericton, York New Brunswick, Canada, at age 65. Record from Richard Segee, July 1997.

    (a) Venner Frank^6 SEGEE, He was in Boston Synphany Orchestra, played fiddle and had group called the Down Easterners. Worked in the CBC newsroom and was called Frank. He was also a Public Relations Consultant at Trombone Halifax, WWII,1st.Editor CBC, Ford Motor Co., Young & Rubicam Ltd, Volkswagen Can/Consult. He 1st.div.c.1947;2nd.sep.5 Apl.1982 Oakville. HEALTH: Had Cancer.

He and Janet Madelon REID were divorced. He was an Elder, St. John's, Oakville, Ontario. He and Dorothy Elizabeth FULLER were divorced. He immigrated.[129] He was born on 1 Oct 1911 at Fredericton, York, New Brunswick, Canada. He was baptized on 23 Jan 1912 at Saint Paul's Presbyterian Church, Fredericton, York, New Brunswick, Canada.[130] He was educated in Sep 1926 at Fredericton High School, Fredericton, York, New Brunswick, Canada.[131] He Left school to work for Lawlor & Cain's Hardware Store until Sept. 1927 on 8 Mar 1927 at Fredericton?, York, New Brunswick, Canada. He married Bertha Alice Marshall, daughter of Emanuel Marshall and Elizabeth Williams, on 12 May 1934 at 40 Court St., Boston, Suffolk, Massachusetts, USA.[132] He was a Doorman at marriage on 12 May 1934 at Boston, Suffolk, Massachusetts, USA. He married Janet Madelon REID, daughter of Clarence REID and Gladys Wanita STONE, in 1941 at Fredericton, York N.B, Can. He married Dorothy Elizabeth FULLER on 28 Jul 1951 at Amherst, Nova Scotia, Canada. He was Says, Public Relations Consultant, former journalist, elder of St. John's Church (Oakville), former member of the Rotary Clubs of Toronto-Eglinton & Oakville, first accredited member of the Canadian Public Relations Society, director of Toronto and national Pub. Relations Societies, chairman of Toronto branch & treasurer of the National, member of the Toronto Men's Press Club (see file for many more) in Sep 1995 at Obituary Notice, Oakville, Ontario, Canada. He died on 18 Sep 1995 at Oakville, Ontario, Canada, at age 83. He was buried on 21 Sep 1995 at Cremated, spread in Memorial Gardens of St. John's United Church, Oakville, Oakville, Ontario, Canada.[133]

i) Richard (Dick) Frank[7] SEGEE, High School Grad.22 Aug.1960,Toronto;Lakeshore Teachers College May 1964,Toronto;BA Degree, McMaster U.29 May 1975;BEd Degree,York U.Nov.1990. He immigrated.[134] He was Teacher 33 yrs(Math, Science, Computers, grades 6-8,retire 31 Dec.97(Halton school board). School taught at: Westbrook, 1964-66, Eastview, 1966-67, Lorne Skuce, 1967-74, Central, 1974-89, Champlain, 1989-97. HEALTH: Narcolepsy (sleep disorder) and Cataplexy 1997 disability past 2 yrs (part time work) Also, was operated on for spinal cord tumor, Sept. 1958 at Toronto General Hospital by Dr. Tom Morley. Record from himself in June 97, letter 30 June 97 w/gene. He had picture ancestor, Sarah(Bonnell) Segee (cardboard) by Horner Photo, Boston ,Ma. He Has Himalayan cat for past 15 yrs (1997). He was educated.[135] He was born on 10 Apr 1942 at Halifax Infirmary, Halifax, Nova Scotia, Canada.[136] He was baptized on 19 Jul 1942 at St. Thomas Church, Stanley, York, New Brunswick, Canada.[137] Vacationed in Havana after driving from Miami Beach, Fl. to Key West, Fl. then flew to Cuba in Feb 1952 at Havana, Cuba. He was associated in Nov 1969.[138] He was retired on 31 Dec 1997 at Halton Board of Education, Ontario, Canada.[139]

(3) Annie[5] Segee was born circa 1874 at Fredericton, York, New Brunswick, Canada. (From Richard Segee of Ontario) on 9 Jun 1998.

(4) Ella[5] Segee married Robert Libby at Fredericton, York, New Brunswick, Canada. She was born circa 1875 at Fredericton, York, New Brunswick, Canada. (From Richard Segee of Ontario) on 9 Jun 1998.

(5) Evangeline (Eva)[5] Segee was born circa 1880 at Fredericton, York, New Brunswick, Canada. (From Richard Segee of Ontario) on 9 Jun 1998.

(6) Arthur L.[5] Segee was born circa 1885 at Fredericton, York, New Brunswick, Canada. He died in 1887 at (2 yrs. 8 months), Fredericton, York, New Brunswick, Canada. (From Richard Segee of Ontario) on 9 Jun 1998.

(7) Harry[5] Segee was born circa 1886 at Fredericton, York, New Brunswick, Canada. He died in 1887 at (age 13 months), Fredericton, York, New Brunswick, Canada. (From Richard Segee of Ontario) on 9 Jun 1998.

b) Elizabeth[4] BUNNELL was Baptist. She was born circa 1849 at Boston, Suffolk Co., Massachusetts, USA.[140] Record from Pre 1851 Chelsea census before 1851 at Chelsea Mass. Census, Chelsea, Massachusetts, USA. HEALTH: Died at birth before 1851. She died circa 1851 at Chelsea, Suffolk Co., Massachusetts, USA.[141]

c) Woodbury⁴ BUNNELL Birth record in file. He was Baptist? He was born on 29 Jun 1851 at Bennington St., East Boston, Suffolk, Massachusetts, USA.[142] He appeared on the census of 1871 at Canada census, Fredericton, York, New Brunswick, Canada.[143] He immigrated in 1871.[144]

d) George⁴ BUNNELL immigrated.[145] He was born circa 1852 at USA. He was Free Christian Baptist. He appeared on the census of 1871 at Canadian Census, Fredericton, York, New Brunswick, Canada.[146]

e) Hannah⁴ BUNNELL Possibly her listed as FC Baptist from Kings County, NB, but listed as Normal School Students, Fredericton, NB Jan.1885.Could also be #71 too? She was born circa 1855 at Fredericton, York, New Brunswick, Canada.[147] She was Free Christian Baptist. She immigrated in 1871.[148] She appeared on the census of 1871 at Canadian Census, Fredericton, York, New Brunswick, Canada.[149] Transcribe by Daniel Johnson on 15 Jan 1885 at The Fredericton Evening Star Newspaper (Thursday), Fredericton, York, New Brunswick, Canada.

f) Evangeline⁴ BUNNELL was born circa 1858 at Westfield?, Kings, New Brunswick, Canada. She was Free Christian Baptist. She immigrated in 1871.[150] She appeared on the census of 1871 at Canadian Census, Fredericton, York, New Brunswick, Canada.[151]

g) Mary⁴ BUNNELL was born in 1860 at Fredericton?, York, New Brunswick, Canada.[152] She was Free Christian Baptist. She immigrated in 1871.[153] She appeared on the census of 1871 at Canadian Census, Fredericton, York, New Brunswick, Canada.[154]

h) James Edward⁴ BUNNELL (Bonnell) was born in Jul 1860 at Saint John/Fredericton, Saint John, New Brunswick, Canada.[155] He appeared on the census of 1871 at Canadian Census, Fredericton, York, New Brunswick, Canada.[156] He was First Church Baptist listed with parents and family. He immigrated circa 1883 to Boston, Massachusetts, USA.[157] He married Minnie COLLINS, daughter of John COLLINS and Mary (--?--), on 10 Mar 1885 at Fredericton, York Co., New Brunswick, Canada. His Child #15 baptism record says Eliz. mom, born out of wed-lock? Record from Boston Diocese record center on 18 Jan 1897 at Boston, Suffolk, New Brunswick,

He married Elizabeth KELLY, daughter of James C. KELLY (Kelley) and Fannie Francis (Annie Francis) BRENNAN, on 7 Mar 1898 at Boston, Suffolk, Massachusetts, USA. He lived on 13 Mar 1899 at 7 Jamaica Place, Boston, Suffolk, Massachusetts, USA.[158] He appeared on the census of 1900 at US Census, Boston, Suffolk, Massachusetts, USA.[159,160] His Child, Elizabeth born but died possibly at birth after 1905? at Jamaica Plain, Suffolk, Massachusetts, USA. His Child.#1-9,not sure where they went after 1887,child.#10-14 given away after Liz. death circa 1910 at Catholic Homes, Boston, Suffolk, Massachusetts, USA. He was listed as "Intemperate" The children were taken away from both of them circa 1910 at Boston Court System, Boston, Suffolk, Massachusetts, USA. He appeared on the census of 1910 at 10 Benton St., Boston, Suffolk, Massachusetts, USA.[161,162] He was General Laborer/Brass worker & Press Finisher at time of death in 1937 at 6 Boardman St. (son George's home), Amesbury, Essex, Massachusetts, USA. He was buried in Feb 1937 at Union Cemetery (Lot E-23), Amesbury, Essex, Massachusetts, USA.[163] He died on 1 Feb 1937 at 6 Boardman St, Amesbury, Essex Co, Mass, at age 76. HEALTH: died of Cerebral Hemorrhage/Hypertension. He was a big man with white hair and loved to smoke a pipe, and drink. He did not drink much while in Amesbury because everyone was too poor to buy any. (Some info. from George W. Bunnell Jr. 11 June 1998) on 1 Feb 1937 at 6 Boardman St. (son George's home), Amesbury, Essex, Massachusetts, USA. Was given a Quaker Service conducted by Ed Mair of the Amesbury Meeting House
on 21 Sep 2002 at Union Cemetery Stone Placement, Amesbury, Essex, Massachusetts, USA during Bunnell/Bertogli Family reunion. He never had a stone.

(1) Chester[5] Bunnell was born after Apr 1885 at Kings, New Brunswick, Canada.

(2) Agnes[5] BUNNELL was Catholic? She immigrated after 1885 to Boston, Suffolk, Massachusetts, USA.[164] She was born after Apr 1885 at Kings, New Brunswick, Canada.

(3) Woodbury[5] BUNNELL (Bonnell) was Catholic. He immigrated after 1885 to Boston, Suffolk, Massachusetts, USA.[165] He was born after Apr 1885 at Kings, New Brunswick, Canada.

(4) Hannah[5] BUNNELL was Catholic. She was born after Apr 1885 at Kings, New Brunswick, Canada.[166] She Lived with Anne on Charles River, Boston, Ma., later So. Carolina with Mary Talbos until death, had cloth knitted by ancestor, possibly Charles Bunnell/Bonnell circa 1930 at Charles River Apartment, Boston, Suffolk, Massachusetts, USA. She died after 1930 at Boston, Suffolk, Massachusetts, USA.

(5) Frederick (Frank)[5] BUNNELL (Bonnell) was Catholic. He immigrated in 1885 to Boston, Suffolk, Massachusetts, USA.[167] He was born in Jun 1885 at Fredericton, York, New Brunswick, Canada.[168,169] He appeared on the census of 1900 at Census, Boston, Suffolk, Massachusetts, USA.[170,171] He lived on 16 Apr 1907 at 29 Ball St., Boston, Suffolk, Massachusetts, USA.[172] He married Agnes (Grace) M. Marcy, daughter of Theodore Marcy and Mary Martin, on 16 Apr 1907 at Boston, Suffolk, Massachusetts, USA.[173,174] He lived on 28 Jan 1924 at 158 Eustis St, Boston, Suffolk, Massachusetts, USA.[175,176] He lived on 10 Dec 1928 at 64 Alpine St., Boston, Suffolk, Massachusetts, USA.[177,178] He died on 30 Apr 1946 at Boston City Hospital, Boston, Suffolk, Massachusetts, USA, at age 60.[179,180] He was buried circa 1 May 1946 at Calvary (New?) Cemetery, Boston, Suffolk, Massachusetts, USA.[181]

(a) Theodore James[6] BUNNELL[182] was born after 1910 at Massachusetts, USA.

(b) Frederick (Frank) James[6] BUNNELL.[183] MILITARY: Officer in US Army circa 1918. He was born on 3 Jan 1922 at 158 Eustis St, Boston, Suffolk, Massachusetts, USA.[184,185] He lived on 9 Sep 1950 at 5 Kenisington St, Roxbury, Suffolk, Massachusetts, USA.[186] He married Alice Jean Ellen Craig, daughter of Milton Craig and Mabel Keenan, on 9 Sep 1950 at Boston, Suffolk, Massachusetts, USA.[187,188] He lived on 26 Oct 1952 at 98 Rossmore Rd., Jamaica Plain, Suffolk, Massachusetts, USA.[189,190] He was listed as Mechanic on 23 Dec 1953 at 98 Rossmore Rd., Jamaica Plain, Suffolk, Massachusetts, USA.[191] He was Listed as Car Inspector on 30 Mar 1956 at 98 Rossmore Rd., Jamaica Plain, Suffolk,

Massachusetts, USA. He was Listed as a Post Office Worker/Clerk on 7 Aug 1957 at 98 Rossmore Rd., Jamaica Plain, Suffolk, Massachusetts, USA.[192] He lived on 12 Dec 1965 at 45 Peter Parley Rd., Boston, Suffolk, Massachusetts, USA.[193,194] He died on 14 Oct 1997 at Jamaica Plain, Suffolk, Massachusetts, USA, at age 75.[195]

    i) Karen Marie[7] BUNNELL[196] married Martin F. Mulvey.[197] She was born on 26 Oct 1952 at Jamaica Plain, Suffolk, Massachusetts, USA.[198]

    ii) Theodore Francis[7] BUNNELL[199] married Donna M. Comeau.[200] He was born on 23 Dec 1953 at Jamaica Plain, Suffolk, Massachusetts, USA.[201]

    iii) Frederick James[7] BUNNELL[202] was born on 30 Mar 1956 at Jamaica Plain, Suffolk, Massachusetts, USA.[203]

    iv) Thomas Austin[7] BUNNELL[204] married Lynne M. Comeau.[205] He was born on 7 Aug 1957 at Jamaica Plain, Suffolk, Massachusetts, USA.[206]

    v) Mary Christine[7] BUNNELL[207] was born on 12 Dec 1965 at Boston, Suffolk, Massachusetts, USA.[208]

(c) Francis Xavier[6] BUNNELL.[209] He was born on 28 Jan 1924 at Boston Hospital, Boston/Roxbury, Suffolk, Massachusetts, USA.[210,211] He lived on 22 May 1948 at 5 Kensington St., Boston, Suffolk, Massachusetts, USA.[212,213] He married Lorraine Theresa Duplace, daughter of Edward Duplace and Catherine Sharkey, on 22 May 1948 at Everett, Middlesex, Massachusetts, USA.[214] He was MILITARY (an unknown value) in 1949 at US Army.[215] He lived on 24 May 1949 at 556 Massachusetts Ave., Boston, Suffolk, Massachusetts, USA.[216] He lived on 8 Jul 1953 at 40 Vallar St., Boston, Suffolk, Massachusetts, USA.[217,218] He lived on 9 Mar 1956 at 593 Broadway, Chelsea, Massachusetts, USA.[219,220] He died on 9 Oct 1974 at VA Hospital, Chelsea, Suffolk, Massachusetts, USA, at age 50.[221,222] He lived on 9 Oct 1974 at 86 Tudor St., Chelsea, Massachusetts, USA.[223] He was buried circa 10 Oct 1974 at Woodlawn Cemetery, Everett, Massachusetts, USA.[224]

    i) Lorraine Theresa[7] BUNNELL[225] was born circa 24 May 1949 at Waltham, Massachusetts, USA.[226]

    ii) Stephen Frances[7] BUNNELL[227] married Susan Lyne Knowles at USA.[228] He was born on 8 Jul 1953 at Waltham, Massachusetts, USA.[229]

        (a) Michael Francis[8] BUNNELL[230]

    iii) Denise Katherine[7] BUNNELL[231] married James G. Bain at USA.[232] She was born on 9 Mar 1956 at Chelsea, Massachusetts, USA.[233]

    (d) Agnes Theresa[6] BUNNELL[234] married John F. Moore at USA.[235] She was born on 10 Dec 1928 at Boston, Suffolk, Massachusetts, USA.[236]

(6) Malvina[5] BUNNELL was Catholic. Record from Boston city birth register 1887,p.216 in 1887. She was born on 24 Jan 1887 at Fredericton, York, New Brunswick, Canada.[237,238] She married Daniel F. Sullivan, son of Bartholomew Sullivan and Ellen Kelliker, on 8 Feb 1909 at Boston, Suffolk, Massachusetts, USA.[239] She lived on 8 Feb 1909 at 66 Warwick st., Boston, Suffolk, Massachusetts, USA.[240]

(7) Melinsa[5] BUNNELL was Catholic. She was born before Feb 1888 at Kings, New Brunswick, Canada. She appeared on the census of 1900 at US Census, Boston, Suffolk, Massachusetts, USA.[241,242]

(8) James Henry[5] BUNNELL Beau was Catholic. He was born on 18 Jan 1896 at Jamaica Plain/Boston, Suffolk, Massachusetts, USA.[243,244] He was baptized on 2 May 1896 at St. Thomas Catholic Church, Jamaica

Plain, Suffolks?, Massachusetts, USA.[245] Born 2 yrs before parents marr on 7 Mar.1898, baptism record says Eliz was mom on 7 Mar 1898 at Boston, Suffolk, Massachusetts, USA. He appeared on the census of 6 Jun 1900 at Census, 8 Jamaica Place, Jamaica Plain, Suffolk, Massachusetts, USA.[246] He appeared on the census of 1910 at US Census, Boston, Suffolk, Massachusetts, USA.[247] He immigrated in 1917 to 23 Centre St., Roxbury, Suffolk, Massachusetts, USA.[248] He appeared on the census of 1920 at US Census, Camp Devine, Massachusetts, USA.[249,250] MILITARY: In 1920 at US Army, Camp Devine, Massachusetts, USA.[251] He was Auto Mechanic 1932 in 1932 at Bronx, New York, USA. He died on 4 Feb 1932 at St. Francis Hospital (12:05 AM), Bronx, Bronx, New York, USA, at age 36.[252] HEALTH: Died of chronic myocarditis/acute cardiodilitation, only age 33 on 4 Feb 1932 at Bronx, New York, USA. He was buried circa 6 Feb 1932 at St. Raymond Cemetery, Bronx, Bronx, New York, USA.[253,254] Some info from Bill Sheridan, of Oxnard, California. He says lived with brother Ben/May, at Yonkers, NY, called Bo/Beau circa 1988 at Oxnard, Ventura, California, USA.

(9) (Un-named)[5] Bunnell was born on 9 Apr 1907 at 10 Benton St., Boston, Suffolk, Massachusetts, USA.[255] He/she died on 19 Apr 1907 at 10 Benton St., Boston, Suffolk, Massachusetts, USA.[256,257] He/she was buried circa 20 Apr 1907 at Mount Benedict Cemetery, Boston, Suffolk, Massachusetts, USA.[258]

(10) Benjamin (Franklin) Francis[5] BUNNELL was Catholic. He lived in 1899 at 55 Cabot St., Jamaica Plain, Suffolk, Massachusetts, USA.[259] He was born on 13 Mar 1899 at Jamaica Plain, Suffolk, Massachusetts, USA.[260,261] He was baptized on 17 Mar 1899 at St. Thomas Catholic Church, Jamaica Plain, Suffolk, Massachusetts, USA.[262] He appeared on the census of 1900 at US Census, Jamaica Plain, Suffolk, Massachusetts, USA.[263] He appeared on the census of 1910 at US Census, Jamaica Plain, Suffolk, Massachusetts, USA.[264] He married May (May) M SHERIDAN, daughter of Rose (--?--), on 26 Sep 1928 at St. Luke's Catholic Church, New York City, New York, New York, USA.[265] He was a nice man and took care of my father's family when he was young circa 1930. He was Bookie in NY? Called Mayor of Van Cortlandt Park East. He obviously held some kind of neighborhood status? circa 1930 at Van Cortlandt Park East, Bronx, New York, USA. He immigrated circa 1935.[266] He Gave me

(Paul) coca cola truck with bottles & tools in 1953 when we stopped over in NYC on way to California, never forgot that in 1953 at Van Cortlandt Park East, Bronx, New York, USA. He died in Jul 1964 at 4320 Van Cortlandt Park East apt. 2C (zip. 10470), Bronx, New York, USA, at age 65.[267] He was buried in Jul 1964 at Caverly Queens Cemetery, Bronx?, New York?, USA.[268] He immigrated circa 1970 to Coral Gables, Florida, USA.[269]

  (a) Genevive[6] Bunnell was born after 1930 at Bronx?, New York, USA. She married ? Breen after 1950 at USA. She lived circa 1975 at Falmouth?, Barnstable?, Massachusetts, USA.[270]

(11) George Woodbury[5] BUNNELL Sr. His Social Security Number was (an unknown value) at 011-05-7100. He was Catholic. He was born on 21 May 1901 at 80 Williams St., Boston, Suffolk, Massachusetts, USA.[271] He was baptized on 9 Jun 1901 at St. Francis de Sales Catholic Church, Roxbury, Massachusetts, USA.[272] He immigrated circa 1910 to Foster Home, Boston, Suffolk, Massachusetts, USA.[273] He, Charles, Joe taken under neglect law by Mr. Proctor, SPCC from Roxbury court by Mr.Pyne,6 May 1915 to 29 Oct.1925-see file circa 1910 at Foster Care, Jamaica Plain, Suffolk, Massachusetts, USA. On 8 Jul 1916 lived at Annry(?) St., Jamaica Plain, Massachusetts, USA. He was educated on 14 Oct 1916 at State Industrial School, Shirley, Massachusetts, USA.[274] He was later a Forman and retired between 1959-62? circa 1920 at Amesbury Hat shop, Amesbury, Essex, Massachusetts, USA. He was listed as a Butcher. Ref. Claude Bunnell records 100-0035-0001-089 in 1920 at Home of Correction, Boston, Suffolk, Massachusetts, USA. He lived in 1920 at 23 Centre St., Boston, Suffolk, Massachusetts, USA.[275] He married Maria Angela BERTOGLI, daughter of Luigi BERTOGLI and Caterina Domenica Maria ORI, on 26 Nov 1920 at Boston, Suffolk, Massachusetts, USA.[276] He lived on 20 Jan 1921 at Warren Ave., Boston, Suffolk, Massachusetts, USA.[277] He lived on 2 Jan 1922 at 4 Boardman St., Amesbury, Essex, Massachusetts, USA.[278] He lived on 20 Dec 1922 at 4 Boardman St., Amesbury, Essex, Massachusetts, USA.[279] He lived on 14 Mar 1924 at Boston, Suffolk, Massachusetts, USA.[280] He lived on 18 Jan 1931 at 4 Horton St., Amesbury, Essex, Massachusetts, USA.[281] He lived on 5 Aug 1940 at 6 Boardman St., Amesbury, Essex,

Massachusetts, USA.[282] He lived in 1951 at 4 Boardman St., Amesbury, Essex, Massachusetts, USA.[283] HEALTH: Died of Emphysema. He also smoked. Moved to California with son James for his health in 1960, but returned. He died on 3 Oct 1964 at Amesbury Hospital, Amesbury, Essex, Massachusetts, USA, at age 63.[284] He was buried on 6 Oct 1964 at St. Joseph Cemetery, Amesbury, Essex, Massachusetts, USA.

    (a) James Henry[6] BUNNELL Sr. He loved camping and fishing. Was very good with his hands as a carpenter, etc. He was Catholic. He was born on 20 Jan 1921 at 4 Boardman St., Amesbury, Essex, Massachusetts, USA.[285] He was baptized on 3 Jul 1921 at St. Joseph Catholic Church, Amesbury, Essex, Massachusetts, USA.[286] He was educated on 10 Sep 1938 at CCC Camp, Salisbury, Essex, Massachusetts, USA.[287] He married Lorraine Muriel VIOLETTE, daughter of Joseph Alfred (Albert) VIOLETTE and Alma BELANGER, on 6 Jun 1941 at St. Joseph Church, Amesbury, Essex County, Ma. He was living here and listed as a Hatter (at Hat Shop). Mass. Vital Records 009-2/199 on 7 Jun 1941 at 6 Boardman St., Amesbury, Essex, Massachusetts, USA. MILITARY: (398 Army Cps,Eng,WWII,Euro/S.Pacif.1942-5)(He had listed in a French Language booklet the following friends - PFC Anthony J. Cataldo of 1053 rd. Eng. PCR group,US Army APO 350, and Gregory Burkr of Co. F, Chester Jones Co., C 1308 Eng. APO 775, US Army, and Selvester D. Hoover, ASN 39289916, 398 Eng. Regiment Co. A. APO 513 c/o PM NY, NY, and PFC H. J. Sweet, RSN 31291039, APO 129, GFRC, US Army) after 20 Sep 1942 at US Army Corps of Engineers. Prepared to go to Europe, overseas shipment. Got shots, equipment, took care of affairs) on 5 Jul 1943 at Camp Claiborne, Arkansas, USA. Troop trains left for Camp Shanks at 2100 on 17 Jul 1943 at Camp Claiborne, Arkansas, USA. Boarded the silent gray hull of the Queen Mary with 20,000 on board, sleeping quarters a major problem with shifts set up, finding a place to sleep was hard. Crossing was smooth, but German subs and planes were always nearby on 23 Jul 1943 at Pier 90, New York City, New York, USA. Arrived, and loaded on troop trains. The 398th. had to stay behind and clean the ship. They did not leave until 1 August) on 30 Jul 1943 at Queen Mary, Greenock, Scotland, Britain. Left Queen Mary and traveled through Scotland to LeMarchant Camp one mile west of Devizes occupying several old buildings for a short while on 1 Aug 1943 at Devizes, Wiltshire, England, Britain. Arrived in England with 398 Eng., G5 Regiment on 1 Aug 1943 at England. Relocated to a hill a mile west of Braunton,

North Devon, C & E Co., pitched pup-tents in fields surrounded by stone walls. Many other companies nearby. A Co. was 3 miles SE of Crowcombe; B Co. & 1st. Batt. at Camp Brymore, one mile west of Cannington, all places near shire of Somerset. D Co. was one mile north of Bideford; Co. F half mile south of Croyde; doing many things there till 31 Dec. 1943, mess halls, housing for 4250 men, laid 5000 feet of water line, reservoir for 150,000 gallons of water, sewer for 40,000 gallons, several miles of roads, plus scores of other projects) on 7 Aug 1943 at Braunton, North Devon, Britain. Hosted Christmas dinner, turkey, sweet potato, cranberry sauce, olives, stuffing to English children at mess hall from GI mess gear. Soldiers saved for candy and gum from their rations. Going home the English children sang Yankee tunes) on 25 Dec 1943 at Braunton, North Devon, Britain. He was issued a German Language Guide with John C. H. Lee, Lt. General instructing us to not trust any German's during the occupation of Germany in 1944 at Germany. Moved 9 miles northwest of town. More construction was ordered on 16 Mar 1944 at Headquarters, Taunton, Somerset, Britain. Completed Naval Supply Depot at Exeter, 10,000 foot runway, 1500 man tent camp with other buildings, Failand Golf Course tented camp for 1500 & buildings, anti-tank range at Kilve Range with roads and buildings at Highbridge POL Depot, and office buildings at Morthoe Camp, roads and parking spaces, 1000 men tent camp at Brymore House Camp with mess hall, sewer lines, The Taunton Shop Detail made 150 timber guard houses and 5000 2-story bed assemblies., 1500 man camp at Alfaxton Park, 1000 man camp at Houndstone and many other locations) on 15 Apr 1944 at Britain. After the invasion of France the 398th. still remained station at Porthcawl, England. Restlessness came over all of us. Moods were high) on 6 Jun 1944 at D-Day, Normandy, France. Basic training, mock & simulated tactical problems at sand-dunes, demolition theories, hikes, rifle marksmanship. Queen's Field Camp near Porthcawl's center was headquarters to port construction exercise, building Bailey Bridges between sand dunes, laying railroad tracks. This hard work went on for 9 1/2 months at Porthcawl before 1 Jul 1944 at Kenfig, Britain. We were finally alerted, mission not known yet. Morale went higher. Our port construction training in Wales would soon come into play. At last we would do something) on 2 Jul 1944 at Porthcawl, Britain. The 2nd. Battalion less Co. D moved by train & convoy to Melbury Park, Dorest, pitched tents and waited for the go-ahead) on 3 Jul 1944 at Britain. Battalion and several companies left for Portland Embarking area. Our heels were cooled with a long wait in rain-drenched camps. Weeks went by on 5 Jul 1944 at Swanage, Dorsetshire, Britain. Finally alerted for crossing the channel on 30 Jul 1944 at English Channel, Britain. Channel crossing began after waiting one year to the day on 1 Aug 1944 at Weymouth, Britain. Landed at 1600 hours and hiked 8 miles to our bivouac. Ships used were the Queen Emma on the 2 August 1944. This crossing made many soldiers sea sick. Morale was good. Upon reaching Utah Beach many will never forget the hulls, stacks, bows and sterns of ships nosed out of their watery graves. This was once a might Nazi stronghold. The hike in was sobering, seeing artillery holes and signs for land mines. Destruction was everywhere. Arriving at bivouac children yelled out to us for gum. That night we all heard front line artillery on 3 Aug 1944 at Utah Beach, Normandy, France. Morning trucks took us here to board trains for Cherbourg. There trucks took us to a field/hill 1 1/2 miles south of the city overlooking the port on 4 Aug 1944 at Chef du Pont, France. Andrew Tully newspaper coverage says: "4 hours after the first wave of assault troops had landed on the beaches on D-Day dawn a battalion from this (398th) outfit swarmed ashore through heavy fire, got its bulldozers operating as soon as they hit the beach, and by sunset had carved the first Allied airstrip on French soil, later to be more than a dozen such strips under fire and always under conditions which would try the toughest South Boston civilian contractor. In Cherbourg, they call it a rough town, lively during the day and full of fist fights and gun play during blackout" on 11 Aug 1944 at Normandy, France.[288] Lt. Col. Griffith was relieved of command and Lt. Col. Addison H. Douglass became new regimental commander. Here, we received the first orders for construction against Germany on 15 Aug 1944 at Cherbourg, France. Work assignments began in Cherbourg with building Regimental and Medical Headquarters and H & S Company moved to Le Mont du Roc 2 miles SE of Cherbourg, First Battalion took over former German gun emplacements and barracks on a hill in view of harbor. Second Battalion occupied Fort du Hommet (nicknamed Fort du Vommit) in Cherbourg's arsenal. After total destruction of the harbor by German's the 398th. brought it back to double function doing a magnificent job, removing all mines and bombs) on 15 Aug 1944 at Cherbourg, France. From photo newspaper of him and newsman Andrew Tully at pillbox near Cherbourg lighting cigarette for Jim. Article says "tough builders of Normandy plane strips under hot Nazi fire win high praise. This is the hangout of the bearded, hard cussing gang that made possible the air invasion and air occupation of France. These engineers, few of whom could get a screen test in the hearts and flowers department, are living a life that would have the bobby sock set gasping if it were put on film. They do a job without which the glamour guys of the fighter and bomber commands could not add to their glamour. Later while watching a crew maneuver a line of German tank cars over a railroad crossing, where power lines dropped dangerously, a yank waltzed over to the crossroads pillbox where I was standing to get a light for his cigarette. Yep, you guessed it, he's a Massachusetts boy. Private James H. Bunnell of 6 Boardman street, Amesbury" circa 17 Aug 1944 at Cherbourg Center, Normandy, France. Promoted from Private to Private First Class. He was an engineer rifleman circa 17 Aug 1944 at Cherbourg?, Normandy, France. German prisoners of war were used for menial work under the supervision of the 398th. The harbor became host to many Victory ships large and small creating a massive construction marvel. Nothing was impossible to the 398th. They could build anything. The salvage of German, American and French equipment was another big program of theirs circa 18 Aug 1944 at Cherbourg, France. Jim was one of the first participants of the 398th. American Army Soldiers in Western Europe football team playing in the first game circa 1 Sep 1944 at Cherbourg, France. First call sounded for the "Forty-and-Eight" trip to an unknown destination leaving at 0600 hours that turned out to be Verdun, Meuse, France. Conditions were horrible at the train station. Leaving at 0800 hours they could not lay or sit in the crowded boxcars because of nails coming through the floors. Losing out on the football title back at Cherbourg all they had to eat was K-rations which passed off as coffee on 8 Dec 1944 at 0500 hours, Cherbourg, France. The 3 day trip was terrible, smelly, cramped, cold and unforgettable. Shaving before arrival impossible, spilling water and bumping into each other, cuts and bleeding everywhere. Arrived late, long after dark. Headquarters were established at 9 Place du Cathedral across from the Verdun Cathedral, and 2nd. Battalion at Caserne Anthouard. Our assignment was to rebuild and remodel for hospital space circa 10 Dec 1944 at Verdun, France. German Field Marshall von Rundstedt's breakthrough was an all out Nazi offensive which concerned all. Many were killed on both sides on 16 Dec 1944 at Ardennes, France. The shield above this gate was adopted to be the shield of the 398th. Words say "Factum est" which means "It is done" circa 20 Dec 1944 at Verdun Gate, Verdun, France. He was MILITARY (All work in Verdun was halted. By 1800 hours the advance partly left by motor convoy to an unknown destination in Luxembourg. At 2000 hours First Battalion followed. There, the 398th. was attached to Task Force Reed, XII Corps, Third Army, and advanced with them to Sandweiler. Here is where Jim saw General George S. Patton on 22 Dec 1944 at 1500 hours, Verdun, France.

Convoy provided by the Twelfth Army Group left at 2000 hours, assembled near Moutfort, heavy enemy air attacks were everywhere. The 398th. was now attached to the Second Cavalry Reconnaissance Squadron Co. A of 808th. Tank Destroyer Batt. Combat Team Costello of 4th. Infantry Div. occupied Ihnen to Mertert to defend crossing by enemy at Moselle River, and later extended 9.6 kilometers between Ihnen and northern Wormeldange on 23 Dec 1944 at Luxembourg. By 1800 hours the 4th. Infantry was relieved every position was watched by the enemy. All the 398th. weapons gotten at Cherbourg; machine guns and rocket launchers were taken by Normandy Base Section. All they had here was what was left by the 4th. Infantry. Ten days later we were finally supplied with M-1's to replace our 03's on 24 Dec 1944 at Christmas Eve, Luxembourg. Spent day improving defense lines between Ihnen and Ahn because of heavy artillery fire. On the first 398th. patrolling mission, one engineer was wounded by an exploding booby trap near Syre on 25 Dec 1944 at Christmas Day, Luxembourg. Pushing back enemy troops, heavy artillery and mortar fire. Patrols went out from Mertert on 26 Dec 1944 at Moselle (near), Luxembourg. Pinned down by heavy gun fire, a patrol manages to escape. 398th assigned to booby trap area for enemy patrols out of Grevenmacher-"Moselle Ghost Town." on 27 Dec 1944 at Machtum, Luxembourg. Germans sent out night patrols for US Army info. from these areas and the east bank of the Moselle River coming within their lines. The 398th. and Second Cavalry invaded German held positions on 28 Dec 1944 at (Early hours), Machtum/Mertert/Grevenmacher, Germany? The 398th. & Second Cavalry attacked German positions and returned at 2345 hours with enemy positions on the Moselle's (River) east side near Wincheringen) on 29 Dec 1944 at (1900 hours), Machtum/Mertert/Grevenmacher, Germany? A 12 man patrol crossed the thin ice of the Moselle River going 3 miles into enemy territory (Wincheringen). They encountered a nest of 5 enemy machine guns. Four men, 3 from the 398th. were cut down. Rescue was impossible and later only one was found alive. Friendly artillery fire came down on Machtum followed by the Second Cavalry Tank attack. A 398th. platoon occupied a hill overlooking Machtum at 1630 hours where a German prisoner was taken for interrogation. Another platoon of the 398th. attacked another hill and removed an enemy strong point. The Germans through a 3 hour attack of 88mm mortar barrage on 31 Dec 1944 at (1900 hours), Machtum/Mertert/Grevenmacher, Germany? The 398th. withdrew because of lack of tank support with no wounded. At 1140 hours a 10 minute air attack began on Wecker, about 30 500 pound bombs.

The 398th. quickly repaired all access areas. It was later found to be American B-17's attacking by mistake. Heavy fighting throughout the day, by air and ground. Many Germans were killed. The 398th. took over their positions with only 9 wounded on 1 Jan 1945 at (0300 hours), Machtum, Germany?[289] On German soil a Nazi patrol attacked our outpost and wounded 2 from the 398th. while in their foxholes. The Germans quickly retreat on 2 Jan 1945 at (night) Moselle River Area, Germany? Reginental Headquarters moved from Biwer to near Bucholz. Col. Douglass slipped on ice and hurt himself. Lt. Col. William S. Kingsbury Jr. assumed command. One Sunday service by our Chaplain cause quite a sight when everyone was singing "Old Rugged Cross" and looking over the Moselle River to the enemy side several saw a Nazi kneeling and praying with us all on 3 Jan 1945 at Bucholz, Germany? German patrol attacked and killed 2 from the 398th at their machine gun position. The ground was now covered with snow and the detection of the white clad German troops were difficult. We wore table cloths and curtains, "Any damn thing. Just as long as we can remain unseen." on 6 Jan 1945 at (night) Moselle River Area, Germany?[290] Another attack was made at Machtum by the Second Cavalry and the 398th. With friendly fire they entered the town from the east and were pinned down in cellars by mortar fire. Other platoons were held up on hills and near a river just south of town. By daybreak the Germans pounded us from Nittel. We had to retreat on 9 Jan 1945 at o200 hours, Moselle River Area, Germany? This town finally fell to our forces on 10 Jan 1945 at Machtum, Germany?[291] On this day we were relieved by the 1252nd. and 1258th. Engineers Combat Battalions. We were no longer "green" thanks to the Second Cavalry. Highlighting Luxembourg can only bring to mind Champagne and schnapps because of the poor water. We learned how effective the German artillery was at Oberdonven, Manternach, Bucholz, Grevenmacher and the lines from Mertert to Ihnen, as far back as Lenningen, Niederdonven and Syre. During the past 31 days snow fell giving many positions away. It was a brave attempt to divert the 11th. Panzer Division who were at Saarburg. The crossing of the Moselle River was a victory on 23 Jan 1945 at Moselle River Area, Germany? Our mission here was complete and we were sent back by motor convoy and train to Sissonne, France where our work orders originated on 24 Jan 1945 at 0600 hours, Luxembourg.[292] From 25 Jan. to 5 July 1945 built camp and hospital and prepared to return to the United States on 25 Jan 1945 at Sissonne, France. Our most respected ceremony by Col. Kingsbury and the Chaplain Jones giving honor to all the men in the 398th. and to pay homage to all free-loving people. Galen F. Ebie played taps on his trumpet while our flag was lowered half-mast on 4 Feb 1945 at Sissone Post Theater, Sissone, France. Over 500 men from the 398th. were recruited (as they called it, "Infantry Draft") and sent to the shrinking front lines in Germany to help end the war quickly. New blood from the states came into the 398th. and cautiously took the place of old ones who left. Tensions were high with the original 398th members left behind with the new rookies. Vailly-sur-Aisne served as a major place for our ceremonies. French turned out in large numbers for appreciation before May 1945 at Sissone, France. The 398th. was included in the redeployment plan for shipment to the Pacific front by way of a 30 day furlough in the United States. We were homeward bound on 15 Jun 1945 at Camp Chicago, Sissone?, France. Drank allotted two bottles of beer and say around for the next 6 days, played Baseball and had close order drills on 5 Jul 1945 at Camp Chicago, Sissone?, France. Boarded French troop trains at St. Erme and the next day arrived at Camp Herbert Tarreyton. Thoughts were that we would soon leave on Liberty ships for the United States, but after a week wait, we boarded the Marine Wolf and crossed the English Channel to Southampton, England on 8 Jul 1945 at St. Erme, France. Waited here for nearly two weeks. Gave us opportunity to visit London and old friends, and travel circa 15 Jul 1945 at Camp Barton Stacey, Southampton?, England. Boarded a British troop train and went to Greenock, Scotland arriving on the 28th.on 27 Jul 1945 at Camp Barton Stacey, Southampton?, England. Upon arrival we boarded and at 1700 hours began our journey home. 15,000 GIs were on board. It is not known that Jim was on board because he served in Japan and never made it home on this trip. His ship was re-routed to the Panama Canal headed to Japan on 28 Jul 1945 at Queen Mary, Greenock, Scotland. Arrived in the area of Japan and was issued a restricted Japanese Phrase Book. Also given an Army issue (green) Soldiers & Sailors Prayer Book

before Oct 1945 at Japan. This was a classification card from the service after his discharge. It said: Order #10,748, classed at 1-C Discharged on 30 Oct 1945. He lived on 28 Jul 1946 at 65 Market St., Amesbury, Essex, Massachusetts, USA.[293] He lived in 1951 at 6 Boardman St., Amesbury, Essex, Massachusetts, USA.[294] He was Living here and was a Meterman. From Mass. Vital Records 009-2/376 on 5 Jan 1953 at 6 Boardman st., Amesbury, Essex, Massachusetts, USA. Worked here for a short time. Record Ref. B318-V05-P47 in Jun 1953 at Lockheed Aircraft Company, Burbank, Los Angeles, California, USA.

He immigrated circa Aug 1953 to 13331 Penny St., Pacoima, Los Angeles, California, USA.[295] He was employed at Stainless Steel, Burbank, California (Sheet Metal worker) from 1953 to c.1970 circa Aug 1953 at Stainless Steel Co., Burbank, Los Angeles, California, USA. He immigrated in 1959 to 20149 Parthinia St., Canoga Park, Los Angeles, California, USA.[296] He immigrated in 1963 to Independence St., Canoga Park, Los Angeles, California, USA.[297] He immigrated circa 1964 to Independence St. (2nd. location), Canoga Park, Los Angeles, California, USA.[298] He immigrated circa 1969 to Off Vanowen St., Canoga Park, Los Angeles, California, USA.[299] He immigrated circa 1971 to Syskiou Campground, Mount Shasta, Syskiou, California, USA.[300] He belonged to the Employees Recreation and Welfare Club. Has card in file signed by president, Don E. Brennan on 28 Apr 1972 at Stainless Steel Products, Burbank, California, USA. He immigrated circa 1974 to Main St., Susanville, Lassen, California, USA.[301] He was Owner of the store circa 1974 at Bunnell Books, Susanville, Lassen, California, USA. He immigrated circa 1976 to Eagle Lake, Lassen, California, USA.[302] While living at Eagle Lake they worked for "Give A Hoot"
of PO Box 24434, San Jose, Ca. Edna Hanes, making owls out of the special large pine cones found in their area. They made 50 cents per cone plus when they put them together, they made between $1 to $1.50 each circa 1976 at Eagle Lake, Susanville area, Lasson, California, USA. Jim and Lorraine received a letter from the Chief of Naval Staff, Vedbaek, Denmark, Office of the SledgePatrol saying: "Having received your letter dealing with voluntary military service in northern Greenland, I sincerely regret to inform you that only Danish subjects, who are or have been officers or non-commissioned officers in the Danish Armed Forces, will be accepted. The reason for this is that the said special military unit among other things have the civil authority as police. Sincerely yours, Mogens N. Guldbrandsen, Commander. (They were hoping to be stationed in Greenland manning a post out in natures wilderness) on 29 Mar 1976 at 602 Main St., Susanville, Lasson, California, USA. He immigrated circa 1977 to Beaverton, Clackamas, Oregon, USA.[303] Worked in this electronics company for just a few years circa Jun 1977 at Techtronics Instruments, Beaverton, Klackamas, Oregon, USA. Job review given by Don Shults. All ranges above job requirements 110% range. Job description was Inspector III on 20 Feb 1981 at Techtronics,

Beaverton, Oregon, USA. Performance and wage review level at 110% getting 13.4% raise to $7.33 per hour. Forms in file on 23 Aug 1981 at Techtronics, Beaverton, Oregon, USA. He participated in an ordinance on 7 Mar 1982 at Techtronics, Beaverton, Oregon, USA.[304] He immigrated in 1986 to 5363 Sand Dune Park Dr., Florence, Lane, Oregon, USA.[305] HEALTH: While having the flue it was determined that he had a heart attack, but did not know it until 1992 while being check out circa 1991 at Home, Florence, Oregon, USA. Went on vacation by Sons, Jim and Lorraine on cruise to Alaska, on Liberian ship, ticket #44080 cruise #6118 for 7 nights on board. Travel agent was Palmdale Tours & Travel, Palmdale Calif. (Ticket in his file.) on 1 Jun 1991 at Air Princess, Balantyne/Vancouver, British Columbia, Canada. He immigrated circa 1992 to 505 Morse St P.O. Box 477, Ryderwood, Cowlizt, Washington, USA.[306] HEALTH: Major stroke 1992 while in hospital for kidney stone problem. Speech and right side paralized. Was also diabetic with congestive heart failure 5/6/96. Stroke and seizure/VA Hospital, Jamaica Plain, Mass./died 5/29/96 of possible heart or stroke brought on by morpheme tablets given that day by the VA which made him sick. He was due to have one foot amputated due to diabetes)(Kaiser Medical #7025-6550) in 1992 at Kaiser Hospital, Long View, Washington, USA. He immigrated circa Jul 1995 to 31 Timber Lane, Marstons Mills, Barnstable, Massachusetts, USA.[307] HEALTH: After coming back from Boston Veterans Hospital, he got sick on morphine they gave him to cut his pain in his feet. They were planning to amputate one foot in the coming days. He throw up dry. Medication was not continued because it was too strong for him. He finally rested until just after 12 midnight when he took sick again and passed away on 28 May 1996 at Marstons Mills, Barnstable, Massachusetts, USA. He died on 29 May 1996 at 31 Timber Ln.Marstons Mills, Hyannis, Barnstable, Massachusetts, USA, at age 75.[308] He was buried on 31 May 1996 at National Cemetery (Otis AFB) Plot 22.0.506, Bourne, Barnstable, Massachusetts, USA.[309] John's Xmas card said that he and Jim's best friend when younger died in Florida riding his bike and got hit by a car. His story goes like this; "He, Jim and I were very close. Until your mother (Lorraine) came into the picture. I think Jim fell in love with her the first time he saw her."

MILITARY: Rebuilt for this years memorial parade, this wall lists all Amesbury residence who served in the wars; includes all Bunnell/Gagne/Bertogli/Violette family. Located across from middle school on old hospital lawn) on 31 May 1999 at Veterans Memorial Wall, Amesbury, Essex, Massachusetts, USA.

i) James Henry[7] BUNNELL Jr. was Catholic. HEALTH: Cat allergies/travel sickness/wears glasses. MILITARY: None. He immigrated.[310] He was born on 20 Sep 1942 at Amesbury Hospital, Amesbury, Essex, Massachusetts, USA. He was baptized in Oct 1942 at Amesbury, Essex, Massachusetts, USA. He immigrated in 1953 to Pacoima, Los Angeles, California, USA.[311] He married Patricia Eleanor (Trisha) Brooks, daughter of ? Brooks and ? ?, on 5 Jan 1963 at St. Joseph Catholic Church, Canoga Park, L.A. Co., California. He and Patricia Eleanor (Trisha) Brooks were divorced circa 1973 at Simi, Ventura, California, USA. He married Janet Sue Shaw, daughter of Albert Henry Shaw Sr. and Roselie Wilma (Rose) Gould, on 6 Jul 1975 at Reno, Nevada. He lived circa 1995 at Valencia, Los Angeles, California, USA.[312] HEALTH: Diagnosed as hypertensive, diabetes and nerve condition from work circa 1997 at Valencia, Los Angeles, California, USA. He was Manager for Ralph's Supermarkets in L.A., Ca. area approx. 36 years, produce departments. Started at Safeway, Canoga Park, Cal. c. 1961 in 1997 at Ralph's Super Market, Los Angeles, Los Angeles, California, USA. He was retired in Mar 2000 at Ralph's Market, Los Angeles, California, USA.[313] HEALTH: Had a facial cancerous spot taken off on 23 Aug 2001 at Los Angeles, California, USA. He and Janet now are both retired traveling all around the country.

(a) Donald James[8] BUNNELL (Allison?) Was a Catholic. He was into Forestry education.[314] He was born on 26 Oct 1964 at Panorama, Los Angeles, California, USA. (Works 2 jobs, still single) in Nov 1999 at California, USA.

(b) Thomas[8] BUNNELL, MILITARY: none. He married (--?--) (--?--).[315] He was Catholic. Son Matt's mom never married. He was born on 12 Feb 1965 at Panorama, L.A. Co., Calif.

i) Matthew^9 BUNNELL (Not Bunnell-under moms name) they never married, but may have given Bunnell back to him. He was born on 29 May 1985 at Fontana, Riverside Co., California. He lived in 1995 at California.^{316} Info from Jim Bunnell 28,Oct.1995.

ii) Gary Martin^9 BUNNELL was born circa Oct 1999 at California, USA.^{317}

(c) Robert Jay^8 BUNNELL, Was Catholic. MILITARY: none. He was born on 21 Jul 1970 at Kaiser Hospital?, Panorama, Los Angeles, California, USA. He immigrated circa 1993 to Roseburg, Oregon, USA.^{318} Info from Lorraine Bunnell 1994 in 1994. He lived in 1994 at Roseburg, Oregon, USA.^{319} He married Karen TERRY circa 1998 at Oregon?, USA.^{320}

i) Nichol (Nikki)^9 BUNNELL was born on 15 Nov 1992 at Yacca Valley, California. Info from Lorraine Bunnell 1994 in 1994. She lived in 1995 at Roseburg, Oregon, USA.^{321} She was educated in Oct 1999 at Roseburg, Oregon, USA.^{322}

ii) Brook LeAnn^9 BUNNELL, Info from Lorraine M. Bunnell 1994 & Jim Bunnell, father in 1994. She lived in 1995 at Roseburg, Oregon, USA.^{323} She was born on 12 Jul 1995 at Roseburg, Oregon, USA.^{324}

ii) Paul Joseph^7 BUNNELL F.A.C.G., U.E. HEALTH: Allerg/vascular/asthama. Surgery -Vericosciel/Gaulbladder/left knee. He immigrated in 1946 to 4 Boardman St., Amesbury, Essex, Massachusetts, USA.^{325} He was born on 28 Jul 1946 at Amesbury Hospital (5:15AM Sun), Amesbury, Essex, Massachusetts, USA, 70 56W 42 51N. He was baptized in Aug 1946 at Sacred Heart Catholic Church (French), Amesbury, Essex, Massachusetts, USA.^{326} He immigrated in 1953 to 13331 Penney St., Pacoima, Los Angeles, California, USA.^{327} He immigrated in 1959 to 10249 Parthenia St., Canoga Park, Los Angeles, California,

USA.[328] Occupation was from 1963 to 1965 at Hemstreet Five & Dime store, (Stock Clerk) Sherman Way, Canoga Park, Los Angeles, California, USA. Next job from 1965 to 1966 until I got drafted in 1965 at Viking Industries (Stockroom Clerk), Chatsworth, Los Angeles, California, USA. MILITARY: Drafted 16 May 1966 to 24 Aug. 1966 (Honorable Medical Discharge. In1967 "A" Company (mine) was nearly wiped out from an attack. US Army No. 56687148 on 16 May 1966 at Fort Riley (US Army - Drafted) (Honorable Medical discharge) 9th. Inv.Div.,4th. of the 447th., Fort Riley, Kansas, USA. From 9 Sept. 1966 to May 1975 on 9 Sep 1966 at Hughes Aircraft Co. (Govt. Property Administrator), Fallbrook Ave., Canoga Park, Los Angeles, California, USA. He married Leslie WHITE, daughter of TV and movie director, Robert Frederick WHITE Sr. and Patricia (Patsy) Doreen MCCOY, on 10 May 1969 at Our Lady of the Valley Catholic Church, Canoga Park, California. He immigrated in 1970 to Hurles Ave., Simi Valley, Ventura, California, USA.[329] He immigrated in 1974 to Roscoe Blvd., Canoga Park, Los Angeles, California, USA.[330] He immigrated in 1975 to Regency Dr., Sagamore (Cape Cod), Barnstable, Massachusetts, USA.[331] From 1975 to 1977 had two book store locations, Wareham and Plymouth, Mass, in 1975 at The World Of Books Inc. (Owner), Cranberry Hwy., Wareham, Bristol, Massachusetts. Other on Court Street, Plymouth, Ma. From 1977 to 1979, transferred to Boise, Id. to head entire northwest states in 1977 at (WESCO) Westinghouse Electric Supply Co. (Branch Manager), Portland, Or. And Boise, Id. He immigrated in 1977 to San Jose, California, USA.[332] In 1977 at San Jose Liquor Store (Clerk), San Jose, California, USA. He immigrated in 1978 to Hughes Ave., West Linn, Montlomouth, Oregon, USA.[333] He immigrated in Jan 1979 to Boise, Idaho, USA.[334] From 2 July 1979 to August 1996, plant closing on 2 Jul 1979 at Augat Inc. (Warehouse Supervisor/Manager), Rt. 28, Mashpee, Barnstable, Massachusetts, USA. He immigrated in May 1980 to 31 Timber Lane, Marstons Mills, Barnstable, Massachusetts, USA.[335] He was author (Author of "Thunder Over New England, Benjamin Bonnell, Loyalist" "The New Loyalist Index, Vol. I, II, III" "Guide To Researching Your Loyalist Ancestors" The House of Robinson, The Robinsons of Rhode Island, Their Gene. & Letters & History of The Robinson & Son Oil Co." Acadian & Cajun Cookbook & Remedies" Cemetery

Inscriptions of The Town of Barnstable, Mass." Screenplays of "Thunder Over New England" and "Holy Smoke! I've Got A Loyalist In My Locker") in 1985. Started work on 4 Aug 1996 at Arrow Electronics (Programming Supervisor for shifts 2 & 3), 25 Upton Dr., Welmington, Massachusetts, USA. He lived in Oct 1997 at 58 Bluestone Dr., Nashua, Hillsboro, New Hampshire, USA. He immigrated in May 1998 to 100 Whitehall Rd. #15, Amesbury, Essex, Massachusetts, USA.[336] HEALTH: Visit to Dr. Harris in Newburyport revealed blood sugars at 358. Flue shot taken in Oct. 1999 is possibly to blame for giving him muscle ach and system problems along with sugars as his as nearly 400 in Feb 2000. HEALTH: Dr. Christopher Harris, had blood work done and found blood sugars at 387 on 7 Apr 2000 at Pentucket Medical Asso., Newburyport, Essex, Massachusetts, USA. HEALTH: Had a facial premalignant spot taken off right forehead. Also waiting to hear about possible left knee surgery again; torn muscle on 7 Feb 2001. HEALTH: Changed doctors from Harris to Ficht and the results were great. Though he tried treating me for my Fybromyalgia unsuccessfully, his treatment of my Diabetes was fantastic; From 200-300 range, he brought my sugars down to 90-110 and they have stayed that way through the rest of 2001 circa present at Dr. Kay Ficht of Lahey, Haverhill, Essex, Massachusetts, USA. HEALTH: Medical exam for the past month came up with a drastic improvement with Glycohemoglobin (long term assessment of diabetes) from 10 to 7.1 (goal is 7). Cholesterol LDL (bad) was 234 (high risk is 160 and over), and the HDL (good) was 149. Heart echo, injected stress test came out good. Left knee is acting up again with constant pain and seizing up. Trying to hold off from another operation on that. All other blood work came out fine circa 13 Jun 2001. HEALTH: 10 AM Torn meniscus in left knee surgery on 17 Aug 2001 at Ana Jakes Hospital, Newburyport, Essex, Massachusetts, USA. HEALTH: Dr. Menachem Kohen, 978-374-3940 confirmed and added diagnoses of Fybromyalgia, Poly Fybromyalgia and Rumatoid Arthritis. On 3 Nov. 2001 after blood test results and added visit, he said I should be on disability because conditions would not improve, and restrictions are wide with much pain in Nov 2001 at 1 Water St., Haverhill, Essex, Massachusetts, USA. Employee's were told today that the programming center would be closed and moved to Reno, Nevada and we would be terminated. I was placed in charge of the closure and movement to Reno.

Completion deadline would be 30 Nov. 2001 on 1 Nov 2001 at Arrow Electronics, 87 Concord St., N. Reading, Massachusetts, USA. HEALTH: Dr. Kay Ficht of the Lahey Group agreed with Dr. Kohen's recommendations for disability on 12 Nov 2001 at Haverhill, Essex, Massachusetts, USA. Today was my last day. I kept other spirits up high and comforted them as terminating employees went through various stages of hate, anger, depression, etc. It was hard keeping myself up to, but I made it and bravely walked out the door at the end on 30 Nov 2001 at Arrow Electronics, 87 Concord St., N. Reading, Massachusetts, USA. Today (2002) I am now on Social Security Disability.

(a) Matthew Paul[8] BUNNELL. HEALTH: Epstien Bar/Allergies/Works out/Physically fit. He was Catholic, now Baptist. MILITARY: None. He Likes wrestling/weight lifting. He was born on 11 Jan 1971 at Encino Hosp., Encino, L.A. Co., Ca. 8:51 AM (118W30 log.34N09 lat.). He was baptized circa Feb 1971 at St. Rosa Lima Catholic Church, Simi Valley, Ventura, California, USA.[337] He immigrated in May 1975 to Cape Cod, Sagamore, Barnstable, Massachusetts, USA.[338] He was Electronics Factory Worker (Augat Inc.,Mashpee,Ma.1991-1996) in 1991 at Augat Inc., Mashpee, Barnstable, Massachusetts, USA. He lived in 1997 at 58 Bluestone Dr., Nashua, Hillsboro, New Hampshire, USA. Engaged to married #12528, Soon Yung Choo (Taylor Morris) in 1997. Employed in Aug 1997 at Webb Plumming Supply Warehouse, Nashua, Hillsboro, New Hampshire, USA. He was associated as a pro-wrestler in Sep 1997 with the World Independent Wrestling, Nashua, Hillsboro, New Hampshire, USA.[339] He married Soon Yung Choo (Taylor Morris) on 18 May 2000 at Hedonism II, Jamaica.[340] Wedding party following their marriage in Jamaica. Over 150 family and friends attended. It had a Hawaii/Jamaica theme. Paul, Matt's dad made homemade meatballs and Italian shells. Andy, Taylor's dad furnished beer and ice and helped the rest of the family setting up. Roy, Matt & Taylor's friend had his band play. One week later they went to Southern California for a week, Hollywood, and a Godzilla convention in Jul 2000 at Liberty Hall, Marstons Mills, Barnstable, Massachusetts, USA.

Matthew won the AWA Wrestling Heavy Weight
Championship Belt and held it for over two months in Sep
2000 at American Legion Hall, Hudson, Hillsboro, New
Hampshire, USA. HEALTH: He was taken to the hospital that
night with a kidney stone attack the same time as his sister,
Jeannine. He finally passed two stones. Came home around 3
AM on 20 Nov 2000 at Nashua, Hillsboro, New Hampshire,
USA. They love raising their three dogs; Miko, Ren and Taco.

(b) Jeannine Marie^8 BUNNELL. HEALTH: Diabetes-
erratic/major allergies/asthma/stomach trouble. She was born
on 27 Jan 1973 at Simi Valley Hospital (2:45 PM Sat.), Simi
Valley, Ventura, California, USA. She was baptized on 23 Jun
1973 at St. Rose of Lima Catholic Church, Simi Valley,
Ventura, California, USA.[341] She immigrated in May 1975 to
Cape Cod, Sagamore, Barnstable, Massachusetts, USA.[342]
She and Joseph Robert MONTESION Jr. were engaged in
1992 at Marstons Mills, Barnstable, Massachusetts, USA but
was canceled.[343] She Worked w/handicap/retarded during
school, knows sign language. Submitted poem to American
Poetry Asso.,1988 and was accepted and published. She
married Eric Napoleon SMITH, son of Gordon Stanley SMITH
and Yvonne May DUPUIS, on 24 Mar 1996 at Mashpee
Baptist Church Mashpee, Barnstable Co. Mass. She lived in
1997 at 58 Bluestone Dr. (parents house), Nashua, Hillsboro,
New Hampshire, USA. She lived in 1997 at 55 Major Dr.,
Nashua, Hillsboro, New Hampshire, USA. Raising children
Bunnell. 1997. HEALTH: Was rushed into surgery to remove a
very large kidney stone while 6 months pregnant. Everything
came out ok and she came home Friday 25 Sept. 1998) on 24
Sep 1998 at Anna Jakes Hospital, Newburyport, Essex,
Massachusetts, USA. HEALTH: She got a back kidney stone
attack the same time her brother Matthew did. Leslie took her
the next morning to the hospital. They told her she could need
dialyses by next year on 20 Nov 2000 at Anna Jakes Hospital,
Newburyport, Essex, Massachusetts, and USA. HEALTH:
Became sick and went to the doctors on 20 June and found that
she had a miscarriage. With the same symptoms last month, it
was possible that she had another miscarriage then (May) too

circa 19 Jun 2001 at Haverhill, Essex, Massachusetts, USA. Eric has a son, Timothy Ryan Conn who also lives with the family as their own son, brother and grandson to Jeannine's parents.

i) Rebecca Marie[9] BUNNELL (Montesion). She was born on 22 Oct 1993 at Cape Cod Hospital (8:52 AM), Hyannis, Barnstable Co., Massachusetts, USA. She lived after 22 Oct 1993 at 31 Timber Lane, Marstons Mills, Barnstable, Massachusetts, USA.[344] At birth,9 lb.8oz,22 inches long. Birth reg.#01037 recorded 10 Nov.93 on 10 Nov 1993. HEALTH: Seizures from high fevers/ADAH disorder in Mar 1994 at 31 Timber Lane, Marstons Mills, Barnstable, Massachusetts, USA. She was baptized in Unity Church, West Barnstable, Barnstable Co., Massachusetts by Rev. Janet. At Baptism, Alma Violette (Mimere-Great Great Grandmother) plate was used for holding water to bless on 9 Apr 1994. She was baptized on 9 Apr 1994 at 31 Timber Lane, (1 PM) Home of grandparents, Paul & Leslie Bunnell, by Rev. Janet Smith of Unity, Marstons Mills, Barnstable, Massachusetts, USA. She lived in 1997 at 55 Major Dr., Nashua, Hillsboro, New Hampshire, USA. HEALTH: Bipolar.

ii) Amanda Marie[9] Smith (Bonnell). HEALTH: (Ear & eye infections) in 1995. She was born on 16 May 1995 at New England Medical Center (12:40 PM), Boston, Suffolk Co., Massachusetts, USA.[345] She came home from hospital. 19 May 1995 (Fri.) on 19 May 1995. Birth was a cesarean, original due date was 25 May.(Reg.#6748-date of rec.2 June 95) Original copy in file. Father is not listed, but he is Eric Smith, husband of Jeannine and father to Amanda on 25 May 1995. She lived in 1996 at Paul & Leslie Bunnell House (grandparents), Marstons Mills, Barnstable, Massachusetts, USA. Found to have heavy Royal lines in 1996. She lived in 1997 at 55 Major Dr., Nashua, Hillsboro, New Hampshire, USA. She lived in 1998 at British Royal Apartments, Whitehall Rd., Amesbury, Essex, Massachusetts, USA.

iii) Hannah Marie[9] Bunnell. She was born on 6 Jan 1999 at Anna-Jaques Hospital, Newburyport, Essex, Mass.[346] Father: Willie Bridges. HEALTH: During this week she had contracted the chicken pox from head to toe circa 31 Jan 2000 at Haverhill, Essex, Massachusetts, USA.

iii) Michael Norman[7] BUNNELL. HEALTH: Diabetes/travel sickness/wears glasses. MILITARY: None. He was Salesman/self employed. He lived with Family at 6 Boardman St.,Amesbury,Ma.1951(directory) in 1951. He was baptized circa 1953 at Sacred Heart Catholic Church, Amesbury, Essex, Massachusetts, USA. He immigrated in 1953 to Pacoima, Los Angeles, California, USA.[347] He was Catholic, but is now Baptist. He was born on 5 Jan 1953 at Amesbury Hospital, Amesbury, Essex, Massachusetts, USA.[348] He married Lorraine LINCOLN, daughter of Ronald Henry LINCOLN Sr. and Joyce Helen Amdisen, on 29 Apr 1972 at Chapel of The Canyon, Topanga Canyon Blvd., Canoga Park, Los Angeles, California. He is presently (2002) a produce salesman for many markets.

(b) Anna Mary (Mae)[6] BUNNELL. A very private, very nice and kind person. She was Catholic. WP Code-2. She immigrated.[349] She was born on 2 Jan 1922 at 4 Boardman St., Amesbury, Essex, Massachusetts, USA.[350] She was baptized on 6 Aug 1922 at St. Joseph Catholic Church, and lived 9 Sparhawk St., Amesbury, Essex, Massachusetts, USA. She married Wilfred GAGNE, son of Joseph E. GAGNE and Josephine M. Duke, on 4 Feb 1946 at St. Joseph Catholic Church), Amesbury, Essex, Massachusetts, USA.[351] She lived in 1951 at 11 Boardman St., Amesbury, Essex, Massachusetts, USA.[352] She was Factory worker in Jan 1983. She died on 20 Jan 1983 at Possibly at work, Exeter, Rockingham, New Hampshire, USA, at age 61. HEALTH: Heart attack on 20 Jan 1983. She was buried on 22 Jan 1983 at On Rt. 150 (Family Lot), Kensington, Rockingham, New Hampshire, USA.[353] Death benefit paid Jan. 1984 Amesbury?, Essex?, Massachusetts, USA.

i) Jeanne Elizabeth[7] GAGNE (Horgan) was Self employed. Has New Hampshire Condo & camp in Maine. She was Catholic ? She was born on 21 Jan 1947 at Amesbury, Essex, Ma.

She married Elphege Joseph (Al) HORGAN in 1965 at New Hampshire or Massachusetts, USA. She married John THOMAS circa 1991 at USA.^{354} She lived in 1995 at Rockingham, New Hampshire, USA. Some info from Louis Bunnell 8 Sept.1995 & Jean, 21 Oct.1995 on 8 Sep 1995. Joanne info. from Grace Fletcher,16 Nov.1995 on 16 Nov 1995. HEALTH: Had surgery on eye, removed small lump because it blocked peripheral vision. She feels vision is still the same, no progress. Info. from Jeanne on email dated 13 May 2001.

(a) Joanne^8 HORGAN was adopted out circa 1965.^{355} Mother was in high school. She was born in 1966 at New Hampshire or Massachusetts, USA. In 1990's, looked up mother from city records & had couple visits after 1990. She was hair dresser in Boston circa 1995 at Boston, Suffolk, Massachusetts, USA. She lived in 1995 at Boston, Suffolk, Massachusetts, USA. Some info from Grace Fletcher 16 Nov.1995.

(b) Joseph Elphege^8 HORGAN. Info from Jean #327,21 Oct.1995. He lived in Exeter, Rockingham Co., Massachusetts 1995. He was born on 27 Feb 1967 at Lowell, Essex Co., Massachusetts. He married (--?--) (--?--) before 1994? at Massachusetts or New Hampshire?

i) Tyler^9 HORGAN living in Exeter, Rockingham Co., Massachusetts 1995. Info from Jean Thomas #327,21 Oct.1995. He was born in Mar 1994 at Massachusetts or New Hampshire?

(c) Audrey Marie^8 HORGAN living in Malden, Massachusetts 1995). Some info from Jean Thomas #327,21 Oct.1995. She was born on 27 Mar 1970 at Newburyport, Essex Co., Massachusetts. She married Harry Leathes before 1989 at New Hampshire or Massachusetts, USA.

i) Nicole^9 (--?--) (Horgan) lived at (living in Malden, Massachusetts 1995). Some info from Jean Thomas & mother, 21 Oct.1995. She was born on 22 Dec 1990 at Exeter Hospital, Exeter, Rockingham, New Hampshire, USA.

ii) Wilfred Charles[7] GAGNE was a Catholic. He was born on 8 Dec 1948 at Amesbury, Essex Co., Massachusetts. MILITARY: Vietnam Veteran, PFC 362 Singnal Co before 1970. Victim of Vietnam & drug era before 1970. He died on 23 Sep 1970 at (At home), Exeter?, Rochingham, New Hampshire, USA, at age 21. HEALTH: Died 23 Sep 1970. He was buried circa 25 Sep 1970 at On Rt. 150 (Family plot), Kensington, Rockingham, New Hampshire, USA. Benefit paid in Massachusetts Dec. 1979 in Dec 1979 at Massachusetts, USA. His SS issued in Mass.(benefit paid Dec.1979) in Dec 1979. MILITARY: Rebuilt for this years memorial day parade, lists all other family members who served in the wars. Located across from middle school on old hospital lawn) on 31 May 1999 at Veterans Memorial Wall, Amesbury, Essex, Massachusetts, USA.

iii) Helen Mae[7] GAGNE married an unknown person at Mass./NH? She was Catholic. She and an unknown person were divorced. She was born on 30 Dec 1950 at Amesbury, Essex Co., Massachusetts. She married (--?--) Roberts before 1975 at Rockingham?, New Hampshire?, USA. She was 1988 owned restaurant in Exeter, NH in 1988 at Exeter, Rockingham, New Hampshire, USA. Some info. from Jean #327,21 Oct.1995 & Grace Rogers on 21 Oct 1995. She lived in 1998 at Exeter, Rockingham, New Hampshire, USA. From Helen (Mother) on 11 Apr 1998.

(a) William (Bill) Alan[8] Roberts was born in Apr 1969 at Exeter?, Rockingham?, New Hampshire?, USA. From Helen (Mother) on 11 Apr 1998. He married Nicole Grant Greenlaw on 20 Jul 2002 at Rockingham, New Hampshire, USA.[356]

(b) Benjamin[8] (--?--) was born in 1972 at Exeter?, Rockingham?, New Hampshire?, USA. From Helen (Mother) on 11 Apr 1998.

(c) (--?--)[8] (--?--) (Gagne) immigrated circa 1975.[357] He was born in 1975 at Massachusetts or New Hampshire? From Grace Rogers 16 Nov.1995 on 16 Nov 1995.

iv) Joseph Philip^7 GAGNE was Catholic? He was born on 10 Sep 1955 at Amesbury, Essex Co., Massachusetts. He married Sue (--?--) before 1989 at New Hampshire or Massachusetts, USA. From Jean Thomas #327,21 Oct.1995 on 21 Oct 1995. He lived on 31 Jan 1999 at South Carolina, USA.^{358} He travel up from South Carolina to visit Grace & family, especially his grandson, Matthew. (From Grace xmas card Dec. 2000) circa Apr 2000.

(a) Lindsay Anna^8 GAGNE was born before 1990.

(b) Sarah^8 GAGNE was born before 1990 at New Hampshire?, USA. She lived on 9 Dec 1999 at New Hampshire?, USA.^{359}

i) Matthew^9 (--?--) was born in Nov 1999 at New Hampshire?, USA.^{360}

(c) Albert Lewis/Louis^6 BUNNELL. He was Catholic. He was born on 20 Dec 1922 at 4 Boardman St., Amesbury, Essex, Massachusetts, USA.^{361,362} He was baptized on 11 Feb 1923 at St. Joseph Catholic Church, 9 Sparhawk St., Amesbury, Essex, Massachusetts, USA. MILITARY: Listed on above ship with address as DD U89, c/o FPO NY NY USO) circa 1942 at On board USS Mergine(?). MILITARY: In 1951 at US Naval Air Base, Atlantic City, Atlantic, New Jersey, USA. He married Grace Nora NEWLIN, daughter of Clarence NEWLIN and Helen MORRISON, on 15 Nov 1951 at 3:15 PM, Atlantic City, Atlantic Co., New Jersey, USA. He and Grace Nora NEWLIN were divorced circa 1959. He married Josephine (Josie/Josey) Bell Randall in 1959 at Massachusetts, USA. He was Construction Worker/Lab, Roy Bros. Amesbury & Grave digger, St. Joseph Cemetery on 7 May 1960 at 20 Arlington St., Amesbury, Essex, Massachusetts, USA.^{363} He lived on 7 May 1960 at 20 Arlington St., Amesbury, Essex, Massachusetts, USA.^{364,365} He lived on 14 Sep 1963 at 39 Dublin St., Amesbury, Essex, Massachusetts, USA.^{366,367} He was buried on 13 Feb 1992 at Union Cemetery, Veterans lot, Essex, Massachusetts, USA.^{368,369} He died on 13 Feb 1992 at 11-12 PM at home, Amesbury, Essex, Massachusetts, USA, at age 69. HEALTH: Heart attack on 13 Feb

1992 at Amesbury, Essex, Massachusetts, USA. He Read paper at kitchen table, heart attack, fell off chair to floor, Bee, girlfriend found c.3 PM, Albert Jr. tried door c.12 PM, but left on 13 Feb 1992 at Amesbury, Essex, Massachusetts, MILITARY: (Rebuilt for this years memorial day parade, lists all from Amesbury who served in the wars, includes other Bunnell/Violette/Gagne/Bertogli family members. Located across from middle school on old hospital lawn) on 31 May 1999 at Veterans Memorial Wall, Amesbury, Essex, Massachusetts, USA.

i) Grace Nora^7 BUNNELL. Married F. Fletcher Rogers 1980's? at Massachusetts? She was Catholic? She married (--?--) (--?--) at Mass/NH? She and (--?--) (--?--) were divorced. She was adopted by Wilfred(#326) & Anna(#77) with permission of Anna's brother, Albert #78. She was born on 29 Jun 1953 at Atlantic City Hospital, Atlantic City, Atlantic Co., New Jersey. Birth record & Western Union Telegram to Mary Bunnell saying b.10:15PM,wt.7-3/4 pounds, easy time, signed Grace on 29 Jun 1953. From Jean Thomas #327,21 Oct.1995 on 21 Oct 1995. She lived in 1998 at Exeter, Rockingham, New Hampshire, USA.[370] This year was their 10th anniversary. Fletch got Grace a diamond & sapphire ring in Dec 2000.

(a) Gregg^8 Rogers lived in 1998 at New Hampshire?, USA.[371] He was employed by (Is in the landscaping business) in 1998 at New Hampshire?, USA. He was Grace xmas card says he is still doing well in his business and is happy with his home but continues to look for that special one in Dec 2000.

(b) Desiree^8 Rogers was born at New Hampshire?, USA. She married Keith Murphy in Oct 2000 at New Hampshire or Massachusetts?, USA.[372]

i) Derek^9 ? was born circa 1994 at Exeter?, Rockingham?, New Hampshire?, USA. From Grace Rogers, grandmother on 11 Apr 1998. He was educated in Dec 2000.[373]

ii) Anna Mackenzie[9] Murphy was born on 4 Nov 1998 at New Hampshire?, USA.[374] She was Grace xmas card says she is in her terrible 2's but is a real sweetie. Very independent. Her hair is bright red in Dec 2000.

ii) Colleen[7] BUNNELL (Bonnell) and Joseph S. Houchmuth were divorced. She lived at Church St., Merrimac, Essex Co., Massachusetts 1995). She immigrated.[375] Daughter from first marriage. She was born on 7 May 1960 at Amesbury, Essex, Massachusetts, USA.[376,377] She married Joseph S. Houchmuth before 1990 at Massachusetts. She married (--?--) LENTINE between 1990 and 1991 at Massachusetts.

(a) (Female)[8] (--?--) was born at Essex Co., Massachusetts?

iii) Albert Louis[7] BUNNELL (Bonnell) Jr. was Catholic? He was born on 9 Feb 1962 at Amesbury, Essex, Massachusetts, USA.[378,379] He married Tina M. ELDREDGE, daughter of Robert C. ELDREDGE Sr. and Rose DONOVAN, in 1994 at Essex Co., Massachusetts? From Albert Jr. 21 Oct.1995 on 21 Oct 1995. He lived in 1999 at 66 High St., Amesbury, Essex, Massachusetts, USA.[380] Moved to New Hampshire approx. 2001.

(a) Benjamin[8] BUNNELL (Bonnell) immigrated.[381] He was born on 1 Oct 1984 at Newburyport, Essex Co., Massachusetts. He lived in 1995 at Amesbury, Essex, Massachusetts, USA. From mother,21 Oct.1995.

iv) Chris/Criss Ann[7] BUNNELL[382] married (--?--) SOUCY 1990's? at New Hampshire? She was born on 14 Sep 1963 at Amesbury, Essex, Massachusetts, USA.[383,384] Now living in New Hampshire (2002).

(d) George Woodbury[6] BUNNELL Jr was Catholic. MILITARY: U.S.Navy. He was born on 14 Mar 1924 at Roxbury, Suffolk, Massachusetts, USA. He was baptized after 14 Mar 1924 at St. Joseph Catholic Church, Amesbury, Essex, Massachusetts, USA. He married Nellie Angela GIARRUSSO, daughter of Domenic GIARRUSSO and Adeline FOSSANO, on 12 May 1946 at Holy Rosary Catholic Church,

Lawrence, Ma. He immigrated circa 1950 to Burbank, Los Angeles, California, USA.[385] HEALTH: Open heart surg.1974/5(bypass) & aneurysm taken out of stomach. While living in Las Vegas, Nv. he had arteries cleared in neck 1997 circa 1974 at Canoga Park, Los Angeles, California, USA. Retired Air conditioning Tech.,1987 was a Realtor with Century 21 after that in 1987 at Woodland Hills, Los Angeles, California, USA. From Lorraine Bunnell & George circa 1990. He immigrated in 1993 to Dell Web Retirement Development, Las Vegas, Nevada, USA. HEALTH: (Due to irregular heartbeats and fibrillations he had a pacemaker put in) on 4 Dec 1998 at Mountain View Hospital, Las Vegas, Nevada, USA. MILITARY: He is listed here with all other Amesbury residence who served in the wars. This wall was rebuilt and completed for this years Memorial Parade. It is located on old Hospital grounds across from doe boy soldier at middle school on 31 May 1999 at Veterans Memorial Wall, Amesbury, Essex, Massachusetts, USA. HEALTH: Did another unblocking of arteries and it came out ok circa 17 Dec 2001 at Mountain View Hospital, Las Vegas, Nevada, USA. He died of congestive heart failure and breathing problems. He was buried at the Veterans Cemetery in Las Vegas, Nevada with full military honors.

i) George Woodbury[7] BUNNELL 3rd was Jehova's Witness. He married Clara SIMMONS. MILITARY: None. He was born on 9 Jun 1949 at Lawrence, Essex Co., Ma. He immigrated circa 1950.[386] He was Member of Strawberry Alarmclock rock group that had a number one hit (Incense and Peppermints) and later became car salesman (awarded best in sales several times) circa 1968. He lived in 1995 at Woodland Hills, and now (2002) in Calabasas, Los Angeles, California, USA.

ii) Richard Jay[7] BUNNELL. MILITARY: None. He and Donna TANTALO were divorced. He was Jehova's Witness. Was in Air Conditioning Business for many years and is now a supervisor. He immigrated circa 1950.[387] He was born on 19 Aug 1954 at Burbank, L.A. Co., Calif. He married Donna TANTALO, daughter of Donald Nicolas TANTALO and Jean EASON, before 1975 at California. His Divorce was final in later half of 1994 in 1994. Info also from wedding announcement of 2nd.marr in Nov 1995. He married Dawn COTELLO on 11 Nov 1995 at California.

(a) Richard Jay^8 BUNNELL Jr. was born at California. He was Laborer/Carpenter? He was born at Ca. He was Jahova's Witness. He lived in 1990 at Little Rock, Los Angeles, California, USA. He married an unknown person on 14 Nov 1998 at Los Angeles?, California, USA. Now lives in Phoenix, Arizona.

(e) Marie J.^{6} BUNNELL was Catholic. She Gave dau.#273 away while husband Sal was in hospital at wedding. She was born on 3 Jun 1925 at Roxbury, Suffolk, Massachusetts, USA. She lived circa 1943 at US Navy Base, Mobile?, Louisiana, USA.^{388} She married Salvatore Cosmo DIDOMENICO, son of Andrea DIDOMENICO and Clotilda S. LASCOLA, on 5 Dec 1943 at St. Joseph Catholic Church, Amesbury, Ma. She lived circa 1946 at 40 School St., Somerville, Suffolk, Massachusetts, USA.^{389} She retired before 1990 circa 1990 at Massachusetts, USA. She lived circa 1995 at 111 McCormack St., Medford, Suffolk, Massachusetts, USA.^{390} HEALTH: Diabetes-shot dependent/Triple bypass,5 arteries 28 Oct.96 at Boston, Suffolk, Massachusetts, USA. Her children held a surprise 75th. birthday party for her. Over 100 people showed up, mostly family from all over. Dinner & dancing at 6:30 to 11:00 PM on 20 May 2000 at Knights of Columbus Hall, 11 Sanborn St., Reading, Massachusetts, USA.

i) Clotilda^7 DIDOMENICO. She was Catholic. She was born on 17 Sep 1944 at Gulfport, Mississippi. She married Eugene J. WARE Sr. on 19 Oct 1968 at Massachusetts. Surprise 25th. Wedding Anniversary party, 20 Nov. 1993,7PM,Dante Club, Graigie St., Somerville, Ma. given by sister, Diana on 20 Nov 1993. She lived in 1995 at 39 Old Farm Rd., Reading, Massachusetts, USA.

(a) Eugene J.^{8} WARE Jr. From Gene Sr.,21 Oct.1995. He was Catholic. He was Hair Dresser & Plays Frankenfurter in Rocky Horror Picture Show in Cambridge, Mass. on weekends. Also in Rock band. A professional actor/singer. He was born on 6 Sep 1969 at Massachusetts?

(b) Johanna Clotilda^8 WARE From Gene Sr.,21 Oct.1995. She was born on 28 Aug 1974 at Massachusetts?

(c) Barry Michael[8] WARE. From Gene Sr.,21 Oct.1995. He was born on 26 Sep 1975 at Massachusetts.

(d) John Salvatore[8] WARE. From Gene.Sr.,21 Oct.1995. He was born on 25 Aug 1995 at Massachusetts?

ii) Mary[7] DIDOMENICO was Catholic. Info. from her mom Marie & Amy's marriage record. She was born on 19 Jun 1946 at Cambridge, Middlesex Co., Ma. She married Robert W. VALLANCE Sr. on 9 Aug 1969 at Massachusetts. She lived in 1995 at Deerfield, New Hampshire, USA.

(a) Robert W.[8] VALLANCE Jr. was born at Malden, Massachusetts. He lived at (living in Massachusetts). He married Tricia (--?--) at Rockingham, New Hampshire, USA. From Robert Sr.,21 Oct.1995. He lived in 2002 at 130A Main St., Raymond, Rockingham, New Hampshire, USA.[391]

(b) Amy Marie[8] VALLANCE was born at Somerville, Massachusetts. She was Catholic. Wedding Reception at Holiday Inn, Manchester, NH, child 1 years old at wedding. She married Jodi Malcolm GRANT circa 18 Aug 1990 at St. Paul's Catholic Church, Candia, Rockingham, New Hampshire, USA.[392] She lived in 2002 at 246 Rt. 27, Raymond, Rockingham, New Hampshire, USA.[393]

i) David Robert[9] GRANT (Vallence?) was Catholic. He was born on 24 Feb 1989 at New Hampshire. From Robert Vallance Sr. David was 1 years old at parents wedding on 21 Oct 1995.

(c) Bobby Jo[8] VALLANCE was born at Malden, Massachusetts. She was Catholic. From wedding invite. They went to Aruba for their honeymoon in May 1995. She married Michael James HUOT on 13 May 1995 at Saturday, St. Paul's Church, Candia, Rockingham, New Hampshire, USA. She Also from Robert Sr., 21 Oct.1995.

i) Korey Micheal^9 HUOT From Robert Sr.,21 Oct. 1995. He was born on 30 Jan 1993 at Massachusetts or New Hampshire?

ii) Zachary^9 HUOT was born after Jun 1995 at Rockingham, New Hampshire, USA.

(d) Darlene^8 VALLANCE was born at Somerville, Massachusetts. She was Catholic. She married Richard Brown at Rockingham, New Hampshire, USA. From Robert Sr.,21 Oct.1995. She lived in 2002 at 1555 Bodwell Rd. Unit 9, Manchester, Rockingham, New Hampshire, USA.^{394}

i) Brandon^9 Brown was born at Rockingham, New Hampshire, USA.

ii) Moran/Morgan^9 Brown was born at Rockingham, New Hampshire, USA.

iii) Andrea (Andrew)^7 DIDOMENICO was Catholic. He and Linda M. LANI were divorced. From Marie DiDomenico. He was born on 30 Dec 1948 at Cambridge, Middlesex Co., Ma. He married Linda M. LANI on 20 Feb 1971 at Ma.? He married Maryann R. D'AMELIO on 16 Apr 1988 at Ma.? He lived in 1995 at 200 West St., Reading, Massachusetts, USA.

(a) Beth Ann^8 DIDOMENICO was Catholic. She was born in Sep 1984 at Massachusetts?

iv) George^7 DIDOMENICO was Catholic. From Marie DiDomenico. He was born on 1 Jul 1953 at Cambridge, Middlesex Co., Ma. He married Martha M. COLOZZI on 2 Jun 1973 at Ma.? He and Martha M. COLOZZI were divorced before 1982? He married Karen FILIBRAUN on 20 Jan 1983? at Massachusetts?, USA. He lived on 25 Dec 1997 at 128 Broadsound Ave (zip 02151), Revere, Suffolk?, Massachusetts, USA. He was North End of Boston on 25 Dec 1997 at Joe Tecce's Restaurant, Boston, Suffolk, Massachusetts, USA. Hobby: Has a 35 foot lobster boat converted into a cruiser. It is docked at Portsmouth, Rhode Island.

They have been to the Virgin Islands among many other places in 1998. He was Continues working for Local #33 out of Boston as well as waiting tables at Joe Tecce's a few nights a week. Busy working on his boat, traveling around Long Island Sound and Connecticut. They are hoping to spend two weeks out at sea next summer. From xmas card 2000 in Dec 2000.

(a) Adriana^8 DIDOMENICO was born before 1983 at Massachusetts, USA. She was educated on 25 Dec 1997 at Villanoua University.[395] She was educated on 1 Dec 1998.[396] She was educated in May 2000 at Villanova University, Lancaster, Pennsylvania, USA.[397] She was Works at the GAP store as manager, nights. From parents xmas 2000 letter circa Jun 2000 at Natick, Massachusetts, USA.

(b) Victoria^8 DIDOMENICO was born before 1983? at Suffolk?, Massachusetts, USA. She was educated on 25 Dec 1997 at Lincoln-Sudbury High School, Massachusetts? USA.[398] She was educated on 1 Dec 1998.[399] She was educated in Dec 2000 at New York University, New York, New York, USA.[400]

(c) Courteney^8 DIDOMENICO was born on 27 Dec 1996 at Revere?, Suffolk, Massachusetts, USA. She is a very outgoing, inquisitive and social child like father and has been walking since Thanksgiving with one tooth in already. Her favorite things are "Blankie" the recycling bin and Barney videos on 25 Dec 1997 at Xmas Card from parents. She was (Christmas card says she enrolled in toddler school, is outgoing and inquisitive, loves the sandbox, water table, her bike and Barney videos) on 1 Dec 1998. Takes ballet and tap once a week. Loves crafts and playing dress up dolls. Will have a Cinderella birthday Christmas vacation week 2000. From parents xmas card. Picture in file in Dec 2000 at Revere, Massachusetts, USA.

v) Diana^7 DIDOMENICO. Her married name was LYDON. She married John Michael FURRIER 17 June 1984 (1 PM) at Saint Anthony's Catholic Church, Somerville Ave., Somerville, Ma. She married Michael Paul (Peter?) LYDON, son of Paul J. LYDON and (--?--) (--?--), 2 Oct.1993 (3PM) at Saint Anthony's Catholic

Church, Somerville, Mass. She and John Michael FURRIER were divorced. She was Catholic. She was born on 13 Mar 1964 at Somerville, Middlesex Co., Ma. Wedding shower at VFW, Medford, Ma. 14 Aug.1993, big reception over 200 people. Wedding Reception at Bon Saison, 158 School St., Everett, Ma on 14 Aug 1993 at VFW, Medford, Massachusetts, USA.

(a) Michael Salvatore[8] LYDON was born 12 or 16 Dec.1994 (8lbs? at Winchester Hospital, Winchester, Massachusetts. He lived at (living 1995, 111 McCormick Ave., Medford, Ma.). He was Catholic. From Marie, the grandmother. And Diana 16 Aug.1995.

(b) Erica Marie[8] LYDON Info given by grandmother, Marie DiDimenico who lives with this family (her daughter) on 12 Jun 1998 at Malden, Massachusetts, USA. She was born circa 1 Aug 1998 at Malden?, Massachusetts, USA. (Birth announcement by phone call from Marie DiDimenico, grandmother) on 14 Aug 1998.

(f) Mabel Teresa[6] BUNNELL was Catholic. She married James Frederick WALSH. She was born on 6 Feb 1927 at Amesbury, Essex Co., Massachusetts. She was baptized on 24 Apr 1927 at St. Joseph Catholic Church, 9 Sparhawk St., Amesbury, Essex, Massachusetts, USA.[401] She was Ran secretary pool in Washington .DC during WWII circa 1942 at Washington D.C., District of Columbia, USA. She They met in Wash. DC during WW II circa 1942 at Washington D. c., District of Columbia, USA. She lived circa 1958 at 29044 Hathoway St., Lavoina, Michigan, USA.[402] HEALTH: Huntington's Corea 1972/3. HEALTH: (Placed into a nursing home for care of her Huntington's. After a long brave fight, she died in 2002 at Michigan, USA.

i) James Frederick[7] WALSH Jr.(Dr.) was born at Massachusetts?, USA. He was Chiropractic Doctor. He married (--?--) (--?--) circa 1990 at Michigan, USA. He was Catholic & Practicing Sciencetology Religion (1993). He lived in 1998 at Michigan, USA.

ii) Gail Christine^7 WALSH Doctor. She married George DEBS Dr., son of John Edward DEBS and (--?--) (--?--), 13 Aug.1986 (5 PM Saturday at St. George Greek Catholic Church, 30 Anna St., Worcester, Massachusetts. She was born at Massachusetts, USA. She was Chiropractic Doctor. She was Greek Orthodox Catholic. She immigrated before 1986.^{403} She lived in 1993 at 12 Waterford Dr. (01602 zip), Worcester, Worcester, Massachusetts, USA.

    (a) Stephanie Mary^8 DEBS was born 24 May 1993 (9 pounds,22 at Worcester?, Worcester Co., Massachusetts. She was Greek Orthodox.

    (b) Jaclyn^8 DEBS was Greek Orthodox. She was born between 1990 and 1991? at Worcester?, Worcester Co., Massachusetts.

iii) Eileen E.M.^{7} WALSH Doctor married Robert Michael BLOCK 19 Oct. 1991 (Saturday) at Ohio/Illinois? She was born at Massachusetts?, USA. She was Catholic. She was Chiropractor - Doctor. She immigrated in 1990.^{404} She lived in 1994 at New York, USA. She From Wedding card,& Xmas card 1994 in 1994. She 20 April 1996 birth announcement of child #1 on 20 Apr 1996.

    (a) Allyson Joanna^8 BLOCK died (living 1996) at (living at Ballston Spa, New York). She was born 20 April 1996 (10:18 AM) at Ballston Spa, New York (possibly). HEALTH: Weight at birth-8 lbs,10 ocs.20 inches long. From birth announcement.

    (b) Jacob^8 BLOCK was born circa 1998 at New York, USA.

(g) Barbara P.^{6} BUNNELL^{405} She was Catholic. She was born on 6 Apr 1928 at Amesbury, Essex, Massachusetts, USA. She was baptized on 13 May 1928 at St. Joseph Catholic Church, 9 Sparhawk St., Amesbury, Essex, Massachusetts, USA. She married Norman BURRELL, son of Otis BURRELL and Mary Connors, on 26 Nov 1949 at St. Joseph Catholic Church, Amesbury, Essex, Massachusetts, USA.^{406,407} His sister Natalie married John J. Labby.

Barbara died on 22 Jul 1970 at home, Amesbury, Essex, Massachusetts, USA, at age 42.[408] She was buried circa 23 Jul 1970 at St. Joseph Cemetery, Amesbury, Essex, Massachusetts, USA.

i) William (Billy)(Willy)[7] BURRELL was Catholic? He was born on 15 Mar 1954 at Amesbury, Essex, Massachusetts, USA.[409] He died on 7 Sep 1982 at Amesbury, Essex, Massachusetts, USA, at age 28.[410] He was buried on 8 Sep 1982 at St. Joseph Cemetery?, Amesbury, Essex, Massachusetts, USA.

ii) Robert[7] BURRELL lived at (living possibly in Amesbury, Mass., near the river). He was Catholic? He was born on 13 Sep 1956 at Amesbury, Essex, Massachusetts, USA.[411]

iii) Mary[7] BURRELL was Catholic? She Looks like father's side, and very pretty girl. She was born before 1958 at Amesbury Hospital?, Amesbury, Essex, Massachusetts, USA. She married Mark (--?--) after 1980 at Amesbury?, Essex, Massachusetts, USA. She lived on 23 May 2000 at Lincoln Court, Amesbury, Essex, Massachusetts, USA.

(a) (--?--)[8] (--?--) was born after 1980 at Essex, Massachusetts, USA. He/she lived on 23 May 2000 at Lincoln Court, Amesbury, Essex, Massachusetts, USA.

(b) (--?--)[8] (--?--) was born after 1980 at Essex, Massachusetts, USA. He/she lived on 23 May 2000 at Lincoln Court, Amesbury, Essex, Massachusetts, USA.

(c) (--?--)[8] (--?--) was born after 1980 at Essex, Massachusetts, USA. He/she lived on 23 May 2000 at Lincoln Court, Amesbury, Essex, Massachusetts, USA.

iv) Stella[7] BURRELL was Catholic? She Looks like mother, very pretty girl. She was born on 11 Aug 1958 at Amesbury, Essex, Massachusetts, USA.[412] She married Dennis BOMBA before 1992 at Massachusetts. She lived in 1995 at 23 Winter St., Amesbury, Essex, Massachusetts, USA.[413] Some above info from Louis Bunnell 8 Sept.1995 on 8 Sep 1995.

(h) Benjamin Franklin[6] BUNNELL was Construction worker (at times for Roy Brothers of Amesbury). He was Catholic.
HEALTH: Killed by back-hoe tractor Rt.495 Amesbury accident. He was Paul Joseph Bunnell, UE God-father and baptized on my Birthday day 17 years before me. MILITARY: Navy (Korea?). He was born on 6 Jun 1929 at Amesbury, Essex, Massachusetts, USA. He was baptized on 28 Jul 1929 at St. Joseph Catholic Church, 9 Sparhawk St., Amesbury, Essex, Massachusetts, USA. He married Madeleine Marie GUILMETTE, daughter of Alexis GUILMETTE and Lea Mercier (Doherty), on 29 Jun 1952 at Sacred Heart Catholic Church, Amesbury, Ma. He lived on 29 Jun 1952 at 4 Boardman St., Amesbury, Essex, Massachusetts, USA.[414,415] He lived on 23 May 1953 at 52 Market St., Amesbury, Essex, Massachusetts, USA.[416] He lived on 27 May 1953 at 31 Whitehall Rd., Amesbury, Essex, Massachusetts, USA.[417] He lived on 4 Sep 1957 at 7 Arlington St., Amesbury, Essex, Massachusetts, USA.[418,419] He immigrated circa 1958 to Pacoima, Los Angeles, California, USA.[420] He died on 19 May 1967 at Route 495 construction site, Amesbury, Essex, Massachusetts, USA, at age 37.[421] He was buried on 22 May 1967 at St. Joseph Cemetery, Amesbury, Essex, Massachusetts, USA.
MILITARY: (Rebuilt for this years memorial day parade, lists other Bunnell/Violette/Gagne/Bertogli relatives. Located across from middle school on old hospital lawn) on 31 May 1999 at Veterans Memorial Wall, Amesbury, Essex, Massachusetts, USA.

i) Jeaninne Marie[7] BUNNELL was Company/Insurance? Nurse. HEALTH: Fell down stairs, cut over eye,10 stitches, pregnant for 3rd.child. My daughter (Paul) is names after her. She was Catholic. She was born on 23 May 1953 at Amesbury, Essex, Massachusetts, USA.[422] She immigrated circa 1955.[423] She married Edwin Bell FAULKNER 3rd., son of Edwin Bell FAULKNER Jr. and ? ?, on 1 Oct 1971 at Massachusetts. She lived circa 1996 at 18 Walden St., Lynn, Massachusetts, USA.

(a) (baby boy)[8] FAULKNER From Madaleine Bunnell 22 Oct.1995. He was Catholic. He was born on 12 Mar 1972 at Massachusetts. He died on 13 Mar 1972 at (in hospital?), Massachusetts.

(b) Allison Ann[8] FAULKNER From birth announcement/1 month old picture in parents file. She lived at Living at 18 Walden St., Lynn, Ma. 01905. She was Catholic? She was born on 6 Nov 1992 at Boston, Suffolk Co., Massachusetts, USA.[424]

(c) Edwin (Little Eddie)[8] FAULKNER was Catholic. He Pregnancy announcement from Madeleine Bunnell,22 Oct.1995 & birth told by Marie DiDemenico 31 May 1996. He was born on 4 Apr 1996 at Lynn/Boston?, Massachusetts, USA.

ii) David Joseph[7] BUNNELL. MILITARY: None. He was Painter/Construction worker. He was Catholic. He immigrated circa 1955.[425] He was born on 27 Feb 1955 at Amesbury, Essex, Massachusetts, USA.[426] He was sports member of the Indoor Field Hockey Team taking part in the YMCA tournament Saturday. Picture in file from Amesbury Newspaper with photo circa 1967 at YMCA, Amesbury, Essex, Massachusetts, USA. He married Patricia MELNICK on 10 Sep 1983 at Ma.? He and Patricia MELNICK were divorced circa 1987. He Divorced 1987? circa 1987. He lived in 1995 at Newburyport, Essex, Massachusetts, USA. From Madeleine Bunnell 22 Oct.1995 on 22 Oct 1995.

(a) Michael Edward[8] BUNNELL lived at (Newburyport, Massachusetts 1995). From Madeline Bunnell 22 Oct.1995. He was born on 29 Apr 1981 at Newburyport, Essex Co., Massachusetts. He was educated in Jun 2000 at Amesbury High School, Amesbury, Essex, Massachusetts, USA.[427]

iii) Paul Arnold[7] BUNNELL. MILITARY: None. He was Catholic. He was born on 4 Sep 1957 at Amesbury, Essex, Massachusetts, USA.[428] He was baptized after 4 Sep 1957 at Sacred Heart Church, Amesbury, Essex, Massachusetts, USA. He married Marcia Jane GRASSO on 12 Oct 1980 at Sacred Heart Church, Merrimac/Amesbury, Essex, Massachusetts, USA. From Madeline, 1994 xmas card in 1994. He lived in 1995 at Merrimac, Essex, Massachusetts, USA.

He and Marcia were divorced on 9 Jun 1999 at Massachusetts Probate & Family Court, Salem, Essex, Massachusetts, USA.[429] He married Janet (--?--) circa 2001 at Essex, Massachusetts, USA.

(a) Adam Sebastean[8] BUNNELL was Catholic. He was born either 2 Sep 1983 or 20 Aug 1983? at Amesbury, Essex Co., Massachusetts. He was baptized on 25 Sep 1983 at Sacred Heart Church, Amesbury, Essex, Massachusetts, USA. He From Madeline, grandmother & xmas card 1994 in 1994. He lived in 1995 at Merrimac, Essex, Massachusetts, USA.

(b) Matthew Paul[8] BUNNELL was Catholic. He was born on 30 Jul 1984 at Amesbury, Essex Co., Massachusetts? He from Madeline, grandmother & xmas card 1994 in 1994. He lived in 1995 at Merrimac, Essex, Essex Co., Massachusetts. He was educated in Jun 2002 at Amesbury High School, Amesbury, Essex, Massachusetts, USA.[430]

(c) Benjamin Franklin[8] BUNNELL From Madeline, grandmother & 1994 xmas card. He lived at Merrimac, Essex Co., Massachusetts 1995. He was Catholic. Named after grandfather. He was born on 8 May 1988 at Amesbury, Essex Co., Massachusetts?

(d) Nathan[8] BUNNELL From 1994 xmas card. He lived at Merrimac, Essex Co., Massachusetts 1995. He was Catholic. He was born on 21 Feb 1990 at Amesbury, Essex Co., Massachusetts?

(e) Seth[8] BUNNELL From 1994 xmas card. He lived at Merrimac, Essex Co., Massachusetts 1995. He was Catholic. He was born on 11 Sep 1994 at Amesbury, Essex Co., Massachusetts.

(f) (--?--)[8] BUNNELL was born circa Feb 2003 at Essex, Massachusetts, USA.

iv) Julie A.[7] BUNNELL was Catholic. She was born on 23 Nov 1958 at Amesbury, Essex, Massachusetts, USA.[431] She married Gilbert Paul CARTIER on 5 Oct 1979 at Sacred Heart Catholic Church, Amesbury, Massachusetts. From Julie in 1993. She was did work at Amesbury Town Hall circa 1994. She lived in 1994 at Amesbury, Essex, Massachusetts, USA.[432]

(a) John Paul[8] CARTIER From Julie 1993 & Madeleine Bunnell 22 Oct.1995. He lived at Newbury, Essex Co., Massachusetts 1995. He was Catholic. He was born on 2 Aug 1980 at Amesbury Hospital, Amesbury, Essex Co., Massachusetts.

(b) Lauren Marie[8] CARTIER From Julie 1993 & Madeleine Bunnell 22 Oct.1995. She lived at Newbury, Essex Co., Massachusetts 1995. She was Catholic. She was born on 13 Aug 1982 at Amesbury, Essex Co., Massachusetts.

(c) Leah Marie[8] CARTIER From Julie 1993 & Madeleine Bunnell 22 Oct.1995. She lived at Newbury, Essex Co., Massachusetts 1995. She was Catholic. She was born on 24 Oct 1983 at Amesbury Hospital, Amesbury, Essex Co., Massachusetts.

v) Neal Gerard[7] BUNNELL was Catholic. He lived at Massachusetts. MILITARY: None. He was born on 4 Feb 1961 at Amesbury, Essex, Massachusetts, USA.[433] He was sports Taking part in the Badminton Tournament held yesterday afternoon at the Amesbury YMCA. Picture in file from Amesbury Newspaper circa 1968 at YMCA, Amesbury, Essex, Massachusetts, USA. He married Terri Anne ODOM (?), daughter of Lonnie ODOM (?), in 1982 at Massachusetts. From Madeleine Bunnell 22 Oct.1995.

(a) Benjamin Lonnie[8] BUNNELL From Madeleine Bunnell 22 Oct.1995. He lived at Massachusetts. He was Catholic? He was born on 6 Feb 1989 at Massachusetts.

(b) Zachary Neal[8] BUNNELL From Madeleine Bunnell 22 Oct.1995. He lived at Massachusetts. He was Catholic? He was born on 1 Apr 1993 at Massachusetts.

(c) Sarah Anne[8] BUNNELL From Madeleine Bunnell 22 Oct.1995. He/she lived at Massachusetts. She was Catholic? He/she was born on 6 Jan 1996 at Massachusetts, USA.

vi) Michelle Marie[7] BUNNELL was Catholic. She lived on 4 Jul 1964 at 4 Boardman St., Amesbury, Essex, Massachusetts, USA.[434,435] She was born on 4 Jul 1964 at Amesbury, Essex, Massachusetts, USA.[436] She married Robert Joseph LEVESQUE on 1 Oct 1982 at Massachusetts. She lived in 1995 at Wells, Maine 1995). Separated and going for divorce Oct.1995. From mother & Madeleine Bunnell 22 Oct.1995. She and Robert were divorced circa 1996 at USA. She lived in Feb 2000 at Gardner Lake Village Apartments, 100 Whitehall Rd., Amesbury, Essex, Massachusetts, USA.

(a) Robert Patrick[8] LEVESQUE From Madeleine Bunnell 22 Oct.1995. He lived at Wells, Maine 1995). He was Catholic. He was born on 20 Apr 1983 at Massachusetts.

(b) Michael Anthony[8] LEVESQUE From Madaleine Bunnell 22 Oct.1995. He lived at (living in Wells, Maine 1995). He was Catholic? He was born on 14 Nov 1984 at Maine?

(c) Christopher Joseph[8] LEVESQUE From Madaleine Bunnell 22 Oct.1995. He lived at (living in Wells, Maine 1995). He was Catholic? He was born on 12 Aug 1988 at Maine.

(i) Elizabeth Catherine[6] BUNNELL was hobby All kinds of dancing. She was Retired bookkeeper for family painting business. She was Catholic. She was born on 18 Jan 1931 at Amesbury, Essex Co., Ma. She was baptized on 19 Apr 1931 at St. Joseph Catholic Church, 9 Sparhawk St., Amesbury, Essex, Massachusetts, USA. She married George Knight PERKINS Jr., son of George Knight PERKINS Sr. and Beatrice THURLOW, on 6 Dec 1947 at St. Joseph Catholic Church, Amesbury, Ma. She lived in 1998 at Newburyport, Essex, Massachusetts, USA.[437]

She was traveled to Florida in February and March, boat trips, visiting friends, seeing a water & light show. Later this same year she went on vacations with her sister Marie to Las Vegas to see their brother George, to Livonia, Michigan to see their sister Mable and to Lake George, New York in Feb 2000. She was travel Planning to drive to Florida for this winter in Jan 2001 at Florida, USA. HEALTH: Operation to remove blockage (Cancer) in bowl area. Successfully removed, no future treatment required. Had blood transfusion and was anemic on 13 Aug 2002 at Ana Jakes Hospital, Newburyport, Essex, Massachusetts, USA.

i) Margaret Ann (Peggy)[7] PERKINS was Catholic. She was born on 4 Dec 1948 at Newburyport, Essex Co., Ma. She married Malcolm Winston WINKLEY on 10 Jun 1972 at Massachusetts. She lived in 1995 at Connecticut, USA. From Peggy, 21 Oct.1995.

(a) Jessica Ethel[8] WINKLEY was buried.[438] HEALTH: Died of Leukemia. She was Catholic. From Malcolm, 21 Oct.1995. She was born on 20 May 1973 at Rockville, Connecticut. She died on 18 Apr 1974 at Connecticut.

(b) Christian Barnes[8] WINKLEY was Catholic. He was born on 25 Feb 1975 at Rockville, Connecticut. Living at home, E. Haddam, Connecticut, USA. He was educated in May 1997 at Colby College, Connecticut?, USA.[439] School record and family update in Dec 1997 at Xmas Card, E. Haddam, Connecticut, USA. He was Expect carpenter and finisher. Did trim in parents home, very beautiful and ornate in Dec 1997 at home, E. Haddam, Connecticut, USA. He was educated in Sep 1998 at University of Connecticut, Connecticut, USA.[440] Went into the contracting business while attending law school at night. He bought an apartment house and is refurbishing it. From Eliz. Perkins xmas newsletter Dec. 1999. Dec. 2000 still has contracting business with brother, Joshua working with him in Dec 1999 at Connecticut, USA. He was engaged in 2000 at Connecticut, USA.[441]

(c) Joshua Edward[8] WINKLEY was Catholic. He was born on 10 Jan 1977 at Rockville, Connecticut. He lived in 1997 at Parents home, E. Haddam, Connecticut, USA. He was educated in Aug 1997 at University College, London, England.[442] Update on family in Xmas card in Dec 1997 at Xmas Card, E. Haddam, Connecticut, USA. He was educated in Jun 1999 at Colby College, USA.[443] He was working in brother Christian's construction business in Dec 2000 at Connecticut, USA.

(d) Matthew Malcolm[8] WINKLEY was Catholic. He was born on 2 Oct 1978 at Middletown, Connecticut. He lived in 1997 at Parents home, E. Haddam, Connecticut, USA. He was educated in Dec 1997 at Salve Regina University, Newport, Rhode Island, USA.[444] He was educated in Dec 1999 at Salve Regina College, Newport, Newport, Rhode Island, USA.[445] He was graduated circa 20 May 2001 at Connecticut, USA.[446]

(e) Travis Robert[8] WINKLEY was Catholic. He was born on 29 Jul 1981 at East Haddam, Connecticut. He lived in Dec 1997 at Parents home, E. Haddam, Connecticut, USA. He was Left athletic interest for guitar and band of four named "Official Xavier Band". He is lead singer and plays rhythm guitar. May play Lacrosses in Spring in Dec 1997 at E. Haddam, Connecticut, USA. He was educated in Jun 1999 at Connecticut, USA.[447]

(f) Caitlin Grace-Ann[8] WINKLEY was Catholic. She was born on 23 Apr 1984 at Meriden, Connecticut. She lived in Dec 1997 at Parents home, E. Haddam, Connecticut, USA. She was educated in Dec 1997 at Middle School, Connecticut, USA.[448] She was educated in Dec 1999 at Mercy High School, Connecticut, USA.[449]

ii) Cheryl Lee[7] PERKINS was Catholic. She was born on 11 Feb 1952 at Newburyport, Essex Co., Ma. She married Richard George SAWLER, son of Richard George SAWLER and Marion Louise KEANE, on 30 Aug 1973 at Byfield, Essex Co., Massachusetts. She and Richard George SAWLER were divorced before 1995. (Info. from Cheryl, 21 Oct. 1995) on 21 Oct 1995.

(a) Bradford Michael[8] SAWLER was Catholic. He was born on 14 Sep 1977 at Newburyport, Essex Co., Massachusetts. He From mother, 21 Oct.1995 on 21 Oct 1995. He was educated in Dec 1999 at Thompson Junior College, New Hampshire?, USA.[450] He was Working as a painter in Dec 2000 at New Hampshire?, USA.

(b) Jaime Robert[8] SAWLER was Catholic. He was born on 19 Jan 1980 at Concord, Massachusetts. From mother, 21 Oct.1995 on 21 Oct 1995. He was educated in Dec 1999 at Bates College, USA.[451]

(c) Hannah Louise[8] SAWLER was Catholic. She was born on 10 Dec 1981 at Beverly, Essex Co., Massachusetts. She was educated in Dec 1999 at Exeter High School, Exeter, New Hampshire, USA.[452] From mother, 21 Oct.1995 and on 21 Oct 2000. She was educated in Dec 2000 at Keene State, New Hampshire, USA.[453]

iii) Jay Edward[7] PERKINS was Catholic. MILITARY: None. He was Painter (took over fathers business). He was born on 16 Apr 1955 at Newburyport, Essex Co., Ma. He married Janie Anne ROCHE on 7 Apr 1979 at Massachusetts. He lived in 1995 at Salisbury, Essex, Massachusetts, USA.[454] (Info. from Jay, 21 Oct.1995).

(a) Justin Edward[8] PERKINS was Catholic. He was born on 17 Feb 1983 at Newburyport, Essex Co., Massachusetts. He lived in 1995 at Salisbury, Essex, Massachusetts, USA. (Info. from Janie, 21 Oct.1995). He was educated in Dec 1999 at Triton High School, Salisbury, Essex, Massachusetts, USA.[455]

(b) Joshua Taylor[8] PERKINS was Catholic. He was born on 9 Jan 1984 at Newburyport, Essex Co., Massachusetts. He lived in 1995 at Salisbury, Essex, Massachusetts, USA. (Info. from Janie,21 Oct.1995). He was educated in Dec 1999 at Triton High School, Salisbury, Essex?, Massachusetts, USA.[456]

(j) Stella Marie[6] BUNNELL (Bonnell) was Catholic. She Possibly born between Ben & Eliz.? She Ring Court was the street/house that Bunnell's rented home from Louis Bartley/Bertogli,#8 uncle.(from Marie DiDememico 16 Aug.1995) This was a big house located in back of the Barn Restaurant downtown Amesbury in Sep 1933. She died in Sep 1933 at 10 Ring Court (at home), Amesbury, Essex, Massachusetts, USA.[457,458] HEALTH: Died stillborn shortly after birth in Sep 1933 at Amesbury, Essex, Massachusetts, USA. She was born on 11 Sep 1933 at Ring Court (at home), Amesbury, Essex Co., Massachusetts. She was buried circa 12 Sep 1933 at St. Joseph Cemetery in Unhallowed Ground near workman's shed, Amesbury, Essex, Massachusetts, USA.[459]

(k) Louis Charles[6] BUNNELL. MILITARY: None. He was Catholic. He was Rand Corp., Newburyport, Mass. & The Polish Club (Bartender), Amesbury, Mass. He was born on 5 Aug 1940 at Amesbury, Essex Co., Massachusetts. He was baptized on 1 Sep 1940 at St. Joseph Catholic Church, 9 Sparhawk St., Amesbury, Essex, Massachusetts, USA. He Went to Amesbury High School, Al Star in sports, Basketball/Football circa 1956 at Amesbury High School, Amesbury, Essex, Massachusetts, USA. He married Frances Brenda SNOW on 31 Jan 1965 at Amesbury, Essex, Massachusetts, USA.[460] He immigrated circa 1968 to Canoga Park, Los Angeles, California, USA.[461] He and Frances Brenda SNOW were divorced before 1970. He married Phillis CARR (Adopted) on 29 May 1971 at Salem, Essex Co., Massachusetts? He and Phillis CARR (Adopted) were divorced circa 1979 at Salem, Essex, Massachusetts, USA.

i) Steven[7] BUNNELL. Living, Amesbury, Essex Co., Massachusetts 1995. From Louis Bunnell 8 Sept.1995. He was born on 20 Aug 1965 at Amesbury, Essex Co., Massachusetts?

ii) Jennifer[7] BUNNELL. Her married name was PSZENNY. She was Catholic. She was born at Amesbury/Newburyport?, Essex Co., Massachusetts. From wedding invite/I was there in Oct 1996. She Church located at 47 Butler Ave in Oct 1996 at Essex, Massachusetts, USA. She married Matthew Lee PSZENNY in Oct 1996 at St. Florence Catholic Church, Wakefield, Essex Co., Massachusetts. Popes secretary sent signed scroll from Vatican to them in Oct 1996. She lived in Jun 1998 at 20 Highland Ave., Salem, Essex, Massachusetts, USA. (From obituary of son, Nicholas) on 23 Jun 1998 at The Daily News (Tuesday), Newburyport, Essex, Massachusetts, USA.

    (a) Nicholas Matthew[8] PSZENNY. From Tele call with Marie DiDimenico who will be great aunt on 12 Jun 1998 at Malden, Massachusetts, USA. He was born on 20 Jun 1998 at Salem?, Essex?, Massachusetts, USA.[462] He died on 21 Jun 1998 at New England Medical Center (Neo Natal Intensive Care Unit) 750 Washington St., Boston, Suffolk, Massachusetts, USA.[463] HEALTH: Baby was induced when no movement or water. Upon arrival, found there was a heart defect, placed on respirator, later taken off and he passed away in the arms of his parents. He was a beautiful baby with long black hair on 21 Jun 1998 at New England Medical Center (Natal Unit), Boston, Suffolk, Massachusetts, USA. He was buried on 25 Jun 1998 at c. 12 noon, St. Mary's Cemetery, Salem, Essex, Massachusetts, USA.[464]

    (b) Allysa Nichol[8] PSZENNY was born on 2 Jul 1999 at Salem, Essex, Massachusetts, USA.[465] She was baptized on 19 Sep 1999 at St. James Catholic Church, Essex, Massachusetts, USA.[466]

iii) Jeffery Charles[7] BUNNELL was born at Amesbury/Newburyport?, Essex Co., Massachusetts. Jeff & mother not planning marriage, mother wants to finish school first. (from them on 14 Aug.1993). He was Catholic. MILITARY: US Army 1996/7, stationed in Hanau, Germany in 1996. From Marriage invite 5 March 1997. reception at same place on 5 Mar 1997.

He married Deanna Louise TRACCHIA, daughter of Donald W. TRACCHIA and (--?--) (--?--), on 5 Apr 1997 at Saint Florence Church (5:45 PM) 47 Butler Ave., Wakefield, Essex, Massachusetts, USA. He lived in 1998 at US Army, Hanau, Germany. Now is stationed and living on base in Kentuckey.

    (a) Jeffery[8] BUNNELL Jr.(?) was Catholic? Info. from parents 1994. He was born in Dec 1993 at Salem, Essex Co., Massachusetts?

    iv) Erin[7] BUNNELL was born at Amesbury/Newburyport?, Essex Co., Massachusetts. She was Catholic. She lived in Jun 1998 at 20 Highland Ave., Salem, Essex, Massachusetts, USA.[467]

(12) Charles O'Connell[5] BUNNELL (Bonnell) was Catholic. From Bapt.record & family members. HEALTH: Alcoholic. He was Labourer? He was born on 7 Nov 1902 at home, street #35, Jamaica Plain, Suffolk, Massachusetts, USA. He was baptized on 23 Nov 1902 at St. Francis De Sales Catholic Church, Roxbury, Suffolk, Massachusetts, USA.[468] He appeared on the census of 1910 at US Census, Boston, Suffolk, Massachusetts, USA.[469] He immigrated on 19 Mar 1916 to Lived with Mrs. Beatrice Cooley, Everett, Massachusetts, USA.[470] On 14 July 1918 runaway taking money,19 Sept.1918 Roxbury Court, placed on probation on 14 Jul 1918 at Massachusetts, USA. He died on 2 Apr 1946 of alcoholism at Boston Sanatorium 496 Massachusetts Ave., Boston, Suffolk, Massachusetts, USA, at age 43.[471,472] He was buried circa 3 Apr 1946 at Saint Mary's cemetery, Dorcester, Massachusetts, USA.[473]

(13) Anna May[5] Bunnell Bonnell Nice lady, owned knitted cloth of Saint John, NB made by an ancestors work, possibly Charles Bonnell/Bunnell while he had a broken leg and grounded from sea travel. She was Catholic. She was born on 14 Mar 1904 at Boston, Suffolk, Massachusetts, USA.[474] She lived on 14 Mar 1904 at 37 Weston St., Boston, Suffolk, Massachusetts, USA.[475,476] She Lived on Charles River, Boston, Ma., then Brocton, Ma., then So. Carolina with Mary Talbos possibly until death circa 1930 at Charles River Apartment, Boston, Suffolk, Massachusetts, USA. She died after 1930 at Boston, Suffolk, Massachusetts, USA.

(14) Mable Elizabeth[5] BUNNELL was Catholic. She was born on 14 May 1905 at 37 Weston St., Boston, Suffolk, Massachusetts, USA.[477] She immigrated circa 1910 to Massachusetts, USA.[478] She appeared on the census of 1910 at US Census, Boston, Suffolk, Massachusetts, USA.[479] She immigrated on 7 Oct 1917 to East Bridgewater, Massachusetts, USA.[480] She lived on 24 Nov 1927 at Milton, Massachusetts, USA.[481,482] She married Edward (Eddy) Charles FAY Sr., son of John FAY and Mary Quigly, on 7 Feb 1930 at Boston, Suffolk, Massachusetts, USA.[483,484] She Married and lived at 195 Everett St. E. Boston circa 8 Feb 1930 at 195 Everett St., East Boston, Suffolk, Massachusetts, USA. HEALTH: Did she have Huntington's Disease? Had erratic behavior, mood swings, appeared drunk? Per Virginia LecLerc of Revere, Ma circa 1954 at Revere, Suffolk, Massachusetts, USA. HEALTH: died of Cerebral Hemerage/had trouble w/memory/confused, age 54 till death (per Virginia,2Jan95)(Huntingtons?) on 27 Mar 1963. She died on 27 Mar 1963 at Possibly at home, Revere, Suffolk, Massachusetts, USA, at age 57.[485] She was buried circa 29 Mar 1963 at New Calvery Cemetery, Roxbury, Suffolk, Massachusetts, USA.[486] From Virginia Leclerc 1992 in 1992.

  (a) Grace[6] FAY was born circa 1940 at Revere, Massachusetts, USA. From Virginia (sister) 1992 in 1992 at Revere, Massachusetts, USA. From daughter Lois March 1997 at Massachusetts, USA.

   i) Lois[7] (--?--). Her married name was Cambria. Living at 221 Suffolk Ave. Revere, Ma.02151 (March 1997). From herself March 9 1997. She was born at Massachusetts.

  (b) Joseph[6] FAY was born circa 1941 at Revere, Massachusetts, USA. From Virginia LeLerc of Revere, Ma in 1992 at Revere, Massachusetts, USA.

  (c) Edward (Eddy)[6] FAY Jr. was born circa 1942 at Revere, Massachusetts, USA. From Virginia LeLerc of Revere, Ma in 1992 at Revere, Massachusetts, USA.

(d) Virginia[6] FAY. Her married name was Leclerc. She married (--?) LECLERC at Massachusetts? She was born in 1943 at Revere, Massachusetts?

(15) Joseph Raymond[5] BUNNELL. HEALTH: Had breathing problem & ? He retired.[487] He was Catholic. He was born on 10 May 1908 at 10 Benton St., Roxbury/Boston, Suffolk, Massachusetts, USA.[488] He immigrated circa 1910.[489] He appeared on the census of 1910 at US Census, Boston, Suffolk, Massachusetts, USA.[490] When family broke up Joe went to Nazareth after 1910 at Nazareth Child Care 420 Pond St., Jamaica, Massachusetts, USA. He was raised by Martin & Delia McDonugh, S. Boston after 1910. He married Agnes Frances CONLEY, daughter of Stephen CONLEY and Mary KANE, on 5 Sep 1937 at Boston, Suffolk, Massachusetts, USA.[491] He lived on 5 Sep 1937 at 124A Dorcester St., Boston, Suffolk, Massachusetts, USA.[492] He lived on 11 Dec 1939 at 550 E. 7th. St., Boston, Suffolk, Massachusetts, USA.[493] He lived in 1981 at 550 E. 7th. St., Boston, Suffolk, Massachusetts, USA.[494] He died on 28 Dec 1991 at Randolph, Norfolk, Massachusetts, USA, at age 83.[495] He lived before 1993 at 75 Orchard St., Randolph, Massachusetts, USA. He was buried circa 1993 at Massachusetts, USA.[496]

(a) Mary Louise[6] BUNNELL was Catholic(ex-nun). She was born on 10 Dec 1939 at Boston, Suffolk Co., Mass.[497,498] She married Henry Franklin (Frank) SCHREIBER, son of Henry Otto SCHREIBER and Esther Lydia WOODBURY, on 30 Dec 1972 at Boston, Suffolk Co., Mass. She lived in 1993 at Randolph, Massachusetts., USA.

i) Elsie Marie[7] SCHREIBER Has pretty bright red hair. She lived at Living 1993 in Randolph, Mass. She was Catholic. She was born on 8 Dec 1979 at Boston, Suffolk Co., Massachusetts.

(b) Joseph Raymond[6] BUNNELL Junior was Catholic. He was born on 7 Jan 1943 at Roxbury/Boston, Suffolk, Massachusetts, USA.[499] He 1987, he & sister had 50th. wedding anniversary party for parents in Randolph, Mass in 1987. He lived in 1998 at 61 Imoor Cr., Randolph, Massachusetts, USA.[500]

(16) Martha T.[5] BUNNELL[501] was born on 6 Feb 1910 at 10 Benton St., Boston, Suffolk, Massachusetts, USA.[502] She died on 8 Mar 1910 at 10 Benton St., Boston, Suffolk, Massachusetts, USA.[503] She was buried circa 9 Mar 1910 at Forrest Hills Cemetery, Boston, Suffolk, Massachusetts, USA.[504]

(17) Frank[5] BUNNELL[505] was born on 12 Feb 1911 at 50 Cabot St., Boston, Suffolk, Massachusetts, USA.[506] He died on 6 Sep 1911 at Boston Floating Hospital, Boston, Suffolk, Massachusetts, USA.[507] He was buried circa 7 Sep 1911 at Calvary Cemetery, Boston, Suffolk, Massachusetts, USA.[508]

i) Benjamin Frank[4] BUNNELL[509] was born in Oct 1866 at Fredericton?, York, New Brunswick, Canada.[510] He immigrated in 1871.[511] He was Free Christian Baptist. He appeared on the census of 1871 at Canadian Census, Fredericton, York, New Brunswick, Canada.[512] He appeared on the census of 1900 at US Census, Boston, Suffolk, Massachusetts, USA.[513,514] He died on 5 Feb 1933 at Home For aged & Infirm, Cambridge, Middlesex, Massachusetts, USA, at age 66.[515,516] He lived on 5 Feb 1933 at 48 Eutis St., Cambridge, Middlesex, Massachusetts, USA.[517] He was buried circa 6 Feb 1933 at Forrest Hills Cemetery, Boston, Suffolk, Massachusetts, USA.[518]

j) Frank[4] BUNNELL was Baptist? He immigrated.[519] He was born in Oct 1866 at New Brunswick, Canada.

k) Charles H.[4] BUNNELL immigrated.[520] He was born in Nov 1868 at Fredericton?, York, New Brunswick, Canada.[521,522] He was Free Christian Baptist. He appeared on the census of 1871 at Canadian Census, Fredericton, York, New Brunswick, Canada.[523] He married Margaret L. FARREN (Farron), daughter of Hugh FARREN, in 1898 at Boston?, Suffolk, Massachusetts, USA.[524] He appeared on the census of 1900 at US Census, Boston, Suffolk, Massachusetts, USA.[525,526] He appeared on the census of 1910 at US Census, Boston, Suffolk, Massachusetts, USA.[527,528] From Donna Doscher,102 Prim Rose Path,Summerville,SC,29483 in 1993 in 1993.

(1) Mary M.[5] BUNNELL immigrated.[529] She was born on 22 Dec 1900 at 96 Leverett St., Boston, Suffolk, Massachusetts, USA.[530] She appeared on the census of 1910 at US Census, Boston, Suffolk, Massachusetts, USA.[531,532] She married Floyd Gilchrist TALBERT circa 1920. She appeared on the census of 1920 at US Census, Cambridge, Middlesex, Massachusetts, USA.[533] From Donna in 1993,mentions Charles & Evangeline? Also, Mary called Mae by Donna in 1993.

 (a) Donna[6] TALBERT married John DOSCHER. She was born after 1925. From Donna 1993 in 1993. She was Owns stitch work of possibly Charles Bonnell made while having a broken leg or something like that at Saint John, NB in mid-1800's. Handed down to her in 1997. She was Likes, art, bridge, travel, grandchildren & friends & computers, reading in Dec 1997. She was Librarian in Dec 1997. As of 25 Dec 1997, Donna TALBERT lived at 102 Prim Rose Path, Summerville, South Carolina, USA 29483.[534] She was Taking flight to Seattle, drive to Vancouver, BC and take cruise on ship "Mercury" to Alaska on 24 Jul 1998 at Trip to Alaska, Alaska, USA. She was retired circa Dec 1998 at South Carolina, USA.[535]

  i) Deborah Linn (Lynn?)[7] She married Steve MCCORMACK. She lived in 1993 at Minnesota, USA. From mother, Donna 1993 in 1993. She lived in 1993 at Amsterdam, Netherlands.[536]

   (a) Dylan[8] MCCORMACK was born circa 1994. From Donna Doscher, grandmother Xmas letter. Says he will start school c. 1999 on 25 Dec 1997.

  ii) Susan[7] DOSCHER married Brian MCCOY, son of Robert MCCOY and Goldie (--?--). From Donna Doscher 1993 in 1993. As of 25 Dec 1997, Susan DOSCHER lived at Prim Rose Path, Summerville, South Carolina, USA 29483.[537]

   (a) Rachel[8] MCCOY From Donna Doscher 1993.

   (b) Camile[8] MCCOY From Donna Doscher 1993.

iii) Charles[7] DOSCHER married an unknown person before 1993.[538] From mother Donna, 1993. He and an unknown person were divorced before 1997.[539] He was engaged on 25 Dec 1997.[540] Info from Donna Doscher in Xmas card on 25 Dec 1997.

(2) Charles Franklin[5] BUNNELL Sr. was born on 20 Oct 1903 at 25 Blue Hill Ave., Boston, Suffolk, Massachusetts, USA.[541,542] He appeared on the census of 1910 at US Census, Boston, Suffolk, Massachusetts, USA.[543,544] He appeared on the census of 1920 at US Census, Cambridge, Middlesex, Massachusetts, USA.[545,546] He married Grace Lillian Hall, daughter of Lawrence Hall and Mary Stillman, on 20 Jun 1925 at Waltham, Middlesex, Massachusetts, USA.[547] He died on 24 Jun 1960 at Symms Hospital, Arlington, Middlesex, Massachusetts, USA, at age 56.[548,549] He was buried circa 25 Jun 1960 at Mt. Pleasant Cemetery, Arlington, Middlesex, Massachusetts, USA.[550]

(a) Charles Franklin[6] BUNNELL Jr. married Ann Freeman at Massachusetts, USA.[551] He was born on 17 Jun 1927 at 62 Prentice St., Cambridge, Middlesex, Massachusetts, USA.[552,553] He says he visited St. John, NB to see relations in 1930's. His fathers uncle was Leo Bunnell who moved to Mass from Saint John after World War I on 16 Jun 2001.

(b) Barbara Rae[6] BUNNELL[554] was born on 10 May 1930 at 134 Oxford St., Cambridge, Middlesex, Massachusetts, USA.[555]

(c) Robert Edward[6] BUNNELL[556] married Shirley Keith at Massachusetts, USA.[557] He was born on 18 Sep 1932 at 134 Oxford St., Cambridge, Middlesex, Massachusetts, USA.[558]

i) Keith Stephenson[7] BUNNELL[559] was born at Massachusetts, USA.[560]

ii) Sara Stillman[7] BUNNELL[561] was born at Massachusetts, USA.[562]

(3) Evangeline[5] BUNNELL was born on 24 Dec 1908 at Boston, Suffolk, Massachusetts, USA.[563] From Donna Doscher 1993 in 1993.

l) Anne (Annie) Mae[4] BUNNELL was Baptist. She immigrated back and forth from Massachusetts.[564] She called her brother Woodbury, "Wood" and talked a lot of him to Donna while she lived with her in South Carolina. She was born on 4 Mar 1875 at Fredericton, York, New Brunswick, Canada.[565] She appeared on the census of 1900 at US Census, Boston, Suffolk, Massachusetts, USA.[566,567] She was informant on mothers death in 1919 at Massachusetts, USA.[568] She died on 29 Sep 1963 at Godard Memorial Hospital, Stoughton, Norfolk, Massachusetts, USA, at age 88.[569] She lived on 29 Sep 1963 at 18 Silver Rd., Stoughton, Norfolk, Massachusetts, USA.[570] She was buried circa 30 Sep 1963 at Forest Hills Cemetery, Boston, Suffolk, Massachusetts, USA.[571] Donna Doscher has 25X30 painting made of yarn of St. John by Charles Bunnell 1858-59 she inherited it in 1993.

m) Mabel[4] BUNNELL was Baptist? She immigrated.[572] She was born in 1877 at New Brunswick, Canada.[573,574]

5. Abraham[3] BUNNELL (Bonnell) was Anglican? He was born circa 1821 at Saint John?, Saint John?, New Brunswick, Canada.[575] He was shipping Was owner & builder #1, 32 shares, Previously registered at Saint John, New Brunswick 1842, constructed at Waterborough 1842, 1 deck, 2 mast, type was a schooner, length 66 ft., 17 ft. wide, depth 6 ft, gross tons 55, registered 1845, reason for closure #4 at Saint John in 1845 in 1842 at Ship "Dolphin", Waterborough, New Brunswick?, Canada.[576] He was into shipping Was owner and builder #1 with 64 shares, constructed at Saint John 1846 with 2 mast, was a schooner, length 63 ft, 20 ft. wide, depth 5 ft, gross tons 98, year registered 1846, official year closure 1847, reason #4 at Saint John in 1847 in 1846 at Ship "British Queen", Saint John, Saint John, New Brunswick, Canada.[577] He was Mariner from Kings County, New Brunswick. See above History 1845 in 1846 at Saint John, Saint John, New Brunswick, Canada. He was in shipping Was owner and builder #1 with 64 shares, previously registered at Saint John 1847, constructed at Kingston, Kings Co., New Brunswick 1840 with 1 deck, 2 mast, type was a schooner, length 66 ft, width 19 ft, depth 6 ft, gross tons 53, year registered 1847, official year closure 1853, reason #4 at Saint John 1853 in 1847 at Ship "Prince Albert", Saint John, Saint John, New Brunswick, Canada.[578] He was Mariner.

See above 1845 History for details in 1847 at Saint John, Saint John, New Brunswick, Canada. Was owner and builder #1 with 64 shares, previously registered at Saint John 1848 and constructed at Kingston, Kings Co., New Brunswick 1842. Has 1 deck, 2 mast and is a schooner, length 60 ft, width 16 ft, depth 5 ft, gross tons 44. Year registered 1849, official year closure 1852, reason #4 at Saint John 1852 in 1848 at Ship "Hazard", Saint John, Saint John, New Brunswick, Canada.[579] He was Boatman, age 30 in 1851 in 1851 at New Brunswick Census, Kings ?, New Brunswick, Canada. He appeared on the census of 1851 at Canadian Census, Westfield Parish, Kings, New Brunswick, Canada.[580] Was owner & builder 31 with 64 shares, registered at Saint John 1852, constructed at Long Reach, Kings Co., New Brunswick 1849 with 1 deck, 2 mast, type was a schooner, length 68 ft, width 19 ft, depth 6 ft, gross tons 57, year registered 1853, year closure 1853, reason #4 at Saint John 1853 in 1852 at Ship "Collingwood", Long Reach, Kings, New Brunswick, Canada.[581] He was Mariner from Kings County, New Brunswick. See above 1845 History for details in 1853 at Saint John, Saint John, New Brunswick, Canada. He was directory (Listed as a Farmer in Hutchinson's New Brunswick Directory 1867-68, page 453) circa 1867 at Long Reach, Westfield, Kings, New Brunswick, Canada.

6. Eleanor[3] BUNNELL (Bonnell) was First Church Baptist. She immigrated.[582] She was born circa 1824 at Westfield/Greenwich, Kings, New Brunswick, Canada.[583,584] She married William DELONG, son of Aaron DELONG U.E. and Mary Kierstead U.E, on 3 Nov 1842 at Westfield, Kings, New Brunswick, Canada.[585] Wedding witnessed by Henry Beattie & Clenina on 3 Nov 1842. Her estate was probated on 2 Aug 1866 at Westfield, Kings, New Brunswick, Canada.[586,587] She appeared on the census of 1871 at Census, Wellington, York, New Brunswick, Canada.[588] She died after 1871 at New Brunswick, Canada.

a) Eliza[4] DELONG From 1871 Fredericton, Willington census, lived w/parents. She was First Church Baptist. She was born circa 1846 at New Brunswick, Canada. She died after 1871 at New Brunswick, Canada?

b) Asa[4] DELONG was Farm Laborer. He From 1871 Fredericton, Willington census, living w/parents. He was First Church Baptist. He was born circa 1847 at New Brunswick, Canada. He died after 1871.

c) Alberta[4] DELONG was Dress Maker. From 1871 Fredericton, Willington census, living w/parents. He was First Church Baptist. He was born circa 1851 at New Brunswick, Canada. He died after 1871.

d) Anna P.J.[4] DELONG: From 1871 Fredericton, Willington census, living w/parents. She was First Church Baptist. She was born circa 1855 at New Brunswick, Canada. She died after 1871.

7. Isaac[3] BUNNELL (Bonnell) was Anglican? He married Jemima (--?--) (Bonnell) at New Brunswick, Canada.[589] He was born circa 1826 at Westfield, Kings Co., New Brunswick, Canada. He married Martha MCLEAN on 4 Mar 1848 at New Brunswick, Canada.[590] He was a Boatman, age 25 in 1851,Westfield,Kings Co., NB census in 1851 at Census, Kings, New Brunswick, Canada. He appeared on the census of 10 Dec 1851 at Canadian Census, Westfield Parish, Kings, New Brunswick, Canada.[591,592] He was in shipping Isaac of Westfield, Mariner (in partnership with brother Ben), #2 owner, 32 shares, previously registered at Saint John 1851, built at Grand Lake 1848, 2 masted schooner, length 68 ft, width 19 ft, depth 6 ft, gross tons 56, year registered 1853, official year closure 1867, reason closure #12 at Mount Desert Island 1866 in 1853 at Ship "Linnet", Grand Lake, Kings, New Brunswick, Canada.[593] He was Mariner with 32 shares in shipping. From AutoInc #37819, Reg.#J853034 found in Ships & Seafarer's of Atlantic Canada CD, Newfoundland in 1853 at Westfield, Kings, New Brunswick, Canada. Possibly him listed in Hutchinson's New Brunswick Directory 1867-68, page 453 with Abraham Bonnell, as Farmers in 1867 at Long Reach, Westfield, Kings, New Brunswick, Canada.

8. Samuel[3] BUNNELL (Bonnell) was Anglican? He was born circa 1827 at Westfield, Kings Co., New Brunswick, Canada. He was in shipping Samuel of Westfield, #2 owner (Partnership with brother Abraham), 32 shares, previously registered at Saint John 1846, built at Kingston 1835, 2 masted schooner, length 63 ft, width 20 ft, depth 5 ft, gross tons 98, registered 1847, official date closure 1851, reason #4 at Saint John 1851 in 1847 at Ship "British Queen", Kingston, Kings, New Brunswick, Canada.[594] He was Mariner and owned 32 shares in shipping. From AutoInc #36629, Reg.#J847140, Saint John found in Ships & Seafarer's of Atlantic Canada CD, Newfoundland in 1847 at Westfield, Kings, New Brunswick, Canada. He was in shipping as Samuel of Westfield, Mariner, owner #1, 64 shares, previously registered at Saint John 1849, built at Maugerville 1837, 2 masted schooner, length 67 ft, width 19 ft, depth 6 ft, gross tons 52, year registered 1851, year officially closure 1853, reason #4 at Saint John 1853 in 1851 at Ship "Argyle", Maugerville, New Brunswick, Canada.[595]

He was Mariner that owned 64 shares in shipping. From AutoInc #37478, Reg.#J851096, Saint John, found in Ships & Seafarer's of Atlantic Canada CD, Newfoundland in 1851 at Westfield, Kings, New Brunswick, Canada. He appeared on the census of 10 Dec 1851 at Canadian Census, Westfield Parish, Kings, New Brunswick, Canada.[596,597] He was Mariner and owner of 64 shares in shipping. From AutoInc #40061, Reg.#J864076, Saint John, found in Ships & Seafarer's of Atlantic Canada, Cd, Newfoundland in 1864 at Saint John, Saint John, New Brunswick, Canada. He was in shipping as Samuel of Saint John, Mariner, owner #1 with 64 shares, constructed at Grand Lake 1864, 2 masted schooner, length 72 ft, width 24 ft, depth 6 ft, gross tons 66, net tons 66, year registered 1864, official year closure 1889, reason #13 at Long Reach, 1888 in 1864 at Ship "Hall and Fairweather", Grand Lake, Kings, New Brunswick, Canada.[598] He left a will on 2 Aug 1866 at Westfield, Kings, New Brunswick, Canada.[599,600] He was in directory (Found on page 88 of Hutchinson's New Brunswick Directory 1867-68. Listed as a wood dealer) circa 1867 at 78 Princess St., Saint John, Saint John, New Brunswick, Canada. He was Trader/Dealer and owner of 32 shares in shipping. From AutoInc #41041, Reg.#J867053, Saint John, found in Ships & Seafarer's of Atlantic Canada CD, Newfoundland in 1867 at Saint John, Saint John, New Brunswick, Canada. He was in shipping as Samuel of Saint John, Trader/Dealer, owner #1, 32 shares, constructed at Boston, 1 deck Steamer, length 56 ft, width 14 ft, depth 6 ft, gross tons 30, net tons 29, registered tonnage 9, 30 horse power, year registered 1867, year officially closure 1875, reason #19 at Musquash 1874 in 1867 at Ship "Bessie B", Boston, Suffolk, Massachusetts, USA.[601]

9. George W[3] Bunnell was Bithinia. He married Bethia (Erthia) Kierstead, daughter of Benjamin Kierstead U.E. and Jemima Bunnell (U.E.), at New Brunswick, Canada. He was born circa 1827 at Westfield Parish, Kings, New Brunswick, Canada. He appeared on the census of 1851 at Canadian Census, Westfield Parish, Kings, New Brunswick, Canada.[602]

10. Graves/Gravest William[3] BUNNELL (Bonnell) was Anglican/Baptist? He was born in Oct 1830 at Saint John, Saint John Co., New Brunswick, Canada.[603] He appeared on the census of 1851 at Canadian Census, Westfield Parish, Kings, New Brunswick, Canada.[604,605] He was Boatman 1851,Westfield, NB/Sea Capt.& Mariner & Sea Capt.1859, & Salesman, Boston, Ma in 1851 at Sea Captain, Westfield, Kings, New Brunswick, Canada. He was shipping Graves of Saint John, Mariner, owner #2, 32 shares, previously registered at Saint John 1847, built at Kingston 1840, 2 masted schooner, length 66 ft, width 19 ft, depth 6 ft, gross tons 53, registered 1853, official closure year 1860, reason closure #13 in

1853 at Ship "Prince Albert", Kingston, Kings, New Brunswick, Canada.[606] He was Mariner and part owner (32 shares) in shipping. From AutoInc #38060, Reg.#J853171 found in Ships & Seafarer's of Atlantic Canada CD, Newfoundland in 1853 at Saint John, Saint John, New Brunswick, Canada. He immigrated circa 1859 to 161 Chelsea St., Charlestown, Suffolk?, Massachusetts, USA.[607] He Lived at 161 Chelsea St., Charlestown, Boston, Ma. Married .by Rev. J.S. Cushman in 1859. He married Hannah M. (Dardy) COTTLE, daughter of Woodbury L. COTTLE and Hannah (Margaret) D. SKINNER (Skimmer), on 19 Sep 1859 at Charlestown, Suffolk, Massachusetts, USA.[608,609] He lived on 7 Nov 1860 at 161 Chelsea St., Charlestown, Suffolk, Massachusetts, USA.[610,611] He left a will on 2 Aug 1866 at Fathers Will, Westfield, Kings, New Brunswick, Canada.[612,613] He died in Jun 1868 at Upper Fredericton, York, New Brunswick, Canada, at age 37.[614,615] He was buried in Jun 1868 at Upper Fredericton?, York?, New Brunswick?, Canada?[616,617] From Bill (William)Bunnell 18 Jan.1997 on 18 Jan 1997 at Concord, New Hampshire, USA.

    a) Graves William^4 BUNNELL (Bonnell)(William Albert)[618] Family may have acquired William Bunnell trunk w/P. Bunnell. He was Baptist. He was born on 7 Nov 1860 at 161 Chelsea St., Malden, Middlesex, Massachusetts, USA.[619,620] He married Irene Pierson SNOW, daughter of Zoeth SNOW 3rd. and Rebecca A. MAYO, on 26 Jun 1890 at Unitarian Church, Brewster, Barnstable, Massachusetts, USA.[621] He lived on 23 Mar 1895 at Malden, Middlesex, Massachusetts, USA.[622,623] He immigrated in 1897.[624] He appeared on the census of 1900 at 23 Rockland Ave., Malden, Middlesex, Massachusetts, USA.[625,626] He appeared on the census of 1910 at Iglew St., Malden, Middlesex, Massachusetts, USA.[627,628] He was at Bowditch & Clapp Co.1913-30.1912 Secretary of Co.& Manager(1912)of Hat Dept(Millinery bus. since 1881) in 1913. He appeared on the census of 1920 at 11 Glen St., Malden, Middlesex, Massachusetts, USA.[629,630] HEALTH: Died of Pneumonia (Sunday)after ill 5 days(home) before 13 Feb 1927. He died on 13 Feb 1927 at 11 Glen St., Malden, Middlesex, Massachusetts, USA, at age 66.[631,632] He was buried after 13 Feb 1927 at Brewster Cemetery (Bunnell Plot #A-701), Brewster, Barnstable, Massachusetts, USA. Some info from Bill (William) Bunnell on 18 Jan 1997.

    (1) Charlotte Lee^5 BUNNELL was born in Sep 1893 at Malden, Middlesex, Massachusetts, USA.[633] She appeared on the census of 1900 at Malden, Middlesex, Massachusetts, USA.[634]

She appeared on the census of 1910 at Malden, Middlesex, Massachusetts, USA.[635] She married Edward (Ned) Bickford KITFIELD, son of Jacob KITFIELD and Daisy Bickford, on 26 May 1917 at Malden, Middlesex, Massachusetts, USA.[636] She died in 1931 at Wallingford, Connecticut, USA.[637] From William Brewster Bunnell 1989 & 1997 in Arizona, now in Concord, NH in 1997.

(2) Greaves W.[5] BUNNELL[638] was born on 23 Mar 1895 at Malden, Middlesex, Massachusetts, USA.[639,640]

(3) William Brewster[5] BUNNELL (Bonnell) Sr. immigrated.[641] He was born on 23 Mar 1895 at 11 Glen St., Malden, Middlesex, Massachusetts, USA. He appeared on the census of 1900 at Malden, Middlesex, Massachusetts, USA.[642] He appeared on the census of 1910 at US Census, Malden, Middlesex, Massachusetts, USA.[643,644] He was 1913-17 worked Bowditch,Clapp, Boston, Ma.1917 to USN after 1913. MILITARY: Atlantic 1919 USNR Ensign troopship troops to/from, discharged Oct.1921.1922-25,3rd.Mate on Oil tanker. Enlisted Jun 1917 USN,USS Amphitrite, NY Harb. OCS, Pelham, NY, Commissioned, Ensign USNR, May 1919 circa 1919. He appeared on the census of 1920 at US Census, Malden, Middlesex, Massachusetts, USA.[645,646] He was found on a passenger list on 24 Feb 1920 at Ellis Island, New York, New York, USA.[647] He was found on a passenger list on 21 Mar 1920 at Ellis Island, New York, New York, USA.[648] He was found on a passenger list on 10 Jul 1920 at Ellis Island, New York, New York, USA.[649] He Worked for dad 1925-28 Atlantic Lumber Co.1929-32,Mem.of Hingham Yacht Club 1935-40 after 1925. He lived on 13 Feb 1927 at 11 Glen St., Malden, Middlesex, Massachusetts, USA.[650,651] He married Constance WEBSTER, daughter of Charles WEBSTER and Jesse Taylor, on 17 Aug 1929 at Nashua, Hillborough, New Hampshire, USA.[652,653] He lived on 17 Nov 1937 at 12 Weston Rd., Hingham, Plymouth, Massachusetts, USA.[654,655] Listed in USN 1942-43 Argentina, NewFoundland, Canada and Pacific in 1942. He died on 30 Jun 1953 at 1019 Main St., Hingham, Plymouth, Massachusetts, USA, at age 58.[656,657] HEALTH: d, Cancer on 30 Jun 1953. He was buried circa 1 Jul 1953 at Brewster, Barnstable, Massachusetts, USA.[658]

(a) William Brewster[6] BUNNELL (Bonnell) Jr. living in Concord, New Hampshire 1997. MILITARY: US Army. He immigrated several places.[659] He was Artist/Framer, Boston U Grad SFAR 1961. Self Employed. From Himself. He was born on 17 Nov 1937 at Boston, Massachusetts. Very interested in family genealogy, good friend and cousin.

(4) Graves William[5] BUNNELL (Bonnell) Jr. His Social Security gotten in Connecticut. He had no children 1st & 2nd.marr,div.1940. Picture of family and him 1907, from William Brewster Bunnell in 1907. He was born on 4 Jun 1907 at Malden, Middlesex, Massachusetts, USA.[660] He appeared on the census of 1910 at Malden, Middlesex, Massachusetts, USA.[661,662] He appeared on the census of 1920 at US Census, Malden, Middlesex, Massachusetts, USA.[663,664] MILITARY: Attend Brewster Academy,Wolfboro,N.H.c.mid.1920's. In US Coast Guard WW II, never left Boston circa 1925. He married Constance (Connie) A. WALLACE, daughter of William E. WALLACE and Florence Wilding, on 7 Jun 1930 at Melrose, Middlesex, Massachusetts, USA.[665,666] He and Constance (Connie) A. WALLACE were divorced circa 1945. He married Eleanor V. SMITH, daughter of Clinton E. SMITH and Maggie Myers, on 11 Oct 1946 at Boston, Suffolk, Massachusetts, USA.[667,668] He was Founder, Bunnell Frame Shop 1947,3 location on Newbury St., Boston, Mass in 1947. He immigrated circa 1952.[669] HEALTH: In Naval Hosp, Boston (met 2nd.wife).Bad Car accident late 1961 in 1961. He died on 10 Feb 1962 at Nashua, New Hampshire(hosp), at age 54. He was buried circa 12 Feb 1962 at Bunnell Plot, Brewster Cemetery, Brewster, Barnstable, Massachusetts, USA. From Bill Bunnell 18 Jan.1997 on 18 Jan 1987.

b) Alice M.[4] BUNNELL was born in 1864 at Charlestown, Suffolk, Massachusetts, USA.[670] She appeared on the census of 1870 at US Census, Charlestown, Middlesex, Massachusetts, USA.[671] She married Charles H. DEARBORN, son of Daniel DEARBORN and Nellie (--?--), on 10 May 1887 at Boston, Suffolk, Massachusetts, USA.[672] She appeared on the census of 1920 at 19 Glen St., Malden, Middlesex, Massachusetts, USA.[673,674] She was buried in 1961.[675] She died in 1961 at Wellsley, Massachusetts (nursing home). HEALTH; Lived in Wellsley Nursing Home in 1961. From Bill (William)Bunnell 18 Jan.1997 on 18 Jan 1997.

c) Ann (Annie) A.[4] BUNNELL was buried.[676] She was born in Jul 1867 at Fredericton, York, New Brunswick, Canada.[677] She appeared on the census of 1870 at Charlestown, Middlesex, Massachusetts, USA.[678,679] She died on 6 Sep 1887 at 39 Auburn St., Boston, Suffolk, Massachusetts, USA, at age 20.[680,681] From Bill (William)Bunnell 18 Jan.1997.She never married on 18 Jan 1997.

11. William[3] BUNNELL (Bonnell/Bunel) Henry bir.SJ,1-1,p.66,#324,F14037,RS141 A2/1 county vital rec. He was Anglican. He immigrated.[682] He was born circa 1834 at Greenwich/Westfield, Kings Co. New Brunswick, Canada. He appeared on the census of 10 Dec 1851 at Canadian Census, Westfield Parish, Kings, New Brunswick, Canada.[683] He was Clipper ship Capt/owner of William Bunnell trunk,& rope ring,& yarn picture (Probably brother Charles), St. John 1858/breaking leg in 1858 at Saint John, Saint John, New Brunswick, Canada. He is listed on fathers will on 2 Aug 1866 at Westfield, Kings, New Brunswick, Canada.[684,685] He married Sarah Elizabeth Bunnell on 18 Jan 1874 at Westfield/Greenwich Anglican Church, Westfield/Greenwich, Kings, New Brunswick, Canada.[686] He married Lavina (--?--) after Feb 1874 at New Brunswick, Canada.[687] He died after 1887 at Lost at sea. He was buried after 1887.[688] Trunk w/bro. Gravas & Irene Snow, Cape Cod, Chatham Mariner Muse. auction to Bourne Auction, Hyannis after 1980. From Donna Doscher 1993,poss. made by bro. Charles in 1993.

a) David J.[4] Bunnell Bonnell was born at New Brunswick, Canada? He Fredericton Archives.

b) William B.[4] Bunnell Bonnell was born at Westfield, Kings Co., New Brunswick, Canada.

c) Ernest[4] Bunnell was born in 1875 at Westfield, Kings Co., New Brunswick, Canada.

d) Gurtrude[4] Bunnell was born in 1876 at Westfield, Kings Co. New Brunswick, Canada.

e) Mabel[4] Bunnell From RS141 A2/1 county vitals 1801-99,SJ,1-1,p.195,#399,F14037 birth. She was born on 27 Apr 1878 at Saint John, Saint John Co., New Brunswick, Canada.

f) Ethel[4] Bunnell was born in 1880 at Westfield, Kings Co., New Brunswick, Canada.

g) Ida Adelia[4] BUNNELL (Bonnell) From RS141 A2/1 co.vitals,SJ,1-1,p.195,#398,F14037 birth. She was born on 23 Apr 1882 at Saint John, Saint John Co., New Brunswick, Canada.

h) Louis Eva[4] BUNNELL (Bonnell) From RS141 A2/1 co vitals 1801-99,SJ,1-1,p.195,#400,F14037 birth. She was born on 7 Apr 1885 at Saint John, Saint John Co., New Brunswick, Canada.[689] She died on 22 Sep 1956 at 50 Lexington Ave., Somerville, Middlesex, Massachusetts, USA, at age 71.[690,691] She was buried circa 23 Sep 1956 at Puritan Lawn Cemetery, Peabody, Essex, Massachusetts, USA.[692]

i) Henry Steeves[4] BUNNELL (Bonnell) From RS141 A2/1 county vitals 1801-99, SJ,1-1,p.66,#324,F14037 birth. He was born on 7 Nov 1887 at Saint John, Saint John Co., New Brunswick, Canada.

12. Henry/Harry[3] BUNNELL (Bonnell) married Eliza Ann Dow Bonnell, daughter of John Dow and Phoebe Smith, at New Brunswick, Canada. He was Anglican. He was born in 1836 at Westfield/Greenwich, Kings Co., New Brunswick, Canada.[693] Listed on will 2 Aug 1866 at Westfield, Kings, New Brunswick, USA.[694,695]

a) Eliza[4] BUNNELL (Bonnell) was born at NB or NS, Canada.

b) Frank[4] BUNNELL (Bonnell) was born at New Brunswick/Nova Scotia, Canada.

c) Helen[4] BUNNELL (Bonnell) was born at New Brunswick or Nova Scotia, Canada.

d) John[4] BUNNELL (Bonnell) was born at New Brunswick or Nova Scotia, Canada.

e) Henry[4] BUNNELL (Bonnell) was born at New Brunswick/Nova Scotia Canada.

13. Ophelia/Offie/Affia/Euphemia/Effie³ BUNNELL (Bonnell)⁶⁹⁶ was Anglican. She was born before 1838 at Westfield/Greenwich, Kings, New Brunswick, Canada. Record of connection to parents found in Cleadie Barnett research & records in Jun 2001.

14. Charles³ BUNNELL (Bonnell) was Anglican. He was born before 1838 at Westfield/Greenwich, Kings, New Brunswick, Canada. He was Possible Seaman circa 1860 at Saint John, Saint John, New Brunswick, Canada. He was HEALTH Possibly broke leg in 1860's,left grounded from sea. While sitting on hill over Saint John City he stitched a large cloth showing the entire area and bay. See Dosher file for info circa 1860 at Saint John, Saint John, New Brunswick, Canada. He Stitched picture of St. John harbor with boats c.1860's? The record of his connection to parents was also found in Cleadie Barnett research & records circa 1860 at Saint John Harbour, Saint John, Saint John, New Brunswick, Canada. He left a will on 2 Aug 1866 at Westfield, Kings, New Brunswick, USA.⁶⁹⁷,⁶⁹⁸

15. Alfred L.³ Bunnell (Bonnell) was born in 1838 at Westfield, Kings, New Brunswick, Canada.⁶⁹⁹ He left a will on 2 Aug 1866 at Westfield, Kings, New Brunswick, USA.⁷⁰⁰,⁷⁰¹ He married Mabel (--?--) in 1878 at Saint John, New Brunswick, Canada. He was in shipping as Alfred L. of Portland (Saint John), Mariner owner #3 with 8 shares, constructed at Saint John 1881, 2 masted schooner, length 100 ft, width 27 ft, depth 10 ft, gross tons 198, net tons 170, registered tons 198, registered 1881, officially closure 1882, reason #9 at Caico Island, Bahamas 1882 in 1881 at Ship "E.W. Bonnell", Saint John, Saint John, New Brunswick, Canada.⁷⁰² He was in shipping as Alfred L of Portland (Saint John), Mariner, owner #11, 6 shares, previously registered at Saint John 1886, 3 masted schooner, length 111 ft, width 28, depth 11 ft, gross tons 244, net tons 206, registered tons 228, registered 1886, official closure 1889, reason #22 at Bay of Fundy 1889 in 1886 at Ship "C.E. White", Saint John?, Saint John, New Brunswick, Canada.⁷⁰³ He was in shipping as Alfred L. of Saint John, owner #16, 4 shares, constructed at Saint John 1889, 3 masted schooner, length 127, width 31, depth 11 ft, gross tons 308, net tons 254, registered tons 297, registered 1889, official closure 1897, reason 10, Long Island Sound 1897 in 1889 at Ship "M.L. Bonnell", Saint John?, Saint John, New Brunswick, Canada.⁷⁰⁴ He was baptized after 1894 at Stevens Cemetery, Westfield, Kings, New Brunswick, Canada. He died on 22 Jun 1894 at Westfield, Kings, New Brunswick, Canada.⁷⁰⁵ Also found in Cleadie Barnett research & records in Jun 2001.

D. Joseph^2 BUNNELL (Bonnell)(Bunnele) was Anglican. He was born circa 1790 at Westfield, Kings Co., New Brunswick, Canada. He married Sophia Elizabeth WARD (Wood) on 31 May 1823 at Anglican Church, Westfield, Kings, New Brunswick, Canada.[706] Church record of Marriage say listed as Bachelor, witnessed by John Trott & Peter Fisher on 31 May 1823 at Kings?, New Brunswick, Canada. Estate Mentioned in fathers will getting 25 pounds on 28 Jun 1827 at Will of Father, Westfield/Greenwich Parish, Kings, New Brunswick, Canada. He From 1851 Kings Co., NB Census in 1851 at Census, Westfield, Kings, New Brunswick, Canada. He appeared on the census of 1851 at Canadian Census, Westfield Parish, Kings, New Brunswick, Canada.[707] He immigrated in 1851 to Farmer, Westfield, Kings, New Brunswick, Canada.[708] He appeared on the census of 1871 at Canadian Census, Brooks Ward, Saint John, New Brunswick, Canada.[709]

1. Benjamin^3 BUNNELL (Bonnell) was Anglican. He was born circa 1824 at Westfield, Kings, New Brunswick, Canada. He was baptized in Sep 1824 at Westfield/Greenwich Anglican Church, Westfield/Greenwich, Kings, New Brunswick, Canada.[710] From 1851 Kings Co. NB Census & family records at Fredericton Archives in 1851.

2. James^3 BUNNELL (Bonnell) was Anglican. He was born circa 1831 at Westfield, Kings, New Brunswick, Canada.[711] There is a James Bonnell listed in ST. John City Poll Books 1842-53 by Dorothy Wiggs 1995.He is listed in Kings Ward-Freedom 1848 after 1842. He appeared on the census of circa 1851 at Canadian Census, Westfield Parish, Kings, New Brunswick, Canada.[712] From Fredericton Archives & 1851 Kings Co., NB Census in 1851. He was Mariner/Laborer or shop owner? (1851 census says laborer) in 1851 at New Brunswick, Canada. He died on 3 Jun 1852 at Wards Corner, Saint John, Saint John, New Brunswick, Canada.[713]

3. Mary^3 BUNNELL (Bonnell) was Anglican. She was born circa 1834 at Westfield, Kings Co., New Brunswick, Canada.[714] She appeared on the census of 1851 at Canadian Census, Westfield Parish, Kings, New Brunswick, Canada.[715] She married Robert Porter on 12 Nov 1856 at Westfield, Kings, New Brunswick, Canada.[716]

4. George^3 Bunnell (Bonnell) was Anglican. He was born on 22 Sep 1837 at Westfield, Kings Co., New Brunswick, Canada.[717] From 1851 Kings Co. NB Census & family record at Fredericton Archives in 1851.

He was baptized on 26 Nov 1858 at Anglican Church, Westfield/Greenwich, Kings, New Brunswick, Canada.[718] He married Abigail Jane Marks on 20 Nov 1867 at New Brunswick, Canada.[719] He appeared on the census of 1871 at Canadian Census, Saint John, Saint John, New Brunswick, Canada.[720] He appeared on the census of 1871 at Canadian Census, Lancaster Parish, Saint John, New Brunswick, Canada.[721] He died on 22 Jan 1872 at Parish of Lancaster, Saint john Co. New Brunswick, Canada, at age 34.

    a) George Edwin[4] Bunnell (Bonnell) was born after 1868 at New Brunswick, Canada. He appeared on the census of 1871 at Canadian Census, Lancaster Parish, Saint John, New Brunswick, Canada.[722] He appeared on the census of 1871 at Canadian Census, Saint John, Saint John, New Brunswick, Canada.[723]

    b) Jane Margaret[4] Bunnell (Bonnell) was born before 1871 at New Brunswick, Canada. She appeared on the census of 1871 at Canadian Census, Lancaster Parish, Saint John, New Brunswick, Canada.[724] She appeared on the census of 1871 at Canadian Census, Saint John, Saint John, New Brunswick, Canada.[725]

5. Affey (Euphemia)(Abby) Jane[3] BUNNELL (Bonnell)[726] From Ch.& Marr. rec. film #5359 RS551. She was Anglican. She was born circa 1839 at Westfield, Kings, New Brunswick, Canada.[727] From 1851 Kings Co. NB Census & family record at Fredericton Archives in 1851. She appeared on the census of 1851 at Canadian Census, Westfield Parish, Kings, New Brunswick, Canada.[728] She was baptized on 8 Nov 1857 at Anglican Church, Westfield/Greenwich Parish, Kings, New Brunswick, Canada.[729] She married William Leslie on 8 Apr 1873 at Saint John, Saint John Co., New Brunswick, Canada.[730]

6. Joseph[3] BUNNELL (Bonnell) was Anglican. He was born on 8 Dec 1840 at Westfield, Kings, New Brunswick, Canada.[731] He appeared on the census of 1851 at Canadian Census, Westfield Parish, Kings, New Brunswick, Canada.[732] He was baptized on 26 Nov 1858 at Anglican Church, Westfield/Greenwich Parish, Kings, New Brunswick, Canada.[733] He married Isabella Myles on 2 Jan 1866 at New Brunswick, Canada.[734]

a) George⁴ BUNNELL was born at New Brunswick, Canada.⁷³⁵

b) Joseph⁴ BUNNELL was born at New Brunswick, Canada.⁷³⁶

c) Frederick James⁴ BUNNELL was born on 1 Apr 1847 at Saint John, Saint John, New Brunswick, Canada.⁷³⁷

    (1) Margaret⁵ BUNNELL was born at New Brunswick, Canada.⁷³⁸

    (2) Frederick James⁵ BUNNELL Jr. married Irene Jo (--?--).⁷³⁹ He was born on 1 Apr 1905 at Westbrook, Maine, USA.⁷⁴⁰

        (a) Margaret⁶ BUNNELL was born at New Brunswick?, Canada?⁷⁴¹ She estranged from brother Ben. From Laura & Zwieba Bunnell on 10 Jun 2001. She lived on 10 Jun 2001 at Maine, USA.

        (b) Benjamin William⁶ BUNNELL was born in 1931 at Oregon, USA.⁷⁴² He married Sarah (--?--) circa 1951 at USA.⁷⁴³ He estranged from sister Margaret. From Laura & Zwieba Bunnell on 10 Jun 2001. He lived on 10 Jun 2001 at Barstow, California, USA.

            i) Frank⁷ BUNNELL lived on 10 Jun 2001 at Barstow?, California?, USA. He was Truck Driver on 10 Jun 2001.

            ii) Fred⁷ BUNNELL was born at USA. He lived on 10 Jun 2001 at Barstow?, California?, USA. He was Truck Driver on 10 Jun 2001.

                (a) Sarah⁸ (--?--) was born circa 1978 at USA.

            iii) Lee⁷ BUNNELL was born at USA. He lived on 10 Jun 2001 at Barstow?, California?, USA. He was Truck Driver on 10 Jun 2001.

                (a) Amy⁸ BUNNELL was born circa 1990. She lived on 10 Jun 2001 at Japan.⁷⁴⁴

            iv) Frank Benjamin⁷ BUNNELL married (--?--) Wingerter at USA. He was born in 1953 at New York, USA.⁷⁴⁵

(a) Zwieba Frank Benjamin Wingerter[8] BUNNELL was born circa 1973 at USA.[746] He married Laura (--?--) circa 1993 at USA. MILITARY: Completed Physical Training and will be stationed at Hilo, Hawaii, flying to Seattle, Wa. first on the 28 June 2002. Then we drop the car off for transport to Hawaii on 15 May 2002 at Coast Guard Academy, Washington DC, District of Columbia, USA. MILITARY: Will be on the CGC Kiska. The Coast Guard owns 5 three bedroom houses and one will be for us. First we must stay in a Motel because furniture and things will not arrive for 3-6 weeks. New email is Lauramaynot@yahoo.com. on 4 Jul 2002 at Mokihana St., Hilo, Hawaii, USA. MILITARY: Will leave port for 2 days to 3 weeks on 8 Jul 2002 at CGC Kiska, Hilo, Hawaii, USA.

i) Samuel[9] BUNNELL was born after 1993 at USA.

ii) Sarah[9] BUNNELL was born after 1993 at USA.

iii) Adam[9] BUNNELL was born after 1993 at USA.

(c) Frederick[6] BUNNELL III died before 2001.

(d) David[6] BUNNELL lived on 10 Jun 2001 at Maine, USA.[747]

7. Eliza Ann[3] BUNNELL (Bonnell) was Anglican. She was born circa 1844 at Westfield, Kings, New Brunswick, Canada.[748] She appeared on the census of 1851 at Canadian Census, Westfield Parish, Kings, New Brunswick, Canada.[749] She From 1851 Kings Co., NB Census & family rec. at Fredericton Archives in 1851. She was baptized on 8 Nov 1857 at Anglican Church, Westfield/Greenwich Parish, Kings, New Brunswick, Canada.[750] She was shipping She had 8 shares in the ownership of a ship. From AutoInc #45774 Reg.#J886027 found in Ships & Seafarer's of Atlantic Canada CD, Newfoundland. Says, Eliza of Lancaster (NB) owner #3, constructed at Saint John 1886, 3 masted schooner, length 111 ft, width 28 ft, depth 11 ft, gross tons 244, net tons 206, registered tons 228, registered 1886, official closure 1889, reason #22 at Bay of Fundy 1889. Alfred L. Bonnell had shares in this ship too in 1886 at Ship "C.E. White", Saint John?, Saint John, New Brunswick, Canada.[751]

She was Part owner (4 shares) in ownership of a ship, from AutoInc #46090 Reg.#J889025 found on Ships & Seafarer's of Atlantic Canada CD, Newfoundland in 1889 at Saint John, Saint John, New Brunswick, Canada. She was in shipping as Eliza of Saint John, owner #3 (Alfred L. Bonnell owner too), constructed at Saint John 1889, 3 masted schooner, length 127 ft, width 31 ft, depth 11 ft, gross tons 308, net tons 254, registered tons 297, registered 1889, closure 1897 at Long Island Sound in 1889 at Ship "Martha L. Bonnell", Saint John?, Saint John, New Brunswick, Canada.[752]

8. Allan[3] BUNNELL (Bonnell) was Anglican. He was born in 1851 at Westfield, Kings, New Brunswick, Canada.[753] He appeared on the census of 1851 at Canadian Census, Westfield Parish, Kings, New Brunswick, Canada.[754]

E. Euphemia/Aphia/Effie J.[2] BUNNELL (Bonnell/Burnell) was born on 15 Oct 1792 at Westfield, Kings Co., NB, Canada.[755] She married William H. ALLISON Jr., son of William H. ALLISON Sr. and Ann COURTNEY, circa 1812 at New Brunswick, Canada. She was estate Mentioned in fathers will getting 10 pounds on 28 Jun 1827 at Will of Father, Westfield/Greenwich Parish, Kings, New Brunswick, Canada. She immigrated circa 1845.[756] She died on 3 Jul 1874 at Goodland, Lapeer Co., Michigan USA, at age 81. She was buried circa 5 Jul 1874 at Goodland Cemetery, Lapeer, Michigan, USA. From G.Bodemiller bible records. In Affie's bible it mentions mother's name; Sarah/Sally Jones in 1993.

1. Matilda[3] ALLISON immigrated.[757] From Geneva Bodenmiller of Northville, Michigan, a descendant. She was born after 1812 at New Brunswick, Canada.

2. Thomas (Tom)[3] ALLISON: From Royal Gazette & New Brunswick Advertiser newspaper & Geneva Bodenmiller of Northville, Mich, a descendant. He was born after 1812 at New Brunswick, Canada. He died on 30 Nov 1930 at Off Red Head Beach, New Brunswick, Canada.[758]

3. Ellen[3] ALLISON: From Geneva Bodenmiller of Michigan. She was born after 1812 at New Brunswick, Canada. She married (--?--) TRUE after 1832.

(1) Sarah[3] ALLISON: From Geneva Bodenmiller of Northville, Mich, a descendant. She married John MCCLEAN. She was (possibly named after her grandmother, Bonnell?). She was born after 1812 at New Brunswick, Canada.

(1) William^3 ALLISON From Geneva Bodenmiller of Northville, Michigan, a descendant. He was born after 1812 at New Brunswick, Canada. He was baptized circa 1845 at Port Huron, St. Clair, Michigan, USA.

(1) Effie/Euphemia Jane^3 ALLISON From Geneva Bodenmiller of Michigan. She was born after 1812 at New Brunswick, Canada. She married Benjamin HARRINGTON after 1830.

(1) Charlotte^3 ALLISON From Geneva Bodenmiller of Northville, Mich. She was born after 1812 at New Brunswick, Canada. She married (--?--) MCGEE circa 1835. She immigrated circa 1845.^{759}

(1) Mary Ann^3 ALLISON From Geneva Bodenmiller of Michigan. She was born after 1812 at New Brunswick, Canada. She married (--?--) DORMAN after 1830.

(1) Esther I.^{3} ALLISON was born on 3 May 1832 at Black River, St. John Co., NB, Canada. She immigrated circa 1845.^{760} She married William H. SMITH on 28 Jun 1852. She died on 30 Apr 1917 at Goodland, Lapeer Co., Mich. USA, at age 84. She was buried circa 1 May 1917 at Goodland Cemetery, Lapeer, Michigan, USA. From Geneva Bodenmiller of Northville, Mich. Family descendant in 1993.

(1) James Herbert^4 SMITH was born on 26 Aug 1881 at Goodland, Lapeer, Michigan, USA. He married Bessie Mae TIBBENHAM, daughter of William TIBBENHAM and Anna DUNSTER, on 28 Oct 1903. He died on 2 Feb 1956 at Ann Arbor, Washington, Michigan, USA, at age 74. From Geneva Bodenmiller in Michigan in 1993. He Says that his parents are buried at Goodland Cemetery, Lapeer Co., Michigan (Peter Smith and Elizabeth Hines, and Euphenia Bunnell and William Allison) This conflicts with parents listed below? On 25 Dec 1997 at Xmas Card.

(1) Geneva Mae^5 SMITH was born on 25 Jun 1916 at Detroit, Wayne, Michigan, USA. She married Homer Elvin BODENMILLER, son of Tobias Rhinehart BODENMILLER and Cora TROTT, in 1938 at Toledo, Lucas, Ohio, USA. From herself & Smith Bible records in 1993. She lived in 1995 at Aqueduct Ct. (zip 48167), Northville, Lapeer, Michigan, USA. She Giving entire genealogy of family on 25 Dec 1997 at Xmas Card, Northville, Lapeer, Michigan, USA. As of 25 Dec 1997, Geneva Mae SMITH lived at Aquduct Ct., Northville, Lapeer, Michigan, USA, 248-349-3722.

(a) Timothy[6] BODNMILLER was born at Lapeer?, Michigan?, USA. He was Involved in a truck hitting him while driving mothers car. Car was totaled. Truck crossed over two lanes and pushed his car in Mar 1997 at Clarleston, Lapeer, Michigan, USA. From Geneva Bodenmiller, grandmother on 25 Dec 1997 at Xmas Card. HEALTH: After knee surgery he is going to therapy and got ok to return to work on 25 Dec 1997 at Northville, Lapeer, Michigan, USA.

    i) John[7] BODENMILLER was born at Michigan?, USA. He married an unknown person in Apr 1997 at Lapeer?, Michigan?, USA. From Geneva Bodenmiller, grandmother on 25 Dec 1997 at Xmas Card. He was employed on 25 Dec 1997 at Working for Ford Motor Co., Kansas, USA.

    ii) Rhonda[7] BODENMILLER was born at Michigan?, USA. From Geneva Bodenmiller, great grandmother on 25 Dec 1997 at Xmas Card. She was educated on 25 Dec 1997 at Clarleston, Michigan, USA.761

        (a) ?[8] (--?--) was born in Mar 1997 at Clarteston, Michigan, USA. He lived on 25 Dec 1997 at mother's home, Clarleston, Michigan, USA.762 From Geneva Bodenmiller Xmas Card. He is her great grand son on 25 Dec 1997.

(b) Carol[6] BODENMILLER was born at Lapeer?, Michigan?, USA. She was They all ski andplay football (not Carol) in 1997. She is a nurse, but not an RN on 25 Dec 1997.

    i) Christopher[7] (--?--) was born circa 1968. He married an unknown person in 1996. From Geneva Bodenmiller, grandmother on 25 Dec 1997 at Xmas Card.

    ii) Nick[7] (--?--) was born circa 1970. He was educated in 1997 at College. From Geneva Bodenmiller, grandmother on 25 Dec 1997 at Xmas Card.

    iii) Alexander (Alex)[7] (--?--) was born circa 1984. From Geneva Bodenmiller, grandmother on 25 Dec 1997 at Xmas Card.

iv) Clessie[7] (--?--) was born circa 1985. From Geneva Bodenmiller, grandmother on 25 Dec 1997 at Xmas Card.

v) Timothy (Tim)[7] (--?--) was born circa 1986. From Geneva Bondenmiller, grandmother circa 1986 at Xmas Card.

(c) William Earl[6] BODENMILLER was born on 23 Dec 1945 at Michigan ? From Geneva Bodenmiller, mother on 25 Dec 1997 at Xmas Card.

10. Benjamin[3] ALLISON From Geneva Bodenmiller of Northville, Mich., a descendant. He married Mary BELL. He was Possibly named after Ben the loyalist, his grandfather who died 1828. He was born in 1834 at New Brunswick, Canada.

F. Eleanor Ann (Jane)[2] Bunnell (Bonnell) Fanjoy's were very close to Bonnell family. She was Anglican. She was born in 1797 at Harding's Point (Long Reach), Westfield, Kings, New Brunswick, Canada.[763] She married Joseph FANJOY, son of William FANJOY U.E. and Isabella (--?--) U.E, on 20 Aug 1816 at Westfield, Kings, New Brunswick, Canada.[764] She was estate Mentioned in fathers will getting 10 pounds on 28 Jun 1827 at Will of Father, Westfield/Greenwich Parish, Kings, New Brunswick, Canada. She appeared on the census of 1851 at Canadian Census, Long Reach/Westfield, Kings, New Brunswick, Canada.[765] She died on 21 Mar 1856 at Kings, New Brunswick, Canada.[766] She was buried on 23 Apr 1856 at Fanjoy Point Cemetery (Family plot) or Days Landing Private Cemetery, Westfield/Long Reach, Kings, New Brunswick, Canada.[767]

1. Charles Thomas[3] Fanjoy married Elizabeth GORHAM at New Brunswick ? He was born after 1817 at Long Reach/Westfield, Kings, New Brunswick, Canada. From Harold & Emery Fanjoy circa 1985.

2. Isazella (Isabella)[3] FANJOY married Archibald MCCLEAN at New Brunswick, Canada? She was born after 1817 at Westfield, Kings, New Brunswick, Canada.

3. Rebecca[3] FANJOY married John WATSON at New Brunswick ? She was buried.[768] She was born in 1820 at Westfield, Kings Co., New Brunswick, Canada. From Harold & Emery Fanjoy circa 1985.

4. Sarah Ann³ FANJOY was born circa 1822 at Westfield, Kings Co., New Brunswick, Canada. She married George MCLEAN circa 1842 at New Brunswick, Canada. She died on 27 Nov 1849 at New Brunswick, Canada.⁷⁶⁹ She was buried circa 29 Nov 1849 at Fanjoy Point Cemetery, Long Reach, Long Reach/Westfield, Kings, New Brunswick, Canada.⁷⁷⁰ From Harold & Emery Fanjoy circa 1985.

5. James Edwin (Edward) Albert³ FANJOY was buried.⁷⁷¹ From Kristin Cottle 6/25/97 (e-mail-kristin@sisna.com). He changed name from James Edwin to Edward Albert (parents #9 child could be same?). MILITARY: Commission Merchant 1890's. He was Boat builder, then hay dealer in 1876. He was born in 1822 at New Brunswick, Canada. He married Catherine Ann WHELPLEY on 21 Jan 1847 at Kings Co., New Brunswick, Canada. He died in 1909 at New Brunswick, Canada?

6. William James³ FANJOY immigrated.⁷⁷² He was born on 10 Aug 1828 at Westfield, Kings, New Brunswick, Canada.⁷⁷³ He appeared on the census of 1851 at Canadian Census, Long Reach/Westfield, Kings, New Brunswick, Canada.⁷⁷⁴ He was Boatman in 1851 at New Brunswick, Canada. He married Cecelia Olivia LINGLEY, daughter of Peter LINGLEY, on 1 Jun 1864 at Kings, New Brunswick, Canada. He died on 27 Aug 1907 at Everett, Massachusetts, USA, at age 79. He was buried on 29 Aug 1907 at Everett, Massachusetts, USA. From Harold & Emery Fanjoy circa 1986.

    a) Wood⁴ FANJOY was born after 1864.

    b) Mabel⁴ FANJOY was born after 1868.

    c) Violet⁴ FANJOY was born after 1868.

    d) Ethelbert L.⁴ FANJOY was born circa Feb 1868 at Westfield/Long Reach, Kings, New Brunswick, Canada. She died on 23 Aug 1874 at Westfield/Long Reach, Kings, New Brunswick, Canada.⁷⁷⁵ She was buried circa 25 Aug 1874 at Days Landing Private Cemetery, Westfield/Long Reach, Kings, New Brunswick, Canada.⁷⁷⁶

e) Nora C.[4] FANJOY was born circa Aug 1870 at Westfield/Long Reach, Kings, New Brunswick, Canada. She died on 27 Dec 1872 at Westfield/Long Reach, Kings, New Brunswick, Canada.[777] She was buried circa 29 Dec 1872 at Days Landing Private Cemetery, Westfield/Long Reach, Kings, New Brunswick, Canada.[778]

7. Simeon Bonnell[3] FANJOY appeared on the census of 1851 at Canadian Census, Long Reach/Westfield, Kings, New Brunswick, Canada.[779] He married Eleanor MCCLEAN at New Brunswick ? He married Betsy WIGGINS (wife #2) at New Brunswick ? He was born circa 1829 at Westfield, Kings, New Brunswick, Canada.[780]

8. Joseph[3] FANJOY was born circa 1832 at Westfield, Kings, New Brunswick, Canada.[781] He appeared on the census of 1851 at Canadian Census, Long Reach/Westfield, Kings, New Brunswick, Canada.[782] He died on 1 Jul 1868 at Niagara Falls, New York, USA.[783] From Harold & Emery Fanjoy circa 1985.

9. Elizabeth (Eliza)[3] Fanjoy was born circa 1833 at Long Reach/Westfield, Kings, New Brunswick, Canada.[784] She appeared on the census of 1851 at Canadian Census, Long Reach/Westfield, Kings, New Brunswick, Canada.[785] She married William WHEPLEY (Whelples) after 1851 at New Brunswick, Canada. She died on 6 May 1893 at New Brunswick, Canada.[786] She was buried circa 8 May 1893 at Fanjoy Point Cemetery, Long Reach, Long Reach/Westfield, Kings, New Brunswick, Canada. From Harold & Emery Fanjoy circa 1985.

10. Thomas[3] FANJOY was born circa 1835 at Westfield, Kings, New Brunswick, Canada.[787] He appeared on the census of after 1851 at Canadian Census, Long Reach/Westfield, Kings, New Brunswick, Canada.[788] From Harold & Emery Fanjoy circa 1985.

11. George[3] FANJOY was born circa 1839 at Westfield, Kings Co., New Brunswick, Canada. He appeared on the census of after 1851 at Canadian Census, Long Reach/Westfield, Kings, New Brunswick, Canada.[789] From Harold & Emery Fanjoy circa 1985.

12. Benjamin Bunnell[3] Fanjoy He was named after Benjamin Bonnell, the loyalist. He was Anglican? He was shipping Listed as from Kings County, New Brunswick, Mariner, owner #1 with 64 shares, previously registered at Saint John 1838, constructed at Kingston, NB 1834, 2 masted schooner, length 56 ft, width 17 ft, depth 5 ft, gross tons 66, registered 1841, closure 1843, reason #4 at Saint John 1843 in 1841 at Ship "James and Thomas, Saint John, Saint John, New Brunswick, Canada.[790] He was born circa 1840 at Long Reach/Westfield, Kings, New Brunswick, Canada.[791] He was in shipping listed as Benjamin Fanjoy of Saint John, Mariner, owner #1 with 32 shares, previously registered at Saint John 1841, built at Canning 1839, 2 masted schooner, length 69 ft, width 19 ft, depth 6 ft, gross tons 57, registered 1843, closure 1845, reason #4 at Saint John 1845 in 1843 at Ship "Rising Sun", Saint John, Saint John, New Brunswick, Canada.[792] He married Margaret Phoebe SLOCUM before 1845 at New Brunswick?, Canada. He died in 1900 at (possibly) New Brunswick Canada.

    a) Mary Eleanor[4] FANJOY was born in 1845 at Bagdad, New Brunswick, Canada. She married Thomas Gilbert THORNE before 1877. She died in 1937.[793]

        (1) Lillie[5] THORNE was born in 1877 at Johnstone, New Brunswick, Canada. She married Fred Rude HAINES before 1904. She died in 1924 at Fredericton, York, New Brunswick, Canada.[794]

            (a) Kenneth Frederick[6] HAINES was born on 7 Apr 1904 at St Mary's, Fredericton, York, New Brunswick, Canada.[795] He married Electa ALLEN before 1947. He died on 3 May 1991 at Framingham, Massachusetts, USA, at age 87. He was buried circa 5 May 1991 at Sunny Bank Cemetery, Fredericton, York, New Brunswick, Canada.

                i) John Edward[7] HAINES was born on 14 Jul 1947 at Boston, Suffolk, Massachusetts, USA.[796] He married Elizabeth (Beth) McCue circa 1980. He lived on 2 Jan 2001 at 53 James St., Bellingham, Massachusetts, USA.[797]

                    (a) Patricia (Trisha)[8] HAINES was born on 14 Mar 1985 at Framingham, Massachusetts, USA.

(b) Michael (Mike)[8] HAINES was born on 13 Nov 1986 at Framingham, Massachusetts, USA.

(c) Jeffrey[8] HAINES was born on 24 Oct 1988 at Framingham, Massachusetts, USA.[798] He was hobby Jeffrey is very interested in genealogy. Wrote a play for school 2001 on 2 Jan 2001.

(d) Thomas[8] HAINES was born on 15 Apr 1998 at Framingham, Massachusetts, USA.[799]

(e) Steven[8] HAINES was born on 15 Apr 1998 at Framingham, Massachusetts, USA.[800]

(b) Edna[6] HAINES was born on 2 Jul 1905 at St. Mary's, Fredericton, York, New Brunswick, Canada. She died on 3 Feb 1979 at age 73.

(c) Irvine[6] HAINES was born on 26 May 1907 at St. Mary's, Fredericton, York, New Brunswick, Canada. He died on 12 Apr 1979 at age 71.

(d) Greta[6] HAINES was born on 11 Jan 1914 at St. Mary's, Fredericton, York, New Brunswick, Canada. She died on 23 Aug 1973 at age 59.

(e) Roderick[6] HAINES was born on 29 Jul 1915 at St. Mary's, Fredericton, York, New Brunswick, Canada. He died in 1965.

(f) Aubrey[6] HAINES was born on 14 Apr 1917 at St. Mary's, Fredericton, York, New Brunswick, Canada. She died in 2000.

(g) Albert[6] HAINES was born on 5 Feb 1920 at St. Mary's, Fredericton, York, New Brunswick, Canada. He lived on 15 Mar 2001 at Fredericton, York, New Brunswick, Canada.[801]

(h) Thomas[6] HAINES was born on 20 Jan 1922 at St. Mary's, Fredericton, York, New Brunswick, Canada. He lived on 15 Mar 2001 at Florida, USA.

b) Benjamin Arthur^4 FANJOY was also known as Benjamin Arthur Fanjoy. He married Ann Elizabeth MYLES. He married Ann Elizabeth Myle b:1873. d: 1954. He was born in 1865 at New Brunswick, Canada. He was born in 1865 at New Brunswick Canada ? He died in 1938 at New Brunswick, Canada? He died in 1938 at New Brunswick Canada ?

    (1) Isaac Newton^5 FANJOY was also known as Isaac Newton Fanjoy. He was born in 1898 at New Brunswick, Canada. He was born in 1898 at New Brunswick, Canada. He married Muriel Gertrude Seely before 1939. He died in 1967 at New Brunswick, Canada. He died in 1967 at New Brunswick, Canada?

        (a) Emery(living in Nova Scotia, called me when in Boston in 1987)^6 (--?--)

        (b) Harold Newton^6 FANJOY was Treas. of Westfield. United Church pastor Master of St. Martin's Lodge #.30F & AM & member of Luxor Temp. Shrine Scottish Rite. He was born in 1939 at Kings Co. New Brunswick, Canada. He married Marilyn Dorothy (Mareen) BISHOP before 1966. He immigrated in 1974.^{802} He immigrated on 18 Nov 1974.^{803}

            i) Leslie Bennett^7 FANJOY was born in 1966 at New Brunswick, Canada.

            ii) Benjamin^7 FANJOY was born after 1966 at New Brunswick, Canada.

            iii) Gregory Bishop^7 FANJOY was born in 1968 at New Brunswick, Canada.

        (c) Emery^6 FANJOY was born after 1939 at New Brunswick, Canada.

13. Edward (William) Albert^3 FANJOY married Eliza WHIPLEY at New Brunswick, Canada.^{804} He married Katherine/Catherine Ann WHEPLEY at New Brunswick, Canada.^{805} He was born circa 1850 at Westfield, Kings, New Brunswick, Canada.^{806} From Harold & Emery Fanjoy circa 1985.

a) Douglas⁴ FANJOY was born at New Brunswick, Canada. He married Amberzine PARK.

b) William⁴ FANJOY was born at New Brunswick, Canada. He immigrated.[807]

c) Herbert⁴ FANJOY was born at New Brunswick, Canada. He immigrated.[808]

d) Edward⁴ FANJOY was born at New Brunswick, Canada. He immigrated.[809]

e) Bessie⁴ FANJOY. His/her married name was Stillwell. He/she was born at New Brunswick, Canada. He/she married Alfred STILLWELL.

f) Albert Arnold⁴ FANJOY was born at New Brunswick, Canada. He/she married Viola White WELDON on 1 Jan 1895 at New Brunswick, Canada?

g) Charles⁴ FANJOY was born at New Brunswick, Canada. He/she married Albina FANJOY.

h) Georgiana⁴ FANJOY. His/her married name was Jeffrey. He/she was born at New Brunswick, Canada. He/she married Robert JEFFREY.

i) Burpee⁴ FANJOY was born at New Brunswick, Canada.

j) Tom⁴ FANJOY was born at New Brunswick, Canada. He married Winina HETHERINGTON at New Brunswick, Canada?

k) George E.⁴ FANJOY[810] was born in 1849 at New Brunswick, Canada.[811] He married Helen Davidson LINGLEY, daughter of Thomas Astor LINGLEY and Mary Johnston, circa 1870 at New Brunswick, Canada.[812] He died in 1932 at Sagwa, Kings, New Brunswick, Canada.[813] He was buried in 1932 at Sagwa, Kings, New Brunswick, Canada.[814]

G. Simeon[2] BUNNELL[815] was born circa 1798 at Westfield, Kings, New Brunswick, Canada.[816] He was shipping Mariner/Owner #2 with 32 shares in 1825 at Ship "Honesty", Kingston, Kings, New Brunswick, Canada.[817] His estate was probated on 29 Jun 1827 at Greenwich/Westfield, Kings, New Brunswick, Canada.[818,819] He was land/grant Bought part of fathers land for 80 pounds. Brother Isaac bought rest on 22 Mar 1830 at Devil's Back, Greenwich, Kings, New Brunswick, Canada. He appeared on the census of 1870 at US Census, Independence/Clarkston, Oakland, Missouri, USA.[820] He died after 1870 at Independence?, Oakland?, Missouri?, USA.[821]

H. Isaac[2] BUNNELL (Bonnell) Son Ben's bible listing all. He was Anglican/Baptist? He was born on 6 Oct 1799 at Westfield, Kings Co., New Brunswick, Canada.[822] He was Farmer/took fathers farm over at Devil's Back circa 1828 at Devil's Back, Greenwich Parish, Kings, New Brunswick, Canada. He married Lavinia KIMBELL (Kemble) on 28 Dec 1831 at Westfield Anglican Church, Westfield, Kings, New Brunswick, Canada.[823] He appeared on the census of 1851 at Canadian Census, Westfield Parish & Greenwich, Kings, New Brunswick, Canada.[824] Death record in NBNP #2287, d: Long Reach, Monday Morn. ,Isaac 6th. son of Ben age 28 funeral at 11 AM, dads res.(from 24 Aug.1853) on 7 Feb 1882. He died on 7 Feb 1882 at Will dated, Greenwich/Westfield, Kings Co., New Brunswick, Canada, at age 82.[825] He was buried on 12 Feb 1882 at Brown's Flat Baptist Cemetery, Brown's Flat, Kings, New Brunswick, Canada.

    1. Louella[3] BUNNELL (Bonnell) was Anglican/Baptist. From Viola Bonnell of Westfield, NB, never married. She was born after 1832 at Westfield/Greenwich, Kings Co., New Brunswick, Canada.

    2. Gustie[3] BUNNELL (Bonnell) married (--?--) WELDON. She was Anglican. She was born after 1832 at Westfield/Greenwich, Kings Co., New Brunswick, Canada. She From Viola Bonnell of Westfield, NB circa 1986.

        a) Gertie[4] Bunnell (Bonnell) was born at New Brunswick, Canada. She was Baptist?

3. Annie[3] BUNNELL (Bonnell) Could be same as #402. Have Graig brick from St. John, NB. She was Anglican/Baptist. She was born after 1832 at Westfield/Greenwich, Kings, New Brunswick, Canada. She married George CRAIG after 1850 at New Brunswick, Canada. From Viola Bonnell of Westfield, NB circa 1986.

4. Elmira[3] Bunnell (Bonnell) was Anglican/Baptist. She was born circa 1833 at Westfield Parish, Kings, New Brunswick, Canada.[826] She appeared on the census of 1851 at Canadian Census, Westfield Parish, Kings, New Brunswick, Canada.[827] She married William Parker circa 1854 at Westfield, Kings, New Brunswick, Canada.[828]

5. Lavinia Jane[3] BUNNELL (Bonnell) was Anglican/Baptist. She was born circa 1835 at Westfield/Greenwich, Kings, New Brunswick, Canada.[829] She appeared on the census of 1851 at Canadian Census, Westfield Parish, Kings, New Brunswick, Canada.[830] She married Sam DUNHAM in 1863 at Kings Co., New Brunswick, Canada. From Viola Bunnell of Westfield NB circa 1986.

6. Issac[3] BUNNELL (Bonnell) was Baptist? He was born circa 1836 at Westfield/Greenwich, Kings, New Brunswick, Canada.[831] He appeared on the census of 1851 at Canadian Census, Westfield Parish, Kings, New Brunswick, Canada.[832] He died in 1929 at Westfield/Greenwich ? Kings Co., NB, Canada. He was buried in 1929 at Brown's Flat Cemetery, Brown's Flat, Kings, New Brunswick, Canada. From Viola Bunnell of Westfield NB, never married circa 1986.

7. Affy/Euphemia A.[3] BUNNELL (Bonnell) was Anglican/Baptist. She was born circa 1837 at Westfield/Greenwich, Kings, New Brunswick, Canada.[833] She appeared on the census of 1851 at Canadian Census, Westfield Parish, Kings, New Brunswick, Canada.[834] She married Joseph Thomas MCKIEL in 1870 at New Brunswick, Canada? She could be same as #413. From Viola Bunnell of Westfield, NB circa 1986. She Alice Hyerstay,1775 Dorset St.,Charlotte,Vt.05445 says that spouse may be Joseph McKiel (30 June 1997,e-mail on 30 Jun 1997.

8. Mary Eliza[3] BUNNELL (Bonnell) was Anglican/Baptist. She was born circa 1839 at Westfield/Greenwich, Kings, New Brunswick, Canada.[835] She appeared on the census of 1851 at Canadian Census, Westfield Parish, Kings, New Brunswick, Canada.[836]

She married David Graves PERRY on 21 Feb 1866 at Westfield/Greenwich Anglican Church, Westfield, Kings, New Brunswick, Canada.[837] From Viola Bunnell of Westfield, NB circa 1986.

    a) Alfred[4] Perry was Baptist? He was born after Apr 1866 at New Brunswick, Canada.

9. Solomon[3] BUNNELL (Bonnell) was Anglican/Baptist. He was born circa 1841 at Westfield/Greenwich, Kings, New Brunswick, Canada.[838] He appeared on the census of 1851 at Canadian Census, Westfield Parish, Kings, New Brunswick, Canada.[839] He married an unknown person after 1860 at New Brunswick, Canada. He appeared on the census of 1880 at US Census, Hubbard, Trumbull, Ohio, USA.[840,841] He appeared on the census of 1900 at US Census, Salem, Columbiana, Ohio, USA.[842,843] From Viola Bunnell of Westfield, NB circa 1986.

    a) Hartley[4] Bunnell (Bonnell) was Baptist? He had no children. From Ben S. Bonnell bible records. He was born after 1860 at New Brunswick, Canada.

10. David J. (or I)[3] BUNNELL (Bonnell) was Anglican/Baptist. He was born circa 1842 at Westfield/Greenwich, Kings, New Brunswick, Canada.[844] He appeared on the census of 1851 at Canadian Census, Westfield Parish, Kings, New Brunswick, Canada.[845] From Viola Bunnell of Westfield, NB circa 1985.

11. Susan[3] BUNNELL (Bonnell) was Anglican/Baptist. She was born circa 1844 at Westfield/Greenwich, Kings, New Brunswick, Canada.[846] She appeared on the census of 1851 at Canadian Census, Westfield Parish, Kings, New Brunswick, Canada.[847] From Viola Bunnell of Westfield, NB circa 1985.

12. Sarah E.[3] BUNNELL (Bonnell) was Anglican/Baptist. She was born circa 1846 at Westfield/Greenwich, Kings, New Brunswick, Canada.[848] She appeared on the census of 1851 at Canadian Census, Westfield Parish, Kings, New Brunswick, Canada.[849] From Viola Bunnell of Westfield, NB circa 1985.

13. Albert[3] BUNNELL was born circa 1847 at Westfield Parish & Greenwich, Kings, New Brunswick, Canada. He appeared on the census of 1851 at Canadian Census, Greenwich, Kings, New Brunswick, Canada.[850]

14. Robert L.[3] BUNNELL (Bonnell) was Anglican/Baptist. He was born circa 1847 at Westfield/Greenwich, Kings, New Brunswick, Canada.[851] He appeared on the census of 1851 at Canadian Census, Westfield Parish, Kings, New Brunswick, Canada.[852] From Viola Bonnell of Westfield, NB circa 1985.

15. Eleanor (Ellain) Adelia[3] Bunnell (Bonnell) was Anglican/Baptist. She was born in 1849 at Westfield Parish & Greenwich, Kings, New Brunswick, Canada. She appeared on the census of 1851 at Canadian Census, Westfield Parish, Kings, New Brunswick, Canada.[853] She married James (Jim) H. PARKER on 8 Feb 1872 at Westfield, Kings, New Brunswick, Canada.[854] She Also called Eleanor. From Viola Bonnell of Westfield, NB circa 1985.

16. Benjamin S.[3] BUNNELL (Bonnell) was Anglican/Baptist. He was born on 5 Dec 1851 at Westfield/Greenwich, Kings, New Brunswick, Canada.[855] He married Dora G. DAY (Daye) on 13 Oct 1885 at Westfield, Kings Co., New Brunswick, Canada. He died on 6 Nov 1940 at Public Landing, Westfield/Greenwich, Kings Co., New Brunswick, Canada, at age 88. He was buried circa 8 Nov 1940 at Brown's Flat Baptist Cemetery, Brown's Flat, Kings, New Brunswick, Canada. From Viola Bonnell of Westfield, NB circa 1986.

    a) Odbur S.[4] BUNNELL (Bonnell) was Baptist ? or Anglican? He married Minnie PARKER at New Brunswick, Canada? He was born on 6 Nov 1887 at Greenwich, Kings Co., New Brunswick, Canada. He died on 25 Dec 1922 at New Brunswick, Canada, at age 35. He was buried circa 27 Dec 1922 at St. Peter's Anglican Chech Cemetery, Woodman's Point, Kings, New Brunswick, Canada.[856] From Viola Bonnell of Westfield, NB circa 1985 at Woodman's Point/Westfield, Kings, New Brunswick, Canada.

        (1) Henrietta Jenetta[5] Bunnell (Bonnell) married Raymond Haycox at New Brunswick, Canada? She was Anglican. She was born at New Brunswick, Canada?

            (a) Donald[6] Haycox was born at New Brunswick, Canada. He was Baptist?

b) Emery D.[4] BUNNELL (Bonnell) was Baptist ? From Viola Bonnell of Westfield, NB 3 Oct.1983. He was born on 19 Jul 1889 at Greenwich, Kings Co., New Brunswick, Canada. He married Viola PARKER on 22 Jul 1944 at New Brunswick, Canada. He died on 20 Jun 1953 at New Brunswick, Canada, at age 63.

c) Walter C.[4] BUNNELL (Bonnell) From Viola Bonnell of Westfield, NB 3 Oct.1983. He was Baptist ? He was born on 20 Jan 1893 at Greenwich, Kings Co., New Brunswick, Canada. He died on 3 Feb 1920 at Westfield, Kings Co. New Brunswick, Canada, at age 27.

d) Luda M.[4] BUNNELL (Bonnell) From Viola Bonnell of Westfield, NB 3 Oct.1983. She was Baptist? She was born on 14 Apr 1896 at Greenwich, Kings Co., New Brunswick, Canada. She died on 8 Apr 1898 at Greenwich/Westfield, Kings Co., NB, Canada, at age 1.

e) Alfred G.[4] BUNNELL (Bonnell) was Baptist ? From Viola Bonnell of Westfield, NB 3 Oct. 1983. He was born on 14 Aug 1898 at Greenwich, Kings Co., New Brunswick, Canada. He married Adelia ROBICHAUD (Lister) on 6 Oct 1921? at New Brunswick, Canada ? He died on 14 Jan 1967 at New Brunswick, Canada ?, at age 68.

(1) Marjorie Lorraine[5] Bunnell (Bonnell) married Allan Anthony at New Brunswick, Canada? She was Baptist? She was born on 29 Jan 1922 at New Brunswick, Canada?

(2) Walter Gordon[5] Bunnell (Bonnell) married Audrie Shonman at New Brunswick, Canada? He was Baptist? He was born on 10 Aug 1924 at New Brunswick, Canada?

f) Cecil B.[4] BUNNELL (Bonnell) was Baptist ? From Viola Bonnell of Westfield, NB 3 Oct.1983. Possible error with death date 4/Jan.1928 vs. Marr. 24 July 1951 (reversed?). He died on 4 Jan 1900 at New Brunswick, Canada ? He was born on 20 Dec 1900 at Greenwich, Kings Co., New Brunswick, Canada. He married Victoria (--?--) (Bonnell) on 24 Jul 1951 at New Brunswick, Canada ?

g) Ernest G.[4] BUNNELL (Bonnell) was Baptist ? or Anglican? He was born on 9 Oct 1902 at Greenwich, Kings Co., New Brunswick, Canada. He married Reta APPT on 5 Jul 1931 at New Brunswick, Canada.

He died on 29 Sep 1956 at Woodman's Point/Westfield?, Kings?, New Brunswick, Canada, at age 53.[857] He was buried circa 1 Oct 1956 at St. Peter's Anglican Church Cemetery, Woodman's Point/Westfield, Kings, New Brunswick, Canada.[858] From Viola Bonnell of Westfield, NB 3 Oct.1983 on 3 Oct 1983 at Woodman's Point/Westfield, Kings, New Brunswick, Canada.

    (1) Helen[5] Bunnell (Bonnell) was born at New Brunswick, Canada. She married Donald Coleman at New Brunswick, Canada? She was Baptist?

        (a) Donna[6] Coleman. Her married name was Damink. She married Olde Damink at New Brunswick, Canada? She was Baptist? She was born at New Brunswick, Canada.

           i) Andrew[7] Damink

           ii) Donald[7] Damink

    (2) Ralph A.[5] Bunnell (Bonnell) was Baptist? or Anglican? From Benjamin S. Bonnell bible records. He was born in 1939 at Woodman's Point/Westfield, Kings, New Brunswick, Canada. HEALTH: Died young (9 years) in 1939 at Woodman's Point/Westfield, Kings, New Brunswick, Canada. He was buried in 1939 at St. Peter's Anglican Church Cemetery, Woodman's Point/Westfield, Kings, New Brunswick, Canada.[859] He died in 1948 at Woodman's Point/Westfield, Kings, New Brunswick, Canada?[860]

    (3) Lawrence[5] Bunnell (Bonnell). HEALTH: Died young (14 years). He was Baptist? or Anglican? From Benjamin S. Bonnell bible records. He was born in 1947 at Woodman's Point/Westfield, Kings, New Brunswick, Canada. He was buried in 1960 at St. Peter's Anglican Church Cemetery, Woodman's Point/Westfield, Kings, New Brunswick, Canada.[861] He died in 1960 at Woodman's Point/Westfield, Kings, New Brunswick, Canada.[862]

Parent Ascending Line:
Benjamin Bonnell (1700-1798) & Eleanor
Samuel Bonnel (1675-1698) & Abigail
Nathaniel Bonnell (1644-1696) & Susannah Whitehead
William Bunnell (1600-1678) & Ann Wilmot
Benjamin Bunnell (1570-1655) & Rebecca Brooks
Thomas Bunnell (1550-1607) & ?

Loyalist
Isaac Bonnell (1738) Genealogy

I. ISAAC[1] BUNNELL (BONNELL) UE, ESQUIRE was born on 29 Aug 1738 at New Jersey, USA. He was High Sheriff of Middlesex County from 1763 to 1766 at Perth Amboy, Middlesex, New Jersey, USA. He and Grace Fox obtained a marriage license on 3 Dec 1763 at Perth Amboy, New Jersey, USA.[2] He married GRACE FOX U.E., daughter of THOMAS FOX, on 3 Dec 1763 at Perth Amboy, New Jersey, USA. He was (Appointed Barrack master of the province)(Also sold land as Sheriff of Perth Amboy in May 1770) in 1770 at Perth Amboy, Middlesex, New Jersey, USA. He was (Appointed sheriff of Middlesex County New Jersey under Gov. William Franklin who was a close friend and correspondent. Salary was L200 per annum. Served only 1 year before Whigs turned him out in 1776) in Jun 1775 at Perth Amboy, Middlesex, New Jersey, USA. He was jailed (By order of Washington and directed by the Provincial Congress to remain on paroled in Trenton or Cranbury. Leave was given to live elsewhere upon taking the oath not to bear allegiance to King George III. It is possibly Isaac served once in the American militia) in 1776 at Trenton (or Cranbury), New Jersey, USA. MILITARY: (Joined the British army as barrack master on Staten Island) in 1776 at Staten Island, New York, USA. He was (He was a partner of Abraham Veal in sloop, "Lively" which was impressed by Cortlandt Skinner for use of the Army) in 1776 at Perth Amboy, Middlesex, New Jersey, USA. MILITARY: (Was commissioned Lieutenant in the Prince of Wales American Regiment) in 1777 at New York, USA. He immigrated on 18 Oct 1778 to New Jersey, USA.[3] He was confiscate (Property was taken for being a loyalist. His real estate was entailed and therefore not lost to his children and he withdrew his claim for it. Loss was L635 sterling and was compensated L210, and pension of L15 for rest of life) in 1779 at Perth Amboy, Middlesex, New Jersey, USA. He immigrated in 1784 to Nova Scotia, Canada.[4]

---

[2] (Record #351, Isaac Bonnall & William Kannan, both of Perth Amboy (Bound to) William Franklin, Gov., 500 pounds, 3 Dec. 1763. Isaac Bonnell, obtained license of marriage for himself and for Grace Fox of Perth Amboy aforsaid witness John Mackay, consent of Thomas Fox for daughter Grace to be married to Isaac Bonnell 3 Dec. 1763, witnessed by John Smith, Esq.).

[3] Sheriff/Judge/Magistrate(Judgment in NJ 18 Oct. 1778 & sale of house & land 4 June 1780 Middlesex Co. NJ next to William Wright in Woodbridge who was possibly (loyalist) Ben's Capt. in King's American Reg.)(Isaac left on or after 1783 for Nova Scotia).

[4] (From CD #354, passengers & Immigrants lists index 1538-1940. Says he went to Nova Scotia in 1784, with notes that says from Nova Scotia Immigrants to 1817. Listed in Bunnell/Bonnell Newsletter dated May 1999, Vol. 13, p.2)(Also says he bought for 50 guineas, a log hut with windows of greased paper and one lot of land).

He was (Was commissioned as first Justice of the Peace, living in Digby, but jurisdiction was over County of Annapolis. In March he was appointed Judge of the Inferior Court of Common Pleas)(From Halifax NS Archives, Reel R61,vol.169,p.70) on 9 Feb 1784 at Digby, Digby County, Nova Scotia, Canada. He was (On commission to be Justice of Peace for county of Annapolis. From NS Archives at Halifax, reel RG1,vol. 169,p.121-22) on 25 Jul 1785 at Digby?, Annapolis, Nova Scotia, Canada. He was (With Elisha Budd, formed partnership of Bonnell & Budd for business in shipping and commerce. With Ambrose Haight & John Stewart, Deputy Sheriff, they bought one fourth of schooner "Frerbee and Phoebe" of Col. David Fanning. It worked the West Indies but found unsuitable for service. Capt. Adam Walker and Isaac's son, Franklin Bonnell were added to the firm that became Bonnell, Budd & Co. After getting money from Budd's friends in England they built a large ship, "Queen Charlotte" for foreign traffic. In Autumn of 1805 headed for Barbadoes with Timber, fish, commanded by Capt. Walker, some disaster happened because it was never seen again) in Jan 1794 at Nova Scotia, Canada. He was (On commission to be a Justice of the Inferior Court of Common Pleas for Annapolis county. From NS Archives at Halifax, reel RG1,vol.171,p.117) on 24 Dec 1794 at Digby?, Annapolis, Nova Scotia, Canada. He was (Was appointed over Lighthouse, Gut of Annapolis. From Halifax NS Archives reel RG1,vol. 172,p.108) on 31 Aug 1801 at Digby?, Annapolis, Nova Scotia, Canada. (Was on commission to be commissioner for purpose of encouraging emigrants from Europe to settle in western district of Nova Scotia. From NS Archives at Halifax, reel RG1,vol.172,p.132-33 & p.133-35) on 8 Sep 1803 at Digby?, Annapolis, Nova Scotia, Canada. (Was on commission for the establishment and support of a lighthouse at the entrance of the gut of Annapolis. From NS Archives at Halifax, reel RG1,vol.172,p.138) on 8 Sep 1803 at Digby?, Annapolis, Nova Scotia, Canada. He died circa 7 Nov 1806 at Digby, Nova Scotia, Nova Scotia, Canada.[5] He was buried circa 12 Nov 1806 at Trinity Cemetery, Digby, Annapolis, Nova Scotia, Canada.[6] His estate was probated in 1808 at Nova Scotia, Canada.[7]

---

[5](Died 7 or 10 Nov. 1806)(Executors were William F. Bonnell & son-in-law Elisha Budd).

[6](His inscription reads: "In memory of Isaac Bonnell, Esq., who departed this life 7th. J. 1806, age 68 years, 2 months and 9 days.
If usefull life through long protracted years in unassuming worth have claim to praise, if praise is due to him whose liberal hand gave bread and reiment to the laboring poor, if wealth diffused with just and liberal hand the glow of pious gratitude demand, then sure the sacred ashes buried here, deserve the tribute of a grateful tear."

[7](Archives of Nova Scotia at Halifax film #14996 has estate record #N6977).

A. MARY ANN[2] BUNNELL (BONNELL) was born on 5 Sep 1768 at Perth Amboy, Middlesex, New Jersey, British Colony.[8] She married ELISHA BUDD LOYALIST, son of ELISHA BUDD SR. and ANN LYON, on 15 Aug 1789 at Digby?, Annapolis, Nova Scotia, Canada. She died on 4 Sep 1850 at Nova Scotia, Canada, at age 81.[9]

1. DEBORAH[3] BUDD. Info from Paul D. Schenck 310 N. High St., Yellow Springs, Oh. 45387. She was born after 1790 at Digby?, Annapolis, Nova Scotia, Canada. She married an unknown person on 1 Apr 1828 at Digby, Nova Scotia, Canada.

    a) (--?--)[4] BUDD was born at Nova Scotia? He/she Paul D. Schenck 310 N. High St., Yellow Springs,Oh.45387.

2. ISAAC BONNELL[3] BUDD[10] was born on 14 May 1790 at Digby?, Annapolis, Nova Scotia, Canada.[11] He died on 2 Dec 1809 at age 19.[12]

3. JAMES[3] BUDD[13] was born on 26 Nov 1791 at Digby?, Annapolis, Nova Scotia, Canada.[14] He married STATIRA YOUNG on 24 Feb 1839 at Canada.[15] He died on 12 Nov 1877 at age 85.[16]

    a) GEORGE KIMBERLY NICHOLS[4] BUDD[17] was born on 4 Dec 1839.[18] He married MARY ELIZABETH (--?--) on 8 Jan 1863 at Canada.[19] He married SUSANA ELIZABETH EDWARDS on 15 Nov 1895 at Nebraska?, USA.[20]

---

[8](Or possibly c. 1772).
[9](Age 82).
[10]*no title* (Email-lessmann@earthlink.net: Ellen Lessmann, 18 Nov. 2000.
[11]*Bible Record.*
[12]*Bible Record.*
[13]*Bible Record.*
[14]*Bible Record.*
[15]*Bible Record.*
[16]*Bible Record.*
[17]*Bible Record.*
[18]*Bible Record.*
[19]*Bible Record.*
[20]*Bible Record.*

b) ELISHA[4] BUDD[21] was born on 10 May 1842.[22] He married CYNTHIA (--?--) on 4 Jan 1871.[23] He died on 9 Feb 1876 at age 33.[24]

    (1) EDWARD NICHOLS[5] BUDD[25] was born on 9 Jun 1872.[26]

    (2) JAMES ELENWOOD[5] BUDD[27] was born on 25 Aug 1873.[28]

    (3) ELISHA KIMBERLY[5] BUDD[29] was born on 31 May 1875.[30]

c) GRACE SUSANNAH[4] BUDD[31] was born on 10 May 1844.[32] She married JAMES WOOD on 24 Feb 1875.[33] She died on 26 Sep 1915 at age 71.[34]

    (1) NELLIE[5] WOOD[35] was born after 1875.[36] She died after 1875 at Villisca, Iowa, USA.[37,38]

    (2) ARTHUR LEIGH[5] WOOD[39] was born on 26 Feb 1880.[40] He died on 22 Jan 1945 at age 64.[41]

---

[21]*Bible Record.*
[22]*Bible Record.*
[23]*Bible Record.*
[24]*Bible Record.*
[25]*Bible Record.*
[26]*Bible Record.*
[27]*Bible Record.*
[28]*Bible Record.*
[29]*Bible Record.*
[30]*Bible Record.*
[31]*Bible Record.*
[32]*Bible Record.*
[33]*Bible Record.*
[34]*Bible Record.*
[35]*Bible Record.*
[36]*Bible Record.*
[37]Died an infant.
[38]*Bible Record.*

(3) LENA ETHEL[5] WOOD[42] was born on 30 Nov 1881.[43] She died on 21 Jun 1959 at age 77.[44]

(4) ERNEST BUDD[5] WOOD[45] was born on 28 May 1884.[46] He died in Nov 1955 at age 71.[47]

(a) (?)[6] WOOD[48] was born at Nebraska?, USA.[49]

i) ELLEN[7] (--?--)[50] married (?) LESSMANN at Nebraska?, USA.[51] She was born at Nebraska, USA.[52]

d) MERIAM ELISABETH[4] BUDD[53] was born on 24 May 1848 at Nova Scotia, Canada.[54] She was settled They were homesteaders in Nebraska from Nova Scotia after 1872 at Nebraska, USA. She married JAMES DALEY on 18 Dec 1872 at Nova Scotia, Canada.[55]

(1) ELISHA BUDD[5] DALEY[56] was born in 1873.[57]

---

[39] *Bible Record.*
[40] *Bible Record.*
[41] *Bible Record.*
[42] *Bible Record.*
[43] *Bible Record.*
[44] *Bible Record.*
[45] *Bible Record.*
[46] *Bible Record.*
[47] *Bible Record.*
[48] *Bible Record.*
[49] *Bible Record.*
[50] *Bible Record*, Also from Ellen herself in emailed dated 18 Nov. 2000.
[51] *Bible Record*, And from wife Ellen.
[52] *Bible Record*, And from Ellen.
[53] *Bible Record.*
[54] *Bible Record.*
[55] *Bible Record.*
[56] *Bible Record.*

(2) ERNEST[5] DALEY[58] was born in 1875 at Nebraska, USA.[59] He died in 1889.[60]

4. WILLIAM[3] BUDD[61] was born on 8 Jul 1793 at Canada.[62] He died on 15 Nov 1796 at Canada at age 3.[63]

5. CHARLES[3] BUDD[64] was born on 1 Apr 1795 at Digby?, Annapolis, Nova Scotia, Canada.[65] He married an unknown person on 2 May 1839.[66] He died on 24 Apr 1884 at age 89.[67]

6. MARY ANN[3] BUDD[68] was born on 5 Mar 1797 at Canada.[69] She married an unknown person on 15 Oct 1817.[70] She died on 1 Aug 1881 at age 84.[71]

7. WILLIAM FRANKLIN[3] BUDD[72] was born on 8 Apr 1799 at Canada.[73] He died on 29 Aug 1799 at Canada.[74]

---

[57]*Bible Record.*
[58]*Bible Record.*
[59]*Bible Record.*
[60]*Bible Record.*
[61]*Bible Record.*
[62]*Bible Record.*
[63]*Bible Record.*
[64]*Bible Record.*
[65]*Bible Record.*
[66]*Bible Record.*
[67]*Bible Record.*
[68]*Bible Record.*
[69]*Bible Record.*
[70]*Bible Record.*
[71]*Bible Record.*
[72]*Bible Record.*
[73]*Bible Record.*
[74]*Bible Record.*

8. EDWARD JOHN[3] BUDD[75] was born on 23 Oct 1800 at Canada.[76] He married an unknown person on 4 Oct 1823.[77] He died on 5 Dec 1876 at age 76.[78]

9. GRACE[3] BUDD[79] was born on 20 Nov 1802 at Canada.[80] She married an unknown person on 22 May 1820.[81] She died on 3 Dec 1838 at age 36.[82]

10. COTTNAM TONGE[3] BUDD[83] was born on 17 Dec 1804 at Canada.[84] He died on 11 Jan 1806 at Canada at age 1.[85]

11. ELIZABETH TONGE[3] BUDD[86] was born on 26 Feb 1807 at Canada.[87] She married an unknown person on 9 Jul 1828.[88]

B. ELIZABETH[2] BUNNELL (BONNELL) was born circa 1770 at Perth Amboy?, Middlesex, New Jersey, USA. She married WILLIAM COTTMAN TONGE ESQ. on 18 Feb 1793 at Perth Amboy?, Middlesex, New Jersey, USA.

C. WILLIAM FRANKLIN[2] BUNNELL (BONNELL)(COL.) U.E., ESQ immigrated.[89] He was born circa 1775 at Perth Amboy, Middlesex, New Jersey, USA.[90] (He was the God-Son of Gov. William Franklin of New Jersey, son of Benjamin Franklin, and last loyalist governor of New Jersey). (Was the first

---

[75]*Bible Record.*
[76]*Bible Record.*
[77]*Bible Record.*
[78]*Bible Record.*
[79]*Bible Record.*
[80]*Bible Record.*
[81]*Bible Record.*
[82]*Bible Record.*
[83]*Bible Record.*
[84]*Bible Record.*
[85]*Bible Record.*
[86]*Bible Record.*
[87]*Bible Record.*
[88]*Bible Record.*
[89]Col. in service.
[90](Or born 1773).

Postmaster General) circa 1800 at New Brunswick?, Canada. He married ANNA (--?--) circa 1800 at Canada.[91] (On commission to be a Justice of the Peace for Annapolis County. From NS Archives at Halifax, reel RG1,vol.173,p.46) on 26 Jul 1810 at Digby?, Annapolis, Nova Scotia, Canada. MILITARY: (Was Captain promoted to Major of Fourteenth Battalion Regiment of Militia. From Commissions cardex at NS Archives at Halifax, reel RG22,vol. 26,p.378) on 29 Jun 1811 at Digby?, Annapolis, Nova Scotia, Canada. (Commission to be Justice of the Peace of Annapolis County. From Commissions cardex at NS Archives at Halifax, reel RG1,vol.177,p.449) on 17 May 1819 at Digby?, Annapolis, Nova Scotia, Canada. (On commission of Justice of Inferior Court of Common Pleas for Annapolis County. Name listed as W.T. Bonnell. From NS Archives at Halifax, reel RG1,vol.174,p.27) in Nov 1822 at Digby?, Annapolis, Nova Scotia, Canada. (On a commission to be Justice of the Peace for Annapolis Co. From NS Archives at Halifax, reel RG1,vol. 174,p.276) on 2 Mar 1831 at Digby?, Annapolis, Nova Scotia, Canada. (On commission to be Justice of Peace. From NS Archives at Halifax, reel RG1,vol.174,p.325) on 16 Apr 1832 at Digby?, Annapolis, Nova Scotia, Canada. (Was commissioner of schools of western district of Annapolis. From Commissions cardex at NS Archives at Halifax, reel RG1,vol.174,p.336) on 2 May 1832 at Digby?, Annapolis, Nova Scotia, Canada. He died on 16 Feb 1837 at Digby, Nova Scotia, Canada.[92] He was buried on 20 Feb 1837 at Trinity?, Digby, Nova Scotia, Canada.[93] (On commission to be a commissioner of streets in Maitland in place of Alexander Nelson. From Commissions cardex at NS Archives at Halifax, reel RG1,vol.175,p.379) on 28 Feb 1846 at Digby?, Annapolis, Nova Scotia, Canada.

1. WILLIAM FRANKLIN[3] BUNNELL (BONNELL) JR was born in 1809 at Nova Scotia, Canada.[94] He was baptized on 28 Jan 1810 at Trinity?, Digby, Nova Scotia, Canada.[95]

---

[91](Shows up as mother of some children between 1800-1835. From Archives of Nova Scotia at Halifax film #14996 found by Paul Bunnell in Aug. 1999).

[92](Age 62).

[93](Listed as Esquire, age 63. Found in Archives of Nova Scotia, Halifax, film # 14996 by Paul Bunnell in Aug. 1999).

[94](From Warren Wetmore, WebMerlin@MegslNet.net on 16 Aug. 1999).

[95](From Archives of Nova Scotia at Halifax on film #14996 found by Paul Bunnell in Aug. 1999).

He immigrated in 1829 to Gagetown, New Brunswick, Canada.[96] He married ELIZA (ELIZABETH) (D OR S) LELIA VIETS, daughter of ROGER M. VIETS REV, on 16 Aug 1836 at Trinity Church, Digby, Digby, Nova Scotia, Canada.[97] (First Postmaster General of that area) in 1861 at Gagetown, New Brunswick, Canada. (At Archives of Nova Scotia at Halifax on film #14996 found by Paul Bunnell in Aug. 1999 says William F. born 1809, died 1891 in New York (Ref. N5624;obit N16681) in 1999.

    a) WILLIAM FRANKLIN[4] BUNNELL (BONNELL) was born on 9 Jul 1837 at Gagetown?, New Brunswick, Canada.[98] He died on 6 Sep 1837 at Gagetown, New Brunswick, Canada.[99]

    b) GEORGE AUGUSTUS[4] BUNNELL (BONNELL) was Anglican. He was born in 1840 at Gagetown, York, New Brunswick, Canada.[100] He died in 1842 at Gagetown, New Brunswick, Canada.[101] He was buried in 1842 at St. John Anglican Cemetery, Gagetown, New Brunswick, Canada.

    c) ANNING DIGBY[4] BUNNELL (BUNNELL) was born on 10 Dec 1842 at Gagetown, York, New Brunswick, Canada.[102]

    d) VIETS[4] BUNNELL (BONNELL) was born in 1844 at Gagetown, York, New Brunswick, Canada.[103]

    e) CHARLES EDWARD[4] BUNNELL (BONNELL) married HETTIE CLAFIN. He was born on 10 Jun 1846 at Gagetown, York, New Brunswick, Canada.[104]

---

[96](Move info from Warren Wetmore at WebMerlin@MegslNet.net on 16 Aug. 1999).

[97](From Warren Wetmore on 16 Aug. 1999 e-mail) Married on Tuesday morning, William F. Bonnell Jr. of Gagetown, NB to Eliza S. 4th. daughter of Rev. Roger Viets, of former place. From New Brunswick Royal Gazette 24 Aug. 1836, and NB Courier.

[98](From Archives of Nova Scotia at Halifax on film #14996 found by Paul Bunnell in Aug. 1999).

[99](From same source as birth).

[100](From Warren Wetmore e-mail 16 Aug. 1999).

[101]Age 19 months.

[102](From Warren Wetmore e-mail on 16 Aug. 1999).

[103](From Warren Wetmore e-mail on 16 Aug. 1999).

[104](From Warren Wetmore on e-mail 16 Aug. 1999).

(1) RALPH HOLBROOK^5 BUNNELL (BONNELL) was born on 5 Mar 1899 at Littleton, Ma. He married HELEN M. SULLIVAN on 20 Sep 1925 at Mass.?

    (a) BARBARA HOLBROOK^6 BUNNELL (BONNELL) was born at Massachusetts? She married DONALD COLE.

    (b) BEVERLY ANN^6 BUNNELL (BONNELL) was born at (possibly) Massachusetts.

    (c) BRUCE JEFFERSON^6 BUNNELL (BONNELL) was born at (possibly) Massachusetts.

    (d) RALPH HOLBROOK^6 BUNNELL (BONNELL) was born at Massachusetts, USA.

    (e) SHIRLEY HOLBROOK^6 BUNNELL (BONNELL). Her married name was DOE.

f) ANNIE ELIZA^4 BUNNELL (BONNELL) was born on 15 Oct 1848 at Gagetown, York, New Brunswick, Canada.[105]

g) MARGARET LOUISE^4 BUNNELL was born on 2 Sep 1850 at Gagetown, York, New Brunswick, Canada.[106]

h) HENRY S.^{4} BUNNELL (BONNELL) was born circa 1853 at Gagetown, York, New Brunswick, Canada.[107]

---

[105](From Warren Wetmore on e-mail 16 Aug. 1999).
[106](From Warren Wetmore on e-mail 16 Aug. 1999).
[107](From Warren Wetmore on e-mail 16 Aug. 1999).

2. ISAAC BUDD (HENRY?)^3 BUNNELL (BONNELL) was born on 21 Oct 1811 at Trinity?, Digby, Nova Scotia, Canada.[108] He was baptized on 21 Oct 1811 at Trinity Anglican Church, Digby, Digby, Nova Scotia, Canada.[109]

3. GEORGE JAMES^3 BUNNELL (BONNELL) was born on 17 Sep 1813 at Trinity?, Digby, Nova Scotia, Canada.[110]

4. CHARLES BUDD^3 BUNNELL (BONNELL) was born in 1815 at Nova Scotia, Canada.[111] He died in Mar 1844 at Sydney, New South Wales, Australia.[112]

5. EDWARD BUDD^3 BUNNELL (BONNELL) was born in 1817 at Nova Scotia, Canada.[113] He died on 17 Sep 1844 at Nova Scotia?, Canada?[114]

6. MARY ANN SOPHIA^3 BUNNELL (BONNELL) married TIMOTHY ROBERT WETMORE, son of THOMAS WETMORE U.E. and SARAH PETERS, at New Brunswick, Canada. She was born in 1824 at Digby?, Nova Scotia, Canada. She immigrated after 1824 to New Brunswick, Canada.[115]

7. SUSANNAH GRACE^3 BUNNELL (BONNELL) was born in 1824 at Digby, Digby, Nova Scotia, Canada. She died on 11 May 1836 at Digby, Digby, Nova Scotia, Canada.[116]

---

[108](From Archives of Nova Scotia at Halifax on film #14996 by Paul Bunnell in Aug. 1999)(Or born 1812 per Warren Wetmore, WebMerlin@MegslNet.net on 16 Aug. 19990.

[109]From the IGI records via Claude Bunnell, Florida 24 April 2000. Record says his name was Isaac Henry Bonnell).

[110](From Archives of Nova Scotia at Halifax on film #14996 found by Paul Bunnell in Aug. 1999).

[111](From Warren Wetmore at WebMerlin@MegslNet.net on 16 Aug. 1999).

[112]Died of Cholera.

[113](From Warren Wetmore at WebMerlin@ MegislNet.net on 16 Aug. 1999).

[114]Tuesday evening.

[115](Moved from NS to NB with brother William Franklin Jr. and their mother Anna Maria)(Per Warren Wetmore, 17608 Oakwood Dr., Hazel Crest, Il. 60429, dated 18 April 1999).

[116](Archives of Nova Scotia in Halifax says death was 3 May, at age 10, plus her mother was Anna. Found by Paul Bunnell in film # 14996 in Aug. 1999). Also found in New Brunswick Courier newspaper 28 May 1836; says, died Digby, NS Wednesday 11 inst, of Scarlet Feber, Susannag Grace, 2nd. daughter of W.F. Bonnell, Esq, age 12 years.

D. ISAAC² BUNNELL (BONNELL/BONNEL) was born circa 1764 at New Jersey, British Colony.

Parent Ascending Line:
Not proven yet.

Loyalist
Isaac Bunnell (1745) Genealogy

I. Isaac¹ BUNNELL Loyalist (U.E) Lived just a few miles from Benjamin Bonnell. He was born circa 21 Jul 1745 at Redding, Fairfield, Connecticut, USA. He was baptized on 21 Jul 1745 at Redding Congregational Church, Redding, Fairfield, Connecticut, USA. He married Jerusha Sherwood (UE), daughter of John Sherwood (UE) and Hannah Parrock (or Dorman, in 1771 at Newtown, Connecticut, USA. MILITARY: (United Empire Loyalist, UE and refugee) circa 1783. He immigrated in 1783 to Saint John, Saint John, New Brunswick, Canada.[863] (From Kings Co. Registry of Deeds, Hampton, NB, Vol. G1, Folio 91, #922, received Crown grant 14 July 1784, 200 acres, lot 6. Hawseis(?) survey at Clifton, Kingston, NB to William Frost by Jerusha Duggan, formerly wife ti Isaac Bunnell (Bonnell), David Bonnell, deed is dated 24 July 1799. Kings Co. Registry of deeds, vol. N1, Folio 416, #3010, deed vol. G1, Folio 91 #922 sold by William Frost to Henry Jackson, then too David Brown Wetmore, signed by Bonnell children, deed dated 17 Aug. 1814. Also from Story of Sussex & Vicinity, by Grace Aiten, pub. 1967 by Kings Co. Hist. Soc., p. 28, 37-38) on 14 Jul 1784 at Kings, New Brunswick, Canada. He was buried in 1791 at New Brunswick?, Canada. He died in Aug 1791 at (Kierstead), Collina (Stodholm Parish), Kings, New Brunswick, Canada. His estate was probated on 5 Sep 1791 at Hampton, Kings, New Brunswick, Canada.[864] Land/grant (It is believed that this land petition belongs to this family. Found by Carole Bonnell of Bunnell newsletter at Fredericton NB Archives on film #F1043 of RS108 index 1783-1918) in 1804 at Millstream, Sussex Vale, Kings, New Brunswick, Canada. He was a Farmer, and granted land in 1809,190 acres, lot #10 Kings Co., NB in 1809 at Lot # 10, Kings, New Brunswick, Canada. From Doug McQuinn, Saint John, NB 7/5/97. Will dated 1791 on 5 Jul 1997. (More sources of: American Loyalist Claims, by Peter W. Coldham, 1980. Isaac fled Redding, Ct., 15 Nov. 1776 to NY & got commission as Capt.. Got to Kingston, NB 25 Feb. 1786 with large family. Found in Prince of Wales Regiment, capturing rebel Capt. Sullivan A013/21/45-47) on 19 Aug 1998.

A. Daniel² Bunnell (Bonnell) Sr. U.E was born in 1772 at Connecticut, USA. He married (--?--) (--?--) circa 1795 at New Brunswick, Canada? He married Emma (Emmy) SPRAGUE, daughter of William SPRAGUE U.E. and Elizabeth (--?--) U.E, circa 1800 at New Brunswick, Canada? Was a Millwright & Freeman of Saint John, NB 1806 (see reg. of voters, city of Saint John 1785-1862,shelf 46,p.5 in 1806 at Saint John, Saint John, New Brunswick, Canada. Land/grant (Listed on his land petition found by Carole Bonnell at the Fredericton Archives, NB on film #F4179 of RS108 index 1783-1918) in 1817 at We., New Brunswick, Canada. He immigrated before 1841 to Lower Millstream, Penobsquis, New Brunswick, Canada.865 He died on 16 Jan 1841 at Penobsquis, Kings Co, New Brunswick, Canada.866 He was buried circa 17 Jan 1841 at Pioneer Cemetery, Penobsquis, Kings, New Brunswick, Canada.867 Pioneer Cemetery record at Fredericton, NB Archives circa 17 Jan 1841. From Doug McQuin, Saint John, NB 7/5/97 (descends)..

    1. Samuel³ BUNNELL. From Doug McQuinn, Saint John, NB 7/5/97. He was born after 1795? at New Brunswick, Canada?

    2. Crandall³ BUNNELL was born circa 1802 at New Brunswick, Canada. He married Catherine FITZGERALD on 27 Oct 1829 at New Brunswick, Canada? He died on 11 Sep 1847 at Penobsquis/Cardwell Parish?, Kings?, New Brunswick, Canada.868 He was buried circa 13 Sep 1847 at Pioneer Cemetery, Penobsquis/Cardwell Parish, Kings, New Brunswick, Canada.869 From Doug McQuinn, Saint John, NB 7/5/97.

    a) William Calvin⁴ Bunnell was born circa 1831 at New Brunswick, Canada.870 He died on 2 Aug 1844 at Penobsquis/Cardwell Parish, Kings, New Brunswick, Canada.871 He was buried on 4 Aug 1844 at Pioneer Cemetery, Penobsquis/Cardwell Parish, Kings, New Brunswick, Canada.872

    b) Mary Ann⁴ BUNNELL was born circa 1833 at Kings, New Brunswick, Canada. She appeared on the census of 1851 at Canadian Census, Sussex Parish, Kings, New Brunswick, Canada.873

c) James[4] BUNNELL was born circa 1835 at Kings, New Brunswick, Canada. He appeared on the census of 1851 at Canadian Census, Sussex Parish, Kings, New Brunswick, Canada.[874]

d) Emma[4] BUNNELL was born circa 1836 at Kings, New Brunswick, Canada. She appeared on the census of 1851 at Canadian Census, Sussex Parish, Kings, New Brunswick, Canada.[875]

e) Lydia[4] BUNNELL was born circa 1839 at Kings, New Brunswick, Canada. She appeared on the census of 1851 at Canadian Census, Sussex Parish, Kings, New Brunswick, Canada.[876] She married (?) King after 1851 at Penobsquis/Cardwell Parish, Kings, New Brunswick, Canada. She was buried in 1888 at Pioneer Cemetery, Penobsquis/Cardwell Parish, Kings, New Brunswick, Canada.[877] She died in 1888 at Penobsquis/Cardwell Parish, Kings, New Brunswick, Canada.

f) John[4] BUNNELL was born circa 1841 at Kings, New Brunswick, Canada. He appeared on the census of 1851 at Canadian Census, Sussex Parish, Kings, New Brunswick, Canada.[878]

g) Crandell Joseph[4] BUNNELL (Bonnell) From RS141 A2/1 co. vitals (1801-99),K1,5-1,p.127,#247,F13367 (sons birth). He was Baptist. He was born in 1844 at New Brunswick, Canada. He appeared on the census of 1851 at Canadian Census, Sussex Parish, Kings, New Brunswick, Canada.[879] He was directory (From Hutchinson's New Brunswick Directory 1867-68, page 460. Listed as a farmer) circa 1867 at South Branch Kennebecaasis, King's, New Brunswick, Canada. He married Lucinda Alcorn before 1877 at New Brunswick, Canada. He died in 1934 at New Brunswick, Canada. He was buried in 1934 at Cardwell Baptist Cemetery (across the street), Cardwell Parish, Kings, New Brunswick, Canada.[880]

(1) Alfred E.[5] Bunnell was Baptist? He was born in 1877 at New Brunswick, Canada. He died in 1952 at New Brunswick, Canada. He was buried in 1952 at Cardwell Baptist Cemetery, Cardwell Parish, Kings, New Brunswick, Canada.[881]

(2) John W.⁵ Bunnell was born in 1884 at New Brunswick, Canada. He was buried in 1939 at Cardwell Baptist Cemetery, Cardwell Parish, Kings, New Brunswick, Canada.⁸⁸² He died in 1939 at New Brunswick, Canada.

(3) Crandall Joseph⁵ Bunnell (Bonnell) From RS141 A2/1 county vitals (1801-99),K1,5-1,p.127,#247,F13367. He was born on 7 Dec 1891 at Penobsquis, Kings, New Brunswick, Canada. He was buried in 1946 at Cardwell Baptist Cemetery, Cardwell Parish, Kings, New Brunswick, Canada.⁸⁸³ He died in 1946 at New Brunswick, Canada.

(4) Isaac H.⁵ Bunnell was born in 1896 at New Brunswick, Canada. He was buried in 1976 at Cardwell Baptist Cemetery, Cardwell Parish, Kings, New Brunswick, Canada.⁸⁸⁴ He died in 1976 at New Brunswick, Canada.

3. Daniel³ BUNNELL U.E. Jr. married Anna VAIL at New Brunswick, Canada? He Marr.UN#RS551, Fredericton Archives. Bonds at Saint John, both from Sussex Parish, Kings Co. NB. He was born circa 1760 at New Jersey, USA.⁸⁸⁵ MILITARY: In the Prince of Wales American Regiment (From Grace Aiton's book) circa 1783. He immigrated after 1783 to Digby, Nova Scotia, Canada.⁸⁸⁶ He immigrated in 1800.⁸⁸⁷ He was tax list Listed with others with 4 1/2 d. and 3 acres of land with 3 cattle. (From The Story of Sussex and Vicinity New Brunswick, by Grace Aiton, Pub. by Kings Co. Hist. Soc., 1967) in 1800 at Assessment tax rolls, Sussex Vale Parish, Kings, New Brunswick, Canada. He was born circa 1805 at (possibly) Sussex co., New Brunswick, Canada. He married Emma (Amy) Graves, daughter of William Graves Jr. and Emma Armstrong, on 8 Aug 1832 at Saint John, Kings, New Brunswick, Canada.⁸⁸⁸ He At marriage she a Spinster 22 Aug.1832,wit.by John & Lebaron Graves.(listed as Jr.) on 22 Aug 1832. He appeared on the census of 1851 at Census, Sussex Parish, Kings, New Brunswick, USA.⁸⁸⁹ Land/grant (Listed on his land petition and possibly this Daniel, found by Carole Bonnell of Bunnell newsletter at Fredericton NB Archives on film #F4241 of RS108 index 1783-1918) in 1851 at Kings, New Brunswick, Canada. He died after 1851 at New Brunswick, Canada.⁸⁹⁰ Land/grant Grant #6045 from record vol. 41 on 20 Mar 1854 at 29 acres, Studholm, Kings, New Brunswick, Canada. From Doug McQuinn, Saint John, NB 7/5/97 on 5 Jul 1997.

a) Alfred Murray[4] BUNNELL was Baptist. He was a Shoemaker/Bootmaker. He married Nancy A. Ryder at New Brunswick?, Canada?[891] He was born on 23 May 1833 at New Brunswick, Canada.[892] He appeared on the census of 1851 at Canadian Census, Sussex Parish, Kings, New Brunswick, Canada.[893] He married Lucinda Graves, daughter of Charles W. Graves Jr. and Lucy A. Demille, on 15 Jan 1854 at Albert, New Brunswick, Canada.[894] Land/grant (Listed on Land petition of 1857 as son of Daniel. Found at Fredericton Archives, New Brunswick, film # F5935 of RS108 index 1783-1918, found by Carole Bonnell of Bunnell newsletter) in 1857 at Albert, New Brunswick, Canada. Land/grant (Listed on his land petition as son of Daniel, record found by Carole Bonnell of Bunnell newsletter at Fredericton NB Archives on film #F9019 of RS108 index 1783-1918) in 1859 at Albert, New Brunswick, Canada. He married Marie (Mary) Elizabeth Clark, daughter of Charles Howard Clark and Rachel Bunnell (Bonnell), circa 1863 at New Brunswick, Canada.[895] He married Elsie (Alice) Griedner (Guesner)(Gesner) after 1870? He died in 1919 at Montana, USA.[896] He was buried in 1919 at Montana?, USA?

   (1) Oliver H.[5] BUNNELL (Bonnell) died at Montana, USA. He married Genevieve Williams.[897] He was born on 18 Jun 1858 at Albert, New Brunswick, Canada.[898] Immigration: left New Brunswick heading for South Dakota in 1876. He appeared on the census of 1880 at South Dakota, USA.[899]

      (a) Hartley T.[6] BUNNELL was born at South Dakota, USA. He died at Washington, USA. He married Hattie E. Barkdoll. He was source (From Carole Bonnell, P.O. Box 4282 Spanaway, Wa. 98387) on 13 Sep 1998.

         i) Kieth[7] BUNNELL was born at Washington?, USA. Source: (From Carole Bonnell, P.O. Box 4282 Spanaway, Wa. 98387) on 13 Sep 1998.

            (a) Larry[8] BUNNELL (Bonnell) was born at Washington?, USA. He married Carole (--?--) at Washington?, USA?

i) Dean^9 BUNNELL (Bonnell) was born at Washington?, USA. He married (--?--) (--?--) at Washington?, USA. Source: (From mother, publisher of Bunnell/Bonnell Newsletter) on 13 Sep 1998 at P.O. Box 4282, Spanaway, Washington, USA.

    (a) Fletcher^{10} BUNNELL (Bonnell) was born at Washington?, USA. Source: (Zip code - 98387)(From grandmother, Carole Bonnell) on 13 Sep 1998 at P.O. Box 4282, Spanaway, Washington, USA.

    (b) Tabitha^{10} BUNNELL (Bonnell) was born at Washington?, USA. Source: (Zip code 98387)(From grandmother, Carole Bonnell) on 13 Sep 1998 at P.O. Box 4282, Spanaway, Washington, USA.

(2) Aldelia^5 BUNNELL was Baptist. She was born in 1860 at Albert, New Brunswick, Canada.^{900} She lived in 1881 at New Brunswick, Canada.^{901} She married George Schaffer on 16 Feb 1883 at Moncton, New Brunswick, Canada.^{902}

    (a) Oliver^6 Schaffer was born in 1858 at Albert, New Brunswick, Canada.

    (b) Charlton^6 Schaffer was born circa 1861 at Albert, New Brunswick, Canada. He appeared on the census of 1880 at Colorado, USA.^{903}

    (c) Lee^6 Schaffer

(3) Charlton^5 BUNNELL lived at Colorado, USA.^{904} He was born in 1861.^{905}

(4) Burton^5 BUNNELL was born in 1862.^{906}

(5) (?)^5 BUNNELL was born after 1864.

(6) Maudina Rachel[5] BUNNELL (Bonnell) was Baptist. She lived at South Dakota, USA.[907] She was born circa 1865 at New Brunswick, Canada. She married David (--?--) on 7 Apr 1888 at Brule, South Dakota, USA.[908]

    (a) Roy[6] (--?--) (Bunnell/Bonnell) was born at South Dakota, USA.

(7) Evaline[5] BUNNELL was Baptist. She married H. Jackson Kieth. She was born circa 1869 at New Brunswick, Canada.

(8) Edith[5] BUNNELL was F.W. Baptist. She died at Massachusetts, USA. She was born circa 1870 at New Brunswick, Canada. She appeared on the census of 1881 at New Brunswick, Canada.[909]

(9) Lilla[5] BUNNELL was Baptist. She was born circa 1871 at New Brunswick, Canada.

(10) Annadrocey[5] BUNNELL was Baptist. He married Llewwllyn David at Montana, USA. He was born circa 1873 at New Brunswick, Canada.

(11) Fred Lauren[5] BUNNELL (Bonnell) married Mae Wells. He married Helen Johnson.[910] He was born after 1870.[911] He was married 4 times. From Bunnell newsletter, Jan. 19999, vol. 13, #1, p.76)
in Jan 1999.

    (a) Lauren Wells[6] BUNNELL married Emelyn A. Tuttle.

        i) Harris Wells[7] BUNNELL (Bonnell) married Merle Dean.

    (b) William B.[6] BUNNELL (Bonnell) was source (From himself found in Bunnell/Bonnell newsletter dated August/Summer 1998, vol. 12,#3,p.40) in 1998 at Gig Harbor, Washington, USA.

(12) Percy Dell[5] BUNNELL was born after 1870. He lived in 1919 at Bozeman, Montana, USA.[912] He died after 1919 at Montana, USA.[913]

(13) (?)[5] BUNNELL

(14) (?)[5] BUNNELL

(15) (?)[5] BUNNELL

4. Jane[3] BUNNELL. Her married name was Lone. From Doug McQuinn, Saint John, NB 7/5/97. She was born circa 1815 at New Brunswick, Canada? She married Robert LONE on 23 Dec 1839 at Sussex, Kings Co., New Brunswick, Canada.

5. Lucy[3] Bunnell. Her married name was Walters. She married John Walters 09 Feb 1835 or 20 Nov.18 at Connecticut? or Sussex, Kings Co., New Brunswick, Canada. From Doug McQuinn, Saint John, NB 7/5/97. She was born circa 1817 at New Brunswick, Canada.

6. Lovy[3] BUNNELL. Her married name was Hall. She was buried.[914] She was born circa 1824 at New Brunswick, Canada? She married John HALL Sr. circa 1842 at New Brunswick, Canada? She died on 25 Jan 1864 at New Brunswick, Canada? From Doug McQuinn 7/5/97, Saint John, NB on 5 Jul 1997.

    a) Augusta[4] HALL was born at New Brunswick, Canada? She married Levi CONRIGHT at New Brunswick, Canada? From Doug McQuinn, Saint John, NB 7/5/97.

    b) Lucy[4] HALL. She married James MCKINLEY at New Brunswick, Canada? From Doug McQuinn, Saint John, NB 7/5/97. She was born at New Brunswick, Canada?

    c) Emma[4] HALL. From Doug McQuinn, Saint John, NB 7/5/97. She was buried.[915] She was born circa 1845 at New Brunswick, Canada? She died on 18 Feb 1864 at New Brunswick, Canada?

    d) Susan[4] HALL. She was buried.[916] From Doug McQuinn, Saint John, NB 7/5/97. She married John HARRISON at New Brunswick, Canada? She was born circa 1846 at New Brunswick, Canada? She died on 10 Oct 1870 at New Brunswick, Canada?

e) Lovica*4* HALL. Her married name was Kilpatrick. She was buried.[917] From Doug McQuinn, Saint John, NB 7/5/97. She married Alexander KILPATRICK at New Brunswick, Canada? She was born in 1847 at New Brunswick, Canada? She died in 1930 at New Brunswick, Canada?

f) Clarissa*4* HALL. From Doug McQuinn, Saint John, NB 7/5/97. She was buried.[918] She was born circa 1848 at New Brunswick, Canada? She died circa 1849 at New Brunswick, Canada?

g) William*4* HALL married Lily ? at New Brunswick, Canada? From Doug McQuinn, Saint John, NB 7/5/97. He was born circa 1850 at New Brunswick, Canada?

h) John C.*4* HALL. From Doug McQuinn, Saint John, NB 7/5/97. He married Teresa (Trissie) GODDARD at New Brunswick, Canada? He was buried.[919] He was born in 1854 at Jordan Mountain, New Brunswick, Canada.

i) Wealthy A.*4* HALL. Her married name was Law. From Doug McQuinn, Saint John, NB 7/5/97. She married William LAW at New Brunswick, Canada? She was born circa 1856 at New Brunswick, Canada? She died in 1927.

j) Warren*4* HALL was buried.[920] From Doug McQuinn, Saint John, NB 7/5/97. He married Charlotte (Lottie) LOCKHART at New Brunswick, Canada? He was born on 7 Nov 1861 at South Branch, Kings Co., New Brunswick, Canada. He died on 30 Jan 1927 at New Brunswick, Canada?, at age 65.

k) Naomi*4* HALL. She was buried.[921] From Doug McQuinn, Saint John, NB 7/5/97. She was Baptist? She was born on 7 Jan 1864 at Goshen Road, South Branch, Kings Co., New Brunswick, Canada. She married Richard Calvin MCQUINN on 24 Nov 1882 at Baptist Parsonage, Sussex, New Brunswick, Canada. She died on 17 Jul 1950 at Penobsquis, New Brunswick, Canada, at age 86.

7. Emma*3* Bunnell Also from Early Mar. of NB, by Wood-Holt, wit. by J. Schoale of St. John (Yesterdays record says mar. 26 May 1831,wit.William Stone. From descendant Betty Andrews Storey of Wisconsin & Fred Arch.#RS551. She was born in 1808 at Sussex, New Brunswick, Canada.[922] She married Daniel

Goddard, son of Giles Browne Goddard and Johanna Wager, on 10 May 1831 at Sussex, Kings Co., New Brunswick, Canada.[923] (Doug McQuinn, Saint John, NB 7/5/97 & Richard Segee of Ontario research in NB June 1998) on 5 Jul 1997.

    a) John Calvin[4] Goddard: From Betty Andrews Storey,5515 So. Bonnie Ln., Hales Corner,Wi.53130. He was born on 7 Feb 1832 at South Branch, Cardwell Parish, Kings Co. New Brunswick, Canada. He married Lavinia Wells, daughter of Newton WELLS and Lavinia EDGETT, on 24 Dec 1863 at Hopewell Cape, Albert Co., NB, Canada. He died on 24 Sep 1905 at Elgin, Albert Co. NB, Canada, at age 73.

        (1) Lavinia Wells[5] GODDARD. She died at Massachusetts? She From Betty Andrews Storey, 5515 So. Bonnie Ln., Hales Corner,Wi.53130. She married Frank Albert ANDREWS on 31 Mar 1897 at Ipswich, Essex Co., Massachusetts.

8. Elizabeth[3] Bunnell Bunnel Marr. Rec.at Fredericton Archives, NB #RS551 & Early Marr. New Brunswick, by Wood-Holt. She Yesteryears,by Johnson, says marr. 28 July 1831,wit.Samuel John..... & Daniel Bunnell Jr. She was born in Jul 1809 at Sussex Parish, Kings co., New Brunswick, Canada. She married LeBaron Graves, son of William Graves Jr. and Emma Armstrong, on 2 Jul 1831 at Saint John Trinity Church, Saint John, Saint John, New Brunswick, f Canada.[924] She died on 12 Nov 1859 at New Brunswick, Canada?, at age 50. From Doug McQuinn, Saint John, NB 7/5/97 on 5 Jul 1997.

9. Sarah[3] Bunnell (Bonnell) Marr. from Yesterdays, wit. by John Hall & Lebaron Graves. She was born in 1820 at Sussex parish, Kings Co., New Brunswick, Canada. She married William Ode(Ody) DUNFIELD on 9 Apr 1840 at Sussex, Kings Co., New Brunswick, Canada. She died in 1883 at New Brunswick, Canada? From Doug McQuinn, Saint John, NB 7/5/97 on 5 Jul 1997.

    a) Naomi LuLu[4] DUNFIELD Marr. from Yesterdays, wit. by John Hall & Lebaron Graves. She Marr. by G.M. Barrat (NB Courier). She married Charles Wesley WEYMAN, son of Edward WEYMAN Rev. and Naomi LuLu (--?--), on 9 May at New Brunswick, Canada. She was born on 27 Feb 1852 at New Brunswick, Canada.

She died on 10 Apr 1913 at Studholm Parish, Kings, New Brunswick, Canada, at age 61. She was buried circa 12 Apr 1913 at Lower Millstream Baptist Cemetery (Lester Cemetery), Studholm Parish, Kings, New Brunswick, Canada.[925]

    (1) Edward[5] WEYMAN Rev was born at New Brunswick, Canada. He was a Reverend. He was buried.[926] Marriage from Yesterdays, wit .by John Hall & Lebaron Graves.

B. Jemima[2] Bunnell (U.E.) Fredericton Archives, Fredericton, NB. She was born on 4 Jan 1773 at Connecticut.[927] She married Benjamin Kierstead U.E., son of Samuel Kierstead Junior (U.E.) and Mary Johnson U.E, on 16 Jun 1793 at Gagetown, New Brunswick, Canada. She was buried in 1822 at Kierstead Mountain, Kings, New Brunswick, Canada. She died in 1822 at Kings Co., New Brunswick, Canada.[928] From Doug McQuinn, Saint John, NB 7/5/97 on 5 Jul 1997.

    1. John Sherwood Bonnell/Bunnell[3] Kierstead (Governor) Fredericton Archives, NB. (Family was born on his land grant south of Kierstead Mt. Church, road going to Collina. He turned farm over to oldest son Robert & his youngest daughters moved to land on Snider Mt. near his uncle Justus Bunnell. John was called Governor Kierstead & attended hearing in New York concerning the "Anneke" estate which had 16 law suites. Got great experience from it). He was born on 9 Mar 1796 at Kings Co., New Brunswick, Canada.[929] He married Ann Holmes, daughter of (--?--) Holmes, on 4 May 1818 at Kings?, New Brunswick?, Canada? He died on 26 Jun 1864 at Kings?, New Brunswick, Canada, at age 68. (From Fancys Davis family files) on 30 Sep 1998 at Massachusetts, USA.

    a) Eliza Jane[4] Kierstead was born on 18 Feb 1819 at Kierstead Mt., Sussex, Kings, New Brunswick, Canada.[930] She married William Gregg (Grigg), son of (--?--) Gregg, on 17 Nov 1836 at Kings?, New Brunswick, Canada.[931] She died on 28 Apr 1888 at Sussex, Kings, New Brunswick, Canada, at age 69. She was buried on 1 May 1888 at Sussex, Kings, New Brunswick, Canada.[932]

    (1) Susanna[5] Gregg married William E. Marr, son of (--?--) Marr, at Kings, New Brunswick, Canada. She was born circa 1840 at New Brunswick, Canada. She died in 1877.[933]

(a) Miles[6] Marr was born at Kings, New Brunswick, Canada.

(b) Edward[6] Marr was born at Kings, New Brunswick, Canada.

(c) Chesley[6] Marr was born at Kings, New Brunswick, Canada.

(d) Cartilda[6] Marr was born at Kings, New Brunswick, Canada.

(e) Luzetta[6] Marr was born at Kings, New Brunswick, Canada.

(f) Nellie[6] Marr was born at Kings, New Brunswick, Canada.

b) Robert Nelson[4] Kierstead was born on 17 Nov 1820 at New Brunswick?, Canada?[934] He married Lydia Holmes, daughter of George Holmes and Mary Kierstead, after 1840 at Kings?, New Brunswick, Canada. He married Deborah Smith, daughter of George Smith, in 1851 at Kings?, New Brunswick, Canada.[935] He married Emmaline Matticks in 1863 at Kings?, New Brunswick, Canada.[936] He died in Jan 1900 at New Brunswick?, Canada?, at age 79.

c) Eleanor[4] Kierstead. She married Robert Kiest at New Brunswick, Canada. She was born on 23 Dec 1822 at Kings?, New Brunswick, Canada. She died circa 1900 at New Brunswick, Canada.[937]

d) Jemima[4] Kierstead was born on 8 Mar 1824 at New Brunswick, Canada.[938] She married Jacob Schofield on 6 Apr 1842 at New Brunswick, Canada.[939] She died on 18 Jul 1853 at New Brunswick, Canada, at age 29.

e) Lydia[4] Kierstead was born on 5 Feb 1826 at New Brunswick, Canada.[940] She married John Horsman on 14 Mar 1859 at Salisbury, New Brunswick, Canada.[941] She died on 22 Mar 1898 at New Brunswick, Canada, at age 72.

f) Charles Wesley[4] Kierstead married Augusta Beck at New Brunswick?, Canada? He was born on 7 Oct 1827 at New Brunswick, Canada. He was (Doctor) after 1840 at New Brunswick, Canada. He married ? ? after 1873 at Wisconsin?, USA?[942] He died circa 1900 at Wisconsin?, USA?

g) John Holmes[4] Kierstead was born on 2 Apr 1829 at New Brunswick?, Canada?[943] He died on 18 Jan 1836 at New Brunswick, Canada, at age 6.[944] (From Francys Davis records) in Oct 1998.

h) Sarah Ann[4] Kierstead was born on 4 Jun 1831 at New Brunswick, Canada. She died on 23 Dec 1835 at New Brunswick, Canada, at age 4.[945]

i) Isabella[4] Kierstead was born on 25 Jun 1833 at New Brunswick, Canada.[946] She married James McKnight on 21 Oct 1857 at New Brunswick?, Canada? She died on 15 Nov 1908 at New Brunswick, Canada, at age 75.

j) Bethia[4] Kierstead died on 6 Jan 1831 at New Brunswick, Canada.[947] She was born on 12 Apr 1835 at New Brunswick, Canada.

k) Michael Pickles[4] Kierstead was born on 14 Dec 1836 at New Brunswick, Canada.[948] He married Mary Jane Beck on 27 Jan 1858 at New Brunswick, Canada. He married (Widow) Bunnell after 1897 at New Brunswick, Canada. He died in Jul 1903 at New Brunswick?, Canada?, at age 66.

l) Sarah Ann[4] Kierstead (#2) died at Philadelphia, Pennsylvania, USA.[949] She married John McNamara. She was born on 23 Oct 1838 at New Brunswick, Canada.

m) Catherine[4] Kierstead was born on 22 May 1841 at New Brunswick, Canada. She married Thomas Willet Kierstead, son of Thomas David Kierstead and Elizabeth Green (Aunt Betty Tom), on 28 Jan 1864 at New Brunswick?, Canada? She died on 25 Feb 1922 at New Brunswick or Vermont? at age 80.

2. Isaac[3] Kierstead: HEALTH: Died young. He died at Kings Co., New Brunswick, Canada.[950] He was buried.[951] From Fredericton Archives, NB. He was born in 1794 at Kings Co., New Brunswick, Canada.

3. David[3] Kierstead Sr.: From Fredericton Archives, NB. He was born on 7 Mar 1798 at Kings Co., New Brunswick, Canada. He married Sarah Blackney (Bleakney) on 8 Jun 1823 at Kings, New Brunswick, Canada. He died in 1856 at Kings?, New Brunswick?, Canada?

a) Henry Allen[4] Kierstead was born at New Brunswick, Canada. He married Eliza Ann Kierstead, daughter of Gershom Kierstead and Hannah Matilda Marr, at New Brunswick, Canada.

4. Thomas David[3] Kierstead: From Fredericton Archives, NB. He was born on 21 Dec 1799 at Sussex, Kings, New Brunswick, Canada.[952] He married Elizabeth Green (Aunt Betty Tom) on 3 Mar 1827 at Sussex, Kings, New Brunswick, Canada. He died on 10 Oct 1857 at New Brunswick?, Canada?, at age 57.[953]

a) Bethia[4] Kierstead was born on 2 Mar 1828 at Kings?, New Brunswick, Canada.[954]

b) Hannah[4] Kierstead was born on 4 Apr 1830 at Kings?, New Brunswick, Canada.[955]

c) Willet[4] Kierstead was born on 19 Sep 1832 at Kings, New Brunswick, Canada.[956]

d) Edward Weyman[4] Kierstead was born on 26 Apr 1835 at Kings, New Brunswick, Canada.[957]

e) Hannah Elizabeth[4] Kierstead was born on 17 Sep 1837 at Kings?, New Brunswick, Canada.[958]

f) Jemima Filinda[4] Kierstead was Baptist. She was born on 23 Feb 1840 at New Brunswick, Canada.[959] She married Justus Sherwood Bunnell, son of Justus/Justice Bunnell and Margeret Barton Baxter, on 6 Feb 1866 at New Brunswick, Canada. She married Richard Redstone on 15 Nov 1895 at NB? She died on 6 Mar 1928 at Kings?, New Brunswick, Canada, at age 88.[960] She was buried circa 8 Mar 1928 at Kierstead Mountain United Baptist Church Cemetery, Studholm Parish, Kings, New Brunswick, Canada.[961]

(1) Wilda Anne[5] Bunnell was born after Mar 1866 at Kings, New Brunswick, Canada.

(2) Hannah Elizabeth[5] Bunnell. She married Thomas Gilbert Perry at New Brunswick, Canada. She was born on 3 Feb 1867 at New Brunswick, Canada.[962] (A Hannah E. Brunnell of Kings county, NB was listed in Fredericton, NB 15 Jan. 1885 school students list as a First Baptist. This was from the Fredericton Evening Capital newspaper which was listed in Generations, NB Gene. Soc. magazine Issue 66, Winter 1995) on 15 Jan 1885 at Fredericton, York, New Brunswick, Canada.

    (a) Milton G.[6] Perry was born at New Brunswick, Canada.[963] She died at Limerick?, Maine, USA.

(3) Wilda Anne[5] Bunnell. She married (--?--) Casson at New Brunswick?, Canada? She was born on 31 Dec 1868 at Kings?, New Brunswick, Canada.[964]

(4) Adam[5] BUNNELL. Cemetery records found at Fredericton Archives...Mom died same day. He was Baptist. He was born on 2 Oct 1870 at Kings Co., New Brunswick, Canada.[965] He died on 22 Dec 1875 at Studholm Parish, Kings, New Brunswick, Canada, at age 5.[966] He was buried circa 24 Dec 1875 at Keirstead Mountain United Baptist Church Cemetery, Studholm Parish, Kings, New Brunswick, Canada.[967] From Doug McQuinn, Saint John, NB 7/5/97 on 5 Jul 1997.

(5) Weldon Thomas[5] Bunnell was born on 11 Jun 1874 at New Brunswick, Canada. He married Margaret Matilda Fowler on 20 Jun 1897 at New Brunswick?, Canada. He died in 1929 at Studholm Parish, Kings, New Brunswick, Canada. He was buried in 1929 at Kierstead Mountain Baptist Cemetery, Studholm Parish, Kings, New Brunswick, Canada.[968]

    (a) Henry A.[6] Bunnell was born after 1898 at New Brunswick, Canada.

    (b) Lucy Anne[6] Bunnell married Frank Donald Coy at New Brunswick?, Canada? She was buried at Kierstead Mountain Baptist Cemetery, Studholm Parish, Kings, New Brunswick, Canada.[969] She was born on 20 May 1910 at New Brunswick, Canada.[970]

(c) Roy Allen[6] Bunnell married Agnes Lanther? at New Brunswick?, Canada? He was born on 28 Jul 1913 at New Brunswick, Canada.[971]

(6) Hettie Jemima[5] Bunnell. She married Gus Dibblee at New Brunswick?, Canada? She was born on 13 Oct 1876 at New Brunswick, Canada.

(7) Mabel Armintha[5] Bunnell was born on 8 Feb 1880 at New Brunswick, Canada. She married Simon P. Dibblee on 20 Jun 1905 at Saint John, Saint John, New Brunswick, Canada.[972]

g) Thomas Willet[4] Kierstead was born on 28 Oct 1842 at Kings?, New Brunswick, Canada.[973] He married Catherine Kierstead, daughter of John Sherwood Bonnell/Bunnell Kierstead (Governor) and Ann Holmes, on 28 Jan 1864 at New Brunswick?, Canada? He died on 25 Feb 1909 at Ludlow, Vermont, USA, at age 66.[974]

h) Daniel[4] Kierstead was born on 26 Feb 1845 at Kings?, New Brunswick, Canada.[975]

i) Bethia Margaret[4] Kierstead was born on 16 Jul 1848 at Kings?, New Brunswick, Canada.[976]

5. Bethia (Erthia)[3] Kierstead Bethia was sister to Jemima, Isaac Bunnell's wife (from 1851 Kings Co. census). From Fredericton Archives, NB. She married George W Bunnell, son of Benjamin Bunnell (Bonnell) and Sarah DAY (Dey), at New Brunswick, Canada. She was born on 8 Nov 1801 at Kings Co., New Brunswick, Canada. She married William Fowlie on 13 May 1822 at New Canaan, New Brunswick, Canada.[977]

6. Lydia (Lidea)[3] Kierstead. From Fredericton Archives, NB. She was born on 28 Jan 1804 at Kings Co., New Brunswick, Canada.[978] She married David Kelly, son of William Kelly and Abigail Whelpley ?, on 16 Feb 1826 at New Brunswick, Canada.[979] She married George Holmes circa 1836 at New Brunswick, Canada.[980] She died after 1851 at New Brunswick, Canada.

a) Lydia Jane[4] Kelly married George Marr at New Brunswick, Canada. She was born on 20 Jan 1836 at Kierstead Mountain, New Brunswick, Canada. She died in 1924 at New Brunswick, Canada.

7. Gershom[3] Kierstead. From Fredericton Archives, NB. He was born on 22 Sep 1805 at Kings Co., New Brunswick, Canada. He married Mary (Elizabeth?) Worden (Warden) on 15 Feb 1829 at New Brunswick, Canada.[981] He married Hannah Matilda Marr, daughter of Richard Marr and Elizabeth Rouse, on 30 Nov 1835 at New Brunswick, Canada.[982] He married Catherine Mills after 1860? at New Brunswick, Canada.[983] He died on 13 Sep 1878 at New Brunswick, Canada, at age 72.[984]

a) ?[4] Kierstead was born at New Brunswick, Canada. He/she died before 1835? at (Died young), New Brunswick, Canada.

b) ?[4] Kierstead was born at New Brunswick, Canada. He/she died before 1835? at (Died young), New Brunswick, Canada.

c) Elizabeth Ann[4] Kierstead was born on 6 Dec 1836 at New Brunswick, Canada. She died on 28 Nov 1839 at New Brunswick, Canada, at age 2.

d) Sarah Elizabeth[4] Kierstead married John Holmes at New Brunswick, Canada. She was born on 30 Oct 1838 at New Brunswick, Canada. She died on 6 May 1875 at age 36.

e) Eliza Ann[4] Kierstead married Henry Allen Kierstead, son of David Kierstead Sr. and Sarah Blackney (Bleakney), at New Brunswick, Canada. She was born on 2 Nov 1840 at New Brunswick, Canada. She died in 1911 at New Brunswick, Canada.

f) Charlotte Bethia[4] Kierstead married James Jamieson at New Brunswick, Canada. She died on 27 Jul at New Brunswick, Canada. She was born on 28 Oct 1842 at New Brunswick, Canada.

g) Hannah Matilda[4] Kierstead married Silas N. Fowler at New Brunswick, Canada.[985] She was born on 9 Feb 1848 at New Brunswick, Canada. She died in Aug 1887 at New Brunswick, Canada, at age 39.

h) Lydia Jane[4] Kierstead married James H. Ryder at New Brunswick, Canada. She was born on 18 Jul 1854 at New Brunswick, Canada. She died circa 28 Aug 1875 at New Brunswick, Canada.

i) Jemima Amelia[4] Kierstead married Silas Douthwright at New Brunswick, Canada. She was born on 24 Mar 1857 at New Brunswick, Canada. She died circa 1921 at New Brunswick, Canada.

8. Justus[3] Kierstead. From Fredericton Archives, NB. He was born on 19 Jun 1807 at Kings Co., New Brunswick, Canada. He married Eliza Ann Rouse on 5 Jun 1834 at New Brunswick, Canada.[986] He died on 16 Dec 1880 at New Brunswick, Canada, at age 73.

9. Daniel[3] Kierstead. From Fredericton Archives, NB. He was born on 14 May 1809 at Kings, New Brunswick, Canada. He married Huldah (Hulda) Gray, daughter of Abram Talhoe Gray, on 21 Oct 1833 at New Brunswick, Canada.[987] He died on 28 Feb 1882 at New Brunswick, Canada, at age 72.[988]

10. Leonard S.[3] Kierstead was Farmer. From Fredericton Archives, NB. He was F.C. Baptist. He was born on 2 Jan 1811 at Kings, New Brunswick, Canada.[989] He married Mary Jane Moffatt (Moffat) on 18 Sep 1841 at New Brunswick, Canada.[990] He died on 26 Sep 1882 at Kings, New Brunswick, Canada, at age 71.[991] He was buried circa 27 Sep 1882 at Caanan Forks Cemetery, Kings?, New Brunswick, Canada. From Loyalist Lineages of Canada; 1881 Queens co., NB Census in Jun 2002.

a) Gershom[4] Kierstead was born at Kings, New Brunswick, Canada.

b) Alfred James[4] Kierstead was born in 1843 at New Brunswick, Canada. He died in 1905.

c) Ruth[4] Kierstead was born in 1844 at New Brunswick, Canada.

d) Maria Margaret[4] Kierstead married (--?--) Beach at New Brunswick, Canada. She was born in 1846 at New Brunswick, Canada. She died in 1916.

e) Cyrus[4] Kierstead was born on 16 Mar 1849 at Kings, New Brunswick, Canada. He died on 9 Jun 1934 at New Brunswick, Canada, at age 85.

f) Lydia Jane[4] Kierstead married Amos Currie. She was born in Aug 1850 at New Brunswick, Canada. She died in 1897.

    (1) Orland H.[5] Currie

    (2) Emma[5] Currie married Pembroke Northrup.

g) Elijah Leonard[4] Kierstead was born in 1852 at Kings, New Brunswick, Canada. He died in 1929.

h) Susan Matilda[4] Kierstead was born in 1855 at Kings, New Brunswick, Canada. She died in 1886.

i) Annie Mary[4] Kierstead married (--?--) Cole at New Brunswick, Canada. She was born in 1857 at Kings, New Brunswick, Canada. She died in 1911.

j) George Leonard[4] Kierstead was born in 1859 at Kings, New Brunswick, Canada. He died in 1911.

k) Eliza[4] Kierstead was born circa 1861 at Kings, New Brunswick, Canada.

l) David William[4] Kierstead was born in 1865 at Kings, New Brunswick, Canada. He died in 1939.

m) Arthur Wesley[4] Kierstead was born in 1867 at Kings, New Brunswick, Canada. He died in 1893.

11. Sarah[3] Kierstead (Aunt Sally). From Fredericton Archives, NB. She was born on 12 Sep 1813 at Kings Co., New Brunswick, Canada. She married Abraham Kierstead, son of Isaiah Kierstead and Elizabeth Lester, before 1865 at New Brunswick, Canada.[992] She married Thomas Gibbon before 1866 at New Brunswick, Canada.[993] She married Frederick Erb circa 1867 at New Brunswick, Canada.[994] She died in 1897 at New Brunswick, Canada.[995]

12. Deborah[3] Kierstead. from Fredericton Archives, NB. She was born on 13 Dec 1815 at Kings Co., New Brunswick, Canada. She married Nicholas Gregg on 4 Apr 1845 at New Brunswick, Canada.[996]

C. Mary[2] Bunnell U.E. From Fredericton Archives, NB. She was born circa 1775 at Connecticut?, USA.[997] MILITARY: (Came with parents as loyalist refugee's) circa 1783 at Saint John, Saint John, New Brunswick, Canada. She married Charles MCLEAN before 1800 at New Brunswick, Canada.[998] She married Ezekiel Foster Jr. U.E., son of Ezekiel Foster Sr. U.E. and Mary Fogg U.E, circa 1800 at New Brunswick, Canada. She died after 1849 at Collina?, Kings, New Brunswick, Canada.[999] From Doug McQuinn, Saint John, NB 7/5/97 on 5 Jul 1997.

    1. Lidia[3] FOSTER. She married Mr. FENWICK at Kings Co., New Brunswick, Canada? From Fredericton Archives, NB. She was born at Kings Co., New Brunswick, Canada?

    2. Hannah[3] FOSTER. She married Mr. ....ELTY? at Kings Co., New Brunswick, Canada? From Fredericton Archives, NB. She was born at Kings Co., New Brunswick, Canada?

    3. Sarah[3] FOSTER was born at Kings, New Brunswick, Canada. She married Mr. MCFARLAND at Kings Co., New Brunswick, Canada? From Fredericton Archives, NB.

    4. Elizabeth[3] FOSTER. She married Mr. LONG at Kings Co., New Brunswick, Canada? From Fredericton Archives, NB. She was born at Kings Co., New Brunswick, Canada?

    5. Clarisse[3] FOSTER. She married Abraham GRAY at Kings Co., New Brunswick, Canada? From Fredericton Archives, NB. She was born at Kings Co., New Brunswick, Canada?

D. Jerusha[2] BUNNELL married John MCLEOD U.E., son of William MCLEOD U.E. and Elizabeth (--?--). She Possible daughter of Isaac? She was born circa 1777 at Kings Co. New Brunswick, Canada. She was buried after 1821 at Ontario, Canada.

    1. Isaac[3] MCLEOD was born at New Brunswick, Canada.

    2. Jerusha[3] MCLEOD was born at New Brunswick, Canada.

E. Caroline (Katy)[2] BUNNELL (Bonnell) married John MCLEOD U.E., son of William MCLEOD U.E. and Elizabeth (--?--), at New Brunswick, Canada.[1000] She was born circa 1779 at USA? From Doug McQuinn, Saint John, NB 7/5/97.

F. John[2] Bunnell. From Fredericton Archives, NB. He was born in 1779 at USA?[1001] (He was a Millwright, and son of a loyalist) circa 1802 at Kings, New Brunswick, Canada. He married Mary McLean circa 1802 at New Brunswick, Canada. He immigrated in 1813 to Kings, New Brunswick, Canada.[1002] He died in 1831 at Mabou, Cape Breton, New Brunswick, Canada.[1003] After his death,wife/6kids walked to Sussex to her family in 1831 at Sussex, Kings, New Brunswick, Canada. From Doug McQuinn, Saint John, NB 7/5/97 on 5 Jul 1997.

    1. (--?--)[3] BUNNELL was born at New Brunswick, Canada. From Fredericton Archives, NB.

    2. (--?--)[3] BUNNELL was born at New Brunswick, Canada. From Fredericton Archives, NB.

    3. (--?--)[3] BUNNELL was born at New Brunswick, Canada. From Fredericton Archives, NB.

    4. (--?--)[3] BUNNELL was born at New Brunswick, Canada. From Fredericton Archives, NB.

    5. (--?--)[3] BUNNELL was born at New Brunswick, Canada. From Fredericton Archives, NB.

    6. (--?--)[3] BUNNELL was born at New Brunswick, Canada. From Fredericton Archives, NB.

G. Isaac[2] BUNNELL Jr. He was born circa 1781 at Newtown, Connecticut, USA. He immigrated in 1783 to Saint John, Saint John, New Brunswick, Canada.[1004] He was baptized after 1783 at Norton, Kings, New Brunswick, Canada.[1005] (One of the first Deacons of this church). He lived after 1783 at Collina, York, New Brunswick, Canada.[1006] He married Sarah Fowler, daughter of Weaton (Weeden) Fowler U.E. and Elizabeth Sherwood U.E, in Jan 1802 at Kings, New Brunswick, Canada.[1007] Land/grant Grant #517, record vol. E, page 8 on 12 Dec 1809 at 190 acres with 48 others, Mill Stream, Kings, New Brunswick, Canada.

He married Elizabeth BLACKNEY on 24 Jun 1819 at New Brunswick, Canada? (Records from Collina church records, Kierstead Mt. Cemetery, 1851 census, letters of Donald Wright and Herrert Bonnell) in 1851 at Collina, York?, New Brunswick, Canada. He appeared on the census of Jul 1851 at Canadian Census, Studholm Parish, Kings, New Brunswick, Canada.[1008] (At death, he had 12 children.72 grandchildren, 38great-grandchildren. He was a Carpenter at marriage. He was also a Millwright on 18 Jun 1860 at Kings, New Brunswick, Canada. He died on 18 Jun 1860 at Brunswick, Queens Co., New Brunswick, Canada.[1009] He was buried circa 20 Jun 1860 at Kings, New Brunswick, Canada. Also from 22 June 1860 Religious Intelligencer on 22 Jun 1860 at New Brunswick, Canada. (From "Generations", p. 43, Spring 1998 issue, with source from Genealogy of the Anglo-Dutch Esterbrooks Family, by Florence Esterbrooks, 1935) in May 1998 at Fredericton, York, New Brunswick, Canada.

1. Rebecca[3] Bunnell (Bonnell) married Isaac Coy, son of Isaac Bonnell Coy Senior, at New Brunswick, Canada?[1010] (Entire Coy line in my files. Needs more research to determine if Isaac or John is husband, or both?). She was a Baptist? She was born in 1807 at Kings, New Brunswick, Canada.[1011] She married John Coy, son of Edward Coy Jr. and Jane A. Murray, in 1827 at Kings, New Brunswick, Canada.[1012] She appeared on the census of 1881 at New Brunswick, Canada.[1013] She died in 1889 at Kings?, New Brunswick?, Canada? (Some info. from Burt Lightbody, 7 Conyers St., Sumter, SC 29150, on 23 Jan 1998.

a) Alfred[4] Coy was born circa 1839 at Collina, Kings, New Brunswick, Canada. He married Isabella Lightbody, daughter of John Lightbody and Margaret Fraser, circa 1872 at New Brunswick?, Canada?[1014] He immigrated before 1873 to Lowell, Massachusetts, USA. (From Burt Lighbody, 7 Conyers St., Sumter, SC 29150, on 23 Jan 1998.

(1) Maud[5] Coy. She was born on 16 Jan 1873 at Lowell, Massachusetts, USA. She married James Andrew Beyea on 23 Mar 1889. She died on 9 May 1901 at age 28. (From Burt Lighbody, 7 Conyers St., Sumter, SC 29150, on 23 Jan 1998.

(2) Margaret[5] Coy. She married Roland Haslett at Massachusetts?, USA? She was born circa 1875 at Lowell, Massachusetts, USA. (From Raymond V. Haslett, 4 Maple Lane, Quispanies, Kings Co., NB...

Says Margaret married William Frost Haslett? Complete gene on this paper but poor reading, many difference around this part of family) on 20 Aug 1987. (From Burt Lightbody, 7 Conyers St., Sumter, SC 29150, on 23 Jan 1998.

(3) Mary^5 Coy. She married (--?--) Andrews at Massachusetts?, USA? She was born circa 1877 at Lowell, Massachusetts, USA. (From Burt Lightbody, 7 Conyers St., Sumter, SC 29150, on 23 Jan 1998.

(4) Ellen^5 Coy. She married Elias William Long at Lowell?, Massachusetts?, USA? She was born circa 1879 at Lowell, Massachusetts, USA. She died on 14 Aug 1914 at Lowell, Massachusetts, USA. (From Burt Lightbody, 7 Conyers St., Sumter, SC 29150, on 23 Jan 1998.

(5) John^5 Coy was born circa 1881 at Lowell, Massachusetts, USA. (From Burt Lightbody, 7 Conyers St., Sumter, SC 29150, on 23 Jan 1998.

(6) Lillian Isabella^5 Coy was born on 29 Dec 1884 at Lowell, Massachusetts, USA. She married Melville James Burnside on 5 Nov 1907 at Saint John, Saint John, New Brunswick, Canada.[1015] She died on 25 Sep 1955 at age 70. (From Burt Lightbody, 7 Conyers St., Sumter, SC 29159, on 23 Jan 1998.

2. Rachel^3 Bunnell (Bonnell) died at Westfield, Kings Co., New Brunswick, Canada.[1016] She was born on 6 Nov 1814 at Belleisle, New Brunswick, Canada.[1017] She married Charles Howard Clark circa 1832 at New Brunswick?, Canada?[1018]

a) Marie (Mary) Elizabeth^4 Clark was born on 18 Aug 1840 at Corn Hill, Kings, New Brunswick, Canada. She married Alfred Murray BUNNELL, son of Daniel BUNNELL U.E. Jr. and Emma (Amy) Graves, circa 1863 at New Brunswick, Canada.[1019] She died circa Nov 1879 at New Brunswick, Canada.[1020]

(1) (?)^5 BUNNELL (see above)

(2) Maudina Rachel[5] BUNNELL (Bonnell) (see above)

(3) Evaline[5] BUNNELL (see above)

(4) Edith[5] BUNNELL (see above)

(5) Lilla[5] BUNNELL (see above)

(6) Annadrocey[5] BUNNELL (see above)

3. Jennest[3] Bunnell was also known as Jennest Bunnell. She was born at New Brunswick, Canada. She was baptized in 1848 at Collina, New Brunswick, Canada.[1021]

4. Jerusha[3] Bunnell Bunnel. She was born at Springfield, New Brunswick, Canada. She lived in 1822 at Coal Creek, Queens, New Brunswick, Canada. She married Jacob Myers(Mires) on 28 Jan 1822 at Springfield, Kings Co. NB.

5. Mary[3] Bunnell Bacon(#2)husband. Her married name was Mcgregor(#1). She was source (From Family record files at Fredericton Archives listed under Isaac Bunnell) at Fredericton Archives, Fredericton, York, New Brunswick, Canada. She was born on 27 Aug 1810 at New Brunswick, Canada. She lived circa 1824 at Waterboro, Queens, New Brunswick, Canada. She married John McGregor on 5 Jan 1824 at New Brunswick, Canada. She married Daniel Bacon on 24 Jun 1830 at New Brunswick, Canada.

    a) Sarah Ann[4] MCGREGOR was born at Kings?, New Brunswick, Canada.

    b) Eleanor Jane[4] MCGREGOR was born at New Brunswick, Canada.

    c) Ester[4] MCGREGOR was born at New Brunswick, Canada.

    d) Mary[4] MCGREGOR was born at New Brunswick, Canada.

    e) Daniel Smith[4] MCGREGOR was born at New Brunswick, Canada.

f) Isaac Bunnell[4] MCGREGOR was born at New Brunswick, Canada.

g) Lois Parker[4] MCGREGOR was born at New Brunswick, Canada.

h) Eliza Miles[4] MCGREGOR was born at New Brunswick, Canada.

i) Blanche Louise[4] MCGREGOR was born at New Brunswick, Canada.

6. Sarah Ann[3] Bunnell: Children & Family records in files. She was born on 6 Nov 1812 at Hampton, Kings Co., New Brunswick, Canada. In 1830 married, witnessed by Dan Fowler & William Wetmore, by Vicar of Kingston, NB in 1830 at New Brunswick, Canada. She Wood-Holt book says, marr.20 Feb.1830, wit. by L.H. DeVeber of St. John on 20 Feb 1830 at New Brunswick, Canada. She married Gabriel Fowler, son of Samuel Fowler, on 4 Mar 1830 at Kingston or Salt Springs, Kings, New Brunswick, Canada.[1022] She married Howard Gray on 3 Apr 1840 at Kings Co.?, New Brunswick, Canada. She died on 3 Mar 1884 at Fairville, New Brunswick, Canada, at age 71. She was buried circa 4 Mar 1884 at New Brunswick, Canada.[1023]

a) William I.[4] FOWLER was born at King's Co., New Brunswick, Canada. Sarah (Bunnell) Fowler files.

b) Samuel O.[4] FOWLER was born at King's Co., New Brunswick, Canada. Sarah (Bunnell) Fowler files.

c) Sarah E.[4] FOWLER was born at King's Co., New Brunswick, Canada. Sarah (Bunnell) Fowler files.

d) Hiram G.[4] FOWLER was born at King's Co., New Brunswick, Canada. Sarah (Bunnell) Fowler files.

e) Emily A.[4] FOWLER was born at King's Co., New Brunswick, Canada. Sarah (Bunnell) Fowler files.

f) Wilford D.[4] FOWLER was born at King's Co., New Brunswick, Canada. Sarah (Bunnell) Fowler files.

g) Ammon N.⁴ FOWLER was born at King's Co., New Brunswick, Canada. Sarah (Bunnell) Fowler files.

h) Levina V.⁴ FOWLER was born at King's Co., New Brunswick, Canada. Sarah (Bunnell) Fowler files.

i) Isaac W.⁴ FOWLER was born at King's Co., New Brunswick, Canada. Sarah (Bunnell) Fowler files.

j) Newton G.⁴ FOWLER was born at King's Co., New Brunswick, Canada. Sarah (Bunnell) Fowler files.

k) John W.⁴ FOWLER was born at King's Co., New Brunswick, Canada. Sarah (Bunnell) Fowler files.

l) George F. M.⁴ FOWLER was born at King's Co., New Brunswick, Canada. Sarah (Bunnell) Fowler files.

7. Justus Johnston³ Bunnell was born in 1822 at Collina, New Brunswick, Canada. He was baptized on 2 Jun 1848 at Collina, Kings?, New Brunswick, Canada. He married Mary F. Chapman (Fisher) before 1850 at Collina Church, Collina, NB Canada. He died on 1 Dec 1854 at Studholm Parish, Kings, New Brunswick, Canada.¹⁰²⁴ He was buried circa 3 Dec 1854 at Kierstead Mountain Baptist Cemetery, Studholm Parish, Kings, New Brunswick, Canada.¹⁰²⁵

a) Henry Allen⁴ Bunnell (Bonnell) Reverened was born on 13 Apr 1849 at New Brunswick, Canada. He married Rebecca Anne Degosline Gosline, daughter of James Degosline Gosline and Jane Redstone Gosline, circa 1871 at New Brunswick, Canada.

(1) James Johnston⁵ Bunnell (Bonnell) was born on 28 Jul 1872 at New Brunswick, Canada. He died on 18 Jan 1915 at New Brunswick, Canada, at age 42.

(2) Beulah⁵ Bunnell (Bonnell) was born in 1875 at New Brunswick, Canada. She died on 30 Aug 1878 at Studholm Parish, Kings, New Brunswick, Canada.¹⁰²⁶ She was buried circa 1 Sep 1878 at Gosline Cemetery, Studholm Parish, Kings, New Brunswick, Canada.¹⁰²⁷

(3) Edna Elzina^5 Bunnell (Bonnell) was born between 13 Jan 1877 and 1878 at New Brunswick, Canada. She married Alfred Edward Kierstead, son of Christopher Wilson Kierstead and Helen Murphy, on 28 Jun 1899 at New Brunswick, Canada? She died on 27 Nov 1959 at New Brunswick, Canada. From Roy Keirstead -e-mail-kdpncla@aol.com in 1997.

(a) (female)^6 KIERSTEAD married Harold ATHERTON at New Brunswick, Canada? She was born after 1900 at New Brunswick, Canada.

(b) (female)^6 KIERSTEAD married J. Packard CAMPBELL at New Brunswick, Canada? She was born after 1900 at New Brunswick, Canada.

(c) Ellen Edna^6 KIERSTEAD. From Roy E.Kierstead,6931 Kitty Hawk Dr.,Pensacola,Fl.32506-5634 E-mail-kdpncla@aol.com. She married James VAN BUSKIRK (Mr.) at New Brunswick, Canada? She was born in 1906 at New Brunswick, Canada?

(d) Allen Wilson^6 KIERSTEAD. From Roy Keirstead of Florida,e-mail-kdpncla@aol.com in 1997. He was born in 1909 at New Brunswick, Canada.

(e) Charles E. Christopher^6 KIERSTEAD. From Roy Keirstead of Florida;e-mail-kdpncla@aol.com in 1997. He was born in 1911 at New Brunswick, Canada.

(f) Alfred E.^{6} KIERSTEAD married Edna Albert MOODY at New Brunswick, Canada? From Roy Keirstead of Florida;e-mail-kdpncla@aol.com in 1997. He was born on 30 Nov 1912 at New Brunswick, Canada.

(g) George Garfield^6 KIERSTEAD. From Roy Keirstead of Florida;e-mail-kdpncla@aol.com in 1997. He was born in 1914 at Saint John, Saint John Co., New Brunswick, Canada.

(h) Ralph Clayton[6] KIERSTEAD. From Roy Keirstead of Florida;e-mail-kdpncla@aol.com in 1997. He was born in 1916 at New Brunswick, Canada.

(i) Lloyd (Loyd) Allison[6] KIERSTEAD. From Roy Keirstead of Florida;e-mail-kdpncla@aol.com in 1997. He was born circa 1919 at New Brunswick, Canada.

(4) Charles Hazen[5] Bunnell (Bonnell) married E. May. He was born on 14 Sep 1881 at Anagance, Kings, New Brunswick, Canada.[1028] He died on 1 Jan 1957 at Kings Co. NB, Canada, at age 75. He was buried circa 2 Jan 1957 at Browns Flat Baptist Church Cemetery, Browns Flat, Kings, New Brunswick, Canada.

(a) (male)[6] BUNNELL (Bonnell) was born at Browns Flat, Kings Co., New Brunswick, Canada.

(b) (male)[6] BUNNELL (Bonnell) was born at Browns Flat, Kings Co., New Brunswick, Canada.

(c) (Male)[6] BUNNELL (Bonnell) was born at Browns Flat, Kings Co., New Brunswick, Canada.

(d) (Female)[6] BUNNELL (Bonnell) was born at Browns Flat, Kings Co., New Brunswick, Canada.

(5) Frank Bliss[5] Bunnell (Bonnell) married Lillian H. (--?--) (Bonnell) at New Brunswick, Canada? He was born on 20 Aug 1883 at Marysville or Havelock, Kings, New Brunswick, Canada.[1029] He died on 8 Mar 1966 at New Brunswick, Canada, at age 82.

(a) (male)[6] BUNNELL (Bonnell) was born at New Brunswick, Canada.

(b) (male)[6] BUNNELL (Bonnell) was born at New Brunswick, Canada.

(c) (male)[6] BUNNELL (Bonnell) was born at New Brunswick, Canada.

(d) (female)[6] BUNNELL (Bonnell) was born at New Brunswick, Canada.

(6) Herbert T.[5] Bunnell (Bonnell) married Roxy T. White at New Brunswick, Canada. He was born on 14 Dec 1885 at New Brunswick, Canada. He died on 11 May 1958 at New Brunswick, Canada, at age 72.

(a) Eldon W.[6] Bunnell (Bonnell) was born at New Brunswick, Canada. He was Anglican. He married Alma Bean, daughter of Edward Bean and Emmaline Stewart (Lagoof), on 6 Nov 1937 at Trinity Anglican Church, Saint John, Saint John Co., New Brunswick, Canada.

i) John Edward[7] Bunnell (Bonnell) was Anglican. He was born after 1937 at New Brunswick, Canada.

(a) Carrie[8] Bunnell (Bonnell). His married name was Alden. He was born at New Brunswick, Canada?

i) Mallory[9] Alden was born before 1988 at New Brunswick or Ontario, Canada.

(b) Herbert T.[6] Bunnell (Bonnell) Junior was born at New Brunswick, Canada.

(c) Ralph K.[6] Bunnell (Bonnell) was born at New Brunswick, Canada.

b) Lydia[4] Bunnell (Bonnell) was born in 1853 at New Brunswick, Canada.

8. John Stratton (Sherwood?)[3] Bunnell[1030] was Ship Carpenter & Postmaster at Coal Creek) at Coal Creek, New Brunswick, Canada. (From family records file on Isaac Bunnell) at Archives of New Brunswick, Fredericton, York, New Brunswick, Canada. He lived at Coal Creek, Queens?, New Brunswick, Canada. He was born in 1824 at Collina, Kings, New Brunswick, Canada. He married Mary Ann Brown on 9 May 1846 at Saint John, Saint John, New Brunswick, Canada. He died after 1861 at Coal Creek, Chaipman, New Brunswick, Canada. (From John & Celestine Barton, 1024 Salisbury Rd., Moncton, NB, Canada E1E 3V6, in Aug 1998.

a) Charles Spurgeon Hatward[4] BUNNELL (Bonnell) married Lena Hannah BROWN (Bonnell) at New Brunswick, Canada? From RS141 A2/1 co. vitals (1801-99),Qu,4-1,p.110,#3966,F14884 (sons birth). He was born on 25 Dec 1860 at Coal Creek, Chipman, Queens Co., New Brunswick, Canada? He died on 10 Sep 1929 at Coal Creek?, Chipman, Queen's, New Brunswick, Canada, at age 68. (From John & Celestine Barton, 1024 Salisbury Rd., Moncton, NB, Canada E1E 3V6, in Aug 1998.

(1) John Spurgeon[5] BUNNELL (Bonnell) From RS141 A2/1 county vitals (1801-99),Qu,4-1,p.110,#3966,F14884. He was born on 30 Dec 1897 at Coal Creek, Chipman, Queens Co., New Brunswick, Canada. He married Annie Louise Walker on 20 Jan 1919 at South Acton, England. He died on 4 Nov 1966 at Coal Creek?, Chipman, Queen's, New Brunswick, Canada, at age 68. (From John & Celestine Barton, 1024 Salisbury Rd., Moncton, NB, Canada E1E 3V6, in Aug 1998.

(a) Lena Annie[6] BUNNELL was born on 4 Mar 1928 at Chipman, Queen's, New Brunswick, Canada. She married ? ? circa 1950? at New Brunswick?, Canada?

i) Celestine[7] ? Her married name was Barton. She married John Barton at New Brunswick?, Canada? She was born circa 1947? at New Brunswick?, Canada? She lived in Aug 1998 at 1024 Salisbury Rd., Moncton, New Brunswick, Canada.[1031] (Postal code - E1E 3V6, in Aug 1998 at 1024 Salisbury Rd., Moncton, New Brunswick, Canada.

9. Isaac B.[3] Bunnell Bonnell was born in 1826 at Westfield, Kings, New Brunswick, Canada.[1032] He married Berthia Kierstead circa 1848 at Kings, New Brunswick, Canada. Land/grant (Not proven, but believed to be this Isaac's land petition, found by Carole Bonnell of Bunnell newsletter at Fredericton, NB Archives on film #F4239 of RS108 index 1783-1918) in 1850 at Kings, New Brunswick, Canada. He married Jemima Fowlie Bonnell, daughter of William Fowlie and Bethia Kierstead, after 1850 at New Brunswick?, Canada? He appeared on the census of 1851 at Canadian Census, Studholm Parish, Kings, New Brunswick, Canada.[1033] He lived in 1853 at Collina, New Brunswick, USA.[1034] Land/grant (Possibly this Isaac, not proven. Listed as Isaac W, on land petition found by Carole Bonnell of Bunnell newsletter at Fredericton NB Archives on film #F5931 of RS108 index 1783-1918) in 1855 at Queen's, New Brunswick, Canada.

He died on 4 Mar 1885 at Studholm Parish, Kings, New Brunswick, Canada.[1035] He was buried circa 6 Mar 1885 at Newtown Baptist Cemetery, Studholm Parish, Kings, New Brunswick, Canada.[1036]

    a) Sarah A.[4] Bunnell was born in 1849 at New Brunswick?, Canada? She appeared on the census of 1851 at Canadian Census, Studholm Parish, Kings, New Brunswick, Canada.[1037] (From Fredericton Archives, Isaac Bunnell family records) in 1986.

    b) Isaac W.[4] Bunnell was born in 1850 at New Brunswick, Canada. He appeared on the census of 1851 at Canadian Census, Studholm Parish, Kings, New Brunswick, Canada.[1038] He married an unknown person in 1877 at Westmoreland Co., New Brunswick, Canada.

10. George W.[3] Bunnell married Bethie FOWLIE at New Brunswick, Canada.[1039] From Fredericton Archives, NB. He was born in 1832 at New Brunswick, Canada.[1040] He appeared on the census of 1851 at Canadian Census, Studholm Parish, Kings, New Brunswick, Canada.[1041] Land/grant: (Possibly this GWB found by Carole Bonnell of Bunnell newsletter at Fredericton NB Archives on land petition film #F4246 of RS108 index 1783-1918) in 1853 at Queen's, New Brunswick, Canada.

11. Robie[3] Bunnell was born in 1834 at New Brunswick, Canada. He was baptized in 1848 at Collina, New Brunswick, Canada.[1042] He appeared on the census of 1851 at Canadian Census, Studholm Parish, Kings, New Brunswick, Canada.[1043]

12. Daniel/David[3] Bunnell married Mary (--?--) at Kings Co. NB. Canada. He lived circa 1844 at Brunswick, Queen's, New Brunswick, Canada.[1044] He was born in 1844 at Queens Co., NB, Canada. He appeared on the census of 1851 at Canadian Census, Studholm Parish, Kings, New Brunswick, Canada.[1045] He Fredericton Archives, NB in 1986.

    a) Daniel B.[4] Bunnell was born at New Brunswick, Canada.

    b) Elizabeth[4] Bunnell was born at New Brunswick, Canada.

- c) Isaac[4] Bunnell was born at New Brunswick, Canada.

- d) Mary[4] Bunnell was born at New Brunswick, Canada.

- e) Newton[4] Bunnell was born at New Brunswick, Canada.

H. Justus/Justice[2] Bunnell was Baptist. He was born circa Jul 1789 at Kings?, New Brunswick, Canada.[1046] Land/grant: (Listed as Justus I Bunnell on land petition found by Carole Bonnell of Bunnell newsletter at Fredericton NB Archives on film #F4196 of RS108 index 1783-1918) in 1824 at Kings, New Brunswick, Canada. Land/grant: (Listed on land petition of William Edgar found by Carole Bonnell of Bunnell newsletter on film #F4211 of RS108 index 1783-1918 at Fredericton, NB Archives) in 1828 at Queen's, New Brunswick, Canada. Land/grant: (Possibly him listed on land petition found by Carole Bonnell of Bunnell newsletter at Fredericton NB Archives on film #F4192 of RS108 index 1783-1918) in 1832 at Queen's, New Brunswick, Canada. Land/grant: (Listed on Thomas Corey land petition, found by Carole Bonnell of Bunnell newsletter at Fredericton NB Archives on film #F4194 of RS108 index 1783-1918) in 1832 at Queen's, New Brunswick, Canada. He married Margeret Barton Baxter, daughter of Simon Barton Captain(Baxter) and Prudence (--?--), on 22 Feb 1836 at Kings, New Brunswick, Canada.[1047] Land/grant Grant: #1725, record vol. 22, page 90 on 29 Dec 1838 at 200 acres, Sussex, Kings, New Brunswick, Canada. He 1851 Sussex Co., New Brunswick, Canada Census in 1851 at Canadian Census, New Brunswick, Canada. He appeared on the census of 1851 at Canadian Census, Studholm Parish, Kings, New Brunswick, Canada.[1048] He died on 7 Apr 1869 at Studholm Parish, Kings, New Brunswick, Canada. He was buried circa 9 Apr 1869 at Keirstead Mountain United Baptist Church Cemetery, Studholm Parish, Kings, New Brunswick, Canada.[1049] From Doug McQuinn, Saint John, NB 7/5/97.

- g) Justus Sherwood[3] Bunnell was Baptist. He was born on 27 Jul 1839 at New Brunswick, Canada. He appeared on the census of 1851 at Canadian Census, Studholm Parish, Kings, New Brunswick, Canada.[1050] He married Jemima Filinda Kierstead, daughter of Thomas David Kierstead and Elizabeth Green (Aunt Betty Tom), on 6 Feb 1866 at New Brunswick, Canada. He was in directory (Listed as a Farmer on page 444 of Hutchinson's New Brunswick Directory 1867-68) circa 1867 at Fenwick (Millstream), Kings, New Brunswick, Canada. He died on 15 Nov 1892 at Age 53, Kings, New Brunswick, Canada, at age 53.[1051] (Woodlawn Ceme & Keirstead Ceme. records found at Fredericton Archives)(Picture of gravestone in files from

Don Kierstead Sept. 1999) on 15 Nov 1892. He was buried circa 17 Nov 1892 at Keirstead Mountain United Baptist Church Cemetery, Studholm Parish, Kings, New Brunswick, Canada.[1052] From Doug McQuinn, Saint John, NB 7/5/97.

    g) Wilda Anne[4] Bunnell (see above)

    g) Hannah Elizabeth[4] Bunnell (see above)

    g) Wilda Anne[4] Bunnell (see above)

    g) Adam[4] BUNNELL (see above)

    g) Weldon Thomas[4] Bunnell (see above)

    g) Hettie Jemima[4] Bunnell (see above)

    g) Mabel Armintha[4] Bunnell (see above)

Parent Line Ascending:
Gershom Bunnell (1707-1758) & Margaret Johnson
Benjamin Bunnell (1679-1749) & Hannah Plumb
Benjamin Bunnell (1636-) & Rebecca Mallory
William Bunnell (1600-1678) & Ann Wilmot
Benjamin Bunnell (1570-1655) & Rebecca Brooks
Thomas (1550-1607) & ?

Loyalist
Gershom Bunnell Genealogy

I. Gershom[1] BUNNELL Jr. (Loyalist U.E.) married Levina Coy, Loyalist daughter of Edward Coy (Coye/McCoy) Sr. and S. Amy Titus, at New Brunswick, Canada? He was born circa Apr 1732 at Connecticut. MILITARY: Loyalist U.E in 1783. Court records in 1814 shows he vs. .Jacob Carvell & 1808 he vs. Sam Stickney in 1814. Listed as Gershom Bunnil on his land petition, found by Carole Bonnell of Bunnell newsletter at Fredericton NB Archives on film #F4183 on RS108 index 1783-1918) in 1819 at Sunbury, New Brunswick, Canada. He lived on 7 Feb 1820 at Parish of St. Mary's, York, New Brunswick, Canada.[1053] He immigrated in 1821 to Burton, Sunbury, New Brunswick, Canada.[1054] In 1828 the House of Assembly, New Brunswick said he was a Meritorious old soldier of 92, and was given L10, because he was in a destitute condition. Listed on 21 July 1846, Head Quarters, New Brunswick (for relief), from news clipping. He shows up in Supreme Court Rec.1808 with Elisha Freeman etal vs. himself RS42, & 1809 Elisha Plummer vs. himself on 21 Jul 1846. He was buried after 21 Jul 1846 at New Brunswick, Canada. He died after 21 Jul 1846 at New Brunswick, Canada. Some information from Doug McQuinn, of Saint John, New Brunswick 7/5/97.

Parent Line Ascending:
Gershom Bunnell (1707 – 1758) & Margaret Johnson
Benjamin Bunnell (1679 – 1749) & Hannah Plumb
Benjamin Bunnell (1636 -) & Rebecca Mallory
William Bunnell (1600 – 1678) & Ann Wilmot
Benjamin Bunnell (1570-1655) & Rebecca Brooks
Thomas Bunnell (1550 – 1607) & ?

Loyalist
Solomon Bonnell Genealogy

I. Solomon[1] Bunnell (Bonnell) UE immigrated circa 1783 to Annapolis, Nova Scotia, Canada.[1055] Some information from Don Cooper of Nova Scotia Nov. 1999. Around 1784 he received his land grant at Lot 24, north side of Sissibou River, Nova Scotia, Canada. He and Samuel Goldsbury built a Saw Mill in 1784 at North side of Sissibou River, Nova Scotia, Canada. Solomon Sr. is listed in the records office (Draped in black) of Bennington, Vermont where he was listed as a loyalist who killed a few of his neighbors at the Battle of Bennington, was jailed but escaped.

A. Solomon^2 Bunnell (Bonnell) was born before 1783 at USA.

After loyalist David Fitzrandolph and his family reached Weymouth, Nova Scotia from New Jersey in the spring of 1784 he settled on the property of Nathaniel Payson. He had an amiable young daughter named Jane. Her bright smiles and winning manners soon won the admiration of young Solomon Bunnell. His manly bearing, agreeable style and gallant attentions were reciprocated by Jane. Intimacy ripened into love; love begat mutual contract; brightest anticipations of conjugal bliss animated their hearts, and irradiated their happy countenances. One beautiful winter night, as Solomon and Jane sat in the parlour of her father's pleasant and enjoyable home, amid all the elative atmosphere, a change in the programme, for mere edification, was conceived in the varied mind of the young lover. Grasping a gun which unfortunately stood in the corner of the room, he pointed it playfully towards the darling of his heart, dreaming not that the dreadful weapon was loaded, remarked jocosely, "I'll shoot you!" The lovely affianced answered; "Shoot if you want to!" Playfully the trigger was pulled when, lo! The confiding household were awakened instantly from their sweet slumbers by the summons from the death missile, calling their beloved child to a higher sphere! Scarcely was the wounded and bleeding martyr, begging her darling's pardon for these reasons, placed on her couch, when life became suddenly extinct. Appalled and heart-broken, the disconsolate but unintentional slayer fled from the harrowing scene. Everything was done that love and devotion could devise to revere and perpetuate her memory. In a field nearly opposite Comeau's Funiture Store, her lover placed a fine slab to mark the tomb of his beloved. Solomon and his father and family, immediately sold their property and left for parts unknown.

Parent Line Ascending:
There is no record yet, but it is believed he came from the Connecticut Bunnell's.

Loyalist
Aaron Bonnell

Born c. 1779. Married before 1821 at New Brunswick, Canada. Was listed as a loyalist, but obviously a son of a loyalist. Record found at the Provincial Archives, Fredericton, New Brunswick, Canada. Not parents or wife listed.

Loyalist
Ann Bunnell

Born before 1760 in colonies. Settled 1783 at Sissaboo, Nova Scotia, Canada. Married Jonathan Bedford (1760-1790). She settled again around 1790 in Ontario, Canada and possibly died there. Info from Heather Henderson, posted on Genform 18 Feb. 2000. (Could this be possibly a daughter of Solomon, or Isaac?)

Loyalist
Major Daniel Bonnell

Born 1731 possibly Charleston, Prince Frederick Winyaw Parish, South Carolina. Son of Capt. John Bonnell (1695-1768) and Honora (d. 1740). Daniel served as loyalist 18 Oct. 1783 in Georgia and died there on that day. He was a Protestant. Executed for crimes alleged to have been committed against Patriots during the war. He was in the Georgia Militia. From Bunnell/Bonnell newsletter dated Jan. 1999, Vol. 13, #1, page 84. Not known if he had a family.

Parent Line Ascending:
Capt. John Bonnell (1695-1768) & Honora (d. 1740)
Daniel Bonnel (b. c. 1664) & Marie Izambert
Jean Bonel (b.c. 1635) & Marie Lalon

Loyalist
Daniel Bonnell

Born in the colonies. Married after 1780 to Mary Ann Masters UE. They had ten children all possibly born in Nova Scotia? The names of 3 were; John, Thomas and Henry. Parents not listed. From Provincial Archives, Nova Scotia listed under his name in cardex file).

Loyalist
Jesse Bunnells

Born in the colonies. Parents unknown. Was listed as a United Empire Loyalist on New York July 22, 1783 claims for losses that was addressed to Sir Guy Carleton along with several others. Found in Loyalists of Nova Scotia, page 152, by Gilroy.

Loyalist
John Bonnell

I. John[1] Bunnell (Bonnell) U.E was (Part time blacksmith) at Stewiacke Valley, Stewiacke, Colchester, Nova Scotia, Canada. He was (Protestant). He was born in 1750 possibly Burke County, Georgia (Listed Bunnell/Bonnell newsletter Jan. 1999, vol. 13, #1, p.85).[1056] He immigrated after 1750 to Georgia, USA.[1057] (Did farming there which is located half way between Augusta and Savannah) after 1765 at Qgeechee River, Georgia, USA. MILITARY: (Supplied food and stuffs to British troops. Took part in campaigns with British in Georgia and East Florida in King's Rangers, mobile cavalry unit. Incorrectly reported killed at battle of Augusta, Georgia in Sept. 1781, but escaped and evacuated to Savannah in 1782 where he was cut off by rebel troops. Hid in back country between Savannah and Augusta with others until 1783-4 going to St. Augustine, Florida where he was taken to Canada) in 1775. He immigrated in 1784 to Halifax, Halifax, Nova Scotia, Canada.[1058] (Reported that he settled in Dartmouth, across the bay from Halifax, then 50-75 miles to back country of present day Musquodoboit) in 1785 at Nova Scotia, Canada. (He later moved here where they stayed for many years) after 1785 at Stewiacke River Valley, Nova Scotia, Canada. (Put in claim for loses to Crown for personal property and possessions under act of Parliament. Claim for 121.5 Pounds was rejected even though neighbor from Ogeechee River in Georgia vouched for him. Outcome was claimed to be "of suspicious character whose story is scarcely credible." He received claim of 21 pounds on claim of 35 for loses in Georgia)
after 1785. He married Abigail Putnam in 1793 at Musquodoboit, Nova Scotia, Canada.[1059] Land/grant Grant # 517 from vol. E, page 8 (same as Isaac Bunnell-brothers?) on 12 Dec 1809 at 400 acres with 48 others, Mill Stream, Kings, New Brunswick, Canada. Land/grant: (He petitioned the Crown for 350 acres, part he purchased earlier and was granted. The family owned most or part of it all the way to 1984, a Murphy family related. Another part was given to an adopted girl whose family is Purdy and still there in 1980's) in 1815 at Stewiacke Valley, Nova Scotia, Canada. He was buried after 1820 at South Branch Cemetery, Stewiacke, Colchester, Nova Scotia, Canada. He died after 1820 at Stewiacke Valley, Nova Scotia, Canada.[1060] Son of Capt. John Bonnell (1695-1768) and Patience Windham.

    A. (?)[2] Bunnell (Bonnell) was born after 1793.[1061]

    B. (?)[2] Bunnell (Bonnell) was born after 1793.[1062]

    C. Mary[2] Bunnell (Bonnell) married Charles Moor. She was born after 1793.[1063]

    D. William[2] Bunnell (Bonnell) was born after 1793.[1064]

E. Daniel[2] Bunnell (Bonnell) was (Part time blacksmith) at Stewiacke Valley, Stewiacke, Colchester, Nova Scotia, Canada. He was born after 1793.[1065] He married Agnes (Nancy) Kennedy circa 1830 at Stewiacke Valley, Stewiacke, Colchester, Nova Scotia, Canada. He was buried in 1844 at South Branch Cemetery, Stewiacke, Colchester, Nova Scotia, Canada. He died after 1844 at Stewiacke Valley, Stewiacke, Colchester, Nova Scotia, Canada.[1066]

    1. (?)[3] Bunnell (Bonnell) was born before 1837 at Stewiacke Valley, Stewiacke, Colchester, Nova Scotia, Canada.[1067]

    2. (?)[3] Bunnell (Bonnell) was born before 1837 at Stewiacke Valley, Stewiacke, Colchester, Nova Scotia, Canada.[1068]

    3. Robert[3] Bunnell (Bonnell) was buried at South Branch Cemetery, Stewiacke, Colchester, Nova Scotia, Canada.[1069] He was (Farmer & Part time blacksmith) at Stewiacke Valley, Stewiacke, Colchester, Nova Scotia, Canada. He was born in 1837 at Stewiacke Valley (South Branch area), Stewiacke, Colchester, Nova Scotia, Canada.[1070] He married Esther T. Grant in 1866.[1071] He married Ellen (--?--) in 1877.[1072] He married Grace Dickle in 1894.[1073]

        a) Clarica[4] Bunnell (Bonnell) was born in 1867.[1074]

        b) Lewis Fulton[4] Bunnell (Bonnell) was born on 15 Dec 1868 at Stewiacke Valley (South Branh area), Stewiacke, Colchester, Nova Scotia, Canada.[1075] He immigrated after 1876.[1076] He married Mary Alcorn in 1894 at Helena (Area), Montana, USA. He was (Blacksmith shop) after 1894 at Cardston, Alberta, Canada. He immigrated after 1894 to (A small frontier town), Alberta, Canada.[1077] He immigrated in 1905 to Lethbridge, Alberta, Canada.[1078] He died in 1950 at Sacramento, Sacramento, California, USA.

            (1) Sophronia[5] Bunnell (Bonnell) married M. Davies. She was born after 1895.[1079]

            (2) Fulton[5] Bunnell (Bonnell) was born after 1895.[1080]

            (3) Harry[5] Bunnell (Bonnell) was born after 1895.[1081]

            (4) Esther[5] Bunnell (Bonnell) was born in 1900.[1082] She married Alchin Frye in 1917. She died in 1981.

(a) James^6 Frye was born in 1918.^{1083} He married Helen Erickson in 1946. He married Elmar Hall in 1973.

    i) James^7 Frye was born in 1949.^{1084} He married Bonnie Cracknell in 1971.

        (a) Samantha^8 Frye was born in 1975.^{1085}

        (b) Gregory^8 Frye was born in 1977.^{1086}

    ii) Larry^7 Frye was born in 1956.^{1087} He married Michelle Young in 1978.

        (a) Analles^8 Frye was born in 1989.^{1088}

    iii) Leslie^7 Frye was born in 1956.^{1089} She married Derek Franzen in 1975.

        (a) Kelsi^8 Franzen was born in 1987.^{1090}

(b) Alchin^6 Frye was born in 1919.^{1091} He married Virginia Vorseth in 1946. He married Caroline McChesney in 1969.

    i) Carol^7 Frye married David Vasquez. She married Michael Bertero. She was born in 1970.^{1092}

        (a) Carrisa^8 Vasquez was born in 1987.^{1093}

        (b) Ashley^8 Bertero was born in 1989.^{1094}

    ii) Robert^7 Frye was born in 1972.^{1095}

    iii) Bonnie^7 Frye was born in 1952.^{1096} She married George Sanchez in 1971.

        (a) Carin^8 Sanchez was born in 1972.^{1097}

    iv) Alan^7 Frye was born in 1954.^{1098} He died in 1973.

(c) Phillip^6 Frye was born in 1921.^{1099} He married Gail Axelrod in 1942. He married Betty Taylor in 1988.

    i) Todd^7 Frye was born in 1945.^{1100} He married Louise Bennett in 1975.

        (a) Aaron^8 Frye was born in 1976.^{1101}

        (b) Jarem^8 Frye was born in 1978.^{1102}

        (c) Nathan^8 Frye was born in 1981.^{1103}

        (d) Aubrie^8 Frye was born in 1984.^{1104}

    ii) Jane^7 Frye was born in 1950.^{1105}

(d) Louis^6 Frye was born in 1922.^{1106} He married Elizabeth Cox in 1951.

    i) David^7 Frye was born on 17 Feb 1952 at Sacramento, Sacramento, California, USA.^{1107}

    ii) Stephen^7 Frye was born on 19 Nov 1953 at New Orleans, Louisiana, USA.^{1108} He married Sheryl Baker in 1981.^{1109}

        (a) Robert^8 Frye was born in 1982.^{1110}

        (b) Lauren^8 Frye was born in 1984.^{1111}

        (c) Daniel^8 Frye was born in 1986.^{1112}

    iii) Susan^7 Frye was born on 16 Jul 1957 at Burlingame, California, USA.^{1113} She married Bruce Janigian in 1986.

        (a) Alan^8 Janigian was born in 1988.^{1114}

(e) Kenneth^6 Frye was born in 1925.^{1115} He married Lorraine Wrenn in 1960.

i) Eric[7] Frye was born in 1962.[1116] He married Erica LeMoine in 1987.

(f) Mary Anne[6] Frye was born in 1934.[1117] She married William Clementson in 1952. She married Charles Cooper in 1964.

i) Vincent[7] Clementson was born in 1958.[1118]

ii) Laura[7] Clementson was born in 1962.[1119]

iii) Susanna[7] Cooper was born in 1966.[1120]

(5) Percy[5] Bunnell (Bonnell) was born in 1905.[1121]

(6) Kenneth[5] Bunnell (Bonnell) married Helen Neccerato. He was born in 1908.[1122]

c) Jane[4] Bunnell (Bonnell) was born in 1870.[1123]

d) John[4] Bunnell (Bonnell) was born in 1872.[1124]

e) Esther[4] Bunnell (Bonnell) was born in 1874.[1125]

f) Samuel[4] Bunnell (Bonnell) was born in 1876.[1126]

g) Nelson[4] Bunnell (Bonnell) was born in 1879.[1127]

h) Norman[4] Bunnell (Bonnell) was born in 1880.[1128]

4. Margaret[3] Bunnell (Bonnell) was born in 1842 at Stewiacke Valley, Stewiacke, Colchester, Nova Scotia, Canada.[1129] She married James Dunbrack in 1865.

F. Anthony[2] Bunnell (Bonnell) married Mary Vance. He was born after 1793.[1130]

G. Ellaklm[2] Bunnell (Bonnell) was born after 1793.[1131]

Parent Line Ascending:
Capt. John Bonnell (c.1695-1768) & Honora
Daniel Bonnel (b.c. 1664) & Marie Izambert
Jean Bonel (b.c. 1635) & Marie Lalon

Loyalist
John Bonnell

Born possibly in Ogeechee, Georgia. Not sure if this John is above listed John? He joined the East Florida Rangers and then returned to Georgia serving under Col. Brown. Made a claim for losses to the Commission for 121 pounds. They reported that he was of a suspicious character and scarcely credible so claim was denied.

Loyalist
John Bunnell

Born around 1750, Redding, Fairfield County, Connecticut. Son of Gershom Bunnell (1707-1758) and Margaret Johnson. Possibly lived in Waterbury, Connecticut and Wyoming, Pennsylvania and in 1809 received 400 acres, lot #35 in Kings County, New Brunswick, Canada. He was listed as a loyalist. Some info. from Doug McQuinn of Saint John, New Brunswick 5 July 1997.

Parent Line Ascending:
Gershom Bunnell (1707-1758) & Margaret Johnson
Benjamin Bunnell (1679-1749) & Hannah Plumb
Benjamin Bunnell (1636-1696) & Rebecca Mallory
William Bunnell (1600-1678) & Ann Wilmot
Benjamin Bunnell (1570-1655) & Rebecca Brooks
Thomas Bunnell (1550-1607) & ?

Loyalist
Samuel Bonnell

Was granted lot #1 and 26 for 118 acres at Bedford, Frantenac, Quebec, Canada. No family or parents listed. From Atlas Digital Project, The Canadian Country, dated August 1999.

Loyalist
Thomas Bunnel

Parents and family unknown. Found Canadian Archives and listed as a loyalist, but no other information.

Sources

---

[0] Burial record says he was 83, so possibly birth c. 1745? Obit in newspaper says 84 (1744)?

[1] (Possibly between 1770-79).

[2] Left NJ 1779 to NYC, July 1783 to Nova Scotia w/wife/2 child age 10,UEL on ship William.

[3] no title, 2002.

[4] Ibid.

[5] Ibid.

[6] Ibid.

[7] Listed in Vol. 1 of The Atlantic Canadians 1600-1900 by Noel Elliot as living here at this time (ref. 27-261).

[8] (From Provincial Archives of New Brunswick, Fredericton, NB Grant book database records, Vol. !, page, Grant number 15, granted with 60 others. Ben had lot 1 at end of Long Reach. Record says Saint John County, but is really Kings. The date of this grant is also in question because document shows August 1786?) There was a total of 1280 acres for all 60 people.

[9] BunnellBonnellBurnell Family, Says 24th.

[10] BunnellBonnellBurnell Family.

[11] Ibid.

[12] Benjamin Bunnell Senior, Yeoman. Executors were: Thomas Fowler & Isaac Cawsan, both of Long Reach. Witnesses: Joseph Purdy & Sarah Purdy. Executed 17 March 1828, Kingston, NB.
1. Just debt be paid.
2. Wife Sarah, all the profits arising from the farm at Devil's Back, known as Lot #29, together with use of two milk cows and six sheep; with the movables and house hold furniture during her natural period of life or while she lives.
3. Son Benjamin, 25 pounds currency; son Joseph, 25 pounds; son Simeon, 50 pounds; my three daughters, Sarah, Alphia and Eleanor, 10 pounds each if it remains after my sons get their share, if not what remains is to be divided equally among them.

[13] Died on Monday, age 84 according to newspaper.

[14] 19 Feb.1828,Greenwich(?)Kings Co., New Brunswick, Canada. Burial record says he was 83.

[15] Will proved for probate.

[16] BunnellBonnellBurnell Family.

[17] Ibid.

[18] 1783 from NYC to, Saint John, Nova Scotia (New Brunswick), Canada on the ship, William.

[19] This record needs more work. Her and Joseph Purdy signed witness to Benjamin's will (Her father).
[20] BunnellBonnellBurnell Family.
[21] Says she was 67 years old.
[22] Between 1817-21.
[23] Age 30, listed with parents.
[24] Age 28, living with parents.
[25] Age 22, living with parents.
[26] Age 17, living with parents.
[27] (Need more being their son?) Birth is only a guess?

[28] Thursday Eve. She was a Miss when married.
[29] Listed with family, page 72, Division 2.
[30] Listed with family on page 72, Division 2.
[31] Listed with family on page 72, Division 2.
[32] Listed with family on page 72, Division 2.
[33] Listed with family on page 72, Division 2.
[34] Listed with family on page 72, Division 2.
[35] 28 April 1827 age 37 at Greenwich/Westfield Angl.Ch.,Westfield, New Brunswick, Canada. Also found in Cleadie Barnett records.
[36] Maritime History Archives, *Ships & Seafarers of Atlantic Canada* in *no series* (CD; St. John's, Newfoundland, Canada A1C 5S7: Memorial University of Newfoundland, c. 1999), Registration #J833075.
[37] Ibid., Registration #J839018.
[38] Ibid., Registration #J853034, official #035012.
[39] Listed with wife and family at age 62, farmer.
[40] Lists wife Heddy and 12 children on his will, and signs it.
[41] BunnellBonnellBurnell Family, plus in my file.
[42] Another possible death date is 14 Aug. 1866. Left will. Age 78.
[43] BunnellBonnellBurnell Family.
[44] Probate estate administers, son Samuel Bonnell and William Buchanan.
[45] BunnellBonnellBurnell Family.
[46] (Shirley Thomas, e-mail msthomas@uniserve.com 17 Feb. 2000 says birth was 1840 which must be error).
[47] BunnellBonnellBurnell Family.
[48] He was from Kingston. From Cleadie Barnett research & records. Witnessed by Thomas Balyer & Joseph French.

[49] BunnellBonnellBurnell Family.

[50] Listed as Polly French on her fathers will.

[51] BunnellBonnellBurnell Family.

[52] Ibid.

[53] Maritime History Archives, *Ships & Seafarers*, Registration #J835119.

[54] Witnessed by Henry Lingley & Eliza Stevens.

[55] BunnellBonnellBurnell Family.

[56] Listed on fathers will.

[57] BunnellBonnellBurnell Family.

[58] Age 63.

[59] Married on Sunday by William McLeod. Witnessed by John Crabb & Charlotte Herrington. Found in newspapers from vital stats vol. 5 NB Courier.

[60] From Stevens Family records of New Brunswick.

[61] Maritime History Archives, *Ships & Seafarers*, Registration #J840058.

[62] Witnessed by William Brundage & Douglas B. Steeves. From Yesteryears.

[63] By S. Robison, witnessed by Abraham Bunnell & W.A. Coleman (From Marriages Register C, 1978).

[64] Maritime History Archives, *Ships & Seafarers*, Registration #J847040.

[65] Ibid., Registration #J851120, official #035012.

[66] Ibid., Registration #J851013, official #034688.

[67] Ibid., Registration #J853093, official #035080.

[68] Ibid., Registration #J881001, official #080053.

[69] Age 65. Possibly died in Kings Co., or Saint John, Co., NB.

[70] (From cemetery records of Kings Co., NB found at Fredericton Archives & Cleadie Barnett records).

[71] She was a Spinster (surname spelled Bonnell).

[72] Listed as niece of Isaac & Martha Bunnell in census at age 13.

[73] Age 40.

[74] Listed with John Stone, Farmer age 45 and his wife Sarah age 57. Census says he is their son?

[75] (From Cleadie B. Barnett records, Stephen Cemetery, Westfield (Brandy Point).

[76] (From Cleadie Barnett records).

[77] (From Cleadie Barnett records).

[78] (From Cleadie Barnett records).

[79](Between 1880-82).

[80]Listed with wife and as a sea fishery.

[81]John Stevens, records 18 Jan. 2000 (e-mail stevens@gwi.met) Record found in 1889/90 Fairview Directory. It is said that he lived in South Bay, Grand Bay, Sutton and Nerepis besides being born in Westfield.

[82]Listed as Alford L. Bonnell.

[83](John Stevens records show he died on 21 March 1896 age 43 after a 4 year battle with consumption?).

[84]Buried with family. (Question from John Stevens e-mail stevens@gwi.net, who says he died 21 March 1896 age 43?).

[85](surname spelled Bonnell).

[86]Stevens Ceme.,Westfield, Kings Co., New Brunswick, Canada (w/mom/dad).

[87]From John Stevens e-mail stevensj@gwi.net on 18 Jan. 2000.

[88]From John Stevens records 18 Jan. 2000.

[89]Died 1 year, 6 months.

[90](From Cleadie Barnett records).

[91]Maritime History Archives, *Ships & Seafarers*, Registration #J881001, official #080053.

[92]Ibid., Registration #J885011, official #088691.

[93]Ibid., Registration #J886027, official #092354.

[94]Ibid., Registration #J88025, official #094745.

[95]Ibid., Registration #J889025, official #096745.

[96]Was owner of ship, Martha L.Bonnell, built 1889,297 tons, destroyed by fire 5 Jan.1897 (surname spelled Bonnell).

[97]Maritime History Archives, *Ships & Seafarers*, Registered #J890021, official #088651.

[98]New Brunswick?

[99]Near there.

[100]Living near there.

[101]Near there.

[102](surname spelled Bonnell).

[103]Lost at Sea, but listed in Ingleside/Stevens Cem.Kings Co.,NB. age 25.

[104]Age 25.

[105](Possibly stone mention at Stephens Cemetery (Brandy Point) Westfield, Kings Co., NB, age 25).

[106](From Cleadie Barnett records).

[107](Shirley Thomas e-mail msthomas@uniserve.com 17 Feb. 2000 says birth place was Westfield, NB).

[108] BunnellBonnellBurnell Family.

[109] Chelsea,Ma.1840,ship Gypsie,Capt.Simeon Bunnell, brother?,to Canada returned to Boston after 1871.

[110] Info from Dr. Percy Bonnell of New Brunswick, now dead furnish info on 2nd. wife Dora.

[111] Worked in Oil Manufacturing.

[112] BunnellBonnellBurnell Family.

[113] Listed as 30 years old with Sophia Cottle age 21, found in page 207, #2249 of census. He was listed as a laborer.

[114] Age 33 listed as Laborer living with George Harding Family without his wife.

[115] BunnellBonnellBurnell Family.

[116] Heir in fathers will.

[117] BunnellBonnellBurnell Family, And Canada archives, copy in my file.

[118] Listed here with family as a laborer. Also found listed in Vol. 1 of The Atlantic Canadians 1600-1900, by Noel Elliot.

[119] Wife owned lot. Stone says, Father. Picture in file.

[120] BunnellBonnellBurnell Family.

[121] Ibid.

[122] By Rev. Joseph McLeod at his home.

[123] BunnellBonnellBurnell Family.

[124] Moved with parents to & from Boston to Fredericton.

[125] Age 22, born in USA, wife of Robert Legee/Segee, listed with him and child with her parents.

[126] Age 3 months, born in Jan. in New Brunswick, listed with parents & grand-parents Ben Bonnell.

[127] Fredericton to 1917,to Boston to Fredericton.

[128] Rural Cemetery, Fredericton, York New Brunswick, Canada.

[129] Lived at 77 Regent St., Fredericton, NB 1911-?Somerville,Ma.1930-1934, returned to Fredericton, NB for 7 years, Amherst,NS.1951-?Oakville,Ont.1982-95.

[130] By Rev. W. H. Smith.

[131] In Dec. 1926, his grade average was 60% with best mark 80% in language. Returning to school in 1927 the Dec. average was 70%, later to 82%. Moved and went to Somerville High School where he graduated 16 June 1930 in Somerville, Massachusetts.

[132] Married by Justice of the Peace, Christopher D.A. Hourin. Residence: 1577 Columbus Ave., Boston. Cert. 169 (138) registered in Medford, Mass.

[133] Lays under a willow where he and his friends met regularly in a Brown Bag Lunch Group.

[134] 2-2232 Upper Middle Rd.Burlington,Ont,Can.L7P 2Z9 1997,past 22 yrs(townhouse).

[135] Grad. Grade 13, Leaside High School, Toronto, Can. 22 Aug. 1960. Grad. Lakeshore Teachers College, New Toronto, Can. May 1964. Grad. McMaster University, Hamilton, Ontario, Can. w/BA Degree 29 May 1975 (A average in majors Anthropology & Psychology). Grad. York University, Toronto, Can. w/BEd Degree Nov. 1990 in Lib. 1 & 2, Media 1 & 2, Special Ed. 1.

[136] During birth father was fighting ship fire at waterfront with munitions on board. Concerned, a mine sweeper fired torpedoes into its side. Mother heard the firing from the hospital.

[137] By Rector, A. R. Smith. Godparents were: William C. Reid, father & mother.

[138] Relationship with Alfreda Robertson.

[139] Retiring after 33.4 years of service as a Special Needs/Ed. teacher.

[140] Birth is only a guess?

[141] Died at Bir.

[142] BunnellBonnellBurnell Family.

[143] Ibid.

[144] Went back & forth to New Brunswick 1851-1890's.

[145] Went back & forth between New Brunswick,1852-1890's.

[146] Age 19 and a clerk, born in USA.

[147] BunnellBonnellBurnell Family.

[148] Went back & forth between New Brunswick,1850's-1890's.

[149] Age 16, born in New Brunswick and was a dressmaker.

[150] Went back & forth between New Brunswick,1850's-1890's.

[151] Age 13, born in New Brunswick.

[152] BunnellBonnellBurnell Family.

[153] Went back & forth between New Brunswick,1860's-1890's.

[154] Age 11, born in New Brunswick.

[155] Born between 1860 and 1862.

[156] Age 9, born in New Brunswick, listed as student.

[157] To Boston,Ma.c.1883?

[158] BunnellBonnellBurnell Family, VR-Ma025-160/484.

[159] With mother Mary. listed as a Brass Worker.

[160] BunnellBonnellBurnell Family.

[161] Listed as a Brass Finisher.

[162] BunnellBonnellBurnell Family.

[163] No stone, but located between Samuel Gillespie and William Darbyshire. Undertaker was Joseph Donnell.

[164] To Mass. after 1885?

[165] To Mass. after 1885?
[166] Not sure if this person is a duplicate of a daughter who died young.
[167] To Mass. after 1885?
[168] Claude Bunnell database.
[169] BunnellBonnellBurnell Family.
[170] Listed with Grandmother, Mary (Cottle) Bunnell.
[171] BunnellBonnellBurnell Family.
[172] Ibid., VR-Ma025-573/79.
[173] Records says he was son of John & Minnie.
[174] BunnellBonnellBurnell Family.
[175] Listed as a Painter.
[176] BunnellBonnellBurnell Family.
[177] Listed as a Painter.
[178] BunnellBonnellBurnell Family.
[179] Age 59.
[180] BunnellBonnellBurnell Family, VR-Ma026-13/394.
[181] From Claude Bunnell database.
[182] BunnellBonnellBurnell Family.
[183] Ibid.
[184] VR-Ma025-1/5.
[185] BunnellBonnellBurnell Family.
[186] Ibid.
[187] VR-Ma025-19/378.
[188] BunnellBonnellBurnell Family.
[189] Listed as a Rail Road Worker.
[190] BunnellBonnellBurnell Family.
[191] Ibid.
[192] Ibid.
[193] Listed as a Postal Clerk.
[194] BunnellBonnellBurnell Family.
[195] Ibid.
[196] Ibid.
[197] Ibid.

[198]Ibid., VR-Ma025-49/396.
[199]Bunnell|Bonnell|Burnell Family.
[200]Ibid.
[201]Ibid., VR-Ma025-54/352.
[202]Bunnell|Bonnell|Burnell Family.
[203]Ibid., VR-Ma025-23/86.
[204]Bunnell|Bonnell|Burnell Family.
[205]Ibid.
[206]Ibid., VR-Ma025-42/142.
[207]Bunnell|Bonnell|Burnell Family.
[208]Ibid., VR-Ma025-50/13.
[209]Ibid., VR-Ma025-I/30.
[210]VR-Ma025-1/30.
[211]Bunnell|Bonnell|Burnell Family, VR-Ma025-I/30.
[212]Listed as Truck Driver.
[213]Bunnell|Bonnell|Burnell Family, VR-Ma025-16/109 Boston.
[214]Bunnell|Bonnell|Burnell Family.
[215]Ibid.
[216]Ibid.
[217]Listed as in US Army.
[218]Bunnell|Bonnell|Burnell Family.
[219]Listed in US Army.
[220]Bunnell|Bonnell|Burnell Family.
[221]Age 50. retired US Army Sergeant.
[222]Bunnell|Bonnell|Burnell Family.
[223]Ibid., VR-Ma025-23/409.
[224]Bunnell|Bonnell|Burnell Family.
[225]Ibid., VR-Ma025-167/436.
[226]Ibid.
[227]Ibid., VR-Ma017-186/500.
[228]Bunnell|Bonnell|Burnell Family.
[229]Ibid., VR-Ma017-186/500.
[230]Bunnell|Bonnell|Burnell Family.

[231] Ibid., VR-Ma017-193/194.

[232] Bunnell|Bonnell|Burnell Family.

[233] Ibid., VR-Ma017-193/194.

[234] Ibid., VR-Ma025-2/I82.

[235] Bunnell|Bonnell|Burnell Family.

[236] Ibid., VR-Ma025-2/I82.

[237] Boston Vital records VR-Ma025-378/216 say she was born in Fredericton, Canada.

[238] Bunnell|Bonnell|Burnell Family.

[239] Ibid.

[240] Ibid.

[241] Living with Grandmother, Mary (Cottle) Bunnell.

[242] Bunnell|Bonnell|Burnell Family.

[243] Or 18 Feb.

[244] Bunnell|Bonnell|Burnell Family.

[245] 2May1896, St.Thomas,Cath.Ch.JamaicaPlain,Ma.,by Rev.CharlesF.Donahoe,spon,Patrick Dereny/Catherine Murphy.

[246] Listed with Grandmother at her house with his mother, age 4, born Jan. 1896 in Mass.

[247] Bunnell|Bonnell|Burnell Family.

[248] Listed 1917 Boston Directory, living 23 Centre St.Roxbury, Ma.w/father.

[249] Listed as soldier in the dispensary.

[250] Bunnell|Bonnell|Burnell Family.

[251] Ibid.

[252] Ibid.

[253] St. Raymond Cemetery, Bronx, NY (with 2 men, plot owned by bro. Ben).

[254] Bunnell|Bonnell|Burnell Family.

[255] Ibid., VR-MA-25-11/172.

[256] 10 days old.

[257] Bunnell|Bonnell|Burnell Family.

[258] Ibid.

[259] Ibid.

[260] Delay birth registration in 1930 by mother Elizabeth.

[261] Bunnell|Bonnell|Burnell Family.

[262] 17March1899,St.ThomasCath.Ch.JamaicaPlain,Ma.byRev.MarcusE.Madden.Spons,Owen F.Flaherty,Maria Keeley.

[263] BunnellBonnellBurnell Family.

[264] Ibid.

[265] Ibid.

[266] He was a said to be a Bookie in the Bronx and was called Mayor of Cortlandt Park East by his neighbors. (From May's brother who lived in Oxnard, Cal.).

[267] He was called the Mayor of Cortlandt Parl East by neighbors.

[268] Buried w/6 pack Budwieser beer. Next to May.

[269] 2nd.home Coral Gables,Fl.

[270] The visited Paul & Leslie Bunnell's bookstore in Wareham, Mass. with mother May in 1975.

[271] Mass Vital Records 025-511/121 & 551/445.

[272] Baptism done by Rev.C.J.Herlily.

[273] Lived w/Ed.Ryder 139 Lamartine St. (From Catholic Diocese Homeless records, Boston, Ma.).

[274] He was committed there by the state to learn a trade.

[275] Listed as a Laborer. Mass Vital Records 025-2/284 Claude Bunnell database.

[276] From Claude Bunnell database on the family.

[277] Listed as born in Roxbury and was a machinist. Mass Vital Records 009-2/I46. Probably working here during birth of James.

[278] Living here and listed as a Laborer. Mass Vital Records 009-2/I90.

[279] Living here and listed as a Press Operator. Mass Vital Records 009-305/67.

[280] Listed as a General worker. From Mass Vital records 025-I/I00.

[281] Listed as working at the Hat Shop. From Mass Vital Records 009-I/16.

[282] From Mass Vital records 009-2/21. Was working at the Hat Shop as a Hatter (Wife was).

[283] (Listed in the 1951 Amesbury Directory, p.315).

[284] Mass Vital Records 009-I/423. Retired from Merrimac Hat Company. Age 63.

[285] Vital Records, Mass. 009-2/I-46.

[286] Baptized as James Henry Woodbury and later changed to Bunnell in 1930. Bapt. by Rv.Jose.Tuscher.

[287] (He was certified as a senior member of the Red Cross Life Saving Service).

[288] By US Army, *History of 398th. Engineer Regiment* in *no series* (n.p.: By Its Personnel, 1945).

[289] Ibid.

[290] Ibid.

[291] Ibid.

[292] Ibid.

[293] Living here at Paul's birth. Mass. Vital Records 009-3/281.

[294] (Listed in 1951 Amesbury Directory, p. 315).

[295] Pacoima/Canoga Pk/Mt.Shasta,Susanville,Ca.1953/59,71,74.Beaverton,Florence,Or.1977,85.Ryderwood,Wa.1992.Marst.Mill,Ma.95.

[296] Move there from Pacoima, Calif. A modern home with intercoms in every room, fireplace, etc.

[297] Moved here from the Parthinia location. This was a small post war development home.

[298] Moved just down the street into an apartment.

[299] Moved to this apartment after son Paul got married.

[300] Moved here and worked on grounds of campground as maintenance employee's. Lived year round in camper there.

[301] Moved here from Shasta and opened Bunnell Books, and lived above the store in an apartment.

[302] Moved to the lake and lived in mobile home. worked for store in San Jose, picking pine cones from the forest and making owls out of them. They got .50 cent a piece.

[303] Moved here after a short stay with son Paul in West Linn, Oregon to find work.

[304] Job review by Don Shultz, all areas above job requirements 110% rate. Form in file.

[305] Moved here from Beaverton, retired and placed a mobile home on lot next to state park near the ocean.

[306] Found a small town of retired people. No admittance under age 55 to own. They bought a small house on Main St.

[307] After wife died, he went to live at son Paul's home.

[308] Died 1:15 AM at home in Paul & Leslie's arms trying to revive him. After 15 minutes rescue came and worked on him another half hour until taking him to the Cape Cod Hospital in Hyannis where they officially pronounced him dead c.2:30 AM, but he really passed away at home.

[309] With full military honors.

[310] Manager of several Ralph7s Supermarkets in So. California.

[311] 1953,Pacoima,Ca./1959,Canoga Park,Ca./1963,Simi,Ca./1970's Valencia, Ca.

[312] Exact date of move in not known, but earlier then above.

[313] After over 35 years in the produce business he retired, bought a 5th. wheel and truck, and first headed for Oklahoma where Janet's family is, then to Alaska for two months. They plan to travel with address being at son's Robbie's in Oregon.

[314] Studying to be a Forest Ranger.

[315] Status: never.

[316] (Was living with mother).

[317] (Was delivered around 6 weeks early).

[318] From So.Calif. to So. Oregon c.1993.

[319] (Living there from 1994-2000. Plans to buy house).

[320] Not sure of married status. Believed married later c. 1998?

[321] (1995-2000).

[322] (Was in the first grade).

[323] (1995-2000).

[324] (7 lbs., 11 ozs).

[325] Lived in Amesbury from 1946 to 1953.

[326] 1978 Baptized .Mormon at Lake Oswego, Oregon Stake.

[327] Lived there from 1953 to 1959.

[328] Lived there from 1959 to c.1963.

[329] From 1970 to 1974.

[330] From 1974 to May 1975.

[331] From 1975 to 1977.

[332] From 1977 to 1978, stayed with brother Michael & wife Lorraine.

[333] From 1978 to 1979.

[334] From Jan. 1979 to May 1979.

[335] 1953,Pacoima,Ca/1959,Canoga Park,Ca.1975,Cape Cod,Ma,1977,San Jose,Ca/1977,W.Linn,Or/1979,Boise,Id/1979,Cape Cod, Ma. Marstons Mills from 1979 to 1996.

[336] After 45 years, I moved back to my home town, into an apartment over looking Lake Gardner.

[337] Godparents-Mike & Susan Nadeau. Susan his 2nd. Cousin.

[338] 1975,Cape Cod Ma./1977,W.Linn,Or./1979,Boise,Id./1979,Cape Cod Ma., Nashua, NH.

[339] Pro Wrestling.

[340] (They are going on 14 May 2000 and staying 7 days).

[341] Spons: Mike & Susan Nadeau.

[342] 1975,Cape Cod,Ma./1977,W.Linn,Or./1979,Boise,Id./1979,Cape Cod, Ma.

[343] Never Married.

[344] (Later moved to Hyannis, Ma., Nashua, NH, Lowell, Ma. And Aug. 1998 to Amesbury, Ma.).

[345] Cesarean Section. 10.2 pounds, 21 inches long.

[346] (Baby induced, cesarean. Weight 9.6 lbs., 19 inches long, jet black hair).

[347] 1953,Pacoima,Ca./1959,Canoga Park,Ca./1970's,San Jose,Ca./1991,Palmdale,Ca.

[348] Date of this record was 6 Jan. 1953. Cert in files.

[349] Moved to New Hampshire.

[350] Bunnell|Bonnell|Burnell Family, VR-Ma009-2/190 & 385/195.

[351] (from Amesbury Town Hall Marriage Records 6 Jan. 1998).

[352] (Listed in 1951 Amesbury Directory, p. 315).

[353] (with son & husband in family plot).

[354] (Married in Mass. or NH?).

[355] (Adopted out 1865/66?).

[356] Wedding date set and reported by Jean in Thanksgiving Day party photo 2001. Reception at Victoria Inn, 430 High St., Hampton, NH at 2:30 PM.

[357] Adopted out c.1975.

[358] (E-mail address is joegagne@home.com).

[359] (From Grace Rogers Xmas card).

[360] (From Grace Rogers Xmas card 9 Dec. 1999).

[361] Between 20 and 22 Dec. 1922.

[362] Bunnell|Bonnell|Burnell Family, VR-Ma009-305/67.

[363] Bunnell|Bonnell|Burnell Family.

[364] Listed as unemployed.

[365] Bunnell|Bonnell|Burnell Family.

[366] Listed as a Laborer.

[367] Bunnell|Bonnell|Burnell Family.

[368] (Funeral Home-E.V.Jutras & Sons,118 Friend St. Amesbury).

[369] Bunnell|Bonnell|Burnell Family.

[370] E-mail address is: grogers@nh.ultranet.com).

[371] (Moved into uncles house with option to buy, 2 1/2 acres, large garage, plenty of room for his landscaping equipment. The house is a Cape and he was approved to by in Fall).

[372] (From Grace on e-mail 29 Sept. 1998) Married after 9 years together. Fletch and Desiree's father both walked her down the aisle.

[373] In 2nd. grade.

[374] (From Grace e-mail 29 Sept. 1998)(From xmas card, weighed 7 lbs, 1 oz, 19 inches long).

[375] (surname spelled Bunnell).

[376] (From Amesbury Town Hall Records, 6 Jan. 1998).

[377] Bunnell|Bonnell|Burnell Family, VR-Ma009-1/288, says Newburyport.

[378] (From Amesbury Town Hall Birth Records, 6 Jan. 1998).

[379] Bunnell|Bonnell|Burnell Family, VR-Ma009-1/145, says Newburyport.

[380] (Zip-01913).

[381] (surname spelled Bunnell).

[382] Bunnell\Bonnell\Burnell Family.

[383] (From Amesbury Town Hall Birth Records, 6 Jan. 1998).

[384] Bunnell\Bonnell\Burnell Family, VR-Ma009-1/292, says Newburyport.

[385] Moved to Burbank, California 1950-53.Lived at 24210 Mariano St., Woodland Hills, Ca. from 1960's-1990? Living in Las Vegas, Nevada 1993.

[386] c.1950 to Burbank, Calif., then Canoga Park, then Woodland Hills.

[387] c.1950 Burbank, Calif., then Canoga Park, then Woodland Hills, then Palmdale area.

[388] (Lived there from approx. 1943-45?)(Also was at 205 Hardy Court, Gulfport, Mississippi. Husband was a Sergeant).

[389] This was Sal's family home where entire family lived in separate apartments.

[390] At Daughters house (Diana).

[391] Zip 03077.

[392] 10 AM Saturday.

[393] Zip 03077.

[394] Zip 03109. Email banchee5007@cs.com.

[395] In Sophomore year. Will move off campus in coming year with friends.

[396] (Per Christmas card; still at Villanova University and hopes to transfer to Boston College).

[397] Degree in Communications. Parents traveled around Amish country while there.

[398] Is a senior there and plans to attend New York University after she was accepted.

[399] (Per Christmas card; is a freshman at New York University in Manhattan and loves it there. Works part time at The Gap Clothing store).

[400] A junior living with roommate Katie Austin on penthouse apartment on West 15th. NY. During a presidential fundraiser at Katie's home she met President Clinton. From parents xmas card.

[401] 24 April 1927,by Rev. Jon C. Martin, St. Joseph Cath.Ch.,9 Sparhawk St. ,Amesbury, Essex Co. Mass.

[402] Lived there from approx. 1950's to present 1998.

[403] 1980's relocated to Worcester, Mass.

[404] To Ohio/Illinois c.1990? Moved to New York 1994.

[405] Bunnell\Bonnell\Burnell Family.

[406] (From Amesbury Town Hall Marriage Records, 6 Jan. 1998).

[407] Bunnell\Bonnell\Burnell Family, VR-Ma009-2/89.

[408] (From Amesbury Town Hall Death Records, 6 Jan. 1998) Death by hanging.

[409] (From Amesbury Town Hall Birth Records, 6 Jan. 1998).

[410] (of Leukemia)(From Amesbury Town Hall Death Records, 6 Jan. 1998).

[411] (From Amesbury Town Hall Birth Records, 6 Jan. 1998).

[412] (From Amesbury Town Hall Birth Records, 6 Jan. 1998).

[413] Zip 01860.

[414] Listed as a Pipe Layer.

[415] BunnellBonnellBurnell Family, VR-Ma009-1/485.

[416] Ibid., VR-Ma009-1/490.

[417] BunnellBonnellBurnell Family.

[418] Listed as a Laborer.

[419] BunnellBonnellBurnell Family.

[420] Moved to Calif.c.1958, returned to Amesbury several months later.

[421] By backhoe tractor, crushed in accident when operator lowered claw into hole not knowing Benny was in there. Location was at the Haverhill on-ramp on Rt. 110.

[422] BunnellBonnellBurnell Family, VR-Ma009-2/490.

[423] Moved c.1955-58 w/parents to Pacoima, Calif, then back to Amesbury.

[424] 6 pounds 5 1/2 ounces.

[425] Moved w/parents c.1955-58 to Pacoima, Calif., then back to Amesbury, Mass.

[426] BunnellBonnellBurnell Family, VR-Ma009-2/224.

[427] Picture of him with his graduation class in 16 June 2000 (Friday) Amesbury News. (Copy in file under him or cousin Troy Burrell's.

[428] BunnellBonnellBurnell Family, VR-Ma009-2/302.

[429] (Listed in Lawrence newspaper, The Eagle-Tribune, Wednesday 9 June 1999 under Divorces: Marcia G. Bunnell of Merrimac from Paul A. Bunnell of Amesbury).

[430] Graduated and given Kiwanis Award.

[431] BunnellBonnellBurnell Family, VR-Ma009-2/326.

[432] (Gilbert built new house in or around Newbury, Ma. c. 1996?).

[433] BunnellBonnellBurnell Family, VR-Ma009-1/166.

[434] Listed as a Laborer.

[435] BunnellBonnellBurnell Family.

[436] Ibid., VR-Ma009-1/265.

[437] (Lived most of her life in Newburyport. Still does as of 1999).

[438] Connecticut?

[439] Graduated magna-cum laude in May.

[440] Law School.

[441] Became engaged to Renee, a lawyer in Connecticut. Plan to marry in September 2001.

[442] Majoring in Math and Economics.

[443] (Graduated and will relocate to Delaware. From Dec. 1999 xmas newsletter of Eliz. Perkins).

[444] Doing studies and playing in school Jazz band and wants to learn Lacrosse in Spring.

[445] Is a junior majoring in Sociology. (From Dec. 1999 xmas newsletter of Eliz. Perkins).

[446] Will graduate from Salve Regina in May.

[447] Graduated and entered his first year at Marist College in New York. (From Dec. 1999 xmas newsletter of Eliz. Perkins). Dec. 2000 is a sophomore at Martist.

[448] This year earning high honors with all "A's". Plays soccer and on the basketball team. Will attend Mercy High School, sister school to Xavier next Fall.

[449] Is a sophomore and is an aggressive player on the varsity field hockey team. (From Dec. 1999 xmas newsletter of Eliz. Perkins) Dec. 2000 is a Junior at Mercy.

[450] Graduated and has gone into the paint contracting business with a friend. (From DEc. 1999 xmas newsletter of Eliz. Perkins).

[451] Is a sophomore playing football as a defensive lineman on the varsity squad. (From Dec. 1999 xmas newsletter of Eliz. Perkins) Dec. 2000 is in 3rd. year at Bates. Doing well academically and athletically. His team did not do well but he had good year on defense.

[452] Is a senior and plans to attend Keene State College in NH. (From Dec. 1999 xmas newsletter of Eliz. Perkins).

[453] In first semester. (From Xmas letter from grandmother, Elizabeth Perkins Dec. 2000) Planning to take some time off and work for a while.

[454] (Lived here for many years, still does as of 1999).

[455] Is a junior playing basketball and baseball, and has just gotten his drivers license. (From Dec. 1999 xmas newsletter of Eliz. Perkins) Dec. 2000 is a senior and co-captain of the basketball team.

[456] is a sophomore who plays football and basketball, broke his nose at football practice and sidelined for four weeks, but entered the last few games. (From Dec. 1999 xmas newsletter of Eliz. Perkins) Is a junior and plays on the football team and did well as a defensive end. (from xmas card from Elizabeth Perkins Dec. 2000).

[457] Stillborn.

[458] BunnellBonnellBurnell Family, VR-Ma009-1/374.

[459] The baby was still born and not baptized which is why buried in unhallowed grave. Mother tried to find it later but could not because it is unmarked.

[460] (From Amesbury Town Hall Marriage Records, 6 Jan. 1998).

[461] Lived in San Fernando Valley, L.A., Calif. during 1968-72?

[462](Full term, approx. 7 lbs., 21 inches long).

[463](Defective heart).

[464](Funeral Friday 26 June 1998, 9:45 AM at the Murphy Funeral Home, 85 Federal St., Salem, Mass. followed by funeral Mass at 10:30 AM at St. James Catholic Church, Salem)(Wake on 26 June 1998 at Murphy Funeral Home, Salem, Mass. 4-8 PM.

[465](From father, Louis Bunnell 9/11/99).

[466](Reception to be at The Knights of Columbus in Salem, Mass. 1:30 PM).

[467](Zip - 01970. Phone - 978-745-4195).

[468]by Rev.J.J.McCarthy,God-parents,Alexander McCann & Mary Keeley signed by Rev.C.A.O'Brien 11 Nov.1915.

[469]BunnellBonnellBurnell Family.

[470]19 Mar.1916 placed w/Mrs.Beatrice Cooley,Everett,Ma,19 Sep.1916 to 7 Dec.1916 absconded from home,10 May 1917 to Daniel F.Austin, Pondsville, Ma.

[471]Was a Laborer in building trade. Informant was brother Ben Bunnell. Died of Alcoholism.

[472]BunnellBonnellBurnell Family.

[473]Ibid.

[474]Ibid.

[475]With mother Lizzie.

[476]BunnellBonnellBurnell Family.

[477]Ibid., VR-Ma025-553/262.

[478]Was raised by the Fay family in Revere, Mass. after family broke up c.1910? Mr. Fay adopted her.

[479]BunnellBonnellBurnell Family.

[480]7 Oct.1917 E.Bridgewater,21 Nov.1917 Roxbury,22 Feb.1918 Roslindale,30 June 1918 Norwood,2 Mar.1919 Roxbury,Ma.(Mr.May)1922,11 Hammatt Rd.Roslindale.

[481]Living here at time of marriage.

[482]BunnellBonnellBurnell Family, VR-Ma025-2/152.

[483]Or 24 Nov. 1927 per Claude Bunnell database.

[484]BunnellBonnellBurnell Family.

[485]Age 62.

[486]New Calvery Ceme,Roxbury,Ma.(Fay family member worked there).

[487]Retired.

[488]BunnellBonnellBurnell Family, VR-Ma025-577/349.

[489]Sent to Destitute Children's Home, Harrison Ave. to live.

[490]BunnellBonnellBurnell Family.

[491]Ibid., VR-Ma025-16/399.

492 Bunnell|Bonnell|Burnell Family.
493 Ibid.
494 Ibid.
495 Ibid.
496 Roxbury or Dorchester, Ma.?
497 Or 11 Dec.
498 Bunnell|Bonnell|Burnell Family, VR-Ma025-34/129.
499 Ibid., VR-Ma025-9/348.
500 (Phone 978-9866615).
501 Bunnell|Bonnell|Burnell Family, VR-Ma025-9/153.
502 Ibid.
503 Ibid.
504 Bunnell|Bonnell|Burnell Family.
505 Ibid., Vr-Ma025-601/364 & VR-Ma025-17/441.
506 Ibid.
507 Ibid.
508 Bunnell|Bonnell|Burnell Family.
509 Ibid.
510 Ibid.
511 Went back & forth to Massachusetts.
512 Age 6, born in New Brunswick.
513 Listed as a painter.
514 Bunnell|Bonnell|Burnell Family.
515 Age 69.
516 Bunnell|Bonnell|Burnell Family.
517 Ibid.
518 Ibid.
519 Moved back & forth to Massachusetts.
520 Went back & forth from Massachusetts.
521 Birth could be 1869?
522 Bunnell|Bonnell|Burnell Family.
523 Age 3, born in New Brunswick.
524 Bunnell|Bonnell|Burnell Family.

[525] Living with Hugh S. Farren at 96 Leverett St.
[526] BunnellBonnellBurnell Family.
[527] A Brass Molder living at 23 Woodward Ave.
[528] BunnellBonnellBurnell Family.
[529] Moved to South Carolina?
[530] BunnellBonnellBurnell Family.
[531] 9 years old.
[532] BunnellBonnellBurnell Family.
[533] 19 years old, listed as a Cashier living with Aunt Ann.
[534] E-mail - RetDosh@aol.com.
[535] Librarian.
[536] Possibly lived there?
[537] They live next to 102 Prim Rose Path (in-laws- Doscher's).
[538] Not sure of date.
[539] Not sure of date.
[540] Thinking about marriage.
[541] From Charles Franklin Bunnell Jr., son.
[542] BunnellBonnellBurnell Family.
[543] Age 6.
[544] BunnellBonnellBurnell Family.
[545] Single Sheet & Metal worker, age 16 living with Aunt Ann.
[546] BunnellBonnellBurnell Family.
[547] Ibid.
[548] Age 56. Was a Woodworking Foreman.
[549] BunnellBonnellBurnell Family.
[550] Ibid.
[551] Ibid.
[552] From himself 16 June 2001.
[553] BunnellBonnellBurnell Family.
[554] Ibid.
[555] Ibid.
[556] Ibid.
[557] Ibid.

[558] Ibid.
[559] Ibid.
[560] Ibid.
[561] Ibid.
[562] Ibid.
[563] Ibid.
[564] Moved back & forth to Massachusetts.
[565] Bunnell|Bonnell|Burnell Family.
[566] Single.
[567] Bunnell|Bonnell|Burnell Family.
[568] Ibid.
[569] Ibid.
[570] Ibid.
[571] Ibid.
[572] Moved back & forth to Massachusetts.
[573] Birth is only a guess?
[574] Bunnell|Bonnell|Burnell Family.
[575] Ibid.
[576] Maritime History Archives, *Ships & Seafarers*, #J845125.
[577] Ibid., Registration #J846177.
[578] Ibid., Registration #J847139.
[579] Ibid., Registration #J849099.
[580] Listed with family at age 30 as a Boatman.
[581] Maritime History Archives, *Ships & Seafarers*, Registration #J853017, official number 034986.
[582] Housewife.
[583] (Shirley Thomas records say birth was 1838 which is in error, e-mail msthomas@uniserve.com 17 Feb. 2000).
[584] Bunnell|Bonnell|Burnell Family.
[585] Was a Spinster at marriage. From Cleadie Barnett research & records.
[586] Listed on fathers will.
[587] Bunnell|Bonnell|Burnell Family, copy in my file.
[588] From 1871 Fredericton,NB census, living in Wellington, says of German descent this probably in error?
[589] From Cleadie Barnett research & records.

[590] BunnellBonnellBurnell Family.

[591] Listed with family at age 25 and boatman.

[592] BunnellBonnellBurnell Family.

[593] Maritime History Archives, *Ships & Seafarers*, Registration #J853034, official #035012.

[594] Ibid., Registration #J847140.

[595] Ibid., Registration #J851096.

[596] Listed with family at age 24, boatman.

[597] BunnellBonnellBurnell Family.

[598] Maritime History Archives, *Ships & Seafarers*, Registration #j864076, official #050546.

[599] Listed on fathers will, and executor.

[600] BunnellBonnellBurnell Family.

[601] Maritime History Archives, *Ships & Seafarers*, Registration #J867053, official #054489.

[602] Listed with George & Elizabeth Harding and their family as a servant age 23.

[603] Birth could be Oct. 1830-1?

[604] Listed with family at age 20. Boatman.

[605] BunnellBonnellBurnell Family.

[606] Maritime History Archives, *Ships & Seafarers*, Registration #J853171.

[607] To Boston c.1859,lived at 161 Chelsea St.,Charlestown,Mass.

[608] Graves as from Saint John, NB, a Mariner, age 28.

[609] BunnellBonnellBurnell Family.

[610] Listed as Sea Captain from Saint John, NB at sons birth.

[611] BunnellBonnellBurnell Family, VR-Ma017-133/80.

[612] Listed in his will.

[613] BunnellBonnellBurnell Family.

[614] Claude Bunnell database says death at Upper Fredericton, NB from Arsenic (From VR NB Newspapers). Bill Bunnell says he died at sea between NY & Newfoundland?

[615] BunnellBonnellBurnell Family.

[616] Bill Bunnell says, At Sea c.1868-70 between New York & New Foundland,Canada. Claude Bunnell says at Fredericton?

[617] BunnellBonnellBurnell Family.

[618] Birth cert says William Albert per Bill Bunnell Oct. 28. 2002.

[619] Claude Bunnell records say birth was 8 Nov. 1861 at Saint John, NB?

[620] BunnellBonnellBurnell Family.

[621] Ibid., & Bill Bunnell.

[622] Lived her at son William's birth and was a Millinery worker.

[623] BunnellBonnellBurnell Family.

[624] Salesman(1897 10 Summer St. Lived Malden)(1889 boarded at Waverly House & 111 Chauncy St.1913-17.

[625] Was a salesman age 38.

[626] BunnellBonnellBurnell Family.

[627] Listed as a Millinery worker age 48 with wife age 45.

[628] BunnellBonnellBurnell Family.

[629] Listed as the proprietor of the Wholesale Knitting Company, age 58 with wife age 53.

[630] BunnellBonnellBurnell Family.

[631] Age 65, from Saint John, NB and Wholesale Millinery on death record.

[632] BunnellBonnellBurnell Family.

[633] Ibid.

[634] Ibid.

[635] Ibid.

[636] Ibid.

[637] Age 38 giving birth.

[638] BunnellBonnellBurnell Family.

[639] Was he a twin? Record VR-Ma017-449/265.

[640] BunnellBonnellBurnell Family.

[641] At 1019 Main St(possibly Malden?)Grew up Glenn St. Malden, Mass.

[642] BunnellBonnellBurnell Family.

[643] Age 15.

[644] BunnellBonnellBurnell Family.

[645] Age 24, 3rd. Mate, Merchant Marines.

[646] BunnellBonnellBurnell Family.

[647] Listed as crew member of ship, Huguenot, age 24 from Providence, Rhode Island, coming from Port Lobos, Vera Cruz, Mexico. From Ellis Island passenger list.

[648] Was listed as a crew member on ship, Huguenot that departed from Port Lobos, Vera Cruz, Mexico. He was 24 years old. From Ellis Island passenger list.

[649] Listed on ship, Huguenot as crew member age 25, place of residence was New York, coming from Port Lobos, Vera Cruz, Mexico. From Ellis Island passenger lists.

[650] Living here at time of fathers death.

[651] BunnellBonnellBurnell Family.

[652] Salesman age 34 and she was 31, an Artist.

[653] BunnellBonnellBurnell Family.

[654] Living here at time of Bill's birth.

[655] BunnellBonnellBurnell Family.

[656] Of Cancer, age 58.

[657] BunnellBonnellBurnell Family.

[658] Bunnell plot, Brewster, Mass.

[659] Lived in N.H. & Hingham 1984 & to Tucson Arizona 1987.

[660] BunnellBonnellBurnell Family.

[661] Age 7.

[662] BunnellBonnellBurnell Family.

[663] Age 12.

[664] BunnellBonnellBurnell Family.

[665] Per Concord, NH Marr. Record also say 16 Nov. 1929 at Exeter, NH, she age 22 and per 7 June 1930 Melrose, Ma. Marr records? She was a Typist in 1930.

[666] BunnellBonnellBurnell Family.

[667] Was a Salesman and she a Librarian.

[668] BunnellBonnellBurnell Family.

[669] Live,11 Glen St. Malden, Mass. To NH early 1950's, nice Farm in Amherst, NH, commuted to Boston to work.

[670] BunnellBonnellBurnell Family.

[671] Ibid.

[672] Ibid.

[673] Age 54 with husband age 55, a Varnish Manufacturer.

[674] BunnellBonnellBurnell Family.

[675] Massachusetts?

[676] Massachusetts?

[677] BunnellBonnellBurnell Family.

[678] age 3.

[679] BunnellBonnellBurnell Family.

[680] Age 21. Death record says born in Fredericton, NB.

[681] BunnellBonnellBurnell Family.

[682] To/from Mass.

[683] Listed with family at age 17.

684 Listed on fathers will.
685 BunnellBonnellBurnell Family.
686 From Cleadie Barnett research & records. Both have Bunnell surname.
687 From Cleadie Barnett research & records.
688 At sea.
689 Claude Bunnell database says 4 July 1885.
690 Age 71, single. Informant was niece, Gertrude Sherwood living at same address.
691 BunnellBonnellBurnell Family.
692 Ibid.
693 Date of birth from Shirley Thomas (e-mail msthomas@uniserve.com) 17 Feb. 2000.
694 Listed on fathers will.
695 BunnellBonnellBurnell Family.
696 Ibid.
697 Listed on fathers will as 2nd. youngest.
698 BunnellBonnellBurnell Family.
699 (Shirley Thomas e-mail msthomas@uniserve.com 17 Feb. 2000 says birth was 1842) Claude Bunnell's database says he is the son of Heddy Day, but Ben & her were not married until 1859?
700 Listed as youngest on fathers will.
701 BunnellBonnellBurnell Family.
702 Maritime History Archives, *Ships & Seafarers*, Registration #J881001, official #080053.
703 Ibid., Registration #J886027, official #092354.
704 Ibid., Registration #J889025, official #096745.
705 Age 46.
706 Marriage record says Sophia Wood of Westfield. From Cleadie Barnett research & records.
707 Listed with wife and family at age 61 and as a farmer.
708 Farmer in 1851 census.
709 Listed only with wife on page 23, Division 1. Named spelled Bunnele.
710 From Cleadie Barnett research & records.
711 (or 1825?) Cleadie Barnett research & records say 1831.
712 Listed with family at age 26, as laborer.
713 (Killed at age 27 between 1852-55?).
714 From Cleadie Barnett research & records.
715 Listed with family as 17 years old.

[716] Bunnell|Bonnell|Burnell Family.

[717] From Cleadie Barnett research & records.

[718] (as an adult).

[719] Says he was of Lancaster, NB and she from Carleton, NB.

[720] Listed with wife, son, and daughter.

[721] Listed with wife and both children (#009-10-02) Division 2.

[722] Listed with family in Division 2.

[723] Listed with parents and sister.

[724] Listed with family in Division 2.

[725] Listed with parents & brother George E.

[726] Cleadie Barnett research & records also show Abby Jane, may be Affy?).

[727] From Cleadie Barnett research & records.

[728] Listed with family as 12 years old.

[729] From Cleadie Barnett research & records.

[730] Both were listed as from Lancaster, NB (suburb of Saint John).

[731] Or 1841 from Cleadie Barnett research & records.

[732] Listed with family as 10 years old.

[733] (as adult).

[734] Says he was of Fairville, NB and she of Petersville, NB. Found in NB Archives.

[735] From Laura & Zwieba Bunnell 10 June 2001.

[736] From Laura & Zwieba Bunnell 10 June 2001.

[737] From Laura & Zwieba Bunnell 10 June 2001, email zwieba21@nwinternet.com. He is direct descendant.

[738] From Laura & Zwieba Bunnell 10 June 2001.

[739] Not the mother of Ben, Margaret and David. This is Fred's 2nd. wife who had a son Stewart that Fred adopted.

[740] From Zwieba Bunnell 10 June 2001, descendant. Email zwieba21@nwinternet.com. Also from Birth, marriages & Deaths ledger in Westbrook, Maine.

[741] From Laura & Zwieba Bunnell 10 June 2001.

[742] From Laura & Zwieba Bunnell 10 June 2001, email zwieba21@nwinternet.com. He is direct descendant.

[743] In June 2001 ready to have 50th. wedding anniversary.

[744] Living with her mother.

[745] From Laura & Zwieba Bunnell 10 June 2001, email zwieba21@nwinternet.com.

[746] From himself & wife Laura 10 June 2001, email zwieba21@nwinternet.com. His mother made up his name from Bunnell & her maiden name.

[747] From Laura & Zwieba Bunnell.

[748] From Cleadie Barnett research & records.

[749] Listed with family at age 7.

[750] (as adult) From Cleadie Barnett research & records.

[751] Maritime History Archives, *Ships & Seafarers*, Registration #J886027, official #092354.

[752] Ibid., Registration #J889025, official #096745.

[753] Was one month old during 1851 census.

[754] Listed with family. (Could this be Allan Bunnell?) Take note of Allan Bunnell, b. 1843 #6830 who possibly could be this person?

[755] From Bodemiller family bible.

[756] One of first settlers in Lapeer Co., Mich.

[757] She moved to California.

[758] Drowned.

[759] Immigrated to Michigan with family?

[760] One of first settlers in Lapeer Co., Michigan.

[761] Will live with mother until she finishes college.

[762] Living there until Rhonda finishes college.

[763] From Arrivals 99, Our First Ancestors in NB, page 88.

[764] Witnessed by Thomas Fanjoy & Handford Bostwick. From Cleadie Barnett research & records.

[765] Listed with family at age 54 and listed with them is Lavinia Bunnell age 16.

[766] Age 61.

[767] (pictures in file) Her stone is lying flat. It says: In Memory of Elenor Jane, Wife of Joseph Fanjoy who died 21 March 1856 age 61, Reveal thy bosom sacred heart, Take this new treasure to thy trust and give this sacred relict room, To slumber in thy sacred tomb.

[768] Fanjoy Pt.Cemetery,Long Reach,King's Co., New Brunswick, Canada.

[769] Age 27. A Nancy McLean age 9 shows up with Sarah's family in 1851 census as visitor (Possible her daughter?).

[770] Fanjoy Pt. Cemetery, Long Reach, King's Co., New Brunswick, Canada.

[771] 1909, Fernhill Cemetery, Saint John, Saint John Co., New Brunswick, Canada.

[772] Boatman.

[773] From Cleadie Barnett research & records.

[774] Listed with family at age 25 and as a Boatman.

[775] Age 6 years, 6 months.

[776] In with sister Nora. Stone says Safe with Jesus. Stone is broken and lying on ground.

[777] Age 1 year, 5 months.

[778] With sister Ethelbert. Stone says Gone Home, Safe with Jesus. Stone is broken and lying on ground.

[779] Listed with family at age 22, but was absent during census.

[780] From Cleadie Barnett research & records.

[781] From Cleadie Barnett research & records.

[782] Listed with family at age 19.

[783] Drowned at Niagara Falls.

[784] From Cleadie Barnett research & records.

[785] Listed with family at age 18.

[786] At age 60.

[787] From Cleadie Barnett research & records.

[788] Listed with family at age 16.

[789] Listed with family at age 12.

[790] Maritime History Archives, *Ships & Seafarers*, Registered #J841160.

[791] From Cleadie Barnett research & records.

[792] Maritime History Archives, *Ships & Seafarers*, Registered #J843025.

[793] From Jeffrey & John Haines 2 Jan. 2001.

[794] From Jeffrey & John Haines 2 Jan. 2001.

[795] From Jeffrey & John Haines 2 Jan. 2001.

[796] From Jeffrey & John Haines 2 Jan. 2001.

[797] From him & son Jeffrey 2 Jan. 2001. They have lived there 10 years or more.

[798] From himself 2 Jan. 2001.

[799] Twin.

[800] Twin.

[801] Still lives there.

[802] It is understood that he holds a position equal to a state Senator in New Brunswick.

[803] NB Legislature 18 Nov.1974,1978,1982,& as Minister of Supply & Services 1976-82,Chairman of Treas. Board 1982-84.

[804] Wife #1.

[805] Wife #2.

[806] From Cleadie Barnett research & records.

[807] Owned store in New Glasgow, Nova Scotia.

[808] Moved to USA.

[809] Owned store in New Glasgow, Nova Scotia.

[810] _____, *no title* in *no series* (n.p.: Internet site, 2002).

[811] Ibid.

[812] Ibid.

[813] Ibid.

[814] Ibid.

[815] BunnellBonnellBurnell Family.

[816] Ibid.

[817] Maritime History Archives, *Ships & Seafarers*.

[818] Listed on fathers will. Copy in my file.

[819] BunnellBonnellBurnell Family.

[820] Listed as 72 years old, from New Brunswick, Canada, Farm Laborer. Also listed there was a Frank Bunnell, Dressmaker age 20, born c. 1850 in Canada.

[821] BunnellBonnellBurnell Family.

[822] (or 1799-1800).

[823] (Or 22 Dec. 1831 or Saint John).

[824] Listed with family as Farmer at age 50 & listed 51 on Greenwich census.

[825] Cleadie Barnett records state there was an Isaac will dated 5 Feb. 1856?

[826] From Cleadie Barnett research & records.

[827] Listed with family at age 18 & listed on Greenwich census as age 17.

[828] BunnellBonnellBurnell Family.

[829] From Cleadie Barnett research & records.

[830] Listed with family at age 16 at Westfield. There is also a Lavinia age 16 listed as a servant with Joseph & Eleanor (Bunnell) Fanjoy on the same census. Also she is listed again with family on Greenwich 1851 census.

[831] From Cleadie Barnett research & records.

[832] Listed with family at age 15 and on Greenwich census with family.

[833] From Cleadie Barnett research & records.

[834] Listed with family at age 14 in Westfield & listed again with family in Greenwich.

[835] From Cleadie Barnett research & records.

[836] Listed with family at age 12 in Westfield and again with family in Greenwich as age 13.

[837] From Cleadie Barnett research & records.

[838] From Cleadie Barnett research & records.

[839] Listed with family at age 10 in Westfield & again with family in Greenwich as age 11.

[840] This may need checking again?

[841] BunnellBonnellBurnell Family.

[842] A single school teacher. this may need checking again?

[843] BunnellBonnellBurnell Family.

[844] (Or 1843) From Cleadie Barnett research & records.

[845] Listed with family at age 9 in Westfield & again with family in Greenwich as age 10.

[846] From Cleadie Barnett research & records.

[847] Listed with family at age 7 & again with family in Greenwich.

[848] From Cleadie Barnett research & records.

[849] Listed with family at age 5 and listed again with family in Greenwich.

[850] Listed with family as age 4.

[851] From Cleadie Barnett research & records.

[852] Listed with family at age 4.

[853] Listed with family at age 2 and listed again on Greenwich census same year with family.

[854] Marriage records from Cleadie Barnett.

[855] Or 1852.

[856] (From records completed by Cleadie Barnett & her mother C. Gertrude Keating c. 1985).

[857] (From St. Peter's Anglican Church records by Cleadie Barnett 1985).

[858] (From records of Cleadie Barnett 1985).

[859] (From Cleadie Barnett records 1985, buried near father & brother).

[860] Died age 9. (From Cleadie Barnett records 1985).

[861] (From Cleadie Barnett records 1985).

[862] Died age 14. (From Cleadie Barnett records 1985).

[863] (To Saint John 1783, left home in Newtown, Connecticut)(From CD #354 passengers & immigrants lists index 1538-1940, also in Nova Scotia Immigration to 1867).

[864] (Wife was named administrator. From Kings Co., Registry of Probate, 1791, Vol.A,p.15).

[865] (From Fredericton Archives, Isaac Bunnell family records).

[866] (Age 68) From K12A-008 Cardwell Parish, Penobsquis records.

[867] (From Fredericton Archives, Isaac Bunnell family records) Stone says: "By long experience have I known, They sovereign power to save, At thy command I venture down, Securely to the grave." Also listed in Elliott book, Gone But Not Forgotten, vol. 3, p. 180.

[868] Age 44. From K12A-008 Cardwell Parish, Penobsquis records.

[869] With family. Stone is whit slab with rose branch flanked by large leaves, facing west. Stone signed by J & R Milligan. Next to another stone with Daniel Bunnell, b. 1841 & family. From Elliott book, Gone But Not Forgotten, vol. 3, p. 180.

[870] From K12A-008 Cardwell Parish, Penobsquis records.

[871] Age 13. From K12A-008 Cardwell Parish, Penobsquis records.

[872] With family. From Elliott book, Gone But Not Forgotten, vol. 3, p. 180.

[873] Listed with widow mother at age 18.

[874] Listed with widow mother & family at age 14.

[875] Listed with widow mother at age 15.

[876] Listed with widow mother & family at age 12.

[877] With family but not husband. From Elliott book, Gone But Not Forgotten, vol. 3, p.180.

[878] Listed with widow mother & family at age 10.

[879] Listed with mother as widow and other brothers & sisters at age 8.

[880] With family. Stone is polished black granite with flowers at top. From Elliott book, Gone But Not Fogotten, vol. 3, p. 157.

[881] With family. From Elliott book, Gone But Not Forgotten, vol. 3, p. 157.

[882] With family. From Elliott book, Gone But Not Forgotten, vol. 3, p. 157.

[883] With parents & family. From Elliott book, Gone But Not Forgotten, vol. 3, p. 157.

[884] With family. From Elliott book, Gone But Not Forgotten, vol. 3, p. 157.

[885] Grace Aiton's book says born in New Jersey and of Huguenot descent.

[886] Later moved to Kings County, New Brunswick peninsula. (and Penobsquis) Later generations lived at Collina, Millstream and Sussex where they still live. (From Story of Sussex & Vicinity by Grace Aiton's book).

[887] Millwright & made a freeman of Saint John City in 1800. Lived in Sussex Parish, Kings Co., NB.

[888] 1 or 21 Aug.

[889] R1,R2,R6.

[890] Was listed on 1851 census.

[891] (From Carole Bonnell, P>O> Box 4282, Spanaway, Wa. 98387 on 13 Sept. 1998)(They had no children and marriage was short).

[892] (From Emelyn A. Bonnell of 3917 Bryce, Ft. Worth, Tx. 76107 records found in Bunnell/Bonnell Newsletter dated August/Summer 1998 Vol. 12,#3, page 40)(Also from Betsy David of Woodstock, Vt. 22 Dec. 1999).

[893] Listed at age 18 with his grandmother, Mrs. Graves who was a widow age 85 from the USA in 1782 (Loyalist?).

[894] (From Carole Bonnell, P.O. Box 4282, Spanaway, Wa. 98387 on 13 Sept. 1998. She descends from this wife and Alfred)(Lucinda had 6 kids by him, per Betsy David, Woodstock, Vt. 22 Dec. 1999).

[895] (From Carole Bonnell P.O. Box 4282, Spanaway, Wa. 98387 on 13 Sept. 1998)(They were second cousins, per descendant from this 2nd. wife, Betsy David of Woodstock, Vt., 22 Dec. 1999. This wife had 6 daughters by him) At marriage he was 29 years old.

[896] Age 85.

[897] (From Carole Bonnell, P.O. Box 4282, Spanaway, Wa. 98387 on 13 Sept. 1998).

[898] (From Carole Bonnell, P.O. Box 4282, Spanaway, Wa. 98387 on 13 Sept. 1998).

[899] Was there at age 20. He was a Montana Pioneer, had a trading post at the Sioux Rosebud Reservation. Was also a Sioux interpreter.

[900] (From Bunnell newsletter Jan. 1999, vol. 13, #1, p. 76) Or 1855.

[901] Living with Zabah & Amanda Hewitt family.

[902] She was 28 years old.

[903] Living there at age 20.

[904] (Lived there at one time).

[905] (From Bunnell newsletter, Jan. 1999, vol. #13, #1, p.76).

[906] (From Bunnell newsletter Jan. 1999, Vol. 13, #1, p.76).

[907] She was living with her step-brother Oliver when she gave birth to Roy.

[908] She was age 23.

[909] Living with Charles & Rachel Clarke during census. Mother died 1879.

[910] (From William B. Bonnell of Gig Harbor, Wa. found in Bunnell/Bonnell newsletter dated August/Summer, 1998, vol. 12,#3,p.40).

[911] (From Emelyn A. Bonnell, of 3917 Bryce, Ft. Worth, Tx. 76107 found in Bunnell/Bonnell Newsletter, August/Summer 1998, Vol. 12,#3, p.40).

[912] (Lived there when father died).

[913] (He died single).

[914] New Brunswick, Canada?

[915] New Brunswick, Canada?

[916] New Brunswick, Canada?

[917] New Brunswick, Canada?

[918] New Brunswick, Canada?

[919] New Brunswick, Canada?

[920] New Brunswick, Canada?

[921] New Brunswick, Canada?

[922] (Between 1807-08).

[923] (Or Saint John) or 26 May 1831 at Sussex as stated by book, Early Families, by the South Eastern Branch of the New Brunswick Genealogical Society, 1987, page 54.

[924] (Witnessed by J. Waters of Sussex, NB & J. Schoals of Saint John) or 28 July.

[925] Fenwick Cemetery, Berwick. Elliott's book, Gone But Not Forgotten says she is buried with husband at Lower Millstream? Stone is polished black granite.

[926] Fenwick Cemetery, Berwick, New Brunswick, Canada?

[927] (Or 16 June 1773/4).

[928] (He died suddenly).

[929] (The record notes the word "Governor").

[930] (From Francys Davis records Sept. 1998)(She was the first white child born on Kierstead Mt.).

[931] (From Francys Davis records Sept. 1998. He was brother to John Gregg and his grandfather was Hon. Milton Gregg).

[932] (From Francys Davis records Sept. 1998).

[933] Or 1880.

[934] (From Francys Davis records Sept. 1998 in Mass.).

[935] (Or 1852).

[936] (Or 1864).

[937] (Or 1901, died of burns).

[938] (From Francys Davis records Sept. 1998).

[939] (After Jemima's death, she married 3 more times).

[940] (From Francys Davis records Sept. 1998).

[941] (Married by Rev. Joseph Crandall).

[942] (From Francys Davis records Sept. 1998).

[943] (From Francys Davis records Sept. 1998).

[944] (Died of Diphtheria).

[945] (Died of Diphtheria)(From Francys Davis records Sept. 1998).

[946] (From Francys Davis records Sept. 1998).

[947] (Died of Diphtheria)(From Francys Davis records Sept. 1998).

[948] (From Francys Davis records Sept. 1998).

[949] (From Francys Davis records Sept. 1998).

[950] (Died young).

[951] Kings Co., New Brunswick, Canada.

[952] (Or 1800)(From Keirstead Genealogy, page 90).

[953] (From Keirstead Genealogy, page 90).

[954] (From Kierstead Genealogy, page 90).

[955] (From Keirstead Genealogy, page 90).

[956] (From Keirstead Genealogy, page 90).

[957] (From Keirstead Genealogy, page 90).

[958] (From Keirstead Genealogy, page 90).

[959] (From Keirstead Genealogy, page 90).

[960] (From Keirstead Genealogy, page 90)(Picture of gravestone in files, given by Don Kierstead in Sept. 1999. It has her noted on stone but no date) Also listed in Elliott's book, Gone But Not Forgotten. Question as to her death date, 1928 or with son Adam 1875?

[961] (listed with husband on stone but no dates for her. Picture of stone in files, given by Don Kierstead in Sept. 1999). Also listed in Elliott's Gone But Not Forgotten. Son, Adam is with them.

[962] (From Keirstead Genealogy, page 90).

[963] (From herself 18 Nov. 1981, PO Box 182, Limerick, Me. 04048).

[964] (From Keirstead Genealogy, page 90).

[965] (From Keirstead Genealogy, page 90).

[966] (From Keirstead Genealogy, page 90) Age 5.

[967] (Picture of stone in files, given by Don Kierstead in Sept. 1999). Also listed in Elliott's book, Gone But Not Forgotten. One record says mother died same day, but have a 1928 death date for her?

[968] With wife. Stone is a polished black granite. From Elliott's book, Gone But Not Forgotten, page 94.

[969] She is listed on the stone with no death date as of 1990 with husband. Stone is polished black granite with small stylized lily at each upper corner. From Elliott's book, Gone But Not Forgotten, page 94.

[970] (Or born 20 May 1910 as Fredericton Archive records on Isaac Bunnell family states).

[971] (From Keirstead Genealogy, page 90).

[972] From Anne Geall (ageall@ns.sympatico.ca) dated 29 June 2002.

[973] (From Keirstead Genealogy, page 90).

[974] (From Francys Davis records Sept. 1998).

[975] (From Keirstead Genealogy, page 90).

[976] (From Keirstead Genealogy, page 90).

[977] (From Francys Davis records 1998 & SE NBGS book Early Families, page 77, 1987.

[978] (Or the 27th.).

[979] (From Francys Davis records 1998. Their grt.Grandparents were Enoch Arden Markham, grt.grt grandparents of Ethel Irene (Holmes) Joslin.).

[980] (From Francys Davis records 1998. George was widower of Lydia's cousin Mary Kierstead).

[981] Early Families, by SE Branch of NBGS, 1987, p. 77 Records say Elizabeth Worden?

[982] (From Francys Davis records 1998).

[983] (From Francys Davis records 1998)(They had no children).

[984] (From Francys Davis records 1998).

[985] His 1st. marriage.

[986] (From Francys Davis of Mass. 1998 & Early Families, by SE Branch of NBGS, 1987, p. 77.

[987] From Early Families, by SE Branch of NBGS, 1987, p.77.

[988] (From Francys Davis records of Mass. 1998).

[989] Or 1818.

[990] From Early Families, by SE Branch of NBGS, 1987, p. 77.

[991] (From Francys Davis records, Mass. 1998 & Early Families, by SE Branch of NBGS, 1987, p. 77.

[992] #1 husband.

[993] #2 husband.

[994] (From Francys Davis records, Mass. 1998).

[995] (From Francys Davis records, Mass. 1998)(says died 1897/8).

[996] (From Francys Davis records, Mass. 1998 & Early Families, by SE Branch of NBGS, 1987, p. 77.

[997] (Or 1776).

[998] Charles died around 1800.

[999] (From Will Book D22C at Fredericton Archives).

[1000] #2 wife.

[1001] (Or c. 1783?).

[1002] (Owned lot #35 up Millstream a short time in 1813).

[1003] (After death, wife and 6 children walked back to her family's home in Sussex, NB).

[1004] Came with loyalists 1783.

[1005] Bapt by Elder Innis/united w/Bapt Ch.in Norton,Kings Co.

[1006] (He lived in Collina, moved to Norton, then back to Collina. The old cellar of his house where he and his father lived is still there at Bonnell's Corner near Collina, Kings Co., NB. Deeds show last conveyance by first wife 1815 and first by second wife in 1827)(Bought 448 acres in Wakefield, York co., NB 27 Jan. 1814)(Land records from Book 4, p.275, Sold 11 Nov. 1824, Book 14, p.216).

[1007] (From The Gillies Family, from genealogy of the Anglo-Dutch Esterbrooks Family, by Florence Esterbrooks, 1935. And found listed in "Generations", p. 43 of Spring 1998 issue) The book, Arrivals 99 Our First Ancestors in NB says marriage was 3 Jan. 1803 (page 101).

[1008] Listed with family at age 70 and as a Millwright. It is noted that 1787, from American Colonies, now USA.

[1009] (Died at age 79 on a Friday)(Day of death could be 8 July 1860?).

[1010] This Isaac may not be a husband, but possibly a son because of middle name and baptismal record date - 1840?

[1011] (possibly 1808).

[1012] (Family records at Archives says husbands name was Isaac Coy?).

[1013] Listed with husband John Coy.

[1014] (or 28 March 1865).

[1015] From Anne Geall (ageall@ns.sympatico.ca) dated 29 June 2002.

[1016] (Error here! She really died 25 April 1893 at Corn Hill, NB per Bunnell newsletter Nov. 1999 vol. 13 #4,p.129)(Ir first said June 1860, age 1 yr., 6 mos? Was there a baby named Rachel).

[1017] (From Bunnell newsletter Nov. 1999, vol. 13 #4,p.129).

[1018] (From Bunnell newsletter Jan. 1999, vol. 13, #1, p.76).

[1019] (From Carole Bonnell P.O. Box 4282, Spanaway, Wa. 98387 on 13 Sept. 1998)(They were second cousins, per descendant from this 2nd. wife, Betsy David of Woodstock, Vt., 22 Dec. 1999. This wife had 6 daughters by him) At marriage he was 29 years old.

[1020] Age 39.

[1021] (From Fredericton Archives, Isaac Bunnell family records).

[1022] (Or at Hampton - from Betsy David of Woodstock, Vt. 22 Dec. 1999).

[1023] New Brunswick, Canada.

[1024] Age 27.

[1025] Stone is a white slab with weeping willow, signed by F.W. Clear. From Elliott's book, Gone But Not Forgotten, page 88.

[1026] Age 3 years, 7 months. From Gone But Not Forgotten, by Elliott.

[1027] Stone is a white slab with words, :Gone Home and a hand pointing up. Also says Daughter of H. Allen & Rebecca A. Bonnell, and also says "Safe in the arms of Jesus." This info also from Elliott's book.

[1028] Or 1880. From Anne Geall (ageall@ns.sympatico.ca) dated 29 June 2002.

[1029] From Anne Geall (ageall@ns.sympatico.ca) dated 29 June 2002.

[1030] (John Barton records show John Sherwood Bonnell).

[1031] (Postal code - E1E 3V6, phone 852-3580).

[1032] (Could be 1825?).

[1033] Listed with wife Jemima and family age 26 and as a Carpenter.

[1034] (Lived there from 1853-85).

[1035] Age 59.

[1036] Buried with wife. Listed in Elliott's Gone But Not Forgotten, page 127.

[1037] Listed with family at age 2.

[1038] Listed with family at age 1.

[1039] (They were cousins, she was daughter of Benjamin Fowlie & Bithinia Kairstead).

[1040] (Birth could have been 5 Nov. 1800?).

[1041] Listed with family at age 19.

[1042] (From Fredericton Archives of Isaac Bunnell family records).

[1043] Listed with family at age 17.

[1044](From Fredericton Archives on Isaac Bunnell family records).

[1045]Listed as David age 7 with family.

[1046](Or 1790/1).

[1047](Or 6 July 1836)(Witnessed by George Crawford & John Kierstead).

[1048]Listed son & wife at age 64 as Farmer/Prop.

[1049](From Keirstead Genealogy, page 90)(Other record says buried at Woodlawn United Church Cemetery, Pearsonville, NB?)(Buried with wife, and son Adam)(Picture in files of stone sent by Don Kierstead in Sept. 1999) Age 79. Also listed in Elliott's book, Gone But Not Forgotten. With wife.

[1050]Listed with mother/father at age 12.

[1051](From Keirstead Genealogy, page 90).

[1052](From Keirstead Genealogy, page 90)(Another record says he is buried at Woodlawn United Church Cemetery in Pearsonville, New Brunswick)(Picture of stone in files, given by Don Kierstead in Sept. 1999) Also found in Elliott's book, Gone But Not Forgotten. Stone is a square polished gray granite column with urn, signed by R. Bardsley. With wife and son Adam.

[1053]Listed on sister-in-law Sarah (Coy) Plumer's probate record that he was sole executor of.

[1054]Land Grant 1821,lot #1,Burton,Sunbury Co. NB.(also made inv. of estate, Joseph Howland 1796 NB).

[1055](Left colonies after battle of Bennington, Vt. where he killed two men (Patriots), left with wife and 4 children. Son later accidentally girl his girl and disappeared in grief. Immigration record found in Annapolis, Nova Scotia, Canada immigration to 1867, record in CD #354 passenger & immigration lists index 1538-1940. Another listing on same CD says he came to Annapolis in 1782).

[1056](See Jean Bunnell #8546 record for source).

[1057](He was raised in Georgia).

[1058](Sailed as loyalist refugee from St. Augustine Florida).

[1059](See Jean Bunnell #8546 record for source)(Had much difficulties getting minister as described in news article in 1967 in Truro).

[1060](Possibly died between 1820-30).

[1061](See Jean Bunnell #8546 record for source)(b. between 1793-1805).

[1062](See Jean Bunnell #8546 record for source. Born between 1793-1805).

[1063](See Jean Bunnell #8546 record for source. Born between 1793-1805).

[1064](See Jean Bunnell #8546 record for source. Born between 1793-1805).

[1065](See Jean Bunnell #8546 record for source. Born between 1793-1805)(Info. from Louis Bunnell Frye of 6425 Meadowridge Dr., Santa Rosa, California 95409, phone 707-539-2107. This book was found in Archives of Nova Scotia, Halifax by Paul Bunnell in Aug. 1999. A full copy is in his file under Nova Scotia Bunnells).

[1066](Between 1844-60).

[1067](See fathers record for source plus listed on 1837 census but State not given).

[1068](See fathers record for source plus listed on 1837 census but State not given).

[1069](On old Bonnell land grant land like father and grandfather).

[1070](See fathers record for source, plus from 1837 census, but State not given).

[1071](From Robert's fathers source).

[1072](From Roberts fathers source).

[1073](From Roberts fathers source).

[1074](For source see fathers record).

[1075](For source see fathers record)(Raised on Academy hill, site of local schoolhouse in 1870's).

[1076](Ran away from home and ended up in the Montana Territory possibly by railroad, took up horse raising and blacksmith).

[1077](About 50 miles from the U.S. boarder between Cardston and the Blood Indian Reservation, built small log cabin, then wood frame home).

[1078](Moved there and opened a Livery stable and rented rigs and horses).

[1079](Between 1895-1899)(See fathers record for source).

[1080](Between 1895-99)(For source see fathers record).

[1081](Between 1895-99)(For source see fathers record).

[1082](See fathers record for source).

[1083](See fathers record for source).

[1084](See fathers line for source).

[1085](See fathers line for source).

[1086](See fathers line for source).

[1087](Twin with Leslie. See fathers line for source).

[1088](See fathers line for source).

[1089](A twin with Larry. See fathers line for source).

[1090](See fathers line for source).

[1091](See mothers record for source).

[1092](See fathers line for source).

[1093](See mothers line for source).

[1094](See mothers line for source).

[1095](See fathers line for source).

[1096](See fathers line for source).

[1097](See mothers line for source).

[1098](See fathers line for source).

[1099](See mothers record for source).

[1100](See fathers line for source).

[1101](see fathers line for source).

[1102](See fathers line for source).

[1103](See fathers line for source).

[1104](See fathers line for source).
[1105](See fathers line for source).
[1106](See mothers record for source).
[1107](See fathers line for source).
[1108](See fathers line for source).
[1109](Could be a mix up due to poor charting. Sheryl could be wife of David, Stephen's brother?).
[1110](See fathers line for source).
[1111](See fathers line for source).
[1112](See fathers line for source).
[1113](See fathers line for source).
[1114](See mothers side for source).
[1115](See mothers record for source).
[1116](See fathers line for source).
[1117](See mothers record for source).
[1118](See mothers line for source).
[1119](See mothers line for source).
[1120](See mothers side for source).
[1121](See fathers record for source).
[1122](See fathers record for source).
[1123](For source see fathers record).
[1124](For source see fathers record).
[1125](For source see fathers record).
[1126](For source see fathers record).
[1127](For source see fathers record).
[1128](For source see fathers record).
[1129](See fathers record for source).
[1130](See Jean Bunnell #8546 record for source. Born between 1793-1805).
[1131](See Jean Bunnell #8546 record for source. Born between 1793-1805).

Surname Index

Abraham	53	Bassett	137		
Ackerman	75	Baxter	256, 274(2)		
Ackins	39	Beam	77		
Adams	52, 68	Bean	271		
Aiten/Aiton	243, 246(2), 314(2)	Beattie	203		
		Beaty	40		
Alcorn	245, 280	Beaumont	53		
Alden	271(2)	Beaupre	75		
Alexander	35	Beck	254, 255		
Allen	144, 222, 319	Beckwith	46, 48		
		Bedford	278		
Allison	216(6), 217(6)	Belanger	75, 156		
		Bell	60b, 94b, 118, 219		
Allyn	47, 52(5)	Bennett	282		
Alston	60(2), 77	Bentley	94(5)		
Ambroise	68, 92	Bernier	75		
Amdisen	172	Bertero	281(2)		
Anderson	20, 21, 40	Bertogli	127, 155(2), 165, 176, 186		
Andre	21				
Andrews	252(2), 265	Berton	58		
Anguish	39	Bettin	22		
Anthony	230	Beyea	264(2)		
Appt	230	Bickford	207		
Arch	251	Bidder	77		
Armstrong	246, 252	Bill	52(2)		
Arnold	1, 9, 11, 16, 20, 21, 22, 25, 30, 31, 32, 34, 37, 39, 40, 41, 42, 43(3), 44(3), 45(2), 46, 47, 49, 50(2), 51, 52, 61, 77, 80, 110, 112, 123, 129	Billings	47, 53(3)		
		Bishop	224		
		Blackburn	145		
		Blackney/Bleakney	255, 259, 264		
Atherton	269				
Austin	68, 77, 108(2), 109, 116(2), 119, 120(2), 128, 131, 298, 301	Blair	68		
		Blame	68		
		Bliss	94		
Avery	47, 48, 49(2), 52(8), 53(6)	Block	184(3)		
		Bodenmiller	119, 216(5), 217(8), 218(11), 219(4), 310		
Axelrod	282				
Babcock	53	Boggs	140		
Bacon	266	Bolton	53		
Bailey	47, 53	Bomba	185		
Bain	153	Bonnell/Bunnel/Bunnell/Bonnel/Bonneuil, Bonneel/Bonhill/La Bunnell/Bennell 1, 2, 3, 4, 5, 6, 7, 8, 9, 12, 13, 16, 23, 25, 31, 33, 39, 52, 56, 57, 59(2), 60, 64(3), 68, 76, 77(2), 78, 80(4), 83(3), 86, 87(3), 89(3)(1b), 90(4), 91(3), 92, 94, 95, 98(3), 101(2), 102, 103, 104(2), 108(10), 109, 110(2), 113, 114, 119(9), 120(3), 121 (Multiple), 123(Multiple), 124(Multiple), 125(Multiple), 126(Multiple), 127(Multiple), 128-322(Multiple)		
Baker	53(2), 282				
Balmar	92				
Balyer	286				
Bardsley	320				
Barlow	59(3), 77				
Barnett	118, 130, 211(2), 286(2), 287(5), 288(2), 304(2), 308(5), 309(5), 310(3), 311(6), 312(8), 313(12)				
Baronet	103				
Barrat	252	Bostwick	310		
Bartlett	146	Boucher	75		
Barton	271, 272(3), 319				

Bowe	39	Caulder	123
Bowman	68	Caulkins	51b
Boyer	69	Cawson/Cawsan	99, 285
Branscomb	59	Challones	69
Breen	155	Chalmers	133(2)
Brennan	150, 163	Chapman	49, 53, 268
Bridegnor	59(2)	Chester	53(5)
Bridgeman	77(2)	Chipman	82, 90, 129
Bridges	172	Chillas	59
Brittain	95	Choo	169(2)
Bromfield	46, 49	Cladian	130
Brooks	126, 165(3), 231, 275, 276, 284	Clafin	240
		Clark	53, 68, 124, 247(2), 265(2)
Brothers	77		
Brotherton	7, 109, 116(2), 130(2), 131	Clarke	315
		Clawson	60(2)
Brown	20, 33, 40, 53, 75, 77, 78, 80, 81(3), 94, 181(3), 271, 272, 284	Clayton	68
		Clear	319
		Clementson	283(3)
Bruce	39	Clemett/Clewett	77(2), 78
Brundige/Brundage	68, 69, 95(5), 102, 287	Clinton	10, 11, 21, 22, 25, 30, 31, 35, 41, 298
Brundride	78	Cocket	40
Buchanan	286	Codington	78
Buckley/Bulkeley	68, 72(2)	Coffin	88, 89(5), 90, 91
Budd	233(2), 233b, 234(7), 235(5), 237(4), 238(4)		
		Coldham	243
Buddington	53	Cole	78, 241, 261
Bulyea	91	Coleman	39, 231(2), 287
Burkr/Burke(?)	156		
Burnet	33	Collins	149(2)
Burnham	77	Colozzi	181(2)
Burns	92(2)	Colt	53
Burnside	265	Comeau	152(2), 277
Burrell	69, 184(2), 185(4), 299	Comely	86
		Conley	198(2)
Burrows	53	Conn	171
Bushnell	53	Connors	184
Butler/Butlers	53, 77, 146(4)	Conrad	77, 78
		Conright	250
Butt	39	Cook	59
Bygote	123	Cooke	39
Bysell	39	Cooley	196, 301
Cain	147	Cooper	68, 77, 78, 283(2)
Camp	15		
Campbell	16, 40, 68(2), 82, 269	Corey	68, 274
		Cornier	75
Canby	86(2)	Cornwallis	31
Carnes	8	Cote	75
Carleton	278	Cotello	178
Carr	194(2)	Cottle	106(2), 145(2), 206(2), 220, 289, 291, 293
Cartier	189(4)		
Casson	257	Courtney	216
Cataldo	156	Cousins	86

Cowan	139	Dickenson/Dickinson	68, 77(2), 78, 92
Cowperthwaite	86	Dickerson	16, 59(2)
Cox	35, 68, 282	Dickle	280
Coy	257, 264(8), 265(4), 276(2), 318(2)	DiDomenico	179(3), 180, 181(4), 182(4), 187
Crab/Crabb/Crabtree	90(2), 91(3), 92(3), 93(2), 96, 102, 111, 119, 130, 137(2), 144, 287	Dillon	59
		Dionne	75
Cracknell	281	Doe	241
Graig	134, 151(2), 227(2)	Doherty	186
		Donahoe	293
Craigie	46	Donnell	290
Cram	68(2), 77(2), 77	Donovan	177
		Dorman	217, 243
Cranbury	39	Doscher	145, 199, 200(6), 201(2), 202(2), 209, 303
Crandall	316, 320		
Crofering	68	Doucet	75
Crofts	69	Douglass	158, 161
Cronwell	68	Douthwright	260
Currie	261(3)	Dow	210(2)
Curtis	14	Drake	14
Cutter	68	Drummond	58, 68
Cyr	75	Duffill	68
Daboll	52	Duggan	243
Daley	236, 237	Duke	172
Dalling	118	Dumont	75
Dalton	140	Dunbrack	283
D'Amelio	181	Duncan	82(3), 119
Damink	231(3)	Dunfield	252(2)
Daniel	86, 92	Dunham	69, 227
Darbyshire	290	Dunster	217
Darrow	53	Duplace	152(2)
Dart	53(2)	Dupuis	170
David	249, 314(3), 319(2)	Eason	178
		Easterbrooks (Easty Brooks)	131(2)
Davies	280	Ebie	162
Davis	53, 68, 253, 255, 316(13), 317(8), 318(5)	Edgar	274
		Edgecomb	52, 53
Davison	78, 81(2)	Edgett	252
Dawling	68	Edward (King VII)	128
Day/Daye/Dey	1, 14, 20, 26, 32, 92, 96(2), 102(3), 111, 135(2), 136, 145, 229, 258, 308	Edwards	234
		Egbert	69
		Eldridge	52(2), 53(2), 177(2)
Dearborn	208(2)		
Debs	184(4)	Elkin	132(5), 133
Degosline/Gosline	268(3)	Elliot	285, 313(2), 314(7), 315, 317(5), 319(4)
Delong	102, 111, 119, 203(4), 204(2)		
		Ellis	7, 92
Dennis	85(2)	Elms	77
Dereny	293	Erb	261
DeVeber	267	Etre	42(2), 45, 46(2), 48
Devober(?)	77		
Dibblee	258(3)	Erickson	281

Esterbrook	264(2), 318(2)	Gagne	75, 165, 172(2), 174(3), 175(3), 176, 186
Fairbanks	85	Gagnon	75
Fanjoy	95, 102, 219(7), 220(9), 221(10), 222(3), 224(11), 225(12), 310(4), 312	Gallup	52(2)
		Gard	60
		Gardner	40
Fanning	233	Geall	317, 319(3)
Farren/Farron	199(2)	George (King) III	2, 76, 78, 114, 128, 232
Faulkner	186(3), 187(2)		
		Giarrusso	125, 177(2)
Fay	197(5), 198	Gibbon	261
Fenwick	262	Gibbs	68
Ferguson	40(2)	Gillespie	290
Ficht	168(2), 169	Gillies	318
Filibraun	181	Glannon	60
Fish	53	Glover	68
Fisher	75, 268	Goddard	251, 252(4)
Fitzgerald	120, 244	Gold	67
FitzRandolph	23, 84, 125(2), 277	Goldbury	276
		Goold	73
Flaherty	293	Gorham	219
Fletcher	40	Gould	165
Flewelling	59, 60(2), 77(3), 78(2), 88, 89(3), 133	Grant	90b, 119, 180(2), 280
Flexner	118	Grasso	187
Fogg	262	Graves	246(3), 247(2), 252(4), 253, 265, 314
Ford	16		
Fossano	177	Gray	260(2), 262, 267
Foster	104(2), 262(7)		
		Green	69, 255, 256, 274
Fowler	59, 60(2), 76, 77, 80, 99, 132, 257, 259, 263(2), 267(15), 268(12), 285		
		Gregg/Grigg	253(3), 261, 316
Fowlie	258, 272(2), 273, 319	Gregory	60, 77, 78
		Griedner/Guesner/Gesner	247(2)
Fox	9, 126, 232(3), 232b(2)	Griffith	92, 101, 158
		Guilmette	127, 186(2)
Franklin	9, 20, 35, 37, 124(2), 126(2), 232, 232b, 238(2), 242b	Haight	233
		Hains/Haines	67, 68(2), 70, 129, 222(4), 223(11), 311(4)
Franzen	281(2)		
Fraser	264	Hale (Dale?)	78(2)
Freeman	9, 46, 48, 53, 54, 201, 276	Hall	201(2), 250(5), 252(2), 253, 281
French	30, 31, 34, 92(2), 102, 130, 136, 286, 287		
		Hallam	47
		Halsey	48, 53
Frink	69	Halstead	39
Frinks	37, 44	Ham	77
Frost	77, 78, 243(2)	Hammilton	68
		Hampton	68, 85(2)
Frye	280(12), 282(15), 283(2), 320	Handford	68
		Hanes	163
Fuller	147(2)	Hanse	39
Furrier	182, 183		

Harding	53, 75, 77, 78, 80(2), 81, 91(3), 97, 101, 114(2), 117, 119(2), 128, 289, 305	Howland	320
		Hoyl	68
		Hrange	68
Harrington	217	Huggeford	58
Harris	60, 68, 77, 78, 168	Hughes	124
		Hulburt	53
Harrison	86(2), 250	Humbold	68
Harvey	39	Humphreys	92, 101
Haslett	264(3), 265	Huot	180, 181(2)
Hater (Hayter?)	78	Hutchinson	68, 85
Haulling (Flewelling?)	77	Hyde	46
Haverhill	117	Hyerstay	227
Haviland	92	Inis	68
Hawk	269	Innis	318
Hay	133	Izambert	278, 284
Haycox	229(2)	Jackson	243
Hayter	78	Jaques	52
Heans	114(2), 120	Jaquish	11, 12, 129
Hearns	69	Jamieson	259
Hebert	75	Janigian	282(2)
Hempstead	49, 53	Jayne	123
Henderson	278	Jefferey/Jeffrey	68, 225
Henyen	40	Jernell	125
Heppard	40	Johnson	104b, 123, 149, 249, 252, 253, 275, 276, 284(2)
Herlily	294		
Herrett	68	Johnston	77, 134(2), 144, 225
Herrington	287		
Hesfand	68	Jones	14, 53, 92, 108, 110, 119, 120, 129, 156, 161, 216
Heston	68		
Hetherington	225	Judd	53, 69
Hewitt	315	Kane	198
Higham	120	Kannan	232b
Hill	40, 53, 58	Kautzman	77, 78
Hines	217	Keane	193
Hoit	92	Keating	313
Holden	77, 78	Keeley	293
Holder	132	Keenan	151
Holdren	123	Keirstead/Kierstead	76, 203, 205(2), 253((8), 254(6), 256(11), 258(6), 259(11), 260(10), 261(12), 269(15), 270(4), 272(2), 274(3), 275(2), 316(6), 317(14), 319, 320(6)
Holdridge	52		
Holland	68(2), 81		
Hollingshead	86		
Holmes	254(2), 258(2), 259, 317		
		Keith	201, 249
Holt	53	Kelliker	153
Holty	92	Kelly/Kelley	150(2), 258(2), 259
Homfray	32		
Hoover	156	Kennedy	78, 280
Horgan	173(6)	Kenson	53
Horner	85	Kiest	254
Horsman	254	Kilbenbock	68
Horton	58, 77	Kilburn	53
Houchmuth	177(2)	Kilpatrick	251
Hourin	289	Kimble/Kemble	91, 92, 93(2), 96, 102, 226
Howe	16		

Kingsbury	161(2)	Likens	8
Kingsland	77	Lincoln	172(2)
Kinney	53	Lingley	68, 73, 137(2), 220(2), 225(2), 287
Kitfield	207		
Knapp	68	Lips	78
Knowles	153	Lisk	77
Kohen	168, 169	Livingston	92
Kustts(?)	68	Lockhart	251
Laffan	68	Lone	250
Lagoof	271	Long	262, 265
Lalon	278, 284	Looseley	77
Lamb	53	Louis (XIV)	124
Lamereux/Lamoreux	68(2)	Love	133
Lane	69	Lovett	39
Langhborough	85	Lowey	92, 101
Lani	181	Lucas	101
Langlois	75	Lucey	68
Lanther(?)	258	Ludlow	35, 75
Lascola	179	Lydon	182(3), 183(2)
Latham	47, 48, 52, 53(6)		
		Lynch	120
Latimer	46	Lyon	234
LaTour	75	Machado	120
Latwyche	35	Machum	133
Lavison (Davison?)	77	MacKay	232b
Law	251	Madden	293
Lawlor	147	Mair	150
Leathes	173	Major	60
Leblanc	75	Mallary/Mallory	77, 275, 276, 284
Leclerc	75, 197(3), 198(2)		
		Mallinson	52
Ledyard	43, 45, 47(6), 48(5), 49(5), 51, 53(3)	Malone	60
		Marchant	75
Lee	15, 77, 78, 86, 157	Marcy	151(2)
		Markham	317
Leeds	52, 53	Marks	213
Legee	289	Marr	253(2), 254(6), 256, 259(3)
Leger	145		
Legrange	31	Marrin	8b
LeMoine	283	Marshall	147(2)
Lent	69	Martin	35, 75, 151, 298
Lentine	177		
Leonard	20, 30, 35	Mason	52(2)
Lesier (Lester?)	77	Massillon	14
Leslie	213	Master	8
Lessmann	234b, 236	Masters	278
Lester	52, 53, 54(3), 77, 78, 261	Matticks	254
		Maybec(?)	68
Leuridan	124	Mayo	206
Levasseur	75	McCall	77
Levesque	75, 190(4)	McCann	301
Lewis	54	McCarthy	301
Lightbody	264(4), 265(5)	McChesney	281

McClean/McLean	102, 204, 216, 219, 220, 221, 262, 310	Morin	75
		Morgan	53(4), 54
McClellan	139	Morley	147
McColgan	69	Morrell	125
McCordick.McCordock	78, 139, 140	Morris	9, 169(2)
McCormack	200(3)	Morrison	175
McCoy	167, 200(4), 276	Morrow	33
		Moxley	53, 54
McCue	222	Mueller	134
McDonald	69	Muheau (Maheau?)	91
McDonugh	198	Mulvey	152
McFarland	262	Munger	68
McGee	217	Munrow	40
McGregor	266(6), 267(4)	Murphy	40, 176, 177, 269, 279, 293
McKeel/McKiel	92(9), 227(2)	Murray	264
McKenzie	146(2)	Murrey	40
McKinley	250	Myers/Mires	68, 208, 213, 266
McKnight	255		
McLean	263	Myles	224(2)
McLeod	262(4), 263(2), 287, 289	Nadeau	75, 296(2)
		Nase	83, 84, 87, 88(2), 89, 98, 103
McNamara	255		
McNeal	68, 69	Neccerato	283
McQuinn	243, 244(2), 246, 250(7), 251(8), 252(3), 253, 257, 262, 263(2), 274, 276, 284	Neal	39, 104, 130
		Nelson	239
		Newlin(3)	
Mead	33	Newman	60
Melanson	75	Norris	11
Melnick	187(2)	Northrup	261
Menzies	59	Nubell	39
Mercier	186	Nutter	92
Merrill	50	Oblenis	59
Merrit	77	O'Brien	301
Mersereau	58	Odell	94
Michaud	75	Odom	189(2)
Micheau	91	O'Donald	78
Miles	77	Ogden	39, 60(2), 68(2), 131(2)
Miller	40, 45, 112, 116, 118, 123		
		Olive	59, 69
Millett	44(2)	Oram	78, 132(2)
Mills	54, 259	Ori	155
Minor	53, 54	Osborn	68
Misseroen	124	Ouellette	75
Moffatt/Moffat	260	Paddock	68
Mo(?)oreau	92	Palmer	54
Montesion	170, 171	Parent	75
Montgomery	46, 48, 50, 55(2)	Park	225
		Parker	68, 77, 227, 229(2), 230
Moody	124, 269		
Moor	279	Parmale	77, 78, 91
Moore	53, 54, 84(2), 109, 130, 153	Parr	67, 72(2)
		Parrock	243
Mopley	39	Parsons	125

Paterson	12, 13, 129	Robinson/Robison	14, 45, 287
Patton	159	Roche	193
Payson	277	Rodin	68
Peatt	126	Roe (Doe)	82(2)
Peddle	86	Rogers	59, 173(2), 174(2), 176(4), 297(2)
Peel	68(2)		
Pelletier	75	Rome	35
Pendleton	53	Rouse	259, 260
Perkins	53(3), 54(6), 190(2), 191, 193(3), 194, 300(11)	Rowley	53
		Roy	75
Perrine	58	Rudolph	15
Perry	77, 78, 82(7), 83(6), 102, 128b(2), 129, 228(2), 257(3)	Ruggles	35, 68
		Russell	119
Peters	94, 95, 242	Ryder	247, 260, 294
Philip (Prince)	120		
Phillippe	124	Sanchez	281(2)
Phillips	31	Sanford	53
Picard	75	Sawler	193(6)
Pinkney	60(4)	Schaffer	248(4)
Place	68	Schenck	234
Plumb	50, 275, 276, 284	Schofield	254
		Schooley	8
Plummer/Plumer	276, 320	Schreiber	198(3)
Porter	119, 212	Scovil	88(2)
Powell	85(2)	Seabury	54
Prentis	53	Seely	224
Prior	53	Sefs	68
Protor	155	Segee	145(3), 252
Pszenny	195(4)	Serjeant	146(4), 147(2), 148(10), 289
Purdy	60, 78, 95(3), 96, 99(2), 101, 102, 130, 131(5), 132(13), 133(9), 134(4), 279, 285, 286		92
		Sewell	118
		Seymour	49, 53
Putnam	118, 119, 279	Shapley	43(2), 48(2), 49, 54
Pyne	155	Shaw	68
Quigly	197	Sharkey	152
Quinton	87	Shaw	165(2)
Randall	175	Sheridan	154(2)
Rathburn	119	Sherwood	69, 88, 89(9), 90(2), 243(2), 263, 308
Recce	68		
Redding	68	Shipton	72
Redstone	256	Shoemaker	123
Reed	40	Sholes	54
Reid	147(2), 290	Shonman	230
Reily	92, 101	Shotwell	69
Remsen	92, 101	Shults/Shultz	163, 295
Richards	54	Siely	68
Richardson	85	Simmons	178
Richie	142(2)	Simion	68
Rider	92(2), 101	Skinner/Skimmer	145, 206, 232
Rivington	20		
Roberts	174(2)	Slocum	222
Robertson	290		
Robichaud	230		

Smith	46, 53, 68, 77, 78, 86(2), 118, 170(2), 171(2), 208(2), 210, 217(5), 232b, 254(2), 289, 290	Thorne	222(2)
		Thorpe	60
		Thurlow	190
Snow	194(2), 206(2), 209	Thurston	144
		Tibbenham	217(2)
Soucy	177	Tift	53
Sprague	244(4)	Tilley	45
Sproul	60(2)	Titus	78
Squires	59	Tom	255, 256, 274
Stackhouse	69(2)		
Stanton	48, 53(2), 54(3)	Tonge	238
		Tool	68
Starr (Star)	53(2), 54(2)	Townsend	40, 78
Stebbens	60	Tracchia	196(2)
Stedman	54	Trott	92, 217
Steeves	14, 102	Trumbull	45, 49
Stephens	78	Tufts	141
Stevens/Steeves	11, 102, 137(3), 140, 287(3), 288(8)	Tully	60, 68, 158(2)
Stewart	35, 233, 271	Tuscher	294
Stillman	53, 201	Underhill	86
Stillwell (Stithwell)	85, 225(2)	Upham	45(2), 46, 47, 50
Stockwell	133(2)		
Stone	139(7), 140, 147, 251, 287	Urien	78
		Vail	77, 246
Storey	251, 252(2)	Vaillancourt	75
Stow	53	Vallance	180(6), 181
Strader	78	Van Buskirk	46, 269(2)
Stricht	77	Vance	283
Strickland	85(2)	Vanderbeck	75
Stupton	67	Van Otto	40
SullivanSullivan	153(2), 241, 243	Van Winkle	123(2), 125
		Varrep	40
Supplee/Supple	60, 77, 78, 91	Vasquez	281(2)
		Veal	232
Suter	92, 101	Vedbaek	163
Sutton	77	Vergasson	118
Sweet	156	Vermulle	77
Talbert	200(2)	Viets	240, 240b
Talbos	151	Violet/Violette	74(2), 75, 156(2), 165, 176, 186
Talbot	75		
Tantalo	178(3)	Von Beaverhoudt	10
Tardif	75	Vorseth	281
Tarron	40	Wager	252
Taylor	68, 69, 207, 282	Wales	53, 128
		Walker	233(2), 272
Tecce	182	Wallace	92(3), 134, 135(3), 208(3)
Terry	166		
Th(?)	85	Walsh	183(2), 184(2)
Thanks	68		
Theal	90, 130	Walter	78
Thibadeau	74(2), 75	Walters	250
Thomas	92, 173(4), 175, 176, 286, 288, 304, 308(2)	Walworth	54
		Wansuc	53

Ward/Wood	14, 33, 39, 54, 96, 102, 212
Warde	69
Warden/Worden	92, 101(2), 104, 130, 259, 317
Ware	179(3), 180(2)
Warren	40
Washington	9, 10, 11, 16, 20, 21, 22, 25, 28, 30, 32, 41, 56(2), 57, 123, 232
Warten	92(2)
Waters	315
Watson	41, 219
Wayne	22
Weade	74
Webster	207(2)
Wedger	54
Weldon	225, 226
Welch	68
Welles	53
Wells	249(3), 252(2)
Welsh	60
Wetmore	239, 240b(6), 241b(3), 242(2), 242b(4), 243, 267
Weyman	252(2), 253
Whelpley/Wheples	92, 220, 221, 224(2), 258
White	13, 167(2), 271
Whitehead	125, 231
Whitlock	50
Whittlesey	54(2)
Wiggs	212
Wiggins	60, 92, 101, 221
Wiiliams	53
William (The Conqueror)	126
Williams	47, 48, 78, 54(4), 92, 147, 247
Willing	68, 69
Wilmot	125, 126(2), 231, 275, 276, 284
Wilson	84, 119, 146
Windham	279
Winkley	191(3), 192(4)
Winn	86
Winslow	78
Wiseman	119
Witmore/Wetmore	68(6), 69, 133(2)
Wogan	39, 40, 45, 52(2), 93, 129(2)
Wood	131, 132(9), 133(7), 134(4), 235(3), 236(3), 308
Woodbridge	54(2)
Woodbury	198, 294
Wood-Holt	251, 252, 267
Woodhouse	39, 40
Woodruff	40
Woodward	85(4)
Woodworth	53(3)
Wrenn	282
Wright	14, 30, 31, 57, 58, 59, 60(2), 76, 77(2), 78, 81(4), 118, 129, 232b
Yeareley/Yearly/Yeasley	68, 77, 78
Yeoman	92
Yherts	33
Young	68, 92(2), 234, 281

Other Publications By The Author

1. The New Loyalist Index Vol. I
   Published by Heritage Books Inc., Bowie, Md. 1989

2. The New Loyalist Index Vol. II
   Published by Heritage Books Inc., Bowie, Md. 1996

3. The New Loyalist Index Vol. III
   Published by Heritage Books Inc., Bowie, Md. 1998

4. Research Guide To Loyalist Ancestors (Revised & Expended Edition)
   Published by Heritage Books Inc., Bowie, Md. 2000

5. American Loyalist Migrations & Documents Guide
   Published by Paul J. Bunnell, UE, Whittier Press Inc., Amesbury, Ma. 2001

6. Cemetery Inscriptions of The Town of Barnstable, Massachusetts, And Its Villages, 1600-1900.
   Published by Heritage Books Inc., Bowie, Md. 1995

7. The House of Robinson; The Robinson's of Rhode Island, Their Genealogy & Letters & The History of The Robinson & Son Oil Company of Baltimore, Maryland
   Published by Heritage Books Inc., Bowie, Md. 1995

8. Acadian & Cajun Cooking & Old Remedies (The Way Memere Made Them)
   Published by Paul J. Bunnell, UE, Whittier Press Inc., Amesbury, Ma. 1997

Loyalty is Everything

ABOUT THE AUTHOR

Paul J. Bunnell, FACG, UE

Loyalty is Everything

For the past twenty-five years, Paul has devoted himself to genealogy and Loyalist studies. Self educated, he later took credited classes from Brigham Young University of Provo, Utah, greatly improving his skills and knowledge in this field. His accomplishments are wide; awarded the Accreditation and Fellowship at the American College of Genealogists of Illinois, and certified and registered lineage member of the United Empire Loyalist Association of Canada, and The Hereditary Order of Descendants of the Loyalists and Patriots of the American Revolution. He has held past and present memberships in over sixty genealogical and writing organizations around the world, including life long memberships and chairman positions. He is also certified with the International Ghost Hunters Society in Paranormal Investigation, and also as a Ghost Hunter. He is a registered BYU blood donor on their genealogical DNA study. His speaking engagements have been in New Jersey, New York, Massachusetts, New Hampshire, Maine, Connecticut and New Brunswick, including TV interviews on Cape Cod, Massachusetts, and Saint John, New Brunswick. In 1989, His Majesty The Prince Philip of Wales (England) accepted his book, Thunder Over New England—Benjamin Bonnell, the Loyalist, at Buckingham Palace. He was also presented with the famous "Loyalist Pin" from the past mayor, Elsie Wayne of Saint John, New Brunswick, Canada (The Loyalist City). Paul has also produced several Internet articles on genealogy, including "Black Loyalist," and "Bonnell/Bunnell Loyalists." And, let's not forget the "Loyalist Ghost of Benjamin Bonnell." Future publications: Life of a Haunted House; The Barnstable House; Tumbleweed; The Nellie Markham Letters; New Loyalist Index; Vol. 4; Native North American and French Marriages; and many other books in progress. Paul enjoys traveling around lecturing or selling books at his vendor table at conventions. He also does Loyalist research for others out of his very large home library.

Other Heritage Books by Paul J. Bunnell:

Cemetery Inscriptions of the Town of Barnstable, Massachusetts, and Its Villages, 1600-1900

Cemetery Inscriptions of the Town of Barnstable, Massachusetts, and its Villages, 1600-1900, with Corrections and Additions

French and Native North American Marriages, 1600-1800

Life of a Haunted House—The Barnstable House of Barnstable, Massachusetts: Genealogy of a Real Haunted House

Research Guide to Loyalist Ancestors: A Directory to Archives, Manuscripts, and Published Sources

Research Guide to Loyalist Ancestors: A Directory to Archives, Manuscripts, Published and Electronic Sources (Updated and Revised)

The House of Robinson—The Robinsons of Rhode Island: Their Genealogy and Letters, and the History of the Robinson & Son Oil Company of Baltimore, Maryland

The New Loyalist Index, Volume I

The New Loyalist Index, Volume II

The New Loyalist Index, Volume III: Including Cape Cod and Islands, Massachusetts, New Hampshire, New Jersey and New York Loyalists

Thunder Over New England—Benjamin Bonnell, the Loyalist: A Loyalist Story and Family Genealogy, Including Other Loyalist Bunnell/Bonnell Genealogies Revised and Updated

www.ingramcontent.com/pod-product-compliance
Lightning Source LLC
Chambersburg PA
CBHW060552230426
43670CB00011B/1784